Big book of Knitting

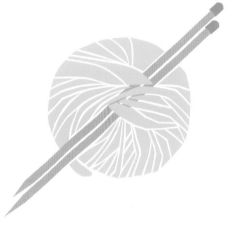

Big book of
Knitting

Everything you need for 100 gorgeous projects

DK

LONDON, NEW YORK, MUNICH,
MELBOURNE, DELHI

UK TEAM

Project Editor Katharine Goddard
Senior Art Editor Nicola Rodway
Managing Editor Penny Smith
Senior Managing Art Editor Marianne Markham
Art Director/Stylist For Photography Isabel de Cordova
Photographer Ruth Jenkinson
Senior Jacket Creative Nicola Powling
Senior Producer, Pre-Production Tony Phipps
Producer Che Creasey
Creative Technical Support Sonia Charbonnier
Art Director Jane Bull
Publisher Mary Ling

INDIA TEAM

Senior Editor Alicia Ingty
Editor Janashree Singha
Senior Art Editor Anchal Kaushal
Art Editor Simran Kaur
Assistant Art Editor Vikas Sachdeva
Managing Editor Glenda Fernandes
Managing Art Editor Navidita Thapa
Production Manager Pankaj Sharma
DTP Designer Sachin Singh

First published in Great Britain in 2013
by Dorling Kindersley Limited,
80 Strand, London WC2R 0RL

Penguin Group (UK)
10 9 8 7 6 5 4 3 2 1
001 – 186656 – Feb/2013

A CIP catalogue record for this book
is available from the British Library.
ISBN 978-1-4093-8294-2

Printed and bound in China by South China Printing Co. Ltd.

Discover more at www.dk.com

Contents

Introduction

This book is suitable for all knitters, whether you have never held a pair of needles before or are an experienced knitter. All key areas are covered – with over 100 patterns, plus tools and materials, and techniques. The Projects chapter contains patterns for a range of skill levels and a variety of techniques. Here you can bring your skills to fruition, knitting garments for all the family, plus a choice of accessories. The children's clothes are given in three sizes, specified by age, while adult garments include four sizes – S (M:L:XL). See the chart, right, for details of sizing.

Each project shows the yarn and stitch tension used, but if you substitute a yarn refer to p.251 for equivalent standard yarn weights from which to choose. Select one that has the same stitch and row count on the ballband as that in the pattern, and always work a tension swatch (see p.259). Adjust your needle size if necessary to achieve the correct stitch tension so that your project comes out at the correct size. Check that the tension swatch in the new yarn looks and feels suitable for the project. Calculate the amount of yarn by yardage/meterage, as the amount needed may vary.

The Stitch pattern gallery shows a selection of knitted fabrics you can make, while the Techniques chapter features more than 200 techniques, from simply understanding a pattern to more complicated cables, lace knitting and colourwork. With *Big Book of Knitting* you'll find everything you need to knit with accuracy, confidence, and flair.

Garment size chart

Women's sizes	To fit bust (approx.)
S (small)	81cm (32in)
M (medium)	91cm (36in)
L (large)	102cm (40in)
XL (extra large)	112cm (44in)

Men's sizes	To fit chest (approx.)
S (small)	97cm (38in)
M (medium)	104cm (41in)
L (large)	112cm (44in)
XL (extra large)	119cm (47in)

Projects: Clothes

Women's classic cardigan

This raglan v-neck cardie in a fine 4-ply yarn makes a versatile fashion garment. Refer to pp.300–302 for detailed information on the various seams you will need to assemble the cardigan. The cuffs can be worn turned back or sitting flat according to the length of your arms.

Essential information

DIFFICULTY Moderate

SIZE To fit an adult female S (M:L:XL)

YARN

Rowan Wool Cotton 4-ply 50g

490 Violet x 7 (8:9:9)

NEEDLES

A: 1 pair of 3mm (UK11/USn/a) needles

B: 1 pair of 3.25mm (UK10/US3) needles

C: 80cm (32in), 3mm (UK11/USn/a) circular needle

A
B
C

TENSION

28sts and 36 rows to 10cm (4in) over st st on 3.25mm (UK10/US3) needles

NOTIONS

2 stitcher holders

Large-eyed needle

7 x 15mm (½in) buttons

SPECIAL ABBREVIATIONS

Y2ON Wind yarn twice over needle

Back

With needles A, cast on 134 (150:158:166) sts.

RIB ROW 1: K2, [p2, k2] to end.

RIB ROW 2: P2, [k2, p2] to end.

Rep the last 2 rows x 6.

Change to needles B and st st.

Work 4 rows.

DEC ROW: K3, skpo, k to last 5sts, k2tog, k3.

Work 7 rows.

Work the last 8 rows x 4 and the dec row again. (122 (138:146:154) sts)

Work 7 rows, ending with a p row.

INC ROW: K4, M1, k to last 4sts, M1, k4.

Work 11 rows.

Rep the last 12 rows x 4 and the inc row again. (134 (150:158:166) sts)

Work straight until back measures 36 (37:37: 37)cm (14¼ (14½:14½:14½)in) from cast on edge, ending with a p row.

Shape raglan armholes

Cast off 6 (8:9:10) sts at beg of next 2 rows. (122 (134:140:146) sts)

NEXT ROW: K3, skpo, k to last 5sts, k2tog, k3.

NEXT ROW: P to end.

Rep the last 2 rows x 31 (35:37:39). (58 (62:64:66) sts)

NEXT ROW: K to end, inc 0 (0:2:0) sts, evenly across row.

RIB ROW 1: P2, [k2, p2] to end.

RIB ROW 2: K2, [p2, k2] to end.

Rep the last 2 rows twice and the first row again.

Cast off in rib.

Left front

With needles A, cast on 67 (75:79:83) sts.

RIB ROW 1: K2, [p2, k2] to last 5sts, p2, k3.

RIB ROW 2: P3, [k2, p2] to end.

Rep the last 2 rows x 6.

Change to needles B and st st.

Work 4 rows.

DEC ROW: K3, skpo, k to end.

Work 7 rows.

Work the last 8 rows x 4 and the dec row again. (61 (69:73:77) sts)

Work 7 rows, ending with a p row.

INC ROW: K4, M1, k to end.

Work 11 rows.

Rep the last 12 rows x 4 and the inc row again. (67 (75:79:83) sts)

Work straight until front measures 36 (37:37: 37)cm (14¼ (14½:14½:14½)in) from cast on edge, ending with a p row.

Shape raglan armhole

NEXT ROW: Cast off 6 (8:9:10) sts, k to end. (61 (67:70:73) sts)

NEXT ROW: P to end.

NEXT ROW: K3, skpo, k to last 3sts, k2tog, k1.

NEXT ROW: P to end.

Rep the last 2 rows x 24 (26:27:28). (11 (13:14:15) sts)

NEXT ROW: K3, skpo, k to end.

NEXT ROW: P to end.

Rep the last 2 rows x 6 (8:9:10). (4sts)

Leave these sts on a stitch holder.

Right front

With needles A, cast on 67 (75:79:83) sts.

RIB ROW 1: K3, [p2, k2] to end.

RIB ROW 2: P2, [k2, p2] to last 5sts, k2, p3.

Rep the last 2 rows x 6.

Change to needles B and st st.

Work 4 rows.

DEC ROW: K to last 5sts, k2tog, k3.

Work 7 rows.

Work the last 8 rows x 4 and the dec row again. (61 (69:73:77) sts)

Work 7 rows, ending with a p row.

INC ROW: K to last 4sts, M1, k4.

Work 11 rows.

Rep the last 12 rows x 4 and the inc row again. (67 (75:79:83) sts)

Work straight until front measures 36 (37:37: 37)cm (14^1/$_4$ (14^1/$_2$:14^1/$_2$:14^1/$_2$)in) from cast on edge, ending with a k row.

Shape raglan armhole

NEXT ROW: Cast off 6 (8:9:10) sts, p to end. (61 (67:70:73) sts)

NEXT ROW: K1, skpo, k to last 5sts, k2tog, k3.

NEXT ROW: P to end.

Rep the last 2 rows x 24 (26:27:28). (11 (13:14:15) sts)

NEXT ROW: K to last 5sts, k2tog, k3.

NEXT ROW: P to end.

Rep the last 2 rows x 6 (8:9:10). (4sts)

Leave these sts on a stitch holder.

Sleeves (make 2)

With needles A, cast on 46 (54:58:62) sts).

RIB ROW 1: K2, [p2, k2] to end.

RIB ROW 2: P2, [k2, p2] to end.

Rep the last 2 rows x 6.

Change to needles B.

Beg with a k row, work in st st.

Work 2 rows.

INC ROW: K3, M1, k to last 3sts, M1, k3.

Work 5 rows.

Rep the last 6 rows x 21 and the inc row again. (92 (100:104:108) sts)

Work straight until sleeve measures 47cm (18^1/$_2$in) from cast on edge, ending with a p row.

Shape raglan tops

Cast off 6 (8:9:10) sts at beg of next 2 rows. (80 (84:86:88) sts)

2nd, 3rd, and 4th sizes

NEXT ROW: K1, skpo, k to last 3sts, k2tog, k1.

NEXT ROW: P to end.

NEXT ROW: K to end.

NEXT ROW: P to end.

Rep the last 4 rows x 2:3:4. (78sts)

1st size only

NEXT ROW: K1, skpo, k to last 3sts, k2tog, k1.

NEXT ROW: P to end.

All sizes

NEXT ROW: K1, skpo, patt to last 3sts, k2tog, k1.

NEXT ROW: P to end.

Rep the last 2 rows x 29. (18sts)

Leave these sts on a spare needle.

Right front and neck edging

With needle C and RS facing, pick up and k105 up right front edge from cast on edge to start of neck shaping, 52 (60:64:68) sts up neck shaping to raglan, k3 from stitch holder, k last st tog with first st on right sleeve, k17. (178 (186:190:194) sts)

RIB ROW 1: P2, [k2, p2] to end.

RIB ROW 2: K2, [p2, k2] to end.

These 2 rows form the rib.

Work 1 more row.

BUTTONHOLE ROW: Rib 3, p2tog, y2on, p2tog, [rib 12, p2tog, y2on, p2tog] x 6, rib to end.

Rib 3 rows.

Cast off in rib.

Left front and neck edging

With needle C and RS facing, k117 across left sleeve, k last st tog with first st on stitch holder, k3, pick up and k52 (60:64:68) sts down left front neck, then 105sts down left front edge to cast on edge. (178 (186:190:194) sts)

RIB ROW 1: P2, [k2, p2] to end.

RIB ROW 2: K2, [p2, k2] to end.

Rep the last 2 rows twice and the first row again.

Cast off in rib.

Making up

Join raglan and neckband seams. Join side and sleeve seams. Sew on buttons.

TOP TIP *When knitting this cardigan, pick up the front and neck edges evenly.*

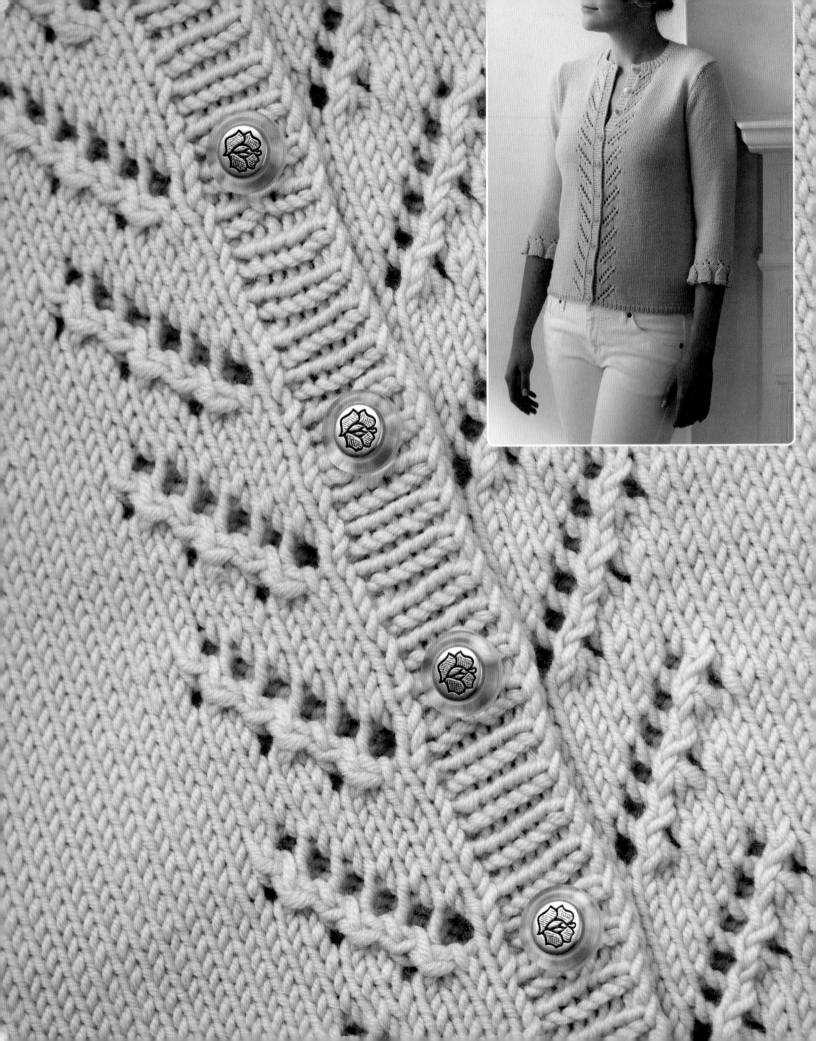

Bell-edge cardigan

This fairly elaborate design provides the opportunity to work lace patterning. The "bell" edging is made by gradually decreasing the initial number of stitches so that the fabric flutes to create this pretty effect.

Essential information

DIFFICULTY Difficult

SIZE To fit an adult female S (M:L:XL)

YARN

Sublime Extra Fine Merino Wool DK 50g

307 Julep x 9 (10:10:11)

NEEDLES

A: 1 pair of 3.25mm (UK10/US3) needles

B: 1 pair of 4mm (UK8/US6) needles

A

B

TENSION

22sts and 28 rows to 10cm (4in) over st st on 4mm (UK8/US6) needles

NOTIONS

Stitch markers

Stitch holder or spare needle

Large-eyed needle

10 x 15mm (½in) buttons

Right panel

(worked over 8sts)

ROW 1: Yrn, sk2p, yrn, k5.

ROWS 2, 4, 6, 8, AND 10: P8.

ROW 3: K1, yrn, k2tog tbl, k5.

ROW 5: K2, yrn, sk2p, yrn, k3.

ROW 7: K3, yrn, k2tog tbl, k3.

ROW 9: K4, yrn, sk2p, yrn, k1.

ROW 11: K5, yrn, k2tog tbl, k1.

ROW 12: P8.

These 12 rows form Right panel.

Left panel

(worked over 8sts)

ROW 1: K5, k3tog, yrn.

ROWS 2, 4, 6, 8, AND 10: P8.

ROW 3: K5, k2tog, yrn, k1.

ROW 5: K3, yrn, k3tog, yrn, k2.

ROW 7: K3, k2tog, yrn, k3.

ROW 9: K1, yrn, k3tog, yrn, k4.

ROW 11: K1, k2tog, yrn, k5.

ROW 12: P8.

These 12 rows form Left panel.

Right front

With needles A, cast on 49 (55:57:61) sts.

ROW 1 (RS): K2, [p1, k1] to last st, k1.

ROW 2: P2, [k1, p1] to last st, p1.

Rep the last 2 rows twice, inc 1st at side edge on last row on 3rd size only. (49 (55: 58: 61) sts) **

Change to needles B and patt.

ROW 1 (RS): K2, work row 1 of Right panel, k39 (45:48:51).

ROW 2: P.

ROWS 3–12: Rep rows 1 and 2 x 5 but working rows 3–12 of Right panel.

These 12 rows form patt.

***Cont in patt until work measures 37cm (14½in) from beg, ending at side edge. Place a marker at centre of last row.

Shape armhole

Cast off 6 (7: 8: 9) sts loosely at beg of next row. Dec 1st at armhole edge on next 5 rows, then on every foll alt row until 36 (40:42:44) sts rem. Cont straight until work measures 11 (13:13: 14)cm (4¼ (5¼:5¼:5½)in) from marker, ending at front edge.

Shape neck

Cast off 9 (9:10:10) sts loosely at beg of next row. Dec 1st at neck edge on every row until 23 (26:27:29) sts rem. Cont straight until front measures 17 (19:20:21)cm (6¾ (7½:8:8¼)in) from marker, ending at armhole edge.

Shape shoulder

Cast off 8 (9:9:9) sts loosely at beg of next and foll alt row. Work 1 row. Cast off rem 7 (8:9:11) sts.

Left front

Work as Right front to **. Change to needles B and patt.

ROW 1 (RS): K to last 10sts, work row 1 of Left panel, k2.

ROW 2: P.

ROWS 3–12: Rep rows 1 and 2 x 5, but working rows 3–12 of Left panel. These 12 rows form patt.

Complete as Right front working from *** to end, reversing the shaping.

Back

With needles A, cast on 101 (113:119:125) sts.
Rep rows 1 and 2 of rib as given for Right front, ignoring reference to increasing.
Change to needles B, and beg k row working in st st until back measures 37cm (14^1/$_2$in) from beg, ending after a p row.

Shape armholes

Cast off 6 (7:8:9) sts loosely at beg of next 2 rows.
Dec 1st at each end of next 5 rows, then on every foll alt row until 75 (83:87:91) sts rem.
Cont straight until back measures same as front to shoulder shaping, ending after a p row.

Shape shoulders

Cast off 8 (9:9:9) sts loosely at beg of next 4 rows, then 7 (8:9:11) sts at beg of next 2 rows.
Slip rem 29 (31:33:33) sts onto a spare needle.

Sleeves (make 2)

With needles B and using the 2 needle method to obtain a loose edge, cast on 109 (119:123:131) sts.
Do not k into back of sts on first row.
K 1 row.

Work bell edging

ROW 1 (RS): P3 (2:4:2), [k7, p5] x 8 (9:9:10), k7, p3 (2:4:2).
ROW 2: K3 (2:4:2), [p7, k5] x 8 (9:9:10), p7, k to end.

ROWS 3–4: As rows 1 and 2.
ROW 5: P3 (2:4:2), [k2tog tbl, k3, k2tog, p5] x 8 (9:9:10), k2tog tbl, k3, k2tog, p to end.
(91 (99:103:109) sts)
ROWS 6 AND 8: Work across row knitting all k sts and purling all p sts.
ROW 7: P3 (2:4:2), [k2tog tbl, k1, k2tog, p5] x 8 (9:9:10), k2tog tbl, k1, k2tog, p to end.
(73 (79:83:87) sts)
ROW 9: P3 (2:4:2), [sk2p, p5] x 8 (9:9:10), sk2p, p to end. (55 (59:63:65) sts)
ROW 10: P.
ROW 11: K2 (1:3:1), [yrn, sk2p, yrn, k3] x 8 (9:9:10), yrn, sk2p, yrn, k2 (1:3:1).
ROW 12: P.
ROW 13: K3 (2:4:2), [yrn, k2tog tbl, k4] x 8 (9:9:10), yrn, k2tog tbl, k to end.
Change to st st and beg p row (for WS) work 7 rows straight.
Shape sleeve by inc 1st at each end of next row, then on every foll 10th (8th:6th:6th) row until there are 61 (69:73:83) sts, then on every foll 10th (10th:8th:8th) row until there are 69 (77:83:87) sts.
Cont straight until sleeve measures 32 (33:33:33)cm (12^1/$_2$ (13:13:13)in) from beg, ending after a p row.

Shape top

Cast off 6 (7:8:9) sts at beg of next 2 rows.
Work 2 (4:4:6) rows straight.

Dec 1st at each end of next row, then on every foll alt row until 41 (47:53:57) sts rem, then on every row until 29 (35:41:45) sts rem.
Cast off loosely.

Neckband

First join shoulders. With needles A and RS facing, k24 (27:31:31) sts evenly round right front neck, k across sts of back neck, finally k24 (27:31:31) sts evenly round left front neck. (77 (89:103:107) sts)
Beg row 2, work 6 rows in rib as on Right front.
Cast off loosely in rib.

Right front border

With needles A and RS facing, k125 (127:129:129) sts evenly up right front edge.
ROW 1: K1, [p1, k1] to end.
ROW 2: K2, [p1, k1] to last st, k1.
ROW 3: Rib 3 (4:4:4), [cast off 2sts in rib, rib 11 – including sts on right needle after cast off] x 9, cast off 2sts, rib to end.
ROW 4: As row 2, casting on 2sts neatly over those cast off.
Rib 2 more rows.
Cast off evenly in rib.

Left front border

Omitting buttonholes, work as Right front border.

Making up

Sew in sleeve tops. Join side and sleeve seams using mattress stitch. Sew on the buttons.

TOP TIP *Loosely cast off the stitches when shaping the sleeves.*

Nautical cardigan

A cardigan shaped with a delicate boat pattern knitted in crisp cotton. The lace stitch for the main body of work has a fair amount of stretch, so remember to change down needle size when working the yoke pattern and top of the sleeves.

Essential information

DIFFICULTY Moderate

SIZE To fit an adult female S (M:L:XL)

YARN

Rico Essentials Cotton DK 50g

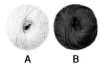

A   **B**

A: 80 White x 9 (10:10:11)

B: 32 Blue x 3

NEEDLES

A: 1 pair of 3.25mm (UK10/US3) needles

B: 1 pair of 3.75mm (UK9/US5) needles

C: 40cm (16in), 3.25mm (UK10/US3) circular needle

TENSION

24sts and 32 rows to 10cm (4in) over patt on 3.75mm (UK9/US5) needles

NOTIONS

Stitch holder and spare needle

Large-eyed needle

8 x 1cm (½in) brass buttons

SPECIAL ABBREVIATIONS

P1 TBL P into back of st

NOTE: The s2kpo must be worked as stated in the instructions to achieve the correct look. Slip them as in k2tog.

Back

Using needles A and yarn B, cast on 109 (121:133:145) sts.

Work 1 row k1 tbl, p1 (twisted) rib then change to yarn A and cont in rib until work measures 7cm (2³/₄in) ending on a WS row.

Change to needles B and start patt as follows:

ROW 1 (RS): K.

ROW 2: K.

ROW 3: *K2tog, yon; rep from *, end k1.

ROW 4: K.

ROW 5: *K1 tbl, yon, k4, s2kpo, k4, yon; rep from *, end k1 tbl.

ROW 6: *P1 tbl, k1, p9, k1; rep from *, end p1 tbl.

ROW 7: *K1 tbl, p1, yon, k3, s2kpo, k3, yon, p1; rep from *, end k1 tbl.

ROW 8: *P1 tbl, k1, p1 tbl, p7, p1 tbl, k1; rep from *, end p1 tbl.

ROW 9: *K1 tbl, p1, k1 tbl, yon, k2, s2kpo, k2, yon, k1 tbl, p1; rep from *, end k1 tbl.

ROW 10: P1 tbl, *k1, p1 tbl, k1, p5, k1, p1 tbl, k1, p1 tbl; rep from * to end.

ROW 11: *[K1 tbl, p1] x 2, yon, k1, s2kpo, k1, yon, p1, k1 tbl, p1; rep from *, end k1 tbl.

ROW 12: P1 tbl, *[k1, p1 tbl] x 2, p3, [p1 tbl, k1] x 2, p1 tbl; rep from * to end.

ROW 13: *[K1 tbl, p1] x 2, k1 tbl, yon, s2kpo, yon, [k1 tbl, p1] x 2; rep from *, end k1 tbl.

ROW 14: P1 tbl, *k1, p1 tbl; rep from * to end.

ROW 15: K1 tbl, *p1, k1 tbl; rep from * to end.

ROW 16: Rep row 14.

These 16 rows form the patt, rep from row 1 until you have completed 5 (5:6:6) full patt reps ending on row 16 of last patt.

Shape armholes and start yoke pattern

Change to needles A.

ROW 1 (RS): Cast off 4 (4:6:6) sts at beg of row, k to end.

ROW 2: Cast off 4 (4:6:6) sts at beg of row, k to end. (101 (113:121:133) sts)

ROW 3: K1, ssk, *yon, k2tog; rep from * to last 3sts, k2tog, k1. (99 (111:119:131) sts)

ROW 4: K1, ssk, k to last 3sts, k2tog, k1.

ROW 5: Using yarn B, k1, ssk, k to last 3sts, k2tog, k1.

ROW 6: Using yarn B, p1, p2tog, p to last 3sts, p2tog tbl, p1.

These 6 rows form the patt, cont to dec 1st at each end of next and foll alt row as written. (89 (101:109:121) sts)

Cont in stripe patt without shaping until armhole measures 19 (20:21:22)cm 7¹/₂ (8:8¹/₄:9)in) from beg ending on a WS row.

Shape back neck

Keeping patt correct, work across 26 (30:32:36) sts, turn, leave rem sts on a spare needle, and work each side separately. Dec 1st at neck edge on the next 2 rows. (24 (28:30:34) sts)

Work WS row. Break yarn and leave sts on a holder to cast off with back later.

With RS facing, rejoin yarn and cast off centre 37 (41:45:49) sts, patt to end of row. Complete to match first side.

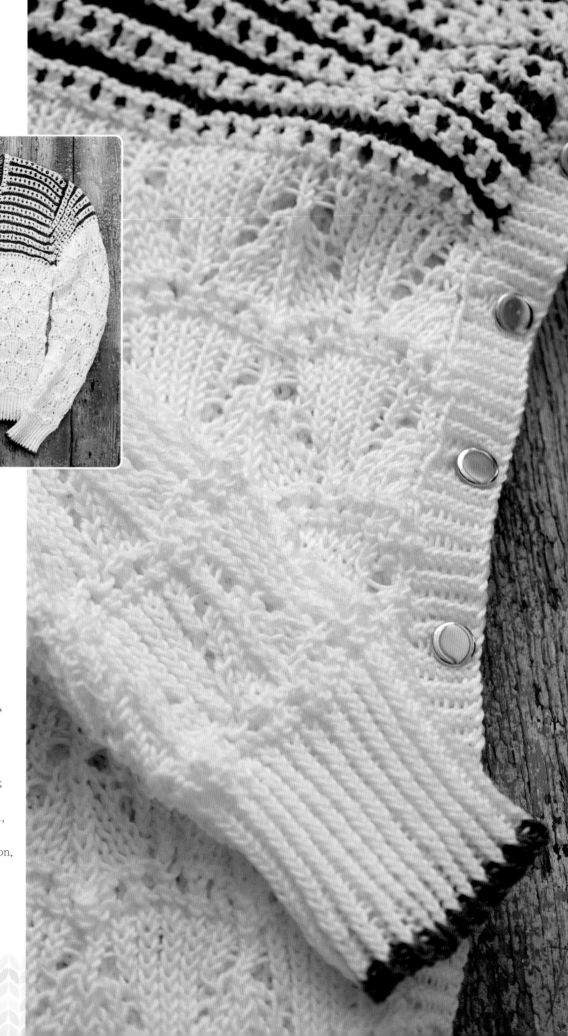

Left front

Using yarn B and needles A cast on 55 (61:67: 73) sts.

Work twisted rib as for Back.

Change to needles B and set patt as follows:

ROW 1 (RS): K.

ROW 2: K.

ROW 3: *K2tog, yon; rep from * to last st, k1.

ROW 4: K.

For 1st and 3rd sizes only

ROW 5: *K1, yon, k4, s2kpo, k4, yon; rep from * to last 7sts, k1, yon, k4, ssk.

ROW 6: P5, k1, p1 tbl, *k1, p9, k1, p1 tbl; rep from * to end.

ROW 7: *K1 tbl, p1, yon, k3, s2kpo, k3, yon, p1; rep from * to last 7sts, k1 tbl, p1, yon, k3, ssk.

ROW 8: P5, k1, p1 tbl, *k1, p1 tbl, p7, p1 tbl, k1, p1 tbl; rep from * to end.

ROW 9: *K1 tbl, p1, k1 tbl, yon, k2, s2kpo, k2, yon, k1 tbl, p1; rep from * to last 7sts, k1 tbl, p1, k1 tbl, yon, k2, ssk.

ROW 10: P3, p1 tbl, k1, p1 tbl, *k1, p1 tbl, k1, p5, [k1, p1 tbl] x 2; rep from * to end.

ROW 11: *[K1 tbl, p1] x 2, yon, k1, s2kpo, k1, yon, p1, k1 tbl, p1; rep from * to last 7sts, [k1 tbl, p1] x 2, yon, k1, ssk.

ROW 12: P2, p1 tbl, [k1, p1 tbl] x 2, *[k1, p1 tbl] x 2, p3, [p1 tbl, k1] x 2, p1 tbl, rep from * to end.

ROW 13: *[K1 tbl, p1] x 2, k1 tbl, yon, s2kpo, yon, [k1 tbl, p1] x 2; rep from * to last 8sts, [k1 tbl, p1] x 2, k1 tbl, yon, ssk, k1.

ROW 14: P1, p1 tbl,*k1, p1 tbl; rep from * to end.

ROW 15: *K1 tbl, p1; rep from *, end k1.

ROW 16: Rep row 14.

For 2nd and 4th sizes only
Work patt as for Back.

All sizes
Work patt as set until you have completed 5 (5:6:6) full patt reps ending on WS row.

Shape armhole and yoke pattern

Change to needles A.
Start to work stripe patt as for Back.
Work armhole shaping.
NEXT ROW (RS): Cast off 4 (4:6:6) sts at beg of row. (51 (57:61:67) sts)
Then work 1 row straight.
Dec 1st at armhole on next 4 rows then on foll alt row. (46 (52:56:62) sts)
Cont to work yoke without shaping until armhole measures 7 (7:8:8)cm (2³/₄ (2³/₄:3:3)in) from beg of shaping ending on a RS row.

Sailing boats chart

Work all odd number (RS) rows from right to left and all even number (WS) rows from left to right.

KEY

	K on RS rows, p on WS rows
●	P on RS rows, k on WS rows
O	Yarnover
ℛ	K into back of st on RS rows, p into back of st on WS rows
╱	K2tog
⋀	S2kpo

Shape front neck

NEXT ROW (WS): Keeping patt correct throughout, cast off 11 (12:13:15) sts at beg of row. (35 (40:43:47) sts)

Then dec 1st at neck edge on the next 6 (6:8:8) rows. (29 (34:35:39) sts)

Then on every foll alt row until 24 (28:30:34) sts rem.

Cont without shaping until the front matches the back, ending on a WS row.

With RS of back facing RS of front and using 3 needles, cast off the front shoulder 24 (28:30:34) sts with the back left shoulder 24 (28:30:34) sts.

Right front

Work rib as Left front then set patt as follows:

Change to needles B.

ROW 1 (RS): K.

ROW 2: K.

For 1st and 3rd sizes only

ROW 3: *K2tog, yon; rep from * end, k2tog, yon, k1.

ROW 4: K.

ROW 5: K2tog, k4, yon, k1 tbl, *yon, k4, s2kpo, k4, yon, k1 tbl; rep from * to end.

ROW 6: *P1 tbl, k1, p9, k1; rep from *, to last 7sts, p1 tbl, k1, p5.

ROW 7: K2tog, k3, yon, p1, k1 tbl, *p1, yon, k3, S2kpo, k3, yon, p1, k1 tbl; rep from * to end.

ROW 8: *P1 tbl, k1, p1 tbl, p7, p1 tbl, k1; rep from * to last 7sts, p1 tbl, k1, p5.

ROW 9: K2tog, k2, yon, k1 tbl, p1, k1 tbl, *p1, k1 tbl, yon, k2, s2kpo, k2, yon, k1 tbl, p1, k1 tbl; rep from * to end.

ROW 10: *[P1 tbl, k1] x 2, p5, k1, p1 tbl, k1; rep from * to last 7sts, [p1 tbl, k1] x 2, p3.

ROW 11: K2tog, k1, yon, [p1, k1 tbl] x 2, *p1, k1 tbl, p1, yon, k1, s2kpo, k1, yon, [p1, k1 tbl] x 2; rep from * to end.

ROW 12: *[P1 tbl, k1] x 2, p1 tbl, p3, [p1 tbl, k1] x 2; rep from * to last 7sts, [p1 tbl, k1] x 2, p3.

ROW 13: K1, k2tog, yon, [k1 tbl, p1] x 2, k1 tbl, *[p1, k1 tbl] x 2, yon, s2kpo, yon, k1 tbl, [p1, k1 tbl] x 2; rep from * to end.

ROW 14: P1 tbl, *k1, p1 tbl; rep from * end.

ROW 15: K1 tbl, *p1, k1 tbl; rep from * to end.

ROW 16: Rep row 14.

For 2nd and 4th sizes only

Complete as Left front.

Start armhole shaping on WS row and front neck shaping on RS row.

Cast off with right back shoulder.

Sleeves (work 2)

Using needles A and yarn B, cast on 49 (49:55:55) sts.

Work rib as for Back until it measures 8 (8:9:9) cm (3 (3:3^1/$_2$:3^1/$_2$)in) ending on a WS row.

Change to needles B.

ROW 1 (RS): K.

ROW 2: K.

ROW 3: K0 (0:3:3), *k2tog, yon, rep from * to last 0 (0:3:3) sts, k0 (0:3:3).

This sets the position for the patt. Cont working as set from row 4 of patt.

At the same time inc 1st at each end of 5th and every foll 6th (4th:4th:4th) row, working the new sts into the patt until there are 81 (73:79:89) sts. Then on every foll 0 (6th:6th:6th) row until there are 81 (89:95:99) sts.

Cont without shaping until you have completed 7 full patt reps ending on row 16.

Shape sleeve head

NEXT ROW: Start working stripe yoke patt. At the same time, cast off 4 (4:6:6) sts at beg of next 2 rows. (73 (81:83:87) sts)

Then dec 1st at each end for next 5 rows. (63 (71:73:77) sts)

Then on every foll alt row until 41 (41:43:45) sts rem.

Cast off.

Front bands

Right front buttonhole band

Using needles A and yarn A, with RS facing and starting at the hem edge of right front, pick up and k111 (111:127:127) evenly up to start of neck shaping.

Work 3 rows of twisted rib as Back.

NEXT ROW (WORK BUTTONHOLES): Rib 5, yon, k2tog, *rib 15 (15:17:17), yon, k2tog; rep from * until you have worked 7 buttonholes, rib to end.

Work 3 more rib rows then cast off in rib.

Left front button band

Starting at the neck edge of the left front, pick up as for Right front.

Work in rib for 7 rows then cast off in rib.

Neckband

Using needle C and yarn A, with RS facing and starting at the edge of the right front, pick up and k7 across the buttonhole band, then pick up and k45 (49:51:57) to shoulder seam, pick up and k37 (41:45:49) across back neck, pick up and k45 (49:51:57) down the left front neck, and 7sts across button band. (141 (153:161:177) sts)

ROW 1 (WS): K to last 7sts, [p1, k1] x 3, p1.

ROW 2: K1 tbl, p1, k1 tbl, yon, k2tog, p1, k1 tbl, *yon, k2tog; rep from * to last 7sts, [k1 tbl, p1] x 3, k1 tbl.

ROW 3: [P1 tbl, k1] x 3, p1 tbl, K to last 7sts, rib to end.

ROW 4: Using yarn B, cast off knitwise.

Making up

Press according to instructions on the ballbands. Join side and sleeve seams, being careful to match the pattern bands. Set in sleeve, matching the centre of the sleeve head to the shoulder seam. Sew buttons onto left front button band. Sew in all loose ends.

Fair Isle cardigan

This colourwork pattern is inspired by traditional Fair Isle. It is a 4-stitch repeat so there's no need to weave the yarns in at the back while you're knitting. Strand them loosely giving a gentle stretch on the needle so the work doesn't lose its elasticity.

Essential information

DIFFICULTY Moderate

SIZE To fit an adult female S (M:L:XL)

YARN

Patons Diploma Gold DK 50g

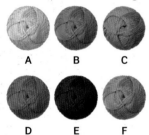

A   B   C

D   E   F

A: 6143 Natural x 5 (5:6:7)

B: 6169 Airforce x 2 (2:2:2)

C: 6307 Warm beige x 1 (2:2:2)

D: 6308 Lilac pink x 1 (1:2:2)

E: 6245 Plum x 1 (1:2:2)

F: 6213 Thyme x 1 (1:1:1)

NEEDLES

A: 1 pair of 3.25mm (UK10/US3) needles

B: 1 pair of 4mm (UK8/US6) needles

A

B

TENSION

22sts and 24 rows to 10cm (4in) over patt on 4mm (UK8/US6) needles

NOTIONS

2 stitch holders or safety pins

Stitch markers

Large-eyed needle

6 (7:8:8) x 18mm (¾in) buttons

Back

With needles A and yarn A, cast on 99 (107:123:131) sts.

Work 12 rows k1, p1 rib, beg alt rows p1.

Change to needles B and cont in st st in patt, stranding yarn not in use loosely across WS of work, reading Fair Isle chart (see p.25) from right to left on RS (k) rows and from left to right on WS (p) rows as follows:

ROW 1 (RS): K1 from A to B, rep 4sts from B to C to last 2sts, k2 from C to D.

ROW 2: P2 from D to C, rep 4sts from C to B to last st, p1 from B to A.

Cont until all 28 patt rows have been worked. These 28 rows form the patt.

Rep them x 1 (1:1:2), then patt 16 (20:28:4) rows more.

Shape armholes

Cont in patt as set, cast off 6 (6:7:8) sts at beg of next 2 rows. (87 (95:109:115) sts)

Dec 1st at both ends of next row and foll 7 (8:9:9) alt rows. (71 (77:89:95) sts)

Patt 39 (41:45:49) rows straight, ending after 16th (24th:10th:18th) patt row.

Shape shoulders

Cast off in patt (with A:with A:in patt).

Place markers 16 (18:22:24) sts in from beg and end of work to indicate shoulders.

Left front

With needles A and yarn A, cast on 52 (56:64:68) sts.

ROW 1 (RS): [K1, p1] to last 2sts, k2.

ROW 2: [K1, p1] to end.

Rep last 2 rows x 5. Change to needles B and cont in patt as follows:

NEXT ROW (RS): Patt to last 6sts, turn and cast on 1st, slip rem 6sts onto safety pin for button band. (47 (51:59:63) sts)

Patt 71 (75:83:87) rows more, ending after 16th (20th:28th:4th) patt row.

Shape armholes and neck

NEXT ROW (RS): Cast off 6 (6:7:8) sts, patt to last 2sts, k2tog.

Dec 1st at both ends of foll 8 (9:10:10) alt rows. (24 (26:31:34) sts)

Keeping armhole edge straight, cont dec at neck edge on 8 (8:9:10) foll 4th rows. (16 (18:22:24) sts)

Patt 7 (9:9:9) rows straight, ending after 16th (24th:10th:18th) patt row. Cast off.

Right front

With needles A and yarn A, cast on 52 (56:64:68) sts.

ROW 1 (RS): K2, [p1, k1] to end.

ROW 2: [P1, k1] to end.

ROW 3 (BUTTONHOLE): K2, yfwd, k2tog, [p1, k1] to end. Rib 9 rows more as set.

NEXT ROW (RS): Rib 6, turn and cast on 1st then slip these 7sts onto safety pin for buttonhole band, with needles B cast on 1st, patt to end. (47 (51:59:63) sts)

Patt 71 (75:83:87) rows more, ending after 16th (20th:28th:4th) patt row.

Shape armhole and neck

NEXT ROW (RS): K2tog, patt to end.

NEXT ROW: Cast off 6 (6:7:8) sts, patt to end.

Dec 1st at both ends of next row and foll 7 (8:9:9) alt rows. (24 (26:31:34) sts)

Keeping armhole edge straight, cont dec at neck edge on 8 (8:9:10) foll 4th rows. (16 (18:22:24) sts)

Patt 7 (9:9:9) rows straight, ending after 16th (24th:10th:18th) patt row. Cast off.

Sleeves

With needles A and yarn A, cast on 51 (55:59:63) sts.

Work 12 rows k1, p1 rib beg alt rows p1.

Change to needles B and beg with 11th patt row cont in patt as back, inc 1st at both ends of 3rd row and 9 (9:11:11) foll 8th rows to 71 (75:83:87) sts, working inc sts into patt as sides.

Work 15 (19:11:15) rows straight, ending after 16th (20th:28th:4th) patt row.

Shape top

Cast off 6 (6:7:8) sts at beg of next 2 rows.

Dec 1st at both ends of next row and every foll alt row to 17sts, ending after WS row.

Cast off 4sts at beg of next 2 rows. Cast off rem 9sts.

Button band

With needles A and yarn A, cast on 1st, then with RS facing [k1, p1] x 2, k2 across 6sts from left front safety pin. (7sts)

NEXT ROW (WS): K1, [p1, k1] x 3.

NEXT ROW: [P1, k1] x 3, k1.

Cont in rib as set until band fits up left front edge to left shoulder, then across back neck to right shoulder. Cast off.

Buttonhole band

Mark button band with pins to indicate buttons, first one on 3rd row of rib, last one level with beg of neck shaping, and rem 4 (5:6:6) sts spaced evenly between (see p.294).

Slip 7sts from right front safety pin onto needles B, then with WS facing join in yarn A, k1, [p1, k1] x 3.

NEXT ROW (RS): K2, [p1, k1] x 2, p1.

Cont in rib as set, working buttonholes at pin positions as follows:

BUTTONHOLE ROW (RS): K2, yfwd, k2tog, p1, k1, p1.

Cont in rib until band fits up right front edge to shoulder. Cast off.

Making up

Press, following instructions on ballband. Sew on front bands and join shoulder seams, matching markers. Join side and sleeve seams. Sew in sleeves. Sew on buttons to correspond with the position of the buttonholes.

Fair Isle chart

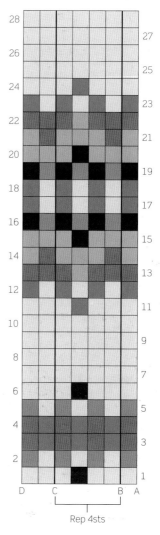

Rep 4sts

KEY

- ☐ Natural
- ■ Airforce
- ■ Warm beige
- ■ Lilac pink
- ■ Plum
- ■ Thyme

TOP TIP *Create the classic edgings with a knit one, purl one rib.*

Essential information

DIFFICULTY Difficult

SIZE To fit an adult female S (M:L:XL)

YARN

King Cole Bamboo Cotton DK 100g

A: 521 Blue x 4 (5:5:6)

B: 530 White x 1 (2:2:2)

NEEDLES

A: 1 pair of 3mm (UK11/USn/a) needles

B: 1 pair of 3.75mm (UK9/US5) needles

TENSION

23sts and 30 rows to 10cm (4in) over patt on 3.75mm (UK9/US5) needles

NOTIONS

1 stitch holder

6 x 15mm (½in) buttons

Large-eyed needle

Chanel-style cardigan

You don't need to be a Fair Isle knitter to work this *haute couture* button-front jacket.

Back

With needles A and yarn A, cast on 101 (117:133:141) sts.

K 9 rows working 1 row in yarn A, 6 rows in yarn B, and 2 rows in yarn A.

Change to needles B and patt as follows:

ROW 1 (RS): K in yarn B.

ROW 2: P in yarn B.

ROWS 3–4: As rows 1 and 2.

ROW 5: K as follows: 2B, [1A, 1B] to last st, 1B.

ROW 6: P in yarn B. **

ROW 7: K in yarn B.

ROWS 8–9: As rows 6 and 7.

ROW 10: P as follows: 2B [1A, 1B] to last st, 1B.

These 10 rows form patt.

Cont in patt until work measures 36cm (14$\frac{1}{4}$in) from beg, measured through centre of work, ending after a WS row.

Shape armholes

Cont in patt, cast off 7 (9:10:11) sts loosely at beg of next 2 rows.

Dec 1st at each end of next 3 (5:7:7) rows, then on every foll alt row until 75 (83:93:97) sts rem. Cont straight until work measures 52 (54:58: 59)cm (20$\frac{1}{2}$ (21:22$\frac{3}{4}$:23)in) from beg, measured through centre of work, ending after a WS row.

Shape shoulders

Cast off 7 (8:9:9) sts loosely at beg of next 4 rows, then 7 (7:9:10) sts at beg of next 2 rows. Slip rem 33 (37:39:41) sts onto a stitch holder and leave.

Right front

Commencing with 49 (57:65:69) sts, work as Back until front measures same as back to armhole shaping, ending at side edge.

Shape armhole

Cont in patt, cast off 7 (9:10:11) sts at beg of next row.

Dec 1st at armhole edge on next 3 (5:7:7) rows, then on every foll alt row until 36 (40:45:47) sts rem.

Cont straight until front measures 5 (6:8:9)cm (2$\frac{1}{4}$ (2$\frac{1}{2}$:3:3$\frac{1}{2}$)in) less than Back up to start of shoulder shaping, ending at front edge.

Shape neck

Cast off 10 (12:13:14) sts loosely all in yarn B at beg of next row.

Dec 1st at neck edge on next 5 rows.
(21 (23: 27:28) sts)

Cont straight until front measures same as Back to shoulder shaping, ending at armhole edge.

Shape shoulder

Cast off 7 (8:9:9) sts loosely at beg of next row and foll alt row.

Work 1 row. Cast off rem sts.

Left front

Work to match Right front.

Sleeves

Commencing with 43 (47:53:55) sts, work as Back to **.

Cont in patt shaping sleeve by inc 1st at each end of next row, then on every foll 8th (6th:4th:4th) row until there are 61 (77:71:85) sts, then on every foll 10th (8th:6th:6th) row until there are 69 (83:97:103) sts, taking extra sts into patt.

Cont straight until sleeve measures 43 (44:46: 46)cm (17 (17$\frac{1}{2}$:18:18)in) from beg, ending after a WS row.

Shape top

Cast off 7 (9:10:11) sts loosely at beg of next 2 rows.

Dec 1st at each end of every RS row until 27 (33:39:47) sts rem, then on every row until 17 (23:29:37) sts rem.

Cast off loosely in yarn B.

Neckband

First join shoulders. With needles B and yarn A, k26 (30:32:34) sts evenly round right front neck, k across back neck sts, finally k26 (30:32:34) sts evenly round left front neck. (85 (97:103:109) sts)

K 8 rows working 1 row in yarn A, 6 rows in yarn B, and 1 row yarn A.

Cast off firmly knitwise in yarn A.

Right border

With needles A and yarn B, k117 (123:130:132) sts evenly along right front edge.

ROW 1 (WS): P in yarn B.

ROWS 2–3: K in yarn A.

ROWS 4–5: K in yarn B.

ROW 6: K52 (58:63:65) sts in yarn B, [cast off 2sts, k8 including st on right needle after cast off] x 4, cast off 2sts, k to end.

ROW 7: K in yarn B, casting on 2sts neatly in each place where sts were cast off.

ROWS 8–9: K in yarn B.

ROW 10: K in yarn A.

Cast off knitwise in yarn A.

Left border

Commencing at neck edge and omitting buttonholes, work to match Right border.

Making up

Sew in sleeve tops. Join side and sleeve seams. Sew on buttons.

Men's cable jacket

This is a straightforward knitting pattern with bold cables worked on the back and front, and makes a great second garment for a newcomer to knitting. The front borders and collar are worked in garter stitch.

Essential information

DIFFICULTY Moderate

SIZE To fit an adult male S (M:L:XL)

YARN

King Cole Merino Blend Chunky 50g

918 Silver x 17 (17:18:19)

NEEDLES

A: 1 pair of 5mm (UK6/US8) needles
B: 1 pair of 6mm (UK4/US10) needles
C: Cable needle

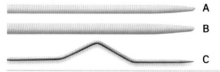

A
B
C

TENSION

14sts and 20 rows to 10cm (4in) over st st on 6mm (UK4/US10) needles

NOTIONS

Large-eyed needle
5 x 3.5cm (1⅜in) buttons

SPECIAL ABBREVIATIONS

P1B P into back of next st
C8B Slip 4sts to cable needle (cn), hold in back, k4, k4 from cn
C8F As C8B but leave cn sts in front of work

Back

With needles A, cast on 74 (78:86:90) sts.
ROW 1 (RS): K2, [p2, k2] to end.
ROW 2: P2, [k2, p2] to end.
Work 8 more rows in rib. **
NEXT ROW: Rib 13 (15:16:18), [M1, rib 3] x 5, M1, rib to last 28 (30:31:33) sts, [M1, rib 3] x 5, M1, rib to end. (86 (90:98:102) sts)
NEXT ROW: P across row noting that on 2nd size only 1st should be increased at centre, and on 3rd size only 1st decreased at centre. (86 (91:97:102) sts)
Change to needles B and patt.
ROW 1 (RS): K10 (12:13:15), *p3, k1 tbl, p3, k8, p3, k1 tbl, p3 *, k22 (23:27:28), work from * to *, k10 (12:13:15).
ROW 2: P10 (12:13:15), *k3, p1b, k3, p8, k3, p1b, k3 *, p22 (23:27:28), work from * to *, p10 (12:13:15).
ROWS 3–8: Rep rows 1 and 2 x 3.
ROW 9: K10 (12:13:15), *p3, k1 tbl, p3, C8B, p3, k1 tbl, p3 *, k22 (23:27:28), work from * to * but working C8F into place of C8B, k to end.
ROW 10: As row 2.
These 10 rows form patt.
Cont in patt until work measures 41cm (16¼in) from beg, ending after a WS row.

Shape armholes

Cast off 5 (6:7:8) sts loosely at beg of next 2 rows.
Dec 1st at each end of next 4 RS rows. (68 (71:75:78) sts)
Cont straight until back measures 61 (63:64:65)cm (24 (25:25¼:26)in) at centre, ending after a WS row.

Shape shoulders

Cast off 8sts at beg of next 4 rows, then 7 (8:9:10) sts at beg of next 2 rows.
Cast off rem 22 (23:25:26) sts loosely.

Right front

Commencing with 34 (38:42:42) sts, work as Back to **.
NEXT ROW: Rib 10 (8:11:13), [M1, rib 3] x 7 (5:4:7), M1, rib to end. (42 (44:47:50) sts)
NEXT ROW: P.
Change to needles B and patt.
ROW 1 (RS): K10 (10:12:13), p3, k1 tbl, p3, k8, p3, k1 tbl, p3, k10 (12:13:15).
ROW 2: P10 (12:13:15), k3, p1b, k3, p8, k3, p1b, k3, p10 (10:12:13).
ROWS 3–8: Rep rows 1 and 2 x 3.
ROW 9: As row 1 but working C8F in place of k8.
ROW 10: As row 2.
These 10 rows form patt.
Cont in patt until work measures 6 rows less than Back up to armhole shaping, thus ending after a WS row.

Shape front slope

NEXT ROW (DEC ROW): K1, k2tog tbl, work to end.
Work 6 rows working dec row again on 4th of these rows. (40 (42:45:48) sts)

Shape armhole

Cast off 5 (6:7:8) sts loosely at beg of next row.
***Cont working front slope, dec spaced as before. At the same time dec 1st at armhole edge on next and every foll RS row until 29 (30:32:34) sts rem.

Cont working front slope, dec only on every 4th row from previous dec until 23 (24:25:26) sts rem.

Cont straight until front measures same as Back to shoulder shaping, ending at armhole edge.

Shape shoulder

Cast off 8sts at beg of next and foll alt row. Work 1 row. Cast off rem sts.

Left front

Commencing with 34 (38:42:42) sts, work as Back to **.

NEXT ROW: Rib 3 (15:19:8), [M1, rib 3] x 7 (5:4:7), M1, rib to end. (42 (44:47:50) sts)

NEXT ROW: P.

Change to needles B and patt.

ROW 1 (RS): K10 (12:13:15), p3, k1 tbl, p3, k8, p3, k1 tbl, p3, k10 (10:12:13).

ROW 2: P10 (10:12:13), k3, p1b, k3, p8, k3, p1b, k3, p10 (12:13:15).

ROWS 3–8: Rep rows 1 and 2 x 3.

ROW 9: As row 1 but working C8B in place of k8.

ROW 10: As row 2.

Cont in patt until work measures same as Right front up to front slope dec row.

NEXT ROW (DEC ROW): Work to last 3sts, k2tog, k1. Work 5 rows working dec row again on 4th of these rows. (40 (42:45:48) sts)

Shape armhole

Cast off 5 (6:7:8) sts loosely at beg of next row. Work 1 row straight.

Complete as Right front working from *** to end.

Sleeves (make 2)

Commencing with 28 (30:30:34) sts, work 10 rows in rib. As on back inc 4 (4:7:5) sts evenly on last row. (32 (34:37:39) sts)

Change to needles B and beg k row work in st st shaping sleeve by inc 1st at each end of 5th row, then on every foll 6th row until there are 44 (46:57:59) sts, then on every foll 8th (8th:8th: 6th) row until there are 52 (56:61:65) sts.

Cont straight until sleeve measures 46 (47:47: 48)cm (18 (18½:18½:19)in) from beg, ending after a p row.

Shape top

Cast off 5 (6:7:8) sts loosely at beg of next 2 rows.

Work 4 (6:6:8) rows straight.

Dec 1st at each end of next and every foll k row until 20 (24:25:29) sts rem, then on every row until 14 (14:15:19) sts rem. Cast off loosely.

Right border and collar

Join shoulder shapings.

With needles A, cast on 10sts.

Work in g st (k every row) until strip, when very slightly stretched, measures 39cm (15½in), ending after an uneven number of rows. **

Shape neck edge

NEXT ROW (INC ROW AND RS): K to last st, M1, k1.

***Cont working inc row on every foll 4th row until there are 18sts, then on every foll 6th row until there are 24 (24:25:25) sts.

Work 5 rows straight.

Shape collar

NEXT ROW: K to last 3sts, turn.

NEXT ROW: S1 firmly, k to end.

NEXT 4 ROWS: Work straight.

Rep the last 6 rows until shaped edge fits from start of right front slope shaping round to centre back of neck, allowing for collar to be slightly stretched.

Cast off loosely.

Left border and collar

First mark positions for 5 buttonholes on right border section, first to be in 7th (8th) rows, last one level with (or up to 8 rows less than) the start of neck edge shaping, and remaining three spaced evenly between (see pp.294–295).

Work as Right border and collar to ** working buttonholes to match markers as follows:

ROW 1: K3, cast off 4sts, k to end.

ROW 2: K casting on 4sts neatly over those cast off.

Shape neck edge

NEXT ROW (INC ROW AND RS): K1, M1, k to end.

Complete to match Right border and collar working from *** to end but noting that 6 rows straight should be worked before shaping collar in place of 5 rows.

Making up

Omitting ribbing, press work on WS following ballband instructions. Sew in sleeve tops. Join side and sleeve seams. Sew on borders and collar sections, joining ends at back of neck. Sew on buttons. Press seams.

TOP TIP *Refer to p.287 for further information about knitting cables.*

Girl's summer bolero

This garment is knitted in one piece and only has one short sleeve seam. Use stitch markers to show the side seams and when you join the sleeves to the main body.

Essential information

DIFFICULTY Moderate

SIZE To fit a child, aged 2-3 (3-4:5-6) years

YARN

Rico Essentials Cotton DK 50g

A   **B**

A: 51 Nature x 3 (4:5)

B: 41 Mint x 1

NEEDLES

A: 80cm (32in), 3.75mm (UK9/US5) circular needle

B: 80cm (32in), 3.25mm (UK10/US3) circular needle

C: 4 x 3.75mm (UK9/US5) double-pointed needles

D: 1 pair of 3.75mm (UK9/US5) needles

A
B
C
D

TENSION

24sts and 32 rows to 10cm (4in) over st st on 3.75mm (UK9/US5) needles

NOTIONS

Stitch markers

1 stitch holder

Large-eyed needle

SPECIAL ABBREVIATIONS

MB Make bobble: (k1, p1, k1, p1, k1, p1, k1) into next st, then pass 2nd, 3rd, 4th, 5th, 6th, and 7th one at a time, over 1st stitch

SM Stitch marker

NOTE: When working the bobbles in the patt panel use a separate length of yarn approx. 20cm (8in) long for each bobble, worked over 2 rows leaving enough yarn to tie them when finished.

Sleeves (make 2)

Using needles D and yarn B, cast on 57 (65: 67) sts.

Beg with a k row work 2 rows of st st.

ROW 3 (RS): K3 (2:3), MB, *k4, MB; rep from * to end, k3 (2:3).

ROW 4: P.

Change to yarn A and cont in st st. Work 4 (4:6) rows.

Cast off 3sts at the beg of the next 2 rows. (51 (59:61) sts)

Break yarn and leave on a stitch holder.

Main body

Using needle A and yarn A, cast on 103 (113:127) sts.

ROW 1 (RS): K19 (21:25), place SM for side, k65 (71:77) across back section, place second SM, k19 (21:25).

ROW 2: P1, M1, p to last st, M1, p1.

ROW 3: K1, M1, k to last st, M1, k1.

ROW 4: Rep row 2.

ROW 5: K1, M1, *k to 1st before SM, M1, k2, M1; rep from * to last st, M1, k1.

This sets the side incs. Cont to inc 1st either side of side stitch markers as set on every foll 10th (8th:8th) row, and inc 1st at each end of every row until there are 27 (29:33) sts in the front section then inc 1st at each end of every foll alt row until there are 34 (38:39) sts in the front sections. Cont with side shapings until there are 35 (39:41) sts in the front sections and 71 (79:83) sts in the back sections. (141 (157:165) sts)

For 3rd size only

Work 4 rows straight.

All sizes

NEXT ROW (WS): Place stitch markers for flower panel – p7 (9:10), place SM, p13, place SM. P to last 20 (22:23) sts, place SM, p13, place SM, p to end.

Start flower panel (see p.35)

NEXT ROW (RS): K7 (9:10) to SM, k4, k2tog, yon, k1, yon, ssk, k4 to SM. K to last 20 (22:23) sts, k4, k2tog, yon, k1, yon, ssk, k4, to SM, k to end. This sets the position for the front panels. Cont working from row 2 of patt or chart (all instructions are for the 13sts between SMs). Cont until you have completed 8 (4:2) rows of patt.

Shape armholes

NEXT ROW (RS): K across 32 (36:38) sts, cast off 6sts, k across back to 3sts before side SM, cast off 6sts, k to end. (32 (36:38) sts in each front section and 65 (73:77) sts in back section)

Join sleeves

NEXT ROW (WS): P across 32 (36:38) sts from front section, with WS of first sleeve facing, p across 51 (59:61) sts from first sleeve, p across back section then with WS of second sleeve facing, p across second sleeve. P to end. (231 (263:275) sts)

Start raglan shaping

NEXT ROW (RS): Patt across 30 (34:36) sts, k2tog, (last 2sts from front section). Ssk (from sleeve), k47 (55:57) across sleeve, k2tog (last 2sts of sleeve section). Ssk, from back, patt across to last 2sts of back section, k2tog (last 2sts from back). Ssk, from sleeve, k47 (55:57), k2tog (last

2sts from sleeve). Ssk from front, k to end. Dec in this way on every foll alt row until you have completed all 19 rows of flower panel.

NEXT ROW (WS): P across front and sleeve sections, p across 22 (24:25) sts from back section, place SM, p13, place second SM, p to end of row. This sets position for the back panel. This sets the patt, cont working from row 2 of patt or chart.

NEXT ROW (RS): Cont working raglan shaping as set. K to SM, k4, k2tog, yon, k1, yon, ssk, k4 to SM, k to end of row.

Cont working as set until you have completed 13 (13:11) rows.

Start bobbles

ROW 1 (WS): P2, [p1 using yarn B, p3 (3:4)] x 1 (1:2), p1 using yarn B. Patt across work to last 7 (7:13) sts, [p1 using yarn B, p3 (3:4)] x 1 (1:2), p1 using yarn B, p2.

ROW 2: K2, [MB using yarn B, k3 (3:4)] x 1 (1:2) MB using yarn B, patt to last 7 (7:13) sts, [MB using yarn B, k3 (3:4)] x 1 (1:2), MB using yarn B, k2.

For 1st and 2nd sizes only

ROW 3: P10, p1 using yarn B, p to last 11sts, p1 using yarn B, p to end.

ROW 4: K10, MB, patt to last 11sts, MB, k10.

For 3rd size only

ROW 3: Patt to end.

ROW 4: Patt to end.

All sizes

ROW 5: P12 (13:14), p1 using yarn B, patt to last 13 (14:15) sts, p1 using yarn B, p to end.

ROW 6 START FRONT NECK SHAPING (RS): Cast off 7 (8:11) sts, work bobble as set complete row.

For 1st and 2nd sizes only

ROW 7: Cast off 7 (8:0) sts, p until you have 5 (6:0) sts on RH needle, p1 using yarn B, p to last 6 (7:0) sts, p1 using yarn B, p to end of row.

For 3rd size only

ROW 7: Cast off 11sts at beg of row, patt to end of row.

All sizes

ROW 8: Dec 1st at each end of this and every foll row until no more sts rem in front section.

At the same time for 3rd size only

ROW 9: Work dec at beg of row p until you have 3sts on RH needle, p1 using yarn B, cont to last 4sts, p1 using yarn B, complete row.

ROW 10: Work bobble as set.

ROW 13: P4 (3:4), [p1 using yarn B, p3 (3:4)] x 2 (3:2), p1 using yarn B, p4 (3:4) across sleeve head, p3 (5:5), [p1 using yarn B, p3 (3:4) x 6, p1 using yarn B, p to end of back section, p4 (3:4), [p1 using yarn B, p3 (3:4)] x 2 (3:2), p1 using yarn B, p to end of sleeve section.

Work bobble as set.

Cont with raglan shaping until there are 13 (17:19) sts in sleeve sections and 27 (31:35) sts in the back section.

Cast off.

Front bands

Using needle B and yarn B, with RS facing and starting at the neck edge of the left front, pick up and k38 (44:54) to the start of the front edge shaping, pick up and k17 (19:17) to cast on edge, pick up and k101 (111:125) across cast on edge, pick up and k17 (19:17) along the shaped edge, then pick up and k38 (44:54) to the neck edge. (213 (239:269) sts)

ROW 1 (WS): P.

ROW 2: K6 (4:4), MB, *k4, MB; rep from * end, k7 (5:5).

ROW 3: P.

Cast off knitwise.

Fold band to WS of work along the bobble row and catch stitch (see p.83) in place as in picture.

Neckband

Using needle B and yarn B, with RS facing and starting at the right front neck, pick up and k13 (14:18) to the beg of sleeves, pick up and k10 (14:16) across the top of the sleeve, pick up and k24 (28:34) across back neck, pick up and k10 (14:16) across top of sleeve then pick up and k13 (14:18) down left front neck. (70 (84:102) sts)

Beg with p row, work 3 rows of st st then cast off knitwise.

Fold to WS and catch stitch in place (see p.83).

Ties (make 2)

Using needles C and yarn B, work i-cord. Cast on 3sts. K3, do not turn, slip sts to other end of double-pointed needles, k3. Cont in this way until the cord measures 25cm (9³/₄in) from beg. Work leaf (on end of i-cord).

NEXT ROW (RS): [K1, yon] x 2. (5sts)

ROW 2 AND EVERY FOLL ALT ROW: P.

ROW 3: K2, yon, k1, yon, k2. (7sts)

ROW 5: K3, yon, k1, yon, k3. (9sts)

ROW 7: K3, s2kpo, k3. (7sts)

ROW 9: K2, s2kpo, k2. (5sts)

ROW 11: K1, s2kpo, k1. (3sts)

ROW 12: P3tog, fasten off and sew in end.

Making up

Sew in all loose ends. Fold the edging on the sleeves to the WS along the bobble row and catch st in place as above. Attach ties to each side of neck at the end of the neckband. Join sleeve seam and sew cast off edge of sleeve to cast off edge of main body. Press.

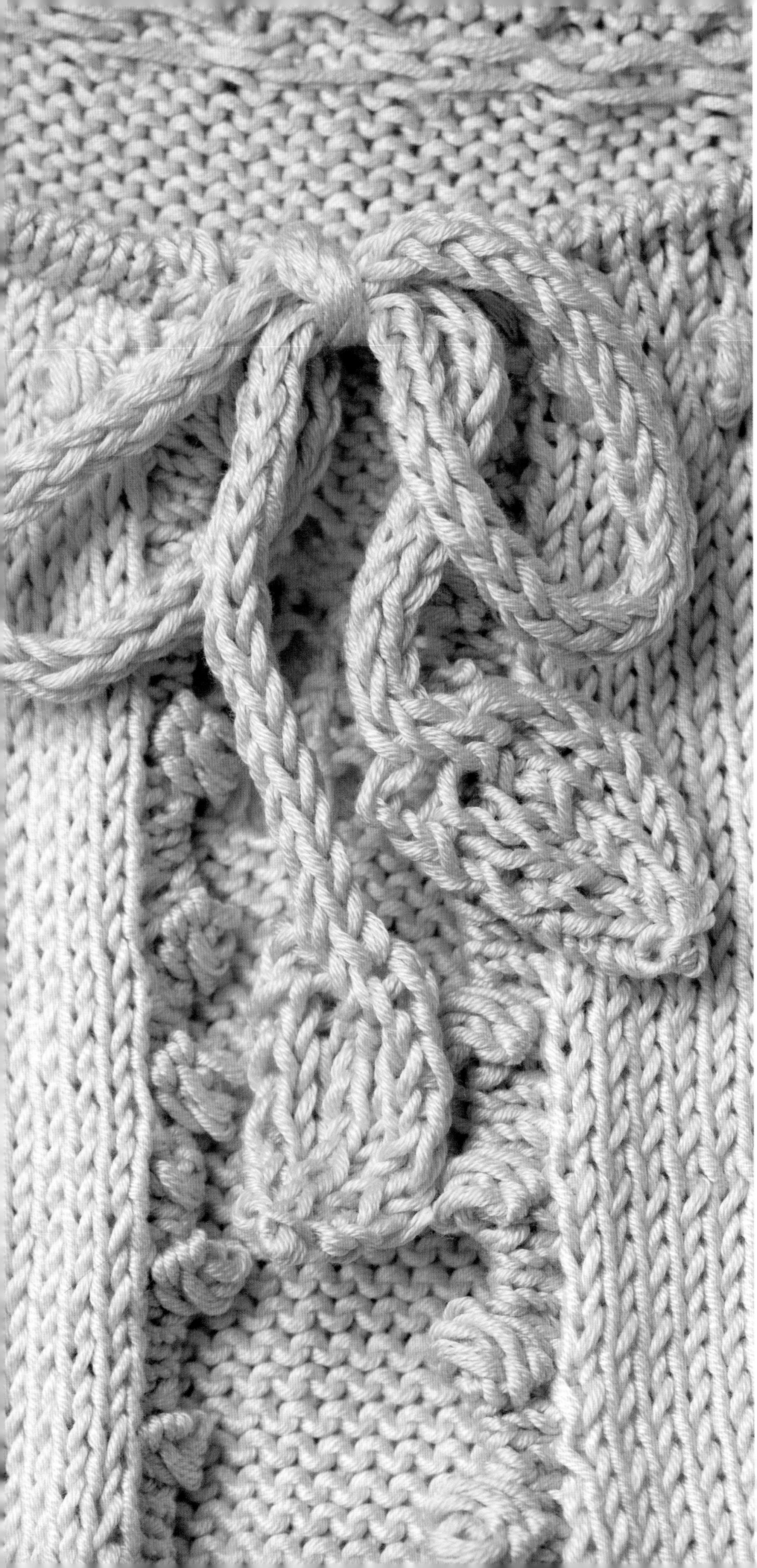

Flower panel

Work all odd number (RS) rows from right to left and all even number (WS) rows from left to right. Flower panel worked over 13sts and 19 rows.

ROW 1 (RS): K4, k2tog, yon, k1, yon, ssk, k4.

ROW 2 AND EVERY FOLL WS ROW EXCEPT ROWS 16 AND 18: P.

ROW 3: K3, k2tog, yon, k3, yon, ssk, k3.

ROW 5: K2, [k2tog, yon] x 2, k1, [yon, ssk] x 2, k2.

ROW 7: K1, [k2tog, yon] x 2, k3, [yon, ssk] x 2, k1.

ROW 9: [K2tog, yon] x 3, k1, [yon, ssk] x 3.

ROW 11: Rep row 7.

ROW 13: K2, k2tog, yon, k5, yon, ssk, k2.

ROW 15: [K1, k2tog, yon, k1, yon, ssk] x 2.

ROW 16: P3, p1 using yarn B, p5 using yarn A, p1 using yarn B, p3.

ROW 17: K2tog, yon, k1, MB in yarn B, k1, yon, s2kpo, yon, k1, MB in yarn B, k1, yon, ssk.

ROW 18: P6, p1 using yarn B, p6.

ROW 19: K6, MB in yarn B, k6.

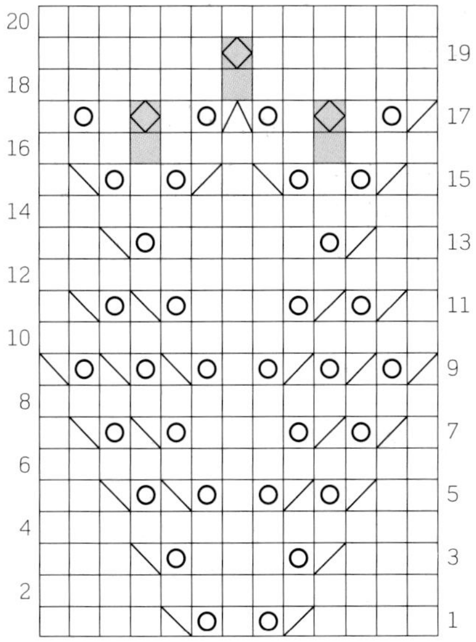

KEY

- Yarnover
- K2tog
- SsK
- S2kpo
- Work in yarn B
- MB in yarn B

Essential information

DIFFICULTY Moderate

SIZE To fit a child, aged 2-3 (4-5:6-7) years

YARN

Debbie Bliss Baby Cashmerino DK 50g

006 Candy Pink x 5 (5:6)

NEEDLES

A: 1 pair of 2.75mm (UK12/US2) needles

B: 1 pair of 3.25mm (UK10/US3) needles

_____ A
_____ B

TENSION

25sts and 44 rows to 10cm (4in) over moss st on
3.25mm (UK10/US3) needles

NOTIONS

Large-eyed needle
5 (6:6) x 12mm (½in) buttons

Child's moss stitch cardigan

This v-neck cardigan for a little girl is given a soft, subtle texture using moss stitch (see p.308), in a cashmere and wool blended yarn.

Back

With needles A, cast on 75 (83:91) sts.
K 3 rows.
Change to needles B.
MOSS ST ROW: K1, [p1, k1] to end.
Cont in moss st until back measures 16 (19: 22)cm (6$^{1}/_{4}$ (7$^{1}/_{2}$:9)in) from cast on edge, ending with a WS row.

Shape armholes

Cast off 5sts at beg of next 2 rows. (65 (73: 81) sts)
Dec 1st at each end of next and 4 (5:6) foll RS rows. (55 (61:67) sts)
Work straight until back measures 28 (32: 36)cm (11 (12$^{1}/_{2}$:14$^{1}/_{4}$)in) from cast on edge, ending with a WS row.

Shape shoulders

Cast off 4sts at beg of next 4 rows and 5 (6:7) sts at beg of foll 2 rows. (29 (33:37) sts)
Cast off.

Left front

With needles A, cast on 39 (43:47) sts.
K 3 rows.
Change to needles B.
ROW 1: [K1, p1] to last 3sts, k3.
ROW 2: K3, [p1, k1] to end.
These 2 rows form moss st with g st edging.
Cont in patt until front measures 16 (19:22)cm (6$^{1}/_{4}$ (7$^{1}/_{2}$:9)in) from cast on edge, ending with row 2.

Shape armhole and front neck

NEXT ROW: Cast off 5sts, patt to last 4sts, k2tog, k2. (33 (37:41) sts)
NEXT ROW: K3, patt to end.

NEXT ROW: Work 2sts tog, patt to last 4sts, k2tog, k2.
Rep the last 2 rows x 4 (5:6). (23 (25:27) sts)
Keeping armhole edge straight, cont to dec at neck edge on every 4th row until 16 (17:18) sts rem. Work straight until front measures same as back to shoulder shaping, ending at armhole edge.

Shape shoulder

Cast off 4sts at beg of next and foll RS row.
Work 1 row.
NEXT ROW: Cast off 5 (6:7) sts, k to end. (3sts)
Cont on these 3sts until band fits halfway across back neck.
Cast off. Mark position for buttons, the first on 4th row, the 5th (6th:6th) two rows below neck shaping, and rem 3 (4:4) spaced evenly between.

Right front

With needles A cast on 39 (43:47) sts.
K 3 rows.
Change to needles B.
ROW 1 (BUTTONHOLE ROW): K1, k2tog, yrn, [p1, k1] to end.
ROW 2: [K1, p1] to last 3sts, k3.
ROW 3: K3, [p1, k1] to end.
These 2 rows form moss st with g st edging.
Working buttonholes to match markers, cont in patt until front measures 16 (19:22)cm (6$^{1}/_{4}$ (7$^{1}/_{2}$:9)in) from cast on edge, ending with row 2.

Shape armhole and front neck

NEXT ROW: K2, skpo, patt to end.
NEXT ROW: Cast off 5sts, patt to end. (33 (37:41) sts)
NEXT ROW: K2, k2tog, patt to last 2sts, work 2tog.
NEXT ROW: [K1, p1] to last 3sts, k3.
Rep the last 2 rows x 4 (5:6). (23 (25:27) sts)

Keeping armhole edge straight cont to dec at neck edge on every 4th row until 16 (17:18) sts rem. Work straight until front measures same as back to shoulder shaping, ending at armhole edge.

Shape shoulder

Cast off 4sts at beg of next and foll RS row.
Work 1 row.
NEXT ROW: Cast off 5 (6:7) sts, k to end. (3sts)
Cont on these 3sts until band fits halfway across back neck. Cast off.

Sleeves (make 2)

With needles A, cast on 35 (39:43) sts.
K 3 rows.
Change to needles B.
MOSS ST ROW: K1, [p1, k1] to end.
Work a further 5 rows.
INC ROW: K1, M1, patt to last st, M1, k1.
Work 7 rows.
Rep the last 8 rows x 10 (11:12) and the inc row again. (59 (65:71) sts)
Cont straight until sleeve measures 25 (28: 31)cm (9$^{3}/_{4}$ (11:12$^{1}/_{4}$)in) from cast on edge, ending with a WS row.

Shape sleeve top

Cast off 5sts at beg of next 2 rows.
Dec 1st at each end of next and 8 (9:10) foll RS rows. (31 (35:39) sts)
Cast off 2sts at beg of next 8 rows. Cast off.

Making up

Join the shoulder seams. Join the cast off edges of the front bands, sew the band to the back of the neck. Join the side and sleeve seams. Sew in the sleeves. Sew on all of the buttons.

New baby's jacket

A little jacket knitted in stocking stitch and garter stitch that's easy to put on a newborn baby. Boys' and girls' buttonholes appear on both sides of the collar.

Essential information

DIFFICULTY Easy

SIZE To fit a newborn baby

YARN

Debbie Bliss Baby Cashmerino DK 50g

003 Pale green x 3

NEEDLES

1 pair of 3.25mm (UK10/US3) needles

TENSION 27sts and 37 rows to 10cm (4in) over st st on 3.25mm (UK10/US3) needles

NOTIONS

1 stitch holder

Large-eyed needle

1 toggle button

Back

Using cable cast on method, cast on 62sts.

ROW 1 (WS): K.

ROWS 2 AND 3: As row 1.

ROW 4 (RS): K.

ROW 5: P.

Last 2 rows set st st. Continue working in st st until work measures 17cm (6³⁄₄in) from cast on edge, ending with a WS row.

Shape arms

NEXT 2 ROWS: Cast on 36sts, k to end. (134sts)

Cont in g st as set for a further 32 rows.

Shape right front

NEXT ROW: K57 and turn, leaving rem 77sts on a stitch holder.

Shape neck

ROW 1 (WS) : K1, skpo, k to end. (56sts)

ROW 2 (RS) : K to last 3sts, k2tog, k1. (55sts)

ROW 3: As row 1. (54sts)

K 11 rows ending with a RS row.

INC ROW (WS): K1, M1, k to end. (55sts)

K 3 rows without shaping.

Cont increasing at neck edge as set by inc row on next and foll 3 alt rows, then at neck edge of foll 2 rows. (61sts)

NEXT ROW: Cast on and k7, k to end. (68sts)

For a girl only

PLACE BUTTTONHOLE: K to last 5sts, cast off 3sts, k1.

NEXT ROW: K2, cast on 3sts, k to end.

For a boy only

K 2 rows.

For boy and girl

SHAPE UNDERARM (RS): Cast off 36sts, k to end. (32sts)

ROW 1 (WS): K5, p to end.

ROW 2 (RS): K to end.

Last 2 rows set st st with g st border.

Rep last 2 rows until work measures 16cm (6¹⁄₄in) from underarm, ending with a RS row.

K 3 rows, cast off.

Shape left front

With RS facing, rejoin yarn to rem sts.

Cast off next 20sts, k to end. (57sts)

ROW 1 (WS): K to last 3sts, k2tog, k1. (56sts)

ROW 2 (RS): K1, skpo, k to end. (55sts)

ROW 3 (WS): As row 1. (54sts)

K 12 rows without shaping, ending with a WS row.

INC ROW (RS): K1, M1, k to end. (55sts)

K 2 rows without shaping.

Cont increasing at neck edge as set by inc row on next and foll 3 alt rows, then at neck edge of foll 2 rows. (61sts)

NEXT ROW (WS): K.

NEXT ROW (RS): Cast on and k7, k to end. (68sts)

For a girl only

K 2 rows.

For a boy only

PLACE BUTTONHOLE: K to last 5sts, cast off 3sts, k1.

NEXT ROW: K2, cast on 3sts, k to end.

For boy and girl

SHAPE UNDERARM (WS): Cast off 36sts, k to end.

ROW 1 (RS): K to end.

ROW 2 (WS): P to last 5sts, k5.

Rep last 2 rows until work measures 16cm (6¹⁄₄in) from underarm, ending with a RS row.

K 3 rows, cast off.

Making up

Join side and underarm seams using mattress stitch (see p.302). Steam gently, and attach the toggle button.

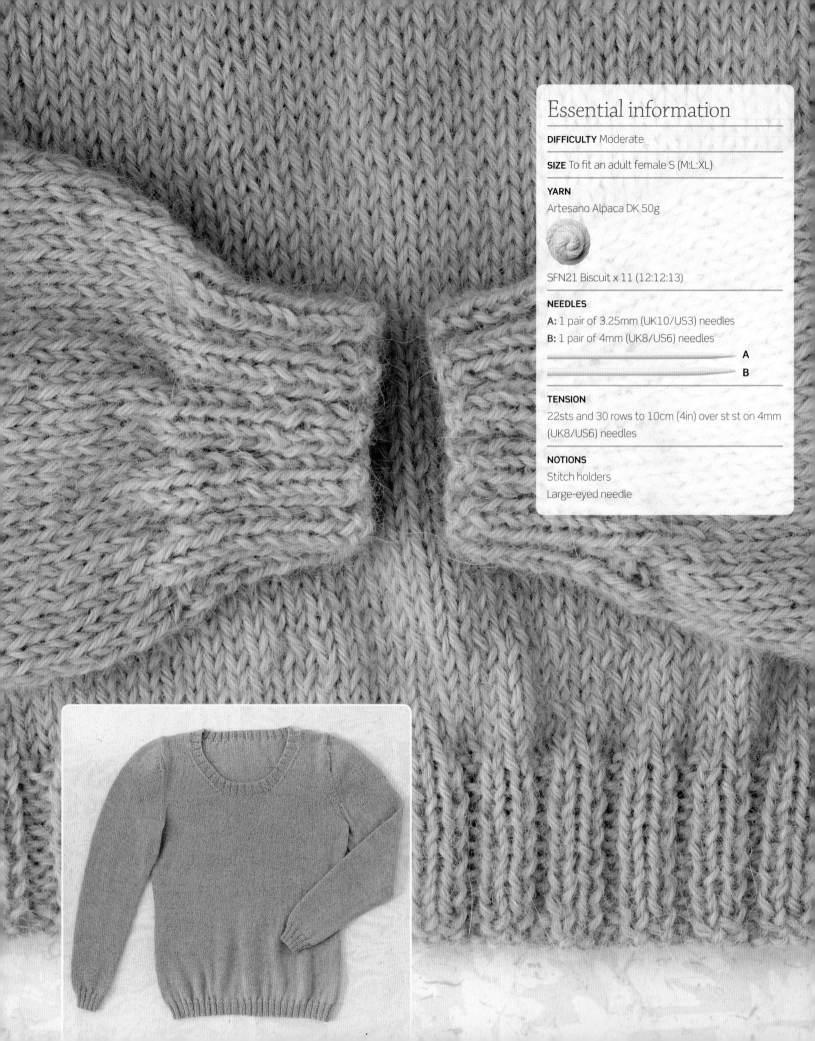

Essential information

DIFFICULTY Moderate

SIZE To fit an adult female S (M:L:XL)

YARN

Artesano Alpaca DK 50g

SFN21 Biscuit x 11 (12:12:13)

NEEDLES

A: 1 pair of 3.25mm (UK10/US3) needles

B: 1 pair of 4mm (UK8/US6) needles

A

B

TENSION

22sts and 30 rows to 10cm (4in) over st st on 4mm (UK8/US6) needles

NOTIONS

Stitch holders

Large-eyed needle

Women's crewneck sweater

This alpaca sweater uses basic stitches to showcase the yarn to its full potential.

Back

With needles A, cast on 110 (122:126:134) sts.
ROW 1: K2, [p2, k2] to end.
ROW 2: P2, [k2, p2] to end.
Rep the last 2 rows x 5, inc 2sts evenly across last row on 3rd size only. (110 (122:128:134) sts)
Change to needles B.
Beg with a k row, cont in st st.
Work 8 rows.
DEC ROW: K6, skpo, k to last 8sts, k2tog, k6.
Work 7 rows.
Rep the last 8 rows x 5, and the dec row again. (96 (108:114:120) sts)
Cont straight until back measures 29cm (11$^{1}/_{2}$in) from cast on edge, ending with a WS row.
INC ROW: K3, M1, k to last 3sts, M1, k3.
Work 5 rows.
Rep the last 6 rows x 3 and the inc row again. (106 (118:124:130) sts)
Cont straight until back measures 45 (46:47:47) cm (17$^{3}/_{4}$ (18:18$^{1}/_{2}$:18$^{1}/_{2}$)in) from cast on edge, ending with a WS row.

Shape armholes

Cast off 5 (6:6:7) sts at beg of next 2 rows. (96 (106:112:116) sts)
NEXT ROW: K2, skpo, k to last 4sts, k2tog, k2.
NEXT ROW: P to end.
Rep the last 2 rows x 5 (8:9:9). (84 (88:92:96) sts rem) **
Cont in st st until back measures 64 (66:67:68)cm (25$^{1}/_{4}$ (26:26$^{1}/_{4}$:26$^{3}/_{4}$)in) from cast on edge, ending with a WS row.

Shape neck

NEXT ROW: K21 (23:24:25) sts, turn and work on these sts for first side of neck shaping.

Dec 1st at neck edge on next 4 rows. (17 (19:20:21) sts)
Work 1 row.

Shape shoulder

Cast off 8 (9:10:10) sts at beg of next row.
Work 1 row.
Cast off rem 9 (10:10:11) sts.
With RS facing, slip centre 42 (42:44:46) sts onto a holder, rejoin yarn to rem sts, k to end.
Complete to match first side of neck shaping.

Front

Work as given for Back to **.

Shape neck

NEXT ROW: K31 (33:34:35) sts, turn and work on these sts for first side of neck shaping.
NEXT ROW: P to end.
NEXT ROW: K to last 3sts, k2tog, k1.
Rep the last 2 rows until 17 (19:20:21) sts rem.
Work straight until front measures the same as back to shoulder, ending at armhole edge.

Shape shoulder

Cast off 8 (9:10:10) sts at beg of next row.
Work 1 row.
Cast off rem 9 (10:10:11) sts.
With RS facing, slip centre 22 (22:24:26) sts onto a holder, rejoin yarn to rem sts, k to end.
Complete to match first side of neck shaping.

Sleeves (make 2)

With needles A, cast on 46 (54:58:62) sts.
Work 12 rows rib as given for Back.
Change to needles B.
Beg with a k row, cont in st st.
Work 8 rows.
INC ROW: K3, M1, k to last 3sts, M1, k3.

Work 5 rows.
Rep the last 6 rows until there are 78 (86:90:94) sts.
Cont straight until sleeve measures 47cm (18$^{1}/_{2}$in) from cast on edge, ending with a p row.

Shape sleeve top

Cast off 5 (6:6:7) sts at beg of next 2 rows.
NEXT ROW: K2, skpo, k to last 4sts, k2tog, k2.
NEXT ROW: P to end.
Rep the last 2 rows x 3 (4:5:5).
Dec 1st as set at each end of next and 5 foll 4th rows. (48 (52:54:56) sts)
NEXT ROW: K2, s1, k2tog, psso, k to last 5sts, k3tog, k2.
NEXT ROW: P to end.
Rep the last 2 rows x 4.
Cast off 4sts at beg of next 2 rows.
Cast off.

Neckband

Join right shoulder.
With RS facing and needles A, pick up and k32 down LS of front neck, k across 22 (22:24:26) sts from centre front holder, pick up and k32 up RS of front neck, 11sts down RS of back neck, k across 42 (42:44:46) sts from back neck holder, pick up and k11 up LS of back neck. (150 (150:154:158) sts)
ROW 1: P2, [k2, p2] to end.
ROW 2: K2, [p2, k2] to end.
Rep the last 2 rows x 2 and the first row again.
Cast off in rib.

Making up

Join left shoulder and neckband seam. Join side and sleeve seams (see p.301). Sew on sleeves.

Ladies' smock top

Based on a traditional design, the smocking is achieved by wrapping stitches.

Essential information

DIFFICULTY Moderate

SIZE To fit an adult female S (M:L:XL)

YARN

Rowan Fine Tweed 4-ply 25g

380 Nappa x 15 (16:17:18)

NEEDLES

A: 1 pair of 3.25mm (UK10/US3) needles

B: 80cm (32in), 3mm (UK11/USn/a) circular needle

C: Cable needle

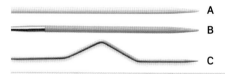

A
B
C

TENSION

25sts and 34 rows to 10cm (4in) over st st on 3.25mm (UK10/US3) needles

NOTIONS

2 stitch holders or spare needles

Large-eyed needle

SPECIAL ABBREVIATIONS

T3R Twist 3 right: slip next st to cable needle (cn) and hold at front, k next 2sts then k st from cn

T3L Twist 3 left: slip next 2sts to cn and hold at back, k next st then k sts from cn

C4B Cross 4 back: slip 2sts to cn and hold at back, k next 2sts from LH needle then k 2sts from cn

P1B P into back of st

W4 Wrap 4sts: with yarn at back, slip next 4sts to cn and hold at front of work, bring yarn forward and wrap around 4sts on cn, slip sts back to LH needle and k1 tbl, p2, k1 tbl

Back

Using needles A, cast on 126 (138:150:166) sts. Work 10 rows of moss st then beg with a k row cont in st st until the work measures 45cm (17³/₄in) from beg ending on a WS row.

Shape armholes

Cast off 5 (5:6:6) sts at the beg of the next 2 rows. (116 (128:138:154) sts)

Then dec 1st at each end of the next 5 rows. (106 (118:128:144) sts)

Dec on next 2 (2:2:3) foll alt rows. (102 (114:124:138) sts)

Cont to work without shaping until the armhole measures 5cm (2¹/₄in) from beg of shaping.

Start smocking block

ROW 1 (RS): K26 (32:37:44), p2, k4, p2, [k1 tbl, p2] x 12, k4, p2, k26 (32:37:44).

ROW 2 AND EVERY FOLL ALT ROW: P26 (32:37:44), k2, p4, k2, [p1b, k2] x 12, p4, k2, p26 (32:37:44).

ROW 3: K26 (32:37:44), p2, C4B, p2, k1 tbl, p2, [W4, p2] x 5, k1 tbl, p2, C4B, p2, k26 (32:37:44).

ROW 5: K26 (32:37:44), p2, k4, [p2, W4] x 6, p2, k4, p2, k26 (32:37:44).

ROW 6: Rep row 2.

Rep rows 3–6 until armhole measures 18 (19:20:21)cm (7 (7¹/₂:8:8¹/₄)in) from beg of shaping ending on a WS row.

NEXT ROW (RS): K26 (30:33:37), turn, leave rem sts on a spare needle and work each side separately. Cast off 3 (3:4:4)sts at beg of WS row then dec 1st at neck edge on every foll row to 18 (22:24:28) sts. Work 1 row straight then break yarn to cast off with front later.

With RS facing, rejoin yarn to rem sts and cast off centre 50 (54:58:64) sts. K to end of row. Dec 1st at neck edge on next row.

Then cast off 3 (3:4:4) sts at beg of RS row. Complete to match first side.

Front

Using needles A, cast on 130 (142:154:170) sts. Work 10 rows of moss st then beg with a k row work in st st until the work measures 35 (36:36:37)cm (14 (14¹/₄:14¹/₄:14¹/₂)in) from beg ending on a WS row.

Set cable and smock panel

ROW 1 (RS): K30 (36:42:50), p2, k3, p2, k4, p2, k3, p2, [k1 tbl, p2] x 12, k3, p2, k4, p2, k3, p2, k30 (36:42:50).

ROW 2 AND EVERY FOLL ALT ROW: P30 (36:42:50), k2, p3, k2, p4, k2, p3, [k2, p1b] x 12, k2, p3, k2, p4, k2, p3, k2, p30 (36:42:50).

ROW 3: K30 (36:42:50) p2, T3L, p2, C4B, p2, T3R, p2, k1 tbl, p2, [W4, p2] x 5, k1 tbl, p2, T3L, p2, C4B, p2, T3R, p2, k30 (36:42:50).

ROW 5: K30 (36:42:50), p2, T3R, p2, k4, p2, T3L, p2, [W4, p2] x 6, T3R, p2, k4, p2, T3L, p2, k30 (36:42:50).

ROW 6: Rep row 2.

Rep rows 3–6 x 3.

ROW 19: K30 (36:42:50), p2, T3L, p2, C4B, p2, T3R, p2, [k1 tbl, p2] x 12, T3L, p2, C4B, p2, T3R, p2, k30 (36:42:50).

ROWS 20–26: Rep rows 2 and 19.

ROW 27: K30 (36:42:50), p2, T3L, p2, C4B, p2, T3R, p2, [W4, p2] x 6, T3L, p2, C4B, p2, T3R, p2, k30 (36:42:50).

ROW 28: Rep row 2.

ROW 29: K30 (36:42:50), p2, T3R, p2, k4, p2, T3L, p2, k1 tbl, p2, [W4, p2] x 5, k1 tbl, p2, T3R, p2, k4, p2, T3L, p2, k30 (36:42:50).

ROW 30: Rep row 2.

ROW 31: Rep row 27.

ROWS 32–38: Rep rows 19 and 2.

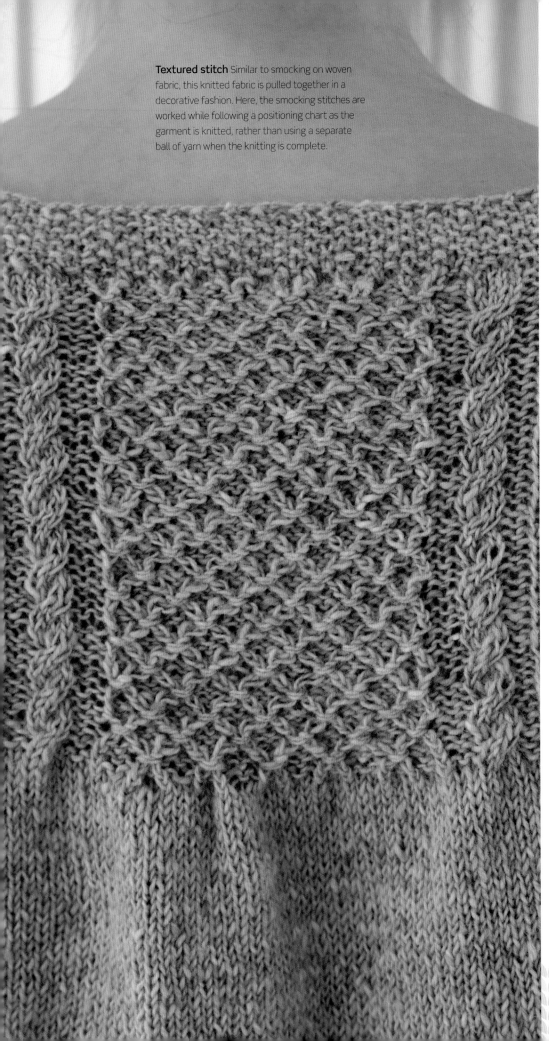

Textured stitch Similar to smocking on woven fabric, this knitted fabric is pulled together in a decorative fashion. Here, the smocking stitches are worked while following a positioning chart as the garment is knitted, rather than using a separate ball of yarn when the knitting is complete.

This sets the patt for central panel, rep from row 3.

NEXT ROW: Shape armhole.
Cast off 5 (5:6:6) sts at beg of next 2 rows. (120 (132:142:158) sts)
Then dec 1st at each end of the next 5 rows. (110 (122:132:148) sts)
Then dec on next 2 (2:3:3) foll alt rows. (106 (118:126:142) sts)
Cont without shaping working patt until the armhole measures 4 (4:5:5)cm ($1^{1}/_2$ ($1^{1}/_2$:$2^{1}/_4$: $2^{1}/_4$)in) from beg of shaping ending on a WS row.

Shape front neck

Keeping patt correct throughout, patt across 35 (39:41:46) sts, turn, leave rem sts on a holder and work each side separately. Cast off 4 (4:5:5) sts at beg of next row. (31 (35:36:41) sts)
Then dec 1st at neck edge on next 5 rows 26 (30:31:35) sts then on every foll alt row until 18 (22:24:28) sts rem.
Cont without shaping until the front matches the back shoulder ending on a WS row. Break yarn and leave sts to cast off with back.
With RS facing, rejoin yarn to rem sts and cast off centre 36 (40:44:50) sts, patt to end of row.
Dec 1st at neck edge on the next row. Cast off 4 (4:5:5) sts from beg of RS row then complete shapings to match first side.

Shoulders

With RS of front facing RS of back, cast off 18 (22:24:28) sts from front and back shoulders together using 3 needles. Do this for both of the shoulders.

Sleeves (make 2)

Using needles A, cast on 66 (66:72:72) sts.
Work 10 rows of moss st.
Beg with a k row work in st st.
At the same time inc 1st at each end of the 10th and every foll 6th row until there are 80 (80:86:102) sts then on every foll 8th row until there are 96 (100:108:112) sts.
Cont without shaping until the sleeve measures 44cm ($17^{1}/_2$in) from beg ending on a WS row.

Shape sleeve head

Cast off 5 (5:6:6) sts at beg of next 2 rows.
(86 (90:96:100) sts)

Dec 1st at each end of the next 7 (7:9:9) rows.
(70 (76:78:82) sts)

Then on every foll alt row until 60 (62:64:66)
sts rem.

Work 1 row straight.

NEXT ROW (RS): Cont to dec on this and every
foll alt row but start smocking panel. K until
you have 11 (12:13:14) sts on RH needle, p2, k1
tbl, [p2, W4] x 5, p2, k1 tbl, p2, k to end of row
working dec as set.

Cont to work smocking panel as set from 4th
row of chart, rep rows 3, 4, 5, and 6 only, and
dec on every alt row until 36 (36:42:42) sts rem
then on next 0 (0:3:3) rows, ending on a WS
row. Then cast off rem 36 (36:36:36) sts.

Neckband

Using needles B, with RS facing and starting at
the left shoulder, pick up and k38 (44:50:54) sts
down to the front neck, pick up and k25
(31:35:39) sts evenly across cast off sts from
front neck, pick up and k38 (44:50:54) sts to the
right shoulder, pick up and k10 down to back
neck. Pick up and k35 (39:43:49) sts evenly
across cast off sts from back neck, then pick up
and k10 to shoulder. (156 (178:198:216) sts)
Work 10 rows of moss st then cast off.

Making up

Join side seam and sleeve seam.
Set in sleeve matching centre of sleeve to
shoulder seam. Sew in loose ends. Press
according to ballband instructions.

Chart for smocked panel

Work all odd number (RS) rows from right to left, and all even number (WS) rows from left to right.
For sleeve panel (worked over 38sts and 6 rows) rep rows 3–6 for the patt.

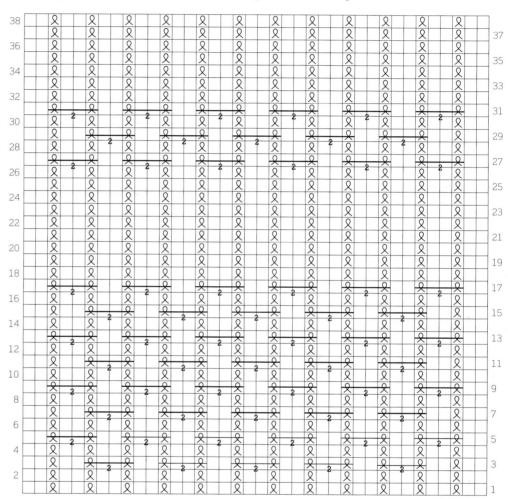

KEY

| ⅄ | K into back on RS rows, p into back on WS rows |

| ⅄ — ₂ — ⅄ | W4 |

Spiral lace sweater

Using a mixture of swirling lacework stitches, this boat-necked sweater requires no shaping for armholes or neck. A Catherine wheel pattern decorates the borders and cuffs, while a little spirals pattern repeats across the body.

Essential information

DIFFICULTY Moderate

SIZE To fit an adult female S (M:L:XL)

YARN

Louisa Harding Mulberry Silk 50g

35 Raspberry x 10 (11:12:13)

NEEDLES

1 pair of 4mm (UK8/US6) needles

TENSION

22sts and 28 rows to 10cm (4in) over little spiral stitch on 4mm (UK8/US6) needles

NOTIONS

Large-eyed needle

SPECIAL ABBREVIATIONS

P2TOG TBL P 2sts tog through back loops

WORK 5TOG S1, k1, psso, k3tog, pass the st resulting from ssk over the st resulting from k3tog

WYIB With yarn in back

Stitches used

Little spirals

Worked over 7sts and 5 rows.

ROW 1 (RS): K1, k2tog, yon, k1, yon, ssk, k1.

ROW 2: P2tog tbl, yon, p3, yon, p2tog.

ROW 3: K1, yon, k2tog, yon, s1, k2tog, psso, yon, k1.

ROW 4: P1, yon, p2tog, p1, p2tog tbl, yon, p1.

ROW 5: K2, yon, s1, k2tog, psso, yon, k2.

Catherine wheel

Worked over 13sts and 17 rows.

ROW 1(RS): K5, s3, yfwd, pass same 3sts back to LH needle, wyib, k3 slipped sts, k5.

ROW 2 AND EVERY FOLL ALT ROW: P.

ROW 3: K3, k3tog, yfwd, inc 2st, yfwd, k3tog tbl, k3.

ROW 5: K1, k3tog, yfwd, k2tog, yfwd, inc 2st, yfwd, ssk, yfwd, k3tog tbl, k1.

ROW 7: [K2tog, yfwd] x 3, k1 tbl, [yfwd, ssk]. Rep x 3.

ROW 9: K1, [yfwd, k2tog] twice, yfwd, s1, k2tog, psso, [yfwd, ssk] twice, yfwd, k1.

ROW 11: [Ssk, yfwd] x 3, k1 tbl, [yfwd, k2tog] x 3.

ROW 13: K1, inc 1st, yfwd, ssk, yfwd, work 5tog, yfwd, k2tog, yfwd, inc 1st, k1.

ROW 15: K3, inc 1st, yfwd, work 5tog, yfwd, inc 1st, k3.

ROW 17: Rep row 1.

Front and back (make 2)

Cast on 131 (139:149:157) sts.

Work 6 rows of g st (k all rows).

ROW 7 (RS): K.

ROW 8: P.

Start Catherine wheel patt placing spirals as follows:

ROW 1 (RS): K10 (11:10:9) *s3p, yfwd, pass same 3sts back to LH needle, wyib, k3 sl sts, k15 (16:15:14); rep from *, end last rep k10 (11:10:9).

ROW 2 AND EVERY FOLL ALT ROW: P.

ROW 3: K8 (9:8:7), *k3tog, yrn, inc 2st, yrn, k3tog tbl, k11 (12:11:10); rep from *, end last rep k8 (9:8:7).

ROW 5: K6 (7:6:5) *k3tog, yrn, k2tog, yrn, inc 2st, yrn, ssk, yrn, k3tog tbl, k7 (8:7:6); rep from *, end last rep k6 (7:6:5).

ROW 7: K5 (6:5:4) *[k2tog, yrn] x 3, k1 tbl, [yrn, ssk] x 3, k5 (6:5:4); rep from * to end.

ROW 9: K6 (7:6:5), [yrn, k2tog] x 2, yrn, s1, k2tog, psso, [yrn, ssk] x 2, yrn, k7 (8:7:6); rep from *, end last rep k6 (7:6:5).

ROW 11: K5 (6:5:4), *[ssk, yrn] x 3, k1 tbl, [yrn, k2tog] x 3, k5 (6:5:4); rep from * to end.

ROW 13: K6 (7:6:5), *inc 1st, yrn, ssk, yrn, work 5 tog, yrn, k2tog, yrn, inc 1st, k7 (8:7:6); rep from *, end last rep k6 (7:6:5).

ROW 15: K8 (9:8:7), *inc 1st, yrn, work 5 tog, yrn, inc 1st, k11 (12:11:10); rep from *, end last rep k8 (9:8:7).

ROW 17: Rep row 1.

ROW 19: K.

Work 3 rows of g st.

15 (16:17:18)cm
6 (6:7:7)in

45 (50:55:60)cm
18 (20:22:24)in

56 (60.5:64.5:68)cm
22 (24:26:27)in

42cm (16½in)

Start main patt (little spirals)

ROW 1 (RS): K.

ROW 2: P.

ROW 3: K.

ROW 4: P.

ROW 5: K9 (7:6:10), *k2tog, yrn, k1, yrn, ssk, k7; rep from *, end last rep k9 (7:6:10).

ROW 6: P8 (6:5:9),*p2tog tbl, yrn, p3, yrn, p2tog, p5; rep from *, end last rep p8 (6:5:9).

ROW 7: K9 (7:6:10) *yrn, k2tog, yrn, s1, k2tog, psso, yrn, k7; rep from *, end last rep k9 (7:6:10).

ROW 8: P9 (7:6:10) *yrn, p2tog, p1, p2tog tbl, yrn, p7; rep from *, end last rep p9 (7:6:10).

ROW 9: K10 (8:7:11), *yrn, s1, k2tog, psso, yrn, k9; rep from *, end last rep k10 (8:7:11).

ROW 10: P.

ROW 11: K.

ROW 12: P.

ROW 13: K3 (13:12:4),*k2tog, yrn, k1, yrn, ssk, k7; rep from *, end last rep k3 (13:12:4).

ROW 14: P2 (12:11:3), *p2tog tbl, yrn, p3, yrn, p2tog, p5; rep from * end last rep p2 (12:11:3).

ROW 15: K3 (13:12:4), *yrn, k2tog, yrn, s1, k2tog, psso, yrn, k7; rep from *, end last rep k3 (13:12:4).

ROW 16: P3 (13:12:4), *yrn, p2tog, p1, p2tog tbl, yrn, p7; rep from *, end last rep p3 (13:12:4).

ROW 17: K4 (14:13:5), *yrn, s1, k2tog, psso, yrn, k9; rep from *, end last rep k4 (14:13:5).

ROW 18: P.

REP ROWS 1–18: Until you have completed 5 (6:7:8) full patt reps.

Work 3 rows of st st then 3 rows of g st.

Work 2 rows of st st then work rows 1–19 of Catherine wheel patt as written for the border. Work 5 rows of g st. Cast off.

Sleeves (work 2)

Cast on 59 (63:63:65) sts.

Work 6 rows of g st.

ROW 7 (RS): K.

ROW 8: P.

Set up border patt.

ROW 1: K10 (11:12:14), *s3, yfwd, pass same 3sts back to LH needle, wyib, k3 slipped sts, k15 (16:15:14); rep from *, end last rep k10 (11:12:14).

This sets the position for the patt, cont working from 2nd row of patt until you have completed all 19 rows.

Work 3 rows of g st.

Start side shaping

ROW 1 (RS): K1, M1, k to last st, M1, k1.

Inc in this way on every foll 4th row.

ROW 2: P.

ROW 3: K.

ROW 4: P.

Start main patt.

ROW 5: K1, M1, k3 (5:5:6) *k2tog, yrn, k1, yrn, ssk, k7; rep from *, end last rep k3 (5:5:6) M1, k1.

This sets the position for the first line of little spirals cont to inc on every foll 4th row working the new sts into the patt, and cont to work from 2nd row of little spirals patt until you have completed all 5 rows.

Work 3 rows of st st.

ROW 13: K1, M1, k12 (2:2:3), *k2tog, yrn, k1, yrn, ssk, k7; rep from *end, k12 (2:2:3) M1, k1.

This sets the position cont working patt and inc until you have 89 (81:81:87) sts then inc on every foll 6th row until there are 95 (95:95:99) sts, working the new sts into the patt.

Cont without shaping until you have completed 5 full patt reps plus 3 rows of st st. Cast off.

Making up

Block pieces (see p.300).

Join shoulder seam for 15 (16:17:18)cm (6 (6¼:6¾:7)in) from sleeve edge.

Sew the sleeves, matching the centre of each sleeve to the shoulder seam, making sure they are even down both front and back. Join side and sleeve seams being careful to match the patterns. Sew in all ends and press according to instructions on the ballband.

TOP TIP *Always count your stitches at the end of each pattern repeat.*

Women's lace hoodie

This garment is knitted in a crisp cotton yarn, making it an ideal cover-up for the beach. Its shape is simple, which shows off the bold lacework. Only three sizes (medium, large, and extra large) are available in this pattern as the sizes are generous.

Essential information

DIFFICULTY Moderate

SIZE To fit an adult female M (L:XL)

YARN

Rico Essentials Cotton DK 50g

80 White x 14 (15:16)

NEEDLES

A: 1 pair of 3.75mm (UK9/US5) needles
B: 1 pair of 4mm (UK8/US6) needles

———————————— A
———————————— B

TENSION

21sts and 24 rows to 10cm (4in) over patt on 4mm (UK8/US6) needles

NOTIONS

2 stitch holders and spare needle
Large-eyed needle

SPECIAL ABBREVIATIONS

M7 [(k1, yon) x 3, k1] all into next st; 7 new sts made – original 1 and 6 more

Back

Using needles B, cast on 111 (133:155) sts.
Work 2 rows of g st.
Work in leaf chain patt as follows:
ROW 1 (RS): Ssk, *[yon, ssk] x 2, k3, [k2tog, yon] x 2, s2kpo, yon, ssk, yon, [k1, yon] x 3, k1 in next st, yon, k2tog, yon, s2kpo; rep from *, end last rep k2tog instead of s2kpo. (131 (157:183) sts)
ROW 2 AND EVERY FOLL ALT ROW: P.
ROW 3: Ssk, *[yon, ssk] x 2, k1, [k2tog, yon] x 2, s2kpo, yon, ssk, yon, k7, yon, k2tog, yon, s2kpo; rep from *, end last rep k2tog. (121 (145:169) sts)
ROW 5: Ssk, *yon, ssk, yon, S2kpo, yon, k2tog, yon, s2kpo, yon, ssk, yon, k7, yon, k2tog, yon, s2kpo; rep from *, end last rep k2tog. (111 (133:155) sts)
ROW 7: Ssk, *yon, ssk, yon, [k1, yon] x 3, k1 into next st, yon, k2tog, yon, s2kpo, [yon, ssk] x 2, k3, [k2tog, yon] x 2, s2kpo; rep from *, end last rep k2tog. (131 (157:183) sts)
ROW 9: Ssk, *yon, ssk, yon, k7, yon, k2tog, yon, s2kpo, [yon, ssk] x 2, k1, [k2tog, yon] x 2, s2kpo; rep from *, end last rep k2tog. (121 (145:169) sts)
ROW 11: Ssk, *yon, ssk, yon, k7, yon, k2tog, yon, s2kpo, yon, ssk, yon, s2kpo, yon, k2tog, yon, s2kpo; rep from *, end last rep k2tog. (111 (133:155) sts)
ROW 12: P.
Rep these 12 rows for patt until you have completed 11 (12:13) full patt reps ending on row 12.

Yoke

ROW 1 (RS): Ssk, *yon, ssk, yon, k7, yon, k2tog, yon, s2kpo, yon, ssk, yon, k1, yon, k2tog, yon, s2kpo; rep from *, end last rep k2tog.
ROW 2: P.
Rep these 2 rows until 12 rows are completed.

Shoulders

NEXT ROW (RS): Patt 35 (44:52) sts cast off centre 41 (45:51) sts, patt across 35 (44:52) sts. Break yarn and leave each shoulder on a holder to cast off with the front later.

Front

Work as for the Back until you have completed 7 (8:9) full patt reps plus a further 11 rows ending on a RS row.

Front neck opening

NEXT ROW (WS): P across 56 (67:78) sts, turn, leave rem sts on a spare needle and work on each side separately.
Cont in patt as set until you have completed 3 full patt reps.
Shape right front neck and start to work yoke patt.
1st size only
NEXT ROW (RS): Cast off 15sts, *k7, yon, k2tog, yon, s2kpo, yon, ssk, yon, k1, yon, k2tog*, yon, s2kpo, yon, ssk, yon: rep from * to *, end, yon, k2tog. (41sts)
2nd size only
NEXT ROW (RS): Cast off 17sts, k4, yon, s2kpo, yon, ssk, yon, * k7, yon, k2tog, yon, s2kpo, yon, ssk, yon, k1, yon*, k2tog, yon, s2kpo, yon, ssk, yon; rep from * to *, ending with yon, ssk. (50sts rem)

NEXT ROW (RS): Cast off 21sts, k5, [yon, ssk, yon, k1, yon, k2tog, yon, s2kpo, yon, ssk, yon, k7, yon, k2tog, yon, s2kpo] x 2, ending with yon, ssk, yon, k1, yon, k2tog, yon, ssk. (57sts)

All sizes

ROW 2: P to last 2sts, p2tog.

This sets the yoke patt. Dec 1st at neck edge on every foll row until 35 (44:52) sts rem. Cont without shaping until the front matches the back. Break yarn and leave sts on a holder.

Left front neck

With RS facing, rejoin yarn to rem sts k1, M1, cont in patt to end of row. (56 (67:78) sts)

Work in patt until work matches Right front ending on a RS row before starting neck shaping.

Shape neck

NEXT ROW (WS): Cast off 15 (17:21) sts at beg of row, p to end. (41 (50:57) sts)

Work yoke patt as for Back, dec 1st at neck edge on every foll row until 35 (44:52) sts rem. Complete to match first side.

Shoulders

With RS of front facing RS of back, cast off front shoulder sts with the back shoulder sts.

Sleeves (make 2)

Using needles B, cast on 45 (51:57) sts.
Work 2 rows of g st.

Start pattern

ROW 1 (RS): K0 (3:6). Work patt from row 1
until you have completed 2 full patt reps.

NEXT ROW (RS): Start side inc – inc 1st at each
end of this and every foll 6th row, working the
new sts into st st until there are 73sts.
Cont without shaping until the sleeve measures
46cm (18in) from beg ending on a WS row
(9 full patt reps).

Hood

Using needles B, cast on 111 (111:133) sts.
Work in patt until you have completed 6 full
patt reps plus a further 11 rows, ending on a
RS row.

NEXT ROW (WS): Cast off 44sts at beg of next 2
rows. (23 (23:45) sts)
Cont working in patt on rem 23 (23:45) sts
until you have completed 4 full patt reps ending
on WS. Cast off.
Join the side of the centre flap to the 44 cast
off sts.

Making up

With RS of the hood facing RS of the main body,
attach the hood by matching the centre of the
hood to the centre back of the garment and
easing the hood to the neck edge.
Sew the sleeves to the main body matching the
centre of the sleeve to the shoulder seam,
making sure it is of equal distance from the
shoulder on the front and back.
Join the side and sleeve seams being careful
to match the pattern.
Sew in all loose ends. Block.

Lacework charts

The top chart shows the patt rep with beg of row sts and the bottom
chart shows the end of row. Read all odd number (RS) rows from
right to left and all even number (WS) rows from left to right.

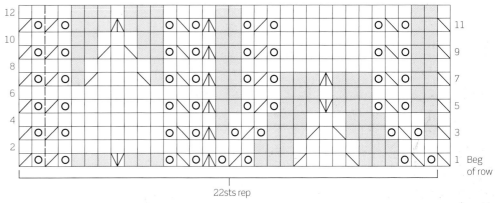

22sts rep

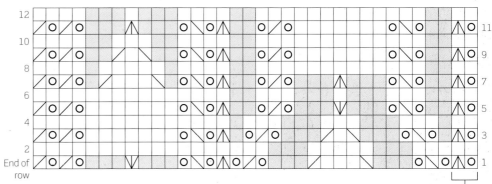

End of row

Last 2sts of above chart

KEY

O	Yarnover
/	K2tog
\	Ssk
/|	S2kpo
V	M7
	No stitch

TOP TIP *Block the lace pattern to get the full effect of the stitch.*

Long line tunic

The background stitch on this garment is a simple two-row-wide seeded rib pattern that is complemented by a bold twisted rib along the bottom hem. The decorative panel that runs down the centre front of the tunic consists of slanting eyelet stitches framed by a twisted rib panel that emphasizes the design.

Essential information

DIFFICULTY Moderate

SIZE To fit an adult female S (M:L:XL)

YARN

King Cole Merino Blend Superwash DK 50g

162 Heather x 12 (13:13:14)

NEEDLES

A: 1 pair of 4mm (UK8/US6) needles

B: 1 pair of 3.25mm (UK10/US3) needles

————————————————————— **A**
————————————————————— **B**

TENSION

22sts and 28 rows to 10cm (4in) over st st using 4mm (UK8/US6) needles

NOTIONS

2 stitch holders and spare needle

Large-eyed needle

SPECIAL ABBREVIATIONS

TW2 K2tog but don't slip off LH needle, now k the first of these 2sts again slipping both sts off needle

Panel

(worked over 38sts)

ROW 1: K9, k2tog, TW2, yfwd, k2, p3, TW2, p3, k2, yfwd, TW2, skpo, k9.

ROW 2 AND EVERY ALT ROW: P15, k3, p2, k3, p15.

ROW 3: K8, k2tog, TW2, yfwd, k3, p3, TW2, p3, k3, yfwd, TW2, skpo, k8.

ROW 5: K7, k2tog, TW2, yfwd, k4, p3, TW2, p3, k4, yfwd, TW2, skpo, k7.

ROW 7: K6, k2tog, TW2, yfwd, k5, p3, TW2, p3, k5, yfwd, TW2, skpo, k6.

ROW 9: K5, k2tog, TW2, yfwd, K6, p3, TW2, p3, k6, yfwd, TW2, skpo, k5.

ROW 11: K4, [k2tog, TW2, yfwd, k1] x 2, k1, p3, TW2, p3, k2, [yfwd, TW2, skpo, k1] x 2, k3.

ROW 13: K3, [k2tog, TW2, yfwd, k1] x 2, k2, p3, TW2, p3, k3, [yfwd, TW2, skpo, k1] x 2, k2.

ROW 15: K2, [k2tog, TW2, yfwd, k1] x 2, k3, p3, TW2, p3, k4, [yfwd, TW2, skpo, k1] x 2, k1.

ROW 17: K1, k2tog, TW2, yfwd, k10, p3, TW2, p3, k10, yfwd, TW2, skpo, k1.

ROW 19: K2tog, TW2, yfwd, k11, p3, TW2, p3, k11, yfwd, TW2, skpo.

ROW 20: As row 2.

These 20 rows form panel.

Back

With needles A, cast on 104 (116:122:128) sts. Work in twisted rib.

ROW 1 (RS): P6 (7:5:3), [TW2, p3] to last 8 (9:7:5) sts, TW2, p6 (7:5:3).

ROW 2: K6 (7:5:3), [p2, k3] to last 8 (9:7:5) sts, p2, k6 (7:5:3).

Rep these 2 rows until rib measures 21cm (8¼in), ending after row 2.

Change to patt.

ROW 1 (RS): K2 (2:5:2), [p1, k5] x 5 (6:6:7), p1, work row 1 of panel, [p1, k5] x 5 (6:6:7), p1, k2 (2:5:2).

ROW 2: P33 (39:42:45), work row 2 of panel, p33 (39:42:45).

ROWS 3–20: Rep rows 1 and 2 x 9 but working rows 3–20 of panel.

These 20 rows form patt.

Cont in patt until work measures 56cm (22¼in), ending after a WS row.

Shape armholes

Cast off 6 (7:8:9) sts at beg of next 2 rows.

Dec 1st at each end of next 5 rows, then on every foll alt row until 76 (84:88:92) sts rem.

Cont straight until work measures 74 (76:77:78)cm (29 (30:30½:30¾)in) from beg, ending after a WS row.

Shape shoulders

Cast off 7 (7:8:8) sts at beg of next 4 rows, then 6 (8:7:9) sts at beg of next 2 rows. Slip rem 36 (40:42:42) sts onto a spare needle.

Front

Work as Back until front measures 18 (20:22:22) rows less than back up to shoulder shaping, ending after a WS row.

Shape neck

NEXT ROW: Work across 25 (27:28:30) sts, turn.
Cont on this group of sts for left half of neck.
Dec 1st at neck edge on next 5 rows. (20 (22:23:25) sts)
Work 12 (14:16:16) rows straight, thus ending at armhole edge.

Shape shoulder

Cast off 6 (7:8:8) sts at beg of next row and foll alt row. Work 1 row.
Cast off rem sts.
With RS facing, slip next 26 (30:32:32) sts on a stitch holder.
Rejoin yarn to rem sts and work 1 row straight.
Complete as left side of neck but working 1 row more than stated before shaping shoulder.

Sleeves (make 2)

With needles A, cast on 51 (53:53:55) sts and k 1 row.
ROW 1 (RS): K1 (2:2:3), [p1, k2] to last 2 (3:3:4) sts, p1, k to end.
ROW 2: P.
ROWS 3–4: As rows 1 and 2.

NEXT ROW: K1 (2:2:3), [p1, k5] to last 2 (3:3:4) sts, p1, k to end.
NEXT ROW: P.
The last 2 rows set the patt for rem of sleeves. Keeping patt correct, dec 1st at each end of next row then on every foll third row until 41 (43:43:45) sts rem.
Cont straight until sleeve measures 12cm (5in) from beg, ending after a p row.
Taking extra sts into patt, now inc 1st at each end of next row, then on every foll 6th (6th: 4th:4th) row until there are 53 (65:59:67) sts, then on every foll 8th (6th:6th:6th) row until there are 69 (77:81:85) sts.
Cont straight until sleeve measures 48cm (19in) from beg, measured through centre of work, ending after a p row.

Shape top

Cast off 6 (7:8:9) sts at beg of next 2 rows.
Work 2 (4:6:6) rows straight.
Dec 1st at each end of next row, then on every foll RS row until 27 (35:39:39) sts rem, then on every row until 21 (27:31:33) sts rem.
Cast off.

Neckband

First join left shoulder. With needles B and RS facing, k across sts on spare needle at back of neck inc 2sts evenly, k17 (19:20:20) sts evenly down left front neck, k across sts on stitch holder, finally k17 (19:20:20) sts evenly up right front neck. (98 (110:116:116) sts)
Work 6 rows in k1, p1 rib.
Cast off evenly in rib.

Making up

Press work on WS following ballband instructions. Join right shoulder. Sew in sleeve tops. Join side and sleeve seams. Press seams.

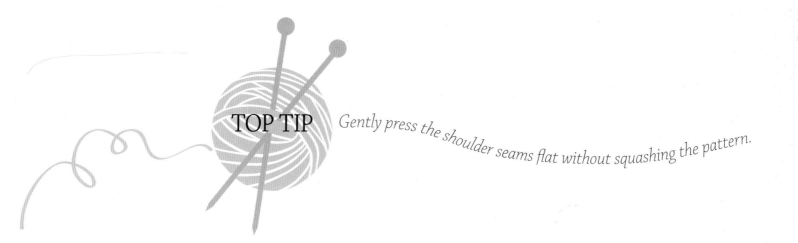

TOP TIP *Gently press the shoulder seams flat without squashing the pattern.*

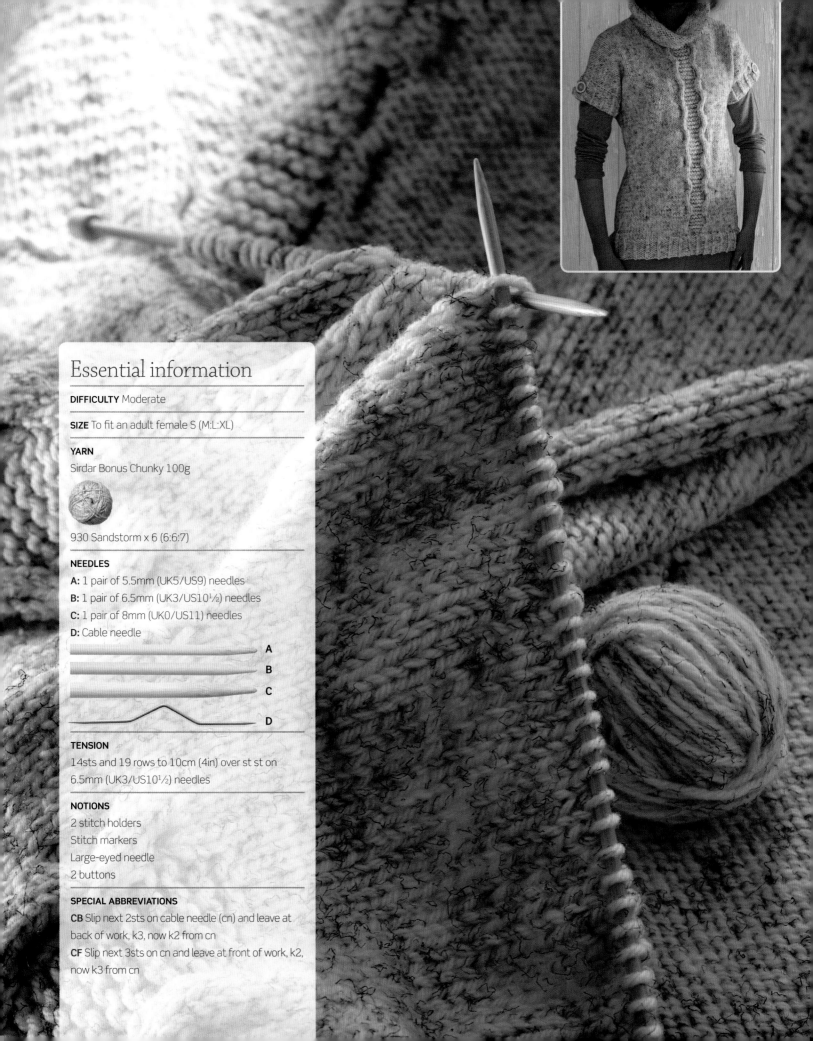

Essential information

DIFFICULTY Moderate

SIZE To fit an adult female S (M:L:XL)

YARN

Sirdar Bonus Chunky 100g

930 Sandstorm x 6 (6:6:7)

NEEDLES

A: 1 pair of 5.5mm (UK5/US9) needles

B: 1 pair of 6.5mm (UK3/US10½) needles

C: 1 pair of 8mm (UK0/US11) needles

D: Cable needle

A

B

C

D

TENSION

14sts and 19 rows to 10cm (4in) over st st on 6.5mm (UK3/US10½) needles

NOTIONS

2 stitch holders

Stitch markers

Large-eyed needle

2 buttons

SPECIAL ABBREVIATIONS

CB Slip next 2sts on cable needle (cn) and leave at back of work, k3, now k2 from cn

CF Slip next 3sts on cn and leave at front of work, k2, now k3 from cn

Rollneck slipover

A simple project that knits up quickly in a chunky yarn, this slipover incorporates overlaid cables and a central garter stitch panel. The buttons on the sleeves add a touch of sophistication, as well as fasten back the cuffs.

Back

Using needles B, cast on 67 (75:79:83) sts.
ROW 1 (RS): K1, [kb, p3] to last 2sts, kb, k1.
ROW 2: K1, [pb, k3] to last 2sts, pb, k1.
These 2 rows form twisted rib.
Work 7 more rows in twisted rib.
NEXT ROW: P, dec 2 (3:4:4) sts evenly across. (65 (72:75:79) sts)
Work in patt.
ROW 1 (RS): K30 (33:35:37), p5 (6:5:5), k30 (33:35:37).
ROW 2: K1, p to last st, k1.
ROWS 3–4: As rows 1 and 2.
ROW 5: K25 (28:30:32), CB, p5 (6:5:5), CF, k25 (28:30:32).
ROW 6: As row 2.
ROWS 7–10: Rep rows 1 and 2 twice.
ROW 11: K22 (25:27:29), CF, k3, p5 (6:5:5), k3, CB, k22 (25:27:29).
ROW 12: As row 2.
These 12 rows form patt.
Cont in patt until work measures 41cm (16¼in) from beg, ending after a WS row.

Shape sleeves

NOTE: For remainder of back do not work "k1" at each end of WS rows.
Working extra sts in st st inc 1st at each end of next 5 rows. (75 (82: 85: 89) sts)
Place a marker 20sts inside one edge.
Cont straight until work measures 18 (20:21: 22)cm (7 (8:8¼:9)in) from marker, ending after a p row.

Shape shoulders

Cast off 6 (5:6:7) sts at beg of next 2 rows, then 5 (6:6:6) sts at beg of next 8 alt rows.
S23 (24:25:27) on a stitch holder and leave.

Front

Work as Back until front measures 10 (12:12:12) rows less than back up to shoulder shaping, ending after a p row.

Shape neck

NEXT ROW: Work across 29 (32: 33:34) sts, turn.
Cont on these sts for left half of neck.
Dec 1st at neck edge on next 3 rows. (26 (29:30:31) sts)
Work 6 (8:8:8) rows straight thus ending at sleeve edge.

Shape shoulder

Cast off 6 (5:6:7) sts at beg of next row, then 5 (6:6:6) sts at beg of next 3 alt rows.
Work 1 row. Cast off rem sts.
With RS facing, s17 (18:19:21) sts on a stitch holder and leave. Neatly rejoin yarn to rem sts and work to end of row.
Complete as left side of neck but working 1 row more than stated before shaping shoulder.

Sleeve borders (make 2)

First join side seams. Using needles A and RS facing, rejoin yarn to top of right front shoulder. Now neatly k49 (57:61:65) sts evenly along front and back armhole edge, cast on 6sts to end of needle holding sts for button underwrap. (55 (63:67:71) sts)

Beg row 2, work 4 rows in twisted rib as on Back.
NEXT ROW (BUTTONHOLE ROW): Rib to last 6sts, cast off 3sts, rib to end.
NEXT ROW: In rib, cast on 3sts neatly over those cast off.
Rib 4 more rows.
Cast off evenly in patt.
Using needles A, cast on 6sts for button underwraps, using this needle, with RS facing and beg at back left shoulder, k49 (57:61:65) sts evenly round left sleeve edge.
Work as first border, noting that the buttonhole row will be:
Rib 3, cast off 3sts, rib to end.

Rollneck

First join left shoulder, omitting sleeve border.
Using needles A, k across sts of back, k14 (16:16:16) sts evenly down left front neck, k across centre front sts, finally k14 (16:16: 16) sts evenly up right front neck. (68 (74: 76: 80) sts)
Beg p row, work 8 rows in st st.
Change to needles C and cont in st st until work measures 19cm (7½in) from beg, ending after a k row.
K 5 rows.
Cast off loosely knitwise.

Making up

Block according to ballband instructions. Join right shoulder, omitting sleeve border, then join polo neck edges. Sew buttons to button underwrap to correspond with the buttonholes.

Fair Isle yoke top

Each band in this simple 4-stitch pattern repeat is different to the last. The plain area of the body is shaped at the sides so that the top fits gently against the waist.

Essential information

DIFFICULTY Moderate

SIZE To fit an adult female S (M:L:XL)

YARN

Patons Diploma Gold DK 50g

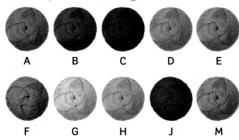

A: 6169 Airforce x 2 (2:2:2)

B: 6298 Charcoal x 1 (2:2:2)

C: 6245 Plum x 1 (1:1:1)

D: 6308 Lilac pink x 1 (1:1:1)

E: 6213 Thyme x 1 (1:1:1)

F: 6237 Taupe x 1 (1:1:1)

G: 6143 Natural x 1 (1:1:1)

H: 6243 Bright aqua x 1 (1:1:1)

J: 6123 Cyclamen x 1 (1:1:1)

M: 6184 Steel x 3 (4:4:4)

NEEDLES

A: 1 pair of 3.75mm (UK9/US5) needles

B: 1 pair of 4mm (UK8/US6) needles

A
B

TENSION

22sts and 25 rows to 10cm (4in) over patt on 4mm (UK8/US6) needles

NOTIONS

2 stitch holders

Large-eyed needle

Back

With needles A and yarn B, cast on 80 (90:100:110) sts.

K 1 more row in yarn B, 2 rows in C, 2 rows in A, 2 rows in M, 2 rows in D, 2 rows in B.

INC ROW (RS): With yarn E, k3 (4:5:6), [kfb, k3] to last 1 (2:3:4) st, k1 (2:3:4). (99 (111:123: 135) sts)

NEXT ROW: P with E.

Stranding yarn not in use loosely across WS of work, read Chart 1 on p.63 from right to left on RS (k) rows and from left to right on WS (p) rows as follows:

ROW 1 (RS): K1 from A to B, rep 4sts from B to C to last 2sts, k2 from C to D.

ROW 2: P2 from D to C, rep 4sts from C to B to last st, p1 from B to A.

ROW 3: As row 1.

P 1 row E.

DEC ROW: With yarn E, k3 (4:5:6), [k2tog, k3] to last 1 (2:3:4) st, k1 (2:3:4). (80 (90:100:110) sts)

P 2 rows in yarn A, 2 rows in C.

INC ROW (WS): With yarn M, p3 (4:5:6), [pfb, p3] to last 1 (2:3:4) st, p1 (2:3:4). (99 (111:123:135) sts)

Change to needles B.

Cont in st st in yarn M only, beg k row work 2 (4:6:8) rows.

Shape sides

DEC ROW: K4, s1 k1 psso, k to last 6sts, k2tog, k4. St st 3 rows.

Rep last 4 rows x 7. (83 (95:107:119) sts)

INC ROW: K4, M1, k to last 4sts, M1, k4. St st 5 rows.

Rep last 6 rows x 7. (99 (111:123:135) sts)

Work 2 (4:6:8) rows straight.

Following chart in the same way as before, work rows 1–10 of Chart 2, see p.63.

Shape armholes

Keeping patt correct, cast off 2 (3:4:5) sts at beg of next 2 rows.

Dec 1st at both ends of next row and foll 9 (10:11:12) alt rows. * (75 (83:91:99) sts)

Patt 29 (31:33:35) rows straight, ending after WS row.

Shape shoulders

NEXT ROW: Cast off in patt 14 (16:18:20) sts, patt until there are 47 (51:55:59) sts on RH needle, cast off rem 14 (16:18:20) sts. Leave centre 47 (51:55:59) sts on a stitch holder.

Front

Work as back to *.

Patt 5 rows straight, ending after WS row.

Shape neck

NEXT ROW: Patt 20 (22:24:26) sts, k2tog, turn, leave rem sts.

Cont on these 21 (23:25:27) sts for left front neck, dec 1st at neck edge on 7 foll alt rows. (14 (16:18:20) sts)

Patt 9 (11:13:15) rows straight, ending after WS row. Cast off in patt.

With RS facing, slip centre 31 (35:39:43) sts onto stitch holder, join in appropriate yarn to 22 (24:26:28) right front sts, k2tog, patt to end.

Work to match first side, reversing shapings.

Sleeves

With needles A and yarn B, cast on 65 (68:71:74) sts.

K 1 more row in yarn B, 2 rows in C, 2 rows in A, 2 rows in M, 2 rows in D, and 2 rows in B.

INC ROW (RS): With yarn E, k6 (5:5:4), [kfb, k3] to last 3 (3:2:2) sts, k3 (3:2:2). (79 (83:87:91) sts)

NEXT ROW: P with yarn E.

Patt 3 rows from Chart 1 as lower border on back. P 1 row in yarn E.

DEC ROW: With yarn E, k6 (5:5:4), [k2tog, k3] to last 3 (3:2:2) sts, k3 (3:2:2). (65 (68:71:74) sts) P 2 rows in yarn A, 2 rows C.

INC ROW (WS): With yarn B, p6 (5:5:4), [pfb, p3] to last 3 (3:2:2) sts, p3 (3:2:2). (79 (83:87:91) sts) Change to needles B.

Shape top

With yarn A, beg k row, cont in st st, cast off 2 (3:4:5) sts at beg of next 2 rows.

Beg with 13th chart row and keeping patt correct as back, cont in patt from Chart 2, at the same time dec 1st at both ends of next row and 15 (16:17:18) foll alt rows. (43sts)

Cont in patt, cast off 6sts at beg of next 4 rows. Cast off rem 19sts.

Neck edging

Join right shoulder seam. With RS facing, using needles A and yarn B pick up and k23 (25:27:29) sts down left front neck, across centre front 31 (35:39:43) sts work as follows: K4 (4:3:3), [k2tog, k3] x 5 (6:7:8), k2 (1:1:0), pick up and k23 (25:27:29) sts up right front neck, then across centre back 47 (51:55:59) sts work as follows: k5 (4:4:3), [k2tog, k3] x 8 (9:10:11), k2 (2:1:1). (111 (121:131:141) sts) K 1 row more in yarn B, 2 rows C, 2 rows A, 1 row D. Cast off firmly knitwise with D.

Making up

Block pieces (see p.300), following instructions on the ballband. Join left shoulder and neck edging. Join side and sleeve seams and sew in sleeves matching pattern where necessary.

Chart 1

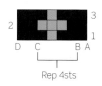

Rep 4sts

KEY

- Airforce
- Charcoal
- Plum
- Lilac pink
- Thyme
- Taupe
- Natural
- Bright aqua
- Cyclamen
- Steel

Chart 2

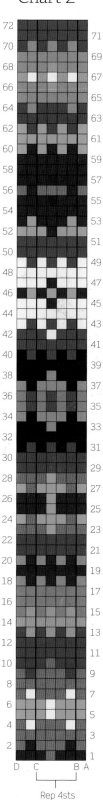

D C   B A

Rep 4sts

TOP TIP   *Keep your balls of yarn separate to prevent the strands tangling.*

Lace-edge summer top

This pretty smock top is worked from the top downwards in a lace-weight yarn. Increases below the neckband form soft gathers. Lengthen the garment to your preferred choice simply by increasing the number of rows knitted.

Essential information

DIFFICULTY Moderate

SIZE To fit an adult female, sizes 10-16 (18-24)

YARN

Debbie Bliss Rialto Lace 50g

09 Cyclamen x 3 (4)

NEEDLES

A: 1 pair of 3.25mm (UK10/US3) needles

B: 80cm (32in), 3.25mm (UK10/US3) circular needle

C: Cable needle

TENSION

31sts and 45 rows to 10cm (4in) over st st on 3.25mm (UK10/US3) needles

NOTIONS

Stitch markers (SM)

2 spare circular needles or spare yarn

Large-eyed needle

SPECIAL ABBREVIATIONS

C6B Cable 6 back: slip 3sts to cable needle (cn) and hold at back, k3 from LH needle then k3 from cn

C6F Cable 6 front: slip next 3sts to cn and hold at front, k3 from LH needle then k3 from cn

T5L Twist 5 left: slip next 3sts to cn and hold at front, p2, k3 from cn

T5R Twist 5 right: slip next 2sts to cn and hold at the back, k3, p2 from cn

NOTE: Use the stitch markers to mark the sleeve sections as all shaping is worked around the stitch marker.

Neckband

Using needles A, cast on 19sts.

ROW 1 (RS): K5, p4, C6B, p2, k2.

ROW 2: K4, p6, k4, p3, k2.

ROW 3: K2, T5L, T5R, T5L, k2.

ROW 4: K2, p3, k4, p6, k4.

ROW 5: K2, p2, C6F, p4, k5.

ROW 6: Rep row 4.

ROW 7: K2, T5R, T5L, T5R, k2.

ROW 8: K4, p6, k5, p2, k2.

Rep rows 1–8 until the band measures 80 (84)cm (31^1/$_2$ (33)in) from beg, ending on a WS row.

Cast off.

With RS together, join the cast on edge with the cast off edge being careful not to twist the band.

Body and sleeves

(marking the sections)

The neckband seam is the centre back. Using a small length of contrasting yarn, place a marker (attach to band using yarn threaded through a needle) 13.5 (14.5)cm (5^1/$_2$ (6)in) either side of the back seam. The back section will be 27 (29)cm (10^1/$_2$ (11^1/$_2$)in).

Place another marker 13cm (5^1/$_4$in) from the back markers. This will be the sleeve section. The front section will be 27 (29)cm (10^1/$_2$ (11^1/$_2$)in). (Place a marker of a different colour at the centre front. This will help you to pick up the sts evenly across this section.) With RS of band facing, starting at the centre back, using needles B, pick up and k33 (39) sts evenly to the first marker, place a marker, pick up and k56 across the sleeve section to the next marker, place a marker, pick up and k66 (78) sts evenly across the front section to the next marker, place a marker, then pick up, and k56 to the next marker, place a marker, then pick up and k33 (39) sts to the centre back. (244 (268) sts)

ROUND 1 (RS): K into front and back of every st to the first marker. (66 (78) sts)

K across 56sts from sleeve section, k into front and back of every st across front section to next marker. (132 (156) sts)

K across 56sts of sleeve section then k into front and back of every st to the centre back. (376 (424) sts)

Shape sleeve

NEXT ROUND: *K until 1st before SM, yon, k1, (slip SM) k1, yon; rep from * to end.

Inc in this way on every foll alt round until there are 112 (118) sts in each sleeve section and 188 (220) sts in the front section.

Work 2 rounds straight. Break yarn.

Divide for front and back.

NEXT ROUND: S94 (110) sts from back section to RH needle. S112 (118) sts from sleeve section to waste yarn or spare circular needle. Rejoin yarn to last st of back section. Cast on 10sts, k across 188 (220) sts from front section, cast on 10sts. S112 (118) sts from sleeve section to waste yarn or spare circular needle, k across 188 (220) sts from back section. Place marker to show beg of round.

There are now 198 (230) sts in front and 198 (230) sts in the back section.

Cont working on these sts without shaping until the work measures 28 (30)cm (11 (12)in) or your desired length from armhole. Break yarn and leave sts on circular needle.

Sleeves (work 2)

S112 (118) sts from sleeve to needles A.
Cast on 5sts at beg of next 2 rows. (122 (128) sts)

Work 1 row straight then inc 1st at each end of next and every foll alt row until there are 134 (140) sts.
Work 2 rows straight.
NEXT ROW (DEC ROW): *K1, k2tog; rep from *, end k2. (90 (94) sts)
Work 10 rows k1, p1 rib, cast off in rib.

Knitted-on border

NOTE: The border can be knitted separately and sewn on to the cast off edge of the garment if you do not want to work a knitted-on border. The last st of every RS row of the border is knitted tog with the next st of the main knitting. Using needles A, cast on 9sts.

ROW 1 (RS): Yon, k2tog, yon, k1, yon, ssk, k3, with RS of main knitting facing, slip the last st from the RH needle to the circular needle holding the main knitting, knit this st tog tbl with first st from main knitting. (10sts) Turn.

ROW 2 (WS): Using needle B, p5, k5.
ROW 3: (Use the circular needle from the main knitting for the rest of the border), yon, k2tog, yon, k3, yon, ssk, k2, k1tog with main knitting tbl. (11sts)
ROW 4: P4, k7.
ROW 5: Yon, k2tog, yon, k2, ssk, k1, yon, ssk, k1, k1tog with main knitting.
ROW 6: P3, k1, ssk, yon x 3, k2tog, k3. (12sts)
ROW 7: Yon, k2tog, yon, ssk, p1, k1, p1 (into 3 yarnovers from previous row), k2tog, yon, k2, k1tog with main.
ROW 8: P4, k5, k2tog, k1. (11sts)
ROW 9: Yon, k2tog, yon, ssk, k1, k2tog, yon, k3, k1tog with main.
ROW 10: P5, k3, k2tog, k1. (10sts)
ROW: 11 Yon, k2tog, yon, s2kpo, yon, k4, k1tog with main.
ROW 12: P6, k1, k2tog, k1. (9sts)
Rep these 12 rows until you have worked all sts from the main knitting – 66 (76) full patt reps if you are working it to sew on later.

Making up

Sew the under arm of the sleeve to the cast off edge. Sew on border to cast off edge if worked separately. Sew in all loose ends. Block carefully.

Chart for border pattern

Work all odd number (RS) rows from right to left, and all even number (WS) rows from left to right.

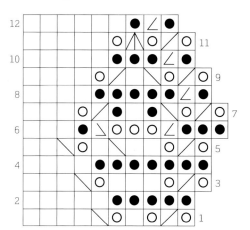

KEY

●	P on RS rows, k on WS rows
O	Yarnover
╱	K2tog
╲	Ssk
⋀	S2kpo
⟋	K2tog on WS rows
⟍	Ssk on WS rows

TOP TIP *Remember to work the neck cables and twists alternately.*

Essential information

DIFFICULTY Moderate

SIZE To fit an adult male S (M:L:XL)

YARN

Debbie Bliss Rialto Aran 50g

36 Sage x 16 (17:19:20)

NEEDLES

A: 1 pair of 4.5mm (UK7/US7) needles
B: 1 pair of 5mm (UK6/US8) needles

A

B

TENSION

18sts and 24 rows to 10cm (4in) over st st on 5mm
(UK6/US8) needles

NOTIONS

1 stitch holder
Large-eyed needle

Men's crew neck sweater

This simple sweater, with 2x2 rib edging in a soft aran yarn, is a wardrobe staple for all men. The shaped shoulders create a comfortable, fitted garment.

Back

With needles A, cast on 102 (114:126:138) sts.
ROW 1: K2, [p2, k2] to end.
ROW 2: P2, [k2, p2] to end.
Rep the last 2 rows x 7.
Change to needles B.
Starting with a k row, cont in st st until the back measures 44 (45:46:47)cm (17^1/$_2$ (17^3/$_4$:18:18^1/$_2$)in) from cast on edge, ending with a p row.

Shape armholes

Cast off 4 (5:6:7) sts at beg of next 2 rows. (94 (104:114:124) sts)
NEXT ROW: K2, skpo, k to last 4sts, k2tog, k2.
NEXT ROW: P to end.
Rep the last 2 rows x 5 (6:7:8). (82 (90:98:106) sts)
Work straight until back measures 64 (66:68:70)cm (25^1/$_4$ (26:26^3/$_4$:27^1/$_2$)in) from beg, ending with a p row.

Shape back neck and shoulders

NEXT ROW: K33 (35:37:39) sts, turn and work on these sts for first side of back neck.
Dec 1st at neck edge on next 4 rows. (29 (31:33:35) sts)
Work 1 row.

Shape shoulder

Cast off 9 (10:11:12) sts at beg of next and foll RS row.
Work 1 row.
Cast off rem 11sts.
With RS facing, slip centre 16 (20:24:28) sts onto a holder, join on yarn to rem sts, k to end.
Complete to match first side.

Front

Work as given for Back until front measures 56 (58:60:62)cm (22^1/$_4$ (22^3/$_4$:23^1/$_2$:24^1/$_2$)in) from beg, ending with a p row.

Shape neck

NEXT ROW: K36 (38:40:42), turn and work on these sts for first side of front neck.
NEXT ROW: P to end.
NEXT ROW: K to last 3sts, k2tog, k1.
Rep the last 2 rows until 29 (31:33:35) sts rem.
Work straight until front measures same as back to shoulder, ending with a WS row.

Shape shoulder

Cast off 9 (10:11:12) sts at beg of next and foll RS row.
Work 1 row.
Cast off rem 11sts.
With RS facing, slip centre 10 (14:18:22) sts onto a holder, join on yarn to rem sts, k to end.
Complete to match first side.

Sleeves (make 2)

Using needles A, cast on 46 (50:54:58) sts.
Work 20 rows rib as given for Back.
Change to needles B.
Beg with a k row cont in st st.
Work 4 rows.
INC ROW: K3, M1, k to last 3sts, M1, k3.
Work 5 rows.
Rep the last 6 rows x 14 and the inc row again. (78 (82:86:90) sts)
Cont straight until sleeve measures 50cm (20in) from cast on edge, ending with a WS row.
Mark each end of last row with a coloured thread.
Work a further 6 rows.

Shape top

NEXT ROW: K2, skpo, k to last 4sts, k2tog, k2.
NEXT ROW: P to end.
Rep the last 2 rows x 5 (6:7:8). (66 (68:70:72) sts)
Cast off 4sts at beg of next 12 rows.
Cast off.

Neckband

Join right shoulder seam.
With RS facing, pick up and k28 down left side of front neck, k10 (14:18:22) sts from centre front holder, pick up and k28 up RS of front neck, k10 down right back neck, k16 (20:24:28) sts from back neck, pick up and k10 up left back neck. (102 (110:118:126) sts)
Starting with row 2, work 7 rows rib as given for Back.
Cast off in rib.

Making up

Join left shoulder and neckband. Sew on sleeve, with last 6 rows to sts cast off at under arm.
Join side and sleeve seams.

Special abbreviations

C5B Cable 5 back: slip next 3sts to cable needle (cn) and hold at back of work, k next 2sts from LH needle then p1, k2 from cn

C5F Cable 5 front: slip next 2sts to cn and hold at front of work, k2 , p1 from LH needle then k2 from cn

T3F Twist 3 front: slip next 2sts to cn and hold at front of work, p1 from LH needle, then k2 from cn

T3B Twist 3 back: slip next st to cn and hold at back of work, k2, from LH needle then p1 from cn

C4B Cross 4 back: slip next 2sts to cn and hold at back of work, k next 2sts from LH needle then k 2sts from cn

C4F Cross 2 front: slip next 2sts to cn and hold at front of work, k next 2sts from LH needle then k 2sts from cn

C6B Cable 6 back: slip next 3sts to cn and hold at back of work, k3 from LH needle then k3 from cn

C6F Cable 6 front: slip next 3sts to cn and hold at front of work, k3 from LH needle then k3 from cn

C2F Cross 2 front: slip next st onto cn and hold at front of work, k next st from LH needle then k st from cn

T2FW Twist 2 front on WS: slip next st to cn and hold at front (WS of work), purl next st from LH needle then k st from cn

T2F Twist 2 front: slip next st onto cn and hold at front of work, purl next st from LH needle, then k st from cn

C2B Cross 2 back: slip next st to cn and hold at the back of work, knit next st from LH needle then k st from cn

T2BW T2 back on WS: slip next st onto cn and hold at back (RS of work), k next st from LH needle then p st from cn

T2B Twist 2 back: slip next st to cn and hold at back of work, k next st from LH needle then p st from cn

Shawl collar aran

A men's cosy sweater with a classic neckline, this pattern includes a variety of cable and rib stitches, which create texture and elasticity in the garment. Refer to the cable and twist stitch patterns and charts on pp.286–297 before you cast on.

Essential information

DIFFICULTY Difficult

SIZE To fit an adult male S (M:L:XL)

YARN

Blacker Designs Pure Organic Corridale with Hebridean 4-ply 50g

Natural fleece x 13 (14:15:16)

NEEDLES

A: 1 pair of of 3.25mm (UK10/US3) needles
B: 1 pair of 4mm (UK8/US6) needles
C: Cable needle
D: 80cm (32in), 3.25mm (UK10/US3) circular needle

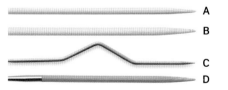

A
B
C
D

TENSION

28sts and 33 rows to 10cm (4in) over 2x2 rib on 4mm (UK8/US6) needles

NOTIONS

2 stitch holder or spare needles
Stitch markers

SPECIAL ABBREVIATIONS

See opposite

Back

NOTE: The rib has an odd stitch in the middle. Using needles A, cast on 165 (181:197:213) sts. Work rib as follows:

ROW 1 (RS): K2, *p2, k2; rep from * until you have worked 82 (90:98:106) sts, p1, k2, *p2, k2; rep from * to end.

ROW 2: P2, *k2, p2; rep from * until you have worked 82 (90:98:106) sts, k1, p2, *k2, p2; rep from * to end.

This sets the position for the rib; cont working as set until the rib measures 10cm (4in) from beg, ending on a WS row.

Change to needles B and work in patt as follows:

ROW 1 (RS): [K2, p2] x 5 (6:7:7), k6 (row 1 of panel A – cable), [p2, k2] x 3 (4:4:5), p2, C2F, p9, (row 1 of panel B – floating leaves), p1, [k2, p2] x 3 (3:4:5), k6, (row 1 of panel A – cable), p6, [k2, p2, C5B, p2, k2], (row 1 of panel C – cross cables), p6, [k6] (panel A – cable), [p2, k2] x 3 (3:4:5), p1, [p2, C2F, p9], (panel B – floating leaves), [k2, p2] x 3 (4:4:5), [k6] (panel A – cable), [p2, k2] x 5 (6:7:7).

This sets up the positions for the cable panels. Cont working from row 2 of cable panels until the work measures 42 (43:44:45)cm (16¹/₂ (17: 17¹/₂:17³/₄)in) from beg, ending on a WS row.

Shape armhole

Keeping patt correct throughout, cast off 6 (6:8:8) sts at beg of next 2 rows. (153 (169:181: 197) sts)

Dec 1st at each end of the next 5 (5:7:7) rows. (143 (159:167:183) sts)

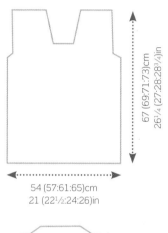

67 (69:71:73)cm
26¹/₄ (27:28:28³/₄)in

54 (57:61:65)cm
21 (22¹/₂:24:26)in

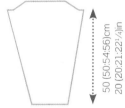

50 (50:54:56)cm
20 (20:21:22¹/₄)in

Then dec 1st at each end of foll alt row. (141 (157:165:181) sts)

Cont without shaping in patt until the armhole measures 25 (26:27:28)cm (9³/₄ (10:10¹/₂:11) in) from beg, ending on a WS row. Leave sts on a spare needle or stitch holder.

Front

Work as for Back until you have completed the armhole shaping plus 1 WS row.

Divide for front neck opening, keeping patt correct throughout, patt across 50 (58:62:70) sts, turn, leave rem sts on a spare needle or stitch holder, and work each side separately.

Dec 1st at neck edge on the foll row then on every foll 4th row until 42 (48:50:54) sts rem. Cont without shaping until the front matches the back shoulder.

With RS facing, rejoin yarn and cast off centre 41sts patt to end of row.

Complete to match first side.

Sleeves (make 2)

Using needles A, cast on 58 (58:66:66) sts. Work in rib as for the Back until the rib measures 8cm (3in) from beg, ending on WS row. Change to needles B and set patt as follows:

ROW 1 (RS): K2, [p2, k2] x 5 (5:6:6), p2 C2F, p9, rib as set to end of row.

This sets the position for the floating leaves patt, cont working from row 2 of patt.

At the same time inc 1st at each end of the next RS row and every foll 4th row until there are 122 (126:128:132) sts, working the new sts into the rib patt.

Cont without shaping until the sleeve measures 50 (52:54:56)cm (20 (20$\frac{1}{2}$:21:22$\frac{1}{4}$)in) from cast on edge ending on a WS row.

Shape sleeve head

Cast off 6sts at the beg of the next 2 rows. (110 (114:116:120) sts)

Cast off 1st at each end of next 2 rows. (106 (110:112:116) sts)

NEXT ROW: K2, p2tog, patt to last 4sts, p2tog, k2.

Cont to dec as set in last row on every foll RS row until 98 (102:104:108) sts rem.

Cast off 4sts at beg of next 4 rows until 82 (86:88:92) sts rem.

Cast off.

Collar

Using 3 needle cast off method (see p.271) and with RS of back facing RS of front, cast off 42 (48:50:54) sts from front shoulder with back, patt across 57 (61:65:73) sts from centre back then cast off rem 42 (48:50:54) sts from shoulder. Leave back sts on a holder.

Using needles D, with RS facing and starting at the base of the front neck, pick up and k52 (54:60:64) sts up to the shoulder, then pick up and k57 (61:65:73) sts across back neck. Pick up and k52 (54:60:64) sts down to the base of front neck. (161 (169:185:201) sts)

ROW 1 (WS): *P2, k2; rep from * for 80 (84:92:100) sts, p1, M1, *k2, p2; rep from * to end. (162 (170:186:202) sts)

Cont in rib as set for 5cm (2$\frac{1}{4}$in) then change to needles B and cont until the collar measures 13cm (5$\frac{1}{4}$in) from beg ending on a WS row. Cast off loosely in rib.

Making up

Block work lightly according to instructions on the ballband. Join side seams and sleeve seam. Sew in sleeve matching the centre of the sleeve to the shoulder seam. Overlap the left side collar with the right side and stitch in place to the cast off edge of the centre front.

Panel A Cable 6 front

(Worked over 6sts and 6 rows)

ROW 1 (RS): K6.

ROW 2 AND EVERY FOLL WS ROW: P6.

ROW 3: C6F.

ROW 5: K6.

ROW 6: P6.

Rep these 6 rows.

Panel A

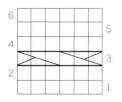

KEY

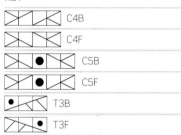

C6F

Panel B Floating leaves

(worked over 13sts and 32 rows)

ROW 1 (RS): P2, C2F, p9.

ROW 2: K8, T2FW, p1, k2.

ROW 3: P2, k1 tbl, p1, C2F, p7.

ROW 4: K6, T2FW, p1, k1, p1, k2.

ROW 5: P2, [k1 tbl, p1] x 2, C2F, p5.

ROW 6: K4, T2FW, [P1, K1] x 2, p1, k2.

ROW 7: P2, [k1 tbl, p1] x 3, C2F, p3.

ROW 8: K2, T2FW, [p1, k1] x 3, p1, k2.

ROW 9: P2, [k1 tbl, p1] x 4, k1 tbl, p2.

ROW 10: K2, [p1, k1] x 3, p1, T2FW, k2.

ROW 11: P3, C2F, [p1, k1 tbl] x 3, p2.

ROW 12: K2, [p1, k1] x 2, p1, T2FW, K4.

ROW 13: P5, C2F, [p1, k1 tbl] x 2, p2.

ROW 14: K2, p1, k1, p1, T2FW, k6.

ROW 15: P7, C2F, p1, k1 tbl, p2.

ROW 16: K2, p1, T2FW, k8.

ROW 17: P9, C2B, p2.

ROW 18: K2 p1, T2BW, k8.

ROW 19: P7, C2B, p1, k1 tbl, p2.

ROW 20: K2, p1, k1, p1, T2BW, k6.

ROW 21: P5, C2B, [p1, k1 tbl] x 2, p2.

ROW 22: K2, [p1, k1] x 2, p1, T2BW, k4.

ROW 23: P3, C2B, [p1, k1 tbl] x 3, p2.

ROW 24: K2, [p1, k1] x 3, p1, T2BW, k2.

ROW 25: P2, [k1 tbl, p1] x 4, k1 tbl, p2.

ROW 26: K2, T2BW, [p1, k1] x 3, p1, k2.

ROW 27: P2, [k1 tbl, p1] x 3, C2B, p3.

ROW 28: K4, T2BW, [p1, k1] x 2, p1, k2.

ROW 29: P2, [k1 tbl, p1] x 2, C2B, p5.

ROW 30: K6, T2BW, p1, k1, p1, k2.

ROW 31: P2, k1 tbl, p1, C2B, p7.

ROW 32: K8, T2BW, p1, k2.

Rep these 32 rows for the patt.

Panel B

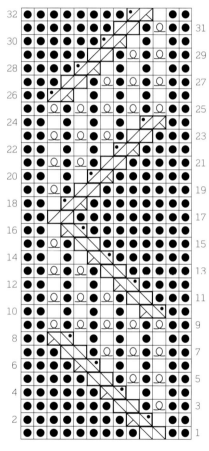

KEY

● P on RS rows, k on WS rows

C2F

C2B

Q K1 tbl

T2FW

T2BW

Panel C

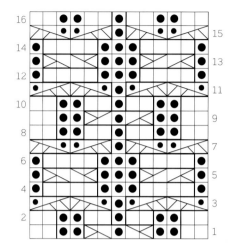

KEY

C4B

C4F

C5B

C5F

T3B

T3F

Panel C Cross cable

(worked over 13sts and 16 rows)

ROW 1 (RS): K2, p2, C5B, p2, k2.

ROW 2: P2, k2, p2, k1, p2, k2, p2.

ROW 3: T3F, T3B, p1, T3F, T3B.

ROW 4: K1, p4, k3, p4, k1.

ROW 5: P1, C4B, p3, C4F, p1.

ROW 6: Rep row 4.

ROW 7: T3B, T3F, p1, T3B, T3F.

ROW 8: Rep row 2.

ROW 9: K2, p2, C5F, p2, k2.

ROW 10: Rep row 2.

ROW 11: Rep row 3.

ROW 12: Rep row 4.

ROW 13: Rep row 5.

ROW 14: Rep row 4.

ROW 15: Rep row 7.

ROW 16: Rep row 2.

Rep these 16 rows for the patt.

Essential information

DIFFICULTY Easy

SIZE To fit an adult male S (M:L:XL)

YARN

Sublime Cashmere Merino Silk DK 50g

223 Latte x 7 (8:8:9)

NEEDLES

A: 1 pair of 3.75mm (UK9/US5) needles

B: 1 pair of 4mm (UK8/US6) needles

TENSION

22sts and 28 rows to 10cm (4in) over st st using 4mm (UK8/US6) needles

NOTIONS

2 stitch holders
Large-eyed needle

Men's sleeveless pullover

A timeless v-necked tank top knitted in stocking stitch with a 2x2 ribbed border. The yarn used here is a cashmere, merino wool and silk blended quality.

Back

With needles A, cast on 106 (118:130:142) sts.

RIB ROW 1: K2, [p2, k2] to end.

RIB ROW 2: P2, [k2, p2] to end.

Rep the last 2 rows x 4 (5:6:7).

Change to needles B.

Beg with a k row cont in st st until back measures 44 (45:46:47)cm (17$\frac{1}{2}$ (17$\frac{3}{4}$:18:18$\frac{1}{2}$)in) from cast on edge, ending with a p row **.

Shape armholes

Cast off 10 (11:12:13) sts at beg of next 2 rows. (86 (96:106:116) sts)

NEXT ROW: K1, skpo, k to last 3sts, k2tog, k1.

NEXT ROW: P to end.

Rep the last 2 rows x 3 (4:5:6). (78 (86:94:102) sts)

Work straight until back measures 65 (67:69:71)cm (26 (26$\frac{1}{4}$:27:28)in) from cast on edge, ending with a WS row.

Shape shoulders

Cast off 8 (9:11:12) sts at beg of the next 2 rows and 9 (10:11:12) sts at beg of foll 2 rows.

Leave rem 44 (48:50:54) sts on a stitch holder.

Front

Work as given for Back to **. (106 (118:130:142) sts)

Shape armholes and neck

NEXT ROW: Cast off 10 (11:12:13) sts, k until there are 42 (47:52:57) sts on the needle, turn, and work on these sts for first side of neck shaping.

NEXT ROW: P to end.

NEXT ROW: K1, skpo, k to last 3sts, k2 tog, k1.

NEXT ROW: P to end.

Rep the last 2 rows x 3 (4:5:6). (34 (37:40:43) sts)

Keeping armhole edge straight cont to dec 1st at neck edge on every RS row until 17 (19:22:24) sts rem.

Cont straight until front measures the same as back to shoulder shaping, ending at armhole edge.

Shape shoulders

Cast off 8 (9:11:12) sts at beg of the next row.

Work 1 row.

Cast off rem 9 (10:11:12) sts.

With RS facing, slip next 2sts on a holder, rejoin yarn to rem sts, k to end.

NEXT ROW: Cast off 10 (11:12:13) sts, p to end. (42 (47:52:57) sts)

NEXT ROW: K1, skpo, k to last 3sts, k2 tog, k1.

NEXT ROW: P to end.

Rep the last 2 rows x 3 (4:5:6). (34 (37:40:43) sts)

Keeping armhole edge straight cont to dec 1st at neck edge on every RS row until 17 (19:22:24) sts rem.

Cont straight until front measures the same as back to shoulder shaping, ending at armhole edge.

Shape shoulders

Cast off 8 (9:11:12) sts at beg of the next row.

Work 1 row.

Cast off rem 9 (10:11:12) sts.

Neckband

Join right shoulder seam.

With RS facing and using needles A, pick up and k50 (52:56:58) sts evenly down left side of front neck, k2 from safety pin, pick up and k50 (52:54:56) sts evenly up RS of front neck, k44 (48:50:54) sts from back neck holder. (146 (154:162:170) sts)

1st and 4th sizes only

ROW 1: K2, [p2, k2] to end.

2nd and 3rd sizes only

ROW 1: P2, [k2, p2] to end.

All sizes

This row sets the rib patt.

ROW 2: Rib 49 (51:55:57), k2tog, skpo, rib to end.

ROW 3: Rib to end.

ROW 4: Rib 48 (50:54:56), k2tog, skpo, rib to end.

ROW 5: Rib to end.

ROW 6: Rib 47 (49:53:55), k2tog, skpo, rib to end.

ROW 7: Rib to end.

Cast off in rib, dec on this row as before.

Armbands

Join left shoulder seam and neckband.

With RS facing and using needles A, pick up and k118 (122:130:134) sts evenly around armhole edge.

ROW 1: K2, [p2, k2] to end.

ROW 2: P2, [k2, p2] to end.

These 2 rows set the rib patt.

Work a further 5 rows.

Cast off in rib.

Making up

Join side and armband seams (see pp.300–302 for more information).

Essential information

DIFFICULTY Moderate

SIZE To fit a child, aged 9-10 (11-12:13-14) years

YARN

Louisa Harding Ondine 100% Cotton 50g

11 Indigo x 11 (12:13)

NEEDLES

A: 1 pair of 3.75mm (UK9/US5) needles
B: 1 pair of 4mm (UK8/US6) needles
C: Cable needle
D: 80cm (32in), 3.75mm (UK9/US5) circular needle
E: 80cm (32in), 4mm (UK8/US6) circular needle

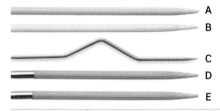

TENSION

28sts and 29 rows to 10cm (4in) over cable and stripe patt on 4mm (UK8/US6) needles

NOTIONS

Spare needle
Large-eyed needle

SPECIAL ABBREVIATIONS

T3B Twist 3 back: slip next st to cable needle (cn) and hold at back, k2 from LH needle then p1 from cn
T3F Twist 3 front: slip next 2sts to cn and hold at front, p1, k2 from cn
C4B Cross 4 back: slip next 2sts to cn and hold at back, k next 2sts from LH needle then k 2sts from cn
C4F Cross 4 front: slip next 2sts to cn and hold at front, k2 then k2 from cn
W1 (K)/(P) Wrap next stitch (knit st)/(purl st)
W1K With yarn at the back, slip next st purlwise, move yarn between needle to front of work, slip same st back to LH needle. Turn work, bringing yarn to purl side between needles. When all short rows worked, work to before wrapped st, insert RH needle under wrap and knitwise into wrapped st, knit together
W1P With yarn at the front, slip next st purlwise, move yarn to back of work between needles. Slip same st back to LH needle. Turn work, bringing yarn to purl side between needles. When all short rows worked, work to before wrapped st, insert RH needle from behind into back loop of wrapped st, place it onto LH needle, purl with next st on LH needle

Child's weekend hoodie

This cabled hoodie is knitted in a cotton summer yarn for a relaxed look.

Back

Using needles A, cast on 114 (128:142) sts.
Set rib as follows:

ROW 1 (RS): K2, *p2, k8, p2, k2; rep from *
to end.

ROW 2: P2, *k2, p2, k4, p2, k2, p2; rep from *
to end.

Rep these 2 rows until you have worked 12 rows
thus ending on a WS row.

Change to needles B and start main patt.

ROW 1 (RS): P4, k8, *p6, k8; rep from *, end, p4.

ROW 2: K4, p8, *k6, p2, k4, p2; rep from * to last
18sts, end, k6, p8, k4.

ROW 3: P4, C4B, C4F, *p6, k8; rep from * to last
18sts, end, p6, C4B, C4F, p4.

ROWS 4 AND 6: Rep row 2.

ROW 5: Rep row 1.

ROW 7: P4, C4F, C4B, *p6, k8; rep from * to last
18sts, p6, C4F, C4B, p4.

Start short row shaping.

ROW 8: Patt as set to last 13sts, W1k, turn.

ROW 9: Patt to last 13sts, W1p, turn.

ROW 10: Patt to last 27sts, W1k, turn.

ROW 11: Patt to last 27sts, W1p, turn.

ROW 12: Patt to last 41sts, W1k, turn.

ROW 13: Patt to last 41sts, W1p, turn.

1st size only

ROW 14: Patt across all sts working into wrap sts
when you get to them.

2nd and 3rd sizes only

ROW 14: Patt to last 55sts, W1k, turn.

ROW 15: Patt to last 55sts, W1p, turn.

2nd size only

ROW 16: Patt to end.

3rd size only

ROW 16: Patt to last 65sts, W1k, turn.

ROW 17: Patt to last 65sts, W1p, turn.

ROW 18: Patt to end.

All sizes cont in cable and stripe patt as follows:

ROWS 1, 3, 5, 7, AND 9 (RS): P4, k8, *p6, k8; rep
from *, end, p4.

ROWS 2, 4, 6 AND 8: K4, p2, k4, p2, *k6, p2, k4, p2;
rep from *, end, k4.

ROWS 10, 12 AND 14: K4, p8, *k6, p8; rep from *,
end, k4.

ROW 11: P4, C4B, C4F, *p6, C4B, C4F; rep from *,
end, p4.

ROW 13: P4, k8, *p6, k8; rep from *, end, p4.

ROW 15: P4, C4F, C4B, *p6, C4F, C4B; rep from *,
end p4.

ROW 16: As row 10.

Rep these 16 rows until the work measures 35
(38:41)cm (14 (15:16¼)in) from beg,
(measured along side edge) ending on a WS row.

Shape armholes

Cast off 3sts at beg of next 2 rows with 108
(122:136) sts rem.

Cont without shaping until armhole measures
19 (20:21)cm (7½(8:8¼)in) from beg of
shaping ending on a WS row. Cast off.

Front

Using needles A, cast on 118 (132:146) sts.
Set up rib as follows:

NOTE: The rib is not the same all across the row.

1st size only

ROW 1 (RS): K2, p2, [k8, p2, k2, p2] x 3, k2, p2,
k2, p3, k2, p4, k2, p3, k2, [p2, k2] x 2, p2, [k8,
p2, k2, p2] x 2, k8, p2, k2.

ROW 2: P2, k2, [p2, k4, p2, k2, p2, k2] x 3, p2, k2,
p2, k3, p2, k4, p2, k3, p2, k2, [p2, k2] x 2, [p2,
k4, p2, k2, p2, k2] x 2, p2, k4, p2, k2, p2.

2nd size only

ROW 1 (RS): K2, p2, [k8, p2, k2, p2] x 2, k8, p2,
[k2, p3] x 4, k2, p4, k2, [p3, k2] x 4, p2, [k8, p2,
k2, p2] x 2, k8, p2, k2.

ROW 2: [P2, k2, p2, k4, p2, k2] x 3, [p2, k3] x 4, p2,
k4, p2, [k3, p2] x 4, [k2, p2, k4, p2, k2, p2] x 3.

3rd size only

ROW 1 (RS): [K2, p2, k8, p2] x 4, [k2, p2] x 2, k2,
p3, k2, p4, k2, p3, [k2, p2] x 3, [k8, p2, k2, p2]
x 3, k8, p2, k2.

ROW 2: [P2, k2, p2, k4, p2, k2] x 4, [p2, k2] x 2,
p2, k3, p2, k4, p2, k3, [p2, k2] x 3, [p2, k4, p2,
k2, p2, k2] x 3, p2, k4, p2, k2, p2.

Rep these 2 rows until you have completed
12 rows.

Change to needles B and start patt.

ROW 1 (RS): P4, k8, [p6, k8] x 2 (2:3), p10
(17:10), k2, p3, k2, p4, k2, p3, k2, p10 (17:10),
k8, [p6, k8] x 2 (2:3), p4.

ROW 2: K4, p8, [k6, p8] x 2 (2:3), k10 (17:10), p2,
k3, p2, k4, p2, k3, p2, k10 (17:10), p8, [k6, p8]
x 2, k4.

ROW 3: P4, C4B, C4F, [p6, C4B, C4F] x 2 (2:3),
p10 (17:10), k2, p3, k2, p4, k2, p3, k2, p10
(17:10), C4B, C4F, [p6, C4B, C4F] x 2 (2:3), p4.

ROW 4: As row 2.

ROW 5: P4, k8, [p6, k8] x 2 (2:3), p10 (17:10),
[T3F, p2] x 2, T3B, p2, T3B, p10 (17:10), k8, [p6,
k8] x 2 (2:3), p4.

ROW 6: K4, p8, [k6, p8] x 2 (2:3), k11 (18:11), p2,
k3, p2, k2, p2, k3, p2, k11 (18:11), p8, [k6, p8]
x 2 (2:3), k4.

ROW 7: P4, C4F, C4B, [p6, C4F, C4B] x 2 (2:3),
p11 (18:11), T3F, p2, T3F, T3B, p2, T3B, p11
(18:11), C4F, C4B, [p6, C4F, C4B] x 2 (2:3), p4.

ROW 8: K4, p8, [k6, p8] x 2 (2:3), k12 (19:12),
p2, k3, p4, k3, p2, k12 (19:12), p8, [k6, p8] x 2
(2:3), k4.

ROW 9: P4, k8, [p6, k8] x 2 (2:3), p12 (19:12),
T3F, p2, C4B, p2, T3B, p12 (19:12), k8, [p6, k8]
x 2 (2:3), p4.

ROW 10: K4, p2, k4, p2, [k6, p2, k4, p2] x 2 (2:3),
k13 (20:13), p2, k2, p4, k2, p2, k13 (20:13), p2,
k4, p2, [k6, p2, k4, p2] x 2 (2:3), k4.

ROW 11: P4, k8, [p6, k8] x 2 (2:3), p13 (20:13), [T3F, T3B] x 2, p13 (20:13), k8, [p6, k8] x 2 (2:3), p4.

ROW 12: K4, p2, k4, p2, [k6, p2, k4, p2] x 2 (2:3), k14 (21:14), p4, k2, p4, k14 (21:14), p2, k4, p2, [k6, p2, k4, p2] x 2 (2:3), k4.

ROW 13: P4, k8, [p6, k8] x 2 (2:3), p14 (21:14), C4F, p2, C4B, p14 (21:14) k8, [p6, k8] x 2 (2:3), p4.

ROW 14: As row 12.

ROW 15: P4, k8, [p6, k8] x 2 (2:3), p13 (20:13), [T3B, T3F] x 2, p13 (20:13), k8, [p6, k8] x 2 (2:3), p4.

ROW 16: As row 10.

ROW 17: P4, k8, [p6, k8] x 2 (2:3), p12 (19:12), T3B, p2, C4B, p2, T3F, P12 (19:12), k8, [p6, k8] x 2 (2:3), p4.

ROW 18: K4, p8, [k6, p8] x 2 (2:3), k12 (19:12), p2, k3, p4, k3, p2, k12 (19:12), p8, [k6, p8] x 2 (2:3), k4.

ROW 19: P4, C4B, C4F, [p6, C4B, C4B] x 2 (2:3), p11 (18:11), T3B, p2, T3B, T3F, p2, T3F, p11 (18:11), C4B, C4F, [p6, C4B, C4F] x 2 (2:3), p4.

ROW 20: K4, p8, [k6, p8] x 2 (2:3), k11 (18:11), p2, k3, p2, k2, p2, k3, p2, k11 (18:11), p8, [k6, p8] x 2 (2:3), k4.

ROW 21: P4, k8, [p6, k8] x 2 (2:3), p10 (17:10), [T3B, p2] x 2, T3F, p2, T3F, p10 (17:10), k8, [p6, k8] x 2 (2:3), p4.

ROW 22: As row 2.

ROW 23: P4, C4F, C4B, [p6, C4F, C4B] x 2 (2:3), p10 (17:10), k2, p3, k2, p4, k2, p3, k2, p10 (17:10), C4F, C4B, [p6, C4F, C4B] x 2 (2:3), p4.

ROW 24: As row 2.

This completes the central patt. Cont with stripe and circle cable as set and rep central patt from row 2 until work measures 35 (38:41)cm (14 (15:16^1/$_4$)in) from beg ending on a WS row.

Shape armholes

Cast off 3sts at beg of next 2 rows. (112 (126:140) sts)

Cont without shaping on these sts in patt until you have completed 4 full central patts from beg of work plus a further 18 rows, thus ending on a WS row.

Shape front neck

Keeping patt correct throughout, work across 56 (63:70) sts, turn, leave rem sts on a spare needle and work each side separately.

NEXT ROW (WS): K2, p2, k12 (19:12), patt to end of row.

RS ROW: Patt 37 (37:51), p12 (19:12), k2, p2. This sets the patt. Cont without shaping as set until the armhole measures 14 (15:16)cm (5^1/$_2$ (6:6^1/$_4$)in) from beg, ending on a RS row.

NEXT ROW (WS): Cast off 10 (12:12) sts at beg of row. (46 (51:58) sts)

Work 1 row straight then cast off 2sts at neck edge on next 2 WS rows. (42 (47:54) sts)

Dec 1st at neck edge on every foll row until 28 (33:42) sts rem. Cont without shaping until the front matches the back shoulder, ending on a WS row. Cast off.

With RS facing, rejoin yarn to centre sts. Cast off centre 6sts, p2, k2, patt to end of row.

Complete to match first side working neck shaping on RS row.

Sleeves (make 2)

Using needles A, cast on 60sts.

Set up rib:

ROW 1 (RS): P1, *k2, p2, k8, p2; rep from *, end, k2, p1.

ROW 2: K1, *p2, k2, p2, k4, p2, k2; rep from *, end, p2, k1.

Rep these 2 rows until you have completed 12 rows.

Change to needles B and work in circle and stripe patt as follows:

ROW 1 (RS): P5, k8, *p6, k8; rep from *, end, p5.

ROW 2: K5, p8, *k6, p8; rep from *, end k5.

This sets the position for the cable patt. **Cont working from row 3 of the Cable and stripe patt (see p.81). At the same time inc 1st at the beg of the next RS row and then on every foll 4th row until there are 96 (106:110) sts working the new sts in p on RS rows and k on WS rows.**

Cont without shaping until the sleeve measures 36 (40:42)cm (14^1/$_4$ (16:16^1/$_2$)in) from beg ending on a WS row. Cast off loosely.

Hood

With RS facing, using needles B and starting at the top of the right neck, pick up and k98 (112:126) sts evenly around the neck.

Work 3 rows of g st.

NEXT ROW (RS): P3, k8, *p6, k8; rep from *, end, p3.

This sets the position for the patt, cont working Cable and stripe patt from row 2 as written for the back until you have worked 16 rows.

Start shaping

NEXT ROW (RS): Cont working in patt as set for 42 (42:56) sts, M1p, patt across 14 (28:14), M1p, patt to end. (100 (114:128) sts)

Inc in same position on every foll 4th (6th:8th) rows until there are 106 (116:130) sts. Working the new sts into the reverse st st between cable patts. Cont without shaping until the hood measures 29 (29:30)cm (11^1/$_2$ (11^1/$_2$:12)in) from beg ending on WS row.

Shape top

NEXT ROW (RS): Patt across 53 (58:65) sts, and turn. Fold hood in half with RS facing and using a third needle, join top seam by casting off both sets of sts tog knitwise (by taking 1st from first needle tog with corresponding st from second needle).

Neck and hood edging

Using needle D and with RS facing, pick up and k17 (20:23) sts to beg of hood, pick up and k58 (58:61) sts to top seam, then pick up and k58 (58:51) sts to beg of neck opening, pick up and k17 (20:23) sts to end. Work 7 rows of g st then cast off.

Making up

Sew sleeves with the cast off edge of the sleeve placed between the armhole shaping on the front and back with the centre of the sleeve matching the shoulder seam. Join side and sleeve seams being careful to match the patterns. Overlap the left neckband with the right band and catch stitch (see p.83) along the centre 6sts cast off. Press according to ballband.

Cable and stripe pattern
(worked over 8sts and 16 rows)

ROW 1 (RS): K8.

ROWS 2, 4, 6, AND 8: P8.

ROW 3: C4B, C4F.

ROW 5: K8.

ROW 7: C4F, C4B.

ROWS 9, 10, 11, 12, 13, 14, 15, AND 16: K.

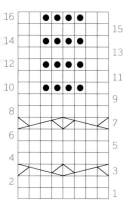

Central front cable pattern
(worked over 18sts and 26 rows)

ROWS 1 AND 3 (RS): K2, p3, k2, p4, k2, p3, k2.

ROWS 2 AND 4: P2, k3, p2, k4, p2, k3, p2.

ROW 5: [T3F, p2] x 2, T3B, p2, T3B.

ROW 6: K1, p2, k3, p2, k2, p2, k3, p2, k1.

ROW 7: P1, T3F, p2, T3F, T3B, p2, T3B, p1.

ROW 8: K2, p2, k3, p4, k3, p2, k2.

ROW 9: P2, T3F, p2, C4B, p2, T3F, p2.

ROW 10: K3, p2, k2, p4, k2, p2, k3.

ROW 11: P3, [T3F, T3B] x 2, p3.

ROWS 12 AND 14: K4, p4, k2, p4, k4.

ROW 13: P4, C4F, p2, C4B, p4.

ROW 15: P3, [T3B, T3F] x 2, p3.

ROW 16: Rep row 10.

ROW 17: P2, T3B, p2, C4B, p2, T3F, p2.

ROW 18: As row 8.

ROW 19: P1, T3B, p2, T3B, T3F, p2, T3F, p1.

ROW 20: As row 6.

ROW 21: [T3B, P2] x 2, T3F, p2, T3F.

ROWS 22, 24, 26: P2, k3, p2, k4, p2, k3, p2.

ROWS 23 AND 25: K2, p3, k2, p4, k2, p3, k2.

KEY

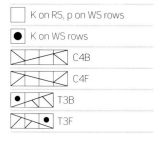

☐	K on RS, p on WS rows
●	K on WS rows
⬚	C4B
⬚	C4F
⬚	T3B
⬚	T3F

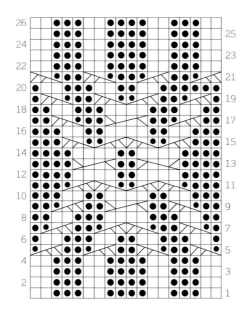

Button placement

22 (24:26)cm
9 (9½:10)in

35 (38:41)cm
14 (15:16½)in

32 (35:38)cm
12½ (14:15)in

Essential information

DIFFICULTY Moderate

SIZE To fit a child, aged 2 (4:6) years

YARN

Rico Essentials Cotton DK 50g

A **B** **C**

A: 38 Navy blue x 4

B: 04 Cherry x 1

C: 33 Cobalt blue x 1

NEEDLES

1 pair of 3.75mm (UK9/US5) needles

TENSION

23sts and 30 rows to 10cm (4in) over st st on
3.75mm (UK9/US5) needles

NOTIONS

Large-eyed needle

6 x 12mm (½in) brass buttons

Child's sailing sweater

Each boat is knitted using a separate small ball of yarn using the intarsia technique (see pp.306–307) to avoid floating it at the back of your knitting.

Back

Using yarn B, cast on 74 (80:86) sts.

Work 8 rows of g st (k all rows).

ROW 1 (RS): K2 in yarn B, k to last 2sts in yarn A, k2 using a small ball of yarn B.

ROW 2: K2 in yarn B, p to last 2sts in yarn A, k2 in yarn B.

Rep these 2 rows twice more. Cont to work in st st with 2 side sts worked in g st.

ROW 7 (PLACE BOATS): K2 in yarn B, k5 (6:7) in yarn A, [k4 in yarn A, k10 (11:12)] in yarn B] x 4, k4 in yarn B, k5 (6:7) in yarn A, k2 in yarn B.

This sets the position for the boats. Cont working boats as set from row 2 of chart and k2 in yarn B at each end of the row until you have worked 4 rows of chart.

Stop working k2 using yarn B at each end of row. Cont to work from chart, working the 2sts at beg and end of row in yarn A.

ROW 11 (ROW 5 OF CHART): K all sts in yarn A.

ROW 12: P4 (5:6) in yarn A, *p5 in yarn C, p9 (10:11) in yarn A; rep from * to end of row.

Cont as set from row 7 of chart until you have completed all 15 rows.

Cont using yarn A until the work measures 20 (21:22)cm (8 (8¼:9)in) from beg, ending on a WS row.

Start stripe yoke patt as follows:

ROWS 1 AND 2: K 2 rows in yarn C (B:C).

ROWS 3–6: Work 4 rows st st in yarn A.

ROWS 7 AND 8: K 2 rows in yarn B (C:B).

ROWS 9–12: Work 4 rows st st in yarn A.

Rep these 12 rows x 2 (3:3).

For 1st and 3rd sizes only

Work rows 1–6.

Change to yarn B and work 7 rows of g st. Cast off.

Front

Work as for Back until you have worked 6 rows of g st on the neckband.

NEXT ROW (BUTTONHOLES): K4, yon, k2tog, [k5 (6:6), yon, k2tog] x 2, k to last 20 (22:22) sts, yon, k2tog, [k5 (6:6) yon, k2tog] x 2, k to end.

NEXT ROW: Work 2 more rows of g st. Cast off.

Sleeves (make 2)

Cast on 44 (50:50) sts in yarn B. Work 8 rows of g st.

INC ROW: Change to yarn A and working in st st beg with k row, inc 1st at each end of this and every foll 6th row until there are 62 (58:68) sts.

At the same time when you have worked 4 rows of st st place boat as follows:

NEXT ROW (RS): K21 (24:24) in yarn A, k4 in yarn B, k to end in second ball of yarn A.

Cont to work the boat from row 2 of chart.

For 2nd and 3rd sizes only

When you have increased to (58:68) sts cont to inc on every foll 8th row until you have (66:70) sts.

All sizes

When you have 62 (66:70) sts, work 3 (1:1) rows thus ending on WS row.

NEXT ROW: Using yarn C (B:C) work 1 full rep of stripe patt as for Back, plus rows 1–4. Cast off loosely.

Making up

Block and sew in loose ends. Overlap the back shoulder band with the front and catch stitch sleeve edge together. To work catch stitch, take a small stitch in seam, with needle going in from right to left. Moving to the right, about 5mm (¼in), make another stitch, again inserting the needle from right and out to left. Moving to the right, take another stitch in the seam inserting the needle from right to left. Continue this pattern, crossing the stitches from left to right. Attach the sleeves matching the centre of each sleeve with the centre of the buttonhole band. Make sure both sides are the same distance from the shoulder. Join the side seam above the red side splits and sleeve seams being careful to match the pattern. Sew the buttons on the front of the sweater to correspond with the buttonholes (see the diagram in the Essential information panel).

Sailing boat chart

Work all RS rows from right to left and all WS rows from left to right.

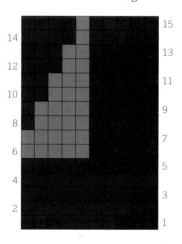

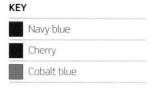

KEY

- ■ Navy blue
- ■ Cherry
- ■ Cobalt blue

Summertime hoodie

An ideal project for the lace beginner, this is a simple garment for a little girl. Make sure you work the s2kpo instruction as stated because this makes the knit stitch in the middle of the border pattern stand out.

Essential information

DIFFICULTY Moderate

SIZE To fit a child, aged 1-2 (3-4:5-6) years

YARN

Sirdar Simply Recycled DK 50g

017 Seashells x 4 (5:6)

NEEDLES

A: 1 pair of 4mm (UK8/US6) needles

B: 1 pair of 4.5mm (UK7/US7) needles

C: 80cm (32in), 3.25mm (UK10/US3) circular needle

D: 50cm (20in), 4mm (UK8/US6) circular needle

A
B
C
D

TENSION

22sts and 30 rows to 10cm (4in) over patt on 4mm (UK8/US6) needles

NOTIONS

2 stitch holders or spare needle

Large-eyed needle

SPECIAL ABBREVIATIONS

K3TOG Knit 3sts tog

Back

Using needles B, cast on 71 (81:91) sts.

ROW 1 (RS): K1,*yon, k3, s2kpo, k3, yon, k1; rep from * to end.

ROW 2: K5, *p1, k4, rep from * replace last k4 with k5.

ROW 3: As row 1.

ROW 4: As row 2.

ROW 5: As row 1.

ROW 6: P.

Rep rows 5 and 6 x 2; (10 rows worked in total). Change to needles A.

NEXT ROW (RS): Ssk, k to last 2sts, k2tog. (69 (79:89) sts)

Beg with a p row, work 3 rows of st st.

Start main patt as follows:

ROW 1 (RS): K5 (10:15), *yon, s2kpo, yon, k11; rep from *, replace last k11 with k5 (10:15).

ROW 2: P.

ROW 3: K3 (8:13), *k2tog, yrn, p3, yon, ssk, k7; rep from *, replace last k7 with k3 (8:13).

ROW 4: P4 (9:14), *k5, p9; rep from *, replace last p9 with p4 (9:14).

ROW 5: K5 (10:15), *yon, k3tog, yon, k11; rep from *, replace last k11 with k5 (10:15).

ROWS 6 AND 8: P.

ROW 7: K.

ROW 9: K12 (3:8), *yon, s2kpo, yon, k11; rep from *, replace last k11 with k12 (3:8).

ROW 10: P.

ROW 11: K10 (1:6), *k2tog, yrn, p3, yon, ssk, k7; rep from *, replace last k7 with k10 (1:6).

ROW 12: P11 (2:7), *k5, p9; rep from *, replace last p9 with p11 (2:7).

ROW 13: K12 (3:8), *yon, k3tog, yon, k11; rep from *, replace last k11 with k12 (3:8).

ROW 14: P.

ROW 15: K.

ROW 16: P.

These 16 rows form the patt rep from 1st row until you have completed 6 (6:7) full patt reps plus 0 (6:0); rows thus ending on a WS row.

Shape shoulders

Cast off 20 (24:28) sts, k until you have 29 (31:33) sts on RH needle then cast off rem 20 (24:28) sts. Leave centre sts on a holder for the back neck.

Front

Work as for Back until you have completed 4 (5:5) full patt reps plus a further 6 (0:6) rows ending on WS row.

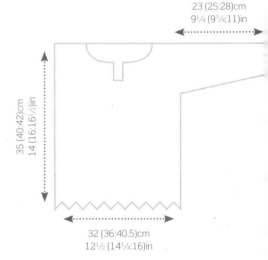

23 (25:28)cm
9¼ (9¾:11)in

35 (40:42)cm
14 (16:16½)in

32 (36:40.5)cm
12½ (14¼:16)in

Shape front neck

NEXT ROW (RS): Cont working in patt as set, work across 32 (37:42) sts, cast off centre 5sts then patt to end.

Leave rem sts on a spare needle and work each side separately.

Cont working in patt on these 32 (37:42) sts for a further 12 rows, ending on a RS row.

NEXT ROW (WS): Cast off 6 (8:10) sts at beg of row then dec 1st at neck edge on every foll row until 20 (24:28) sts rem.

Cont without shaping until the front matches the back shoulder ending on a WS row.

Cast off.

With WS facing, rejoin yarn to rem sts and purl to end of row and complete to match first side, casting off for neck at beg of RS row.

Sleeves (make 2)

Using needles A, cast on 51sts. Work rows 1–10 as for the Back border.

NEXT ROW (RS): K1, M1, k to last st, M1, k1. (53 sts)

(Inc in this way on every foll 6th (4th:4th) row until there are 69 (65:77) sts, then on every foll 0 (6th:6th) row until there are 69 (75:81) sts.

Work 3 more rows of st st, then start patt as follows:

For 1st size only

ROW 1: K11, *yon, s2kpo, yon, k11; rep from * to end.

For 2nd and 3rd sizes only

ROW 1: K1, M1, k10, *yon, s2kpo, yon, k11; rep from *, replace last k11 with k10, M1, k1. (55sts)

This sets position for first row of patt; cont until you have completed row 8 of patt, position next row as follows, working extra sts into patt.

ROW 9: K1, M1, k5 (6:6), *yon, s2kpo, yon, k11; rep from *, replace last k11 with k5 (6:6), M1, k1. (57 (59:59) sts)

Complete patt.

Cont working in patt, working new sts into patt until you have 69 (75:81) sts and have completed 3 (3:4) full patt reps plus a further 0 (9:0) rows ending on a WS row. Cast off loosely.

Hood

Join shoulder seams.

With RS facing, using needles A, and starting at top of right front, pick up and k15 (19:21) sts to shoulder then k across 29 (31:33) sts from back neck and k2tog in centre of back neck, pick up and k15 (19:21) sts to end. (58 (68:74) sts) P 1 row.

Set up patt as follows:

K4, yon, s2kpo, yon, k11, yon, s2kpo, yon, k16 (26:32), yon, s2kpo, yon, k11, yon, s2kpo, yon, k4.

Cont in patt as set until you have completed row 6.

ROW 7: K24 (25:25), M1, k10 (18:24), M1, k24 (25:25). (60 (70:76) sts)

Inc as set on every foll 4th row, working the new sts into the st st central section of the hood until there are 74 (88:94) sts.

ROW 9: K11, yon, s2kpo, yon, k30 (42:48), yon, s2kpo, yon, k11.

This sets the position for patt; cont working as set until there are 74 (88:94) sts then cont without shaping until you have completed 4 full patt reps plus a further 0 (6:6) rows.

Cast off.

Making up

Fold the hood in half with RS facing and sew the top seam.

Border

Using needle C, with RS facing, and starting at base of neck opening on right front, pick up and k12 to beg of hood then pick up and k60 (70:70) sts to top seam then 60 (70:70) sts down to neck edge and 12sts to base of neck opening. (144 (164:164) sts)

Work 5 rows of g st. Cast off.

Overlap the left band with the right band and catch stitch (see p.83) the bottom edge to the centre front cast off sts. Sew in the sleeve, matching the centre to the shoulder seam. Join the side and sleeve seams being careful to match the pattern. Sew in all loose ends.

Chart for main stitch

Worked over 7sts and 5 rows.

Work all odd number (RS) rows from right to left and all even number (WS) rows from left to right.

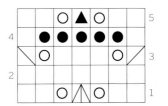

KEY

●	P on RS rows, k on WS rows
○	Yarnover
╱	K2tog
╲	Ssk
╱╲	S2kpo
▲	K3tog

Essential information

DIFFICULTY Easy to moderate

SIZE To fit a baby, aged 0–6 months (1–1½:2–3: 4–5 years)

YARN

The Fibre Company Canopy Aran 50g

Fern x 3 (5:6:7)

NEEDLES

A: 1 pair of 4mm (UK8/US6) needles
B: 1 pair of 4.5mm (UK7/US7) needles

TENSION

18sts and 28 rows to 10cm (4in) over st st on 4.5mm (UK7/US7) needles

NOTIONS

Stitch marker
Large-eyed needle
4 x 12mm (½in) buttons

SPECIAL ABBREVIATIONS

SM Stitch marker

Button-neck child's sweater

This baby and child's sweater is worked with slipped stitches that create long floats. It is knitted in a simple wool blend yarn and a button-up opening along the shoulder seams makes it easy to put on and take off.

Front

Using needles A, cast on 35 (49:57:67) sts. Work in k1, p1 rib for 2.5cm (1in). Change to needles B and set patt as follows:

ROW 1: K11 (18:22:27), place SM, [k1, p1] x 2, s5 wyif, [k1, p1] x 2, place SM, k to end.

ROW 2: P11 (18:22:27), slip SM, [p1, k1] x 2, p5, [p1, k1] x 2, slip SM, p to end.

ROW 3: K to marker, [k1, p1] x 2, k2, p1tog with float, k2, [k1, p1] x 2, k to end.

ROW 4: As row 2.

Work rows 1–4 x 10 (12:14:16).

Set up yoke

ROW 1: [K1, p1] x 3 (2:4:2), *s5 wyif, [k1, p1] x 2; rep from * to last 2 (0:2:0) sts, k1, p1.

ROW 2: [P1, k1] x 3 (2:3:2), *p5, [p1, k1] x 2; rep from * to last 2 (0:4:0) sts, [p1, k1] to end.

ROW 3: [K1, p1] x 3 (2:4:2), *k2, p1tog with float, k2, [k1, p1] x 2; rep from * to last 2 (0:4:0) sts, [k1, p1] to end.

ROW 4: As row 2.

Work yoke patt rows 1–4 x 2 (3:4:5), then rows 1–3 one time more. On patt row 4, cast off neck sts as follows:

Work 11 (18:22:27) sts in patt, cast off centre 13sts, work in patt to end.

Work each shoulder separately, beg with LH shoulder.

DEC ROW: Work in patt as set to last 3sts, k2tog, k1.

Work 1 row in patt.

Rep last 2 rows x 2 (2:3:4).

Keeping in patt, work 1 more complete patt rep (rows 1–4).

Change to needles A and work 5 rows k1, p1 rib. Cast off.

Work right shoulder to match left shoulder, reversing shaping.

Back

Using needles A, cast on 35 (49:57:67) sts. Work in k1, p1 rib for 2.5cm (1in). Change to needles B and work in st st to match front length to yoke.

Begin yoke patt.

ROW 1: [K1, p1] x 3 (2:4:2), *s5 wyif, [k1, p1] x 2; rep from * to last 2 (0:2:0) sts, k1, p1.

ROW 2: [P1, k1] x 3 (2:4:2), *p5, [p1, k1] x 2; rep from * to last 2 (0:4:0) sts, [p1, k1] to end.

ROW 3: [K1, p1] x 3 (2:4:2), *k2, p1tog with float, k2, [k1, p1] x 2; rep from * to last 2 (0:4:0) sts, [k1, p1] to end.

ROW 4: As row 2.

Rep rows 1–4 x 7 (8:9:10).

Change to needles A and work in k1, p1 rib for 2 rows.

BUTTONHOLE ROW: [K1, p1] x 0 (2:2:2), k1, yon, k2tog, [p1, k1] x 1 (2:2:3), yon, k2tog, [p1, k1] x 10 (11:15:18), p1, k2tog, yon, [k1, p1] x 1 (2:2:3), k2tog, yon, [k1, p1] x 0 (2:2:2), end k1.

Work 2 more rows in k1, p1 rib.

Cast off.

Sleeves (make 2)

Using needles A, cast on 20 (24:26:28) sts. Work in k1, p1 rib for 2.5cm (1in). Change to needles B and work 3 rows in st st.

INC ROW: Inc 1st, k to end of row, inc 1st. Rep these 4 rows until you have 32 (36:40:40) sts. Work even until sleeve measures 15.5 (20:25: 30.5)cm (6 (8:9^{3}/$_{4}$:12)in). Cast off all sts.

Making up

Using needles A, pick up and k28 (32:34:38) sts evenly along front neck opening. Work in k1, p1 rib for 5 rows and cast off.

Weave in all ends. Lay front and back flat, face upwards. Place back yoke ribbing over top of front shoulders so ribbing is overlapping. Whip stitch through both layers along 2cm (^{3}/$_{4}$in) of armhole edge. To do this, start with RS facing and the edges together. Insert the large-eyed needle from the RS through the first edge stitch on the right piece and through the first stitch on the left piece from the WS. Pull the yarn through, carry it over the top of the knitting and insert the needle into the next stitch on each piece as before. Repeat this process, taking up 1st from each edge with each stitch. Set in sleeves along armhole edge and sew side and sleeve seams using mattress stitch (see p.302). Weave in ends and block. Sew buttons on front shoulders to match buttonholes.

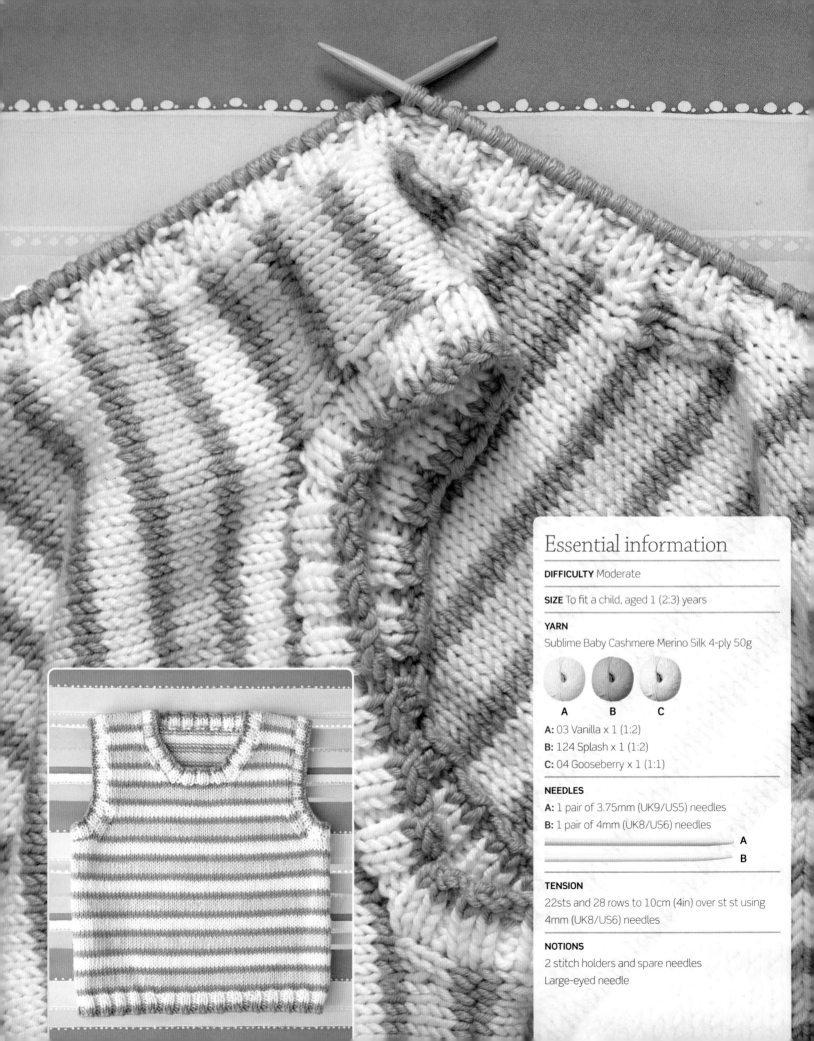

Essential information

DIFFICULTY Moderate

SIZE To fit a child, aged 1 (2:3) years

YARN

Sublime Baby Cashmere Merino Silk 4-ply 50g

A: 03 Vanilla x 1 (1:2)

B: 124 Splash x 1 (1:2)

C: 04 Gooseberry x 1 (1:1)

NEEDLES

A: 1 pair of 3.75mm (UK9/US5) needles

B: 1 pair of 4mm (UK8/US6) needles

TENSION

22sts and 28 rows to 10cm (4in) over st st using
4mm (UK8/US6) needles

NOTIONS

2 stitch holders and spare needles

Large-eyed needle

Tiny tank top

This knitted project, in stocking stitch, has ribbed edges with coloured tipping changing the colour of the stripes. Worked in a soft cashmerino silk yarn, it will make a great garment for either a boy or a girl.

Back

Using needles A and yarn B, cast on 62 (66: 70) sts.

RIB ROW 1 (RS): K2, [p2, k2] to end.

Change to yarn A.

RIB ROW 2: P2, [k2, p2] to end.

These 2 rows form the rib.

Work a further 4 rows, inc 2sts evenly across last row. (64 (68:72) sts)

Change to needles B.

Work in stripe patt of [2 rows in yarn B, 4 rows in yarn C, 2 rows in yarn B, 4 rows in yarn A] throughout.

Beg with a k row, cont in st st until back measures 15 (17:19)cm (6 (6³/₄:7¹/₂)in) from cast on edge, ending with a p row.

Shape armholes

Cast off 6sts at beg of next 2 rows. (52 (56:60) sts)

NEXT ROW: K2, skpo, k to last 4sts, k2tog, k2.

NEXT ROW: P to end.

Rep the last 2 rows x 3 (4:5). (44 (46:48) sts) **

Cont in st st until back measures 26 (29:32)cm (10 (11¹/₂:12¹/₂)in) from cast on edge, ending with a WS row.

Shape back neck

NEXT ROW: K12 (12:13), turn and leave rem sts on a spare needle.

NEXT ROW: P to end.

NEXT ROW: K to last 3sts, k2tog, k1.

NEXT ROW: P to end 11 (11:12) sts.

Shape shoulder.

Cast off.

With RS facing, place centre 20 (22:22) sts on a stitch holder, rejoin yarn to rem sts, k to end.

NEXT ROW: P to end.

NEXT ROW: K1, skpo, k to end.

NEXT ROW: P to end 11 (11:12) sts.

Shape shoulder.

Cast off.

Front

Work as given for Back to **.

Cont in st st until front measures 20 (23:26)cm (8 (9¹/₄:10)in) from cast on edge, ending with a WS row.

Shape front neck

NEXT ROW: K16 (17:18), turn and leave rem sts on a spare needle.

NEXT ROW: P to end.

NEXT ROW: K to last 3sts, k2tog, k1.

NEXT ROW: P to end.

Rep the last 2 rows x 4 (5:5). (11 (11:12) sts)

Work straight until front measures same as back to shoulder, ending at armhole edge.

Shape shoulder.

Cast off.

With RS facing, place centre 12sts on a holder, rejoin yarn to rem sts, k to end.

NEXT ROW: P to end.

NEXT ROW: K1, skpo, k to end.

Rep the last 2 rows x 4 (5:5). (11 (11:12) sts)

Work straight until front measures same as back to shoulder, ending at armhole edge.

Shape shoulder.

Cast off.

Neckband

Join right shoulder seam.

With needle A and yarn A, RS facing, pick up and k24 down LS of front neck, k12 from front neck holder, pick up and k24 up RS of front neck, 6sts down RS of back neck, k20 (22:22) sts from back neck holder, inc 2 (4:4) sts evenly across the back neck sts.

Pick up and k6 up RS of back neck. (94 (98:98) sts)

NEXT ROW: P2, [k2, p2] to end.

This row sets the rib.

Work a further 2 rows.

Change to yarn B.

Work 1 row.

Cast off in rib.

Armbands

Join left shoulder and neckband seam.

With needles A and yarn A, RS facing, pick up and k70 (74:78) sts.

NEXT ROW: P2, [k2, p2] to end.

This row sets the rib.

Work a further 2 rows.

Change to yarn B.

Work 1 row.

Cast off in rib.

Making up

Join side and armband seams (see pp.300–302 for information on seams).

Essential information

DIFFICULTY Moderate

SIZE To fit a child, aged 3 (5:8) years

YARN

Artesano Aran 100g

A   B

A: C864 Midday x 2 (2:3)
B: 5083 Lomond x 1 (1:1)

NEEDLES

A: 1 pair of 6mm (UK4/US10) needles
B: 1.2m (48in), 6mm (UK4/US10) circular
needle (for loop trim)
C: 1 pair of 100cm (39in), 5mm (UK6/US8)
needles, or 5mm (UK6/US8) circular needle
(for neck trim)

A
B
C

TENSION

13sts and 17.5 rows to 10cm (4in) over patt on
6mm (UK4/US10) needles

NOTIONS

Large-eyed needle

SPECIAL ABBREVIATIONS

ML Make a loop

Loop-fringed poncho

Knitted in aran-weight yarn on circular needles, this child's top works up quickly, making a great alternative to a coat for 3–8 year olds. Use your circular needles as if the points are two straight needles and work back and forth.

Right panel

With yarn A and needles A, cast on 32 (38:46) sts.

ROWS 1–4 (1-6:1-4): Starting with a k row, work 4 (6:4) rows in st st.

ROW 5 (7:5): P.

WORK 14 ROWS AS FOLLOWS: [Starting with a k row, work 6 rows in st st.

P 1 row, starting with a k row, work 6 rows in st st.

P 1 row. These 14 rows make up the patt.] Rep x 5 (5:6). (row 88 (90:102))

ROW 89 (91:103): Starting with a k row, work 6 rows in st st.

ROW 95 (97:109): P.

ROW 96 (98:110): Starting with a k row, work 4 (6:4) rows in st st. (99 (103:113) rows) Cast off.

Left panel

Repeat as Right panel.

Right neck trim

RS facing, in yarn A and needles C, pick up and k evenly along the RH edge of the piece.

Turn work, join in yarn B, and starting with a p row, work 3 rows in g st.

Cast off.

Left neck trim

Repeat as for the Right trim.

Joining the panels

Lay the panels in a "v" so that the right trimmed panel edge is level with the cast on edge of the left panel. Slide the cast on edge slightly underneath the right panel trim. Pin in place making sure it is not stretched. For the smoothest join, graft the backs of the yarn A loops of the trim to the cast on edge, otherwise oversew from the inside. Join the back seam in the same way once you have added the loop trim.

Make a loop (ML)

Start to make a k st as normal, but do not slide the stitch off the LH needle. Bring the yarn between the needles from back to front and wrap it around your thumb or finger (always do the same so the loops are of consistent lengths). Take the yarn back between the needles and insert your RH needle into the stitch again. Make another stitch and slide the stitch off the LH needle as normal. There will be one extra stitch now on RH needle. Pass the second stitch over the extra one to lock the loop in place. Tug loop to tighten if necessary.

Loop fringe

RS facing, work to the right away from open centre back seam.

Using yarn A and needles B, pick up and k an even number of stitches all the way around the outer edge of the poncho.

ROW 1: K.

ROW 2: Join in yarn B. K1, [ML, k1]. K1 at end (RS).

ROW 3: K.

ROW 4: K2, [ML, k1].

ROW 5: K.

ROW 6: K1, [ML, k1], k1 at end.

Cast off.

Join back seam as front, and join the neck trim where it meets at right angles. Sew loop trim at centre back join, and sew in all ends.

Essential information

DIFFICULTY Moderate

SIZE To fit a child, aged 2–3 (4–5:6–8) years

YARN

Sublime Baby Cashmere Merino Silk DK 50g

002 Cuddle x 5 (5:6)

NEEDLES

A: 1 pair of 4mm (UK8/US6) needles
B: 80cm (31½in) long, 3mm (UK11/USn⁄a)
circular needle

A
B

TENSION

22sts and 30 rows to 10cm (4in) over st st on 4mm
(UK8/US6) needles

NOTIONS

2 stitch holders
Large-eyed needle

SPECIAL ABBREVIATIONS

Y2ON Wrap yarn twice over needle to make 2sts

Forget-me-not dress

This little dress will look gorgeous on a child aged from two up to eight years. The plain stocking stitch is embellished with a lace-patterned hem and a garter stitch border that is echoed around the neck and armholes.

Back and front alike

Using needles A, cast on 88 (104:120) sts.
K 4 rows.
ROW 1: K10, *k2tog, y2on, Ssk, k12, rep from * to last 14sts, k2tog, y2on, ssk, k10.
ROW 2 AND EVERY ALT ROW: P (k first loop of yon, p second loop of yon).
ROW 3: K8, *[k2tog, y2on, ssk] x 2, k8, rep from * to end of row.
ROW 5: As row 1.
ROW 7: As row 3.
ROW 9: As row 1.
ROW 11: K2, *k2tog, y2on, ssk, k12, rep from * to last 6sts, k2tog, y2on, ssk, k2.
ROW 13: *[K2tog, y2on, ssk] x 2, k8, rep from * to last 8sts, [k2tog, y2on, ssk] x 2.
ROW 15: As row 11.
ROW 17: As row 13.
ROW 19: As row 11.
ROW 20: P.
NEXT ROW: K15 (19:23), k2tog tbl, k1, k2tog, k48 (56:64), k2tog tbl, k1, k2tog, k15 (19:23). (84 (100:116) sts)
Work 9 rows in st st.
NEXT ROW : K14 (18:22), k2tog tbl, k1, k2tog, k46 (54:62) k2tog tbl, k1, k2tog, k14 (18:22). (80 (96:112) sts)
Cont dec 4sts as set out, on every 10th row until there are 56 (72:88) sts.
Cont in st st without further shaping until work measures 33 (38:41)cm (13 (15:16$^1/_4$)in), ending with a WS row.

Shape armhole

Cast off 3sts at beg of next 2 rows.
Dec 1st at each end of the next and every foll alt row as follows:
K2, k2tog tbl, k to last 4sts, k2tog, k2 until there are 38 (50:62) sts.
Cont in st st until work measures 41 (46:51)cm (16$^1/_4$ (18:20$^1/_4$)in), ending with a WS row.

Shape neck

K14 (16:20) sts, turn and leave rem sts on a stitch holder.
NEXT ROW: P.
Dec 1st at neck edge on next and every foll alt row as follows:
K to last 4sts, k2tog, k2 until there are 7 (9:11) sts.
Cont in st st without further shaping until work measures 48 (58:68)cm (19 (22$^3/_4$:26$^3/_4$)in).
Cast off.
Place centre 10 (18:22) sts on a stitch holder.
Rejoin yarn to rem sts and k to the end of row.
NEXT ROW: P.
Dec 1st at neck edge on next and every foll alt row as follows:
K2, k2tog tbl, k to the end of the row until there are 7 (9:11) sts.
Cont in st st without further shaping until work measures 48 (58:68)cm (19 (22$^3/_4$:26$^3/_4$)in).
Cast off.

Neckband

Join shoulder seams.
Using needle B, with RS facing and beginning at left shoulder seam, pick up and k14 (20:26) sts down left front neck, k10 (18:22) sts across centre front neck, k14 (20:26) sts up right front neck, k14 (20:26) sts down right back neck, k10 (18:22) sts across centre back neck, k14 (20:26) sts up left back neck 76 (116:148) sts.
WORKING IN THE ROUND: K 1 row.
P 2 rows.
Cast off.

Armbands

Join side seams.
Using needle B and with RS facing, pick up and k66 (74:82) sts, evenly around armhole.
WORKING IN THE ROUND: K 1 row.
P 2 rows.
Cast off.

Making up

Sew in ends. Block carefully (see p.300).

Baby daisy dress

This square-neck dress is decorated with openwork stitch and embroidered daisies.

Essential information

DIFFICULTY Moderate

SIZE To fit a baby, aged 3 (6:12:18) months

YARN

Sirdar Calico DK 50g

A   **B**   **C**

A: 723 White x 1   **B:** 733 Banana x 1

C: 735 Shrimp x 3 (4:4:5)

NEEDLES

A: 1 pair of 4mm (UK8/US6) needles

B: 1 pair of 3.5mm (UKn/a/US4) needles

C: 80cm (32in), 3.5mm (UKn/a/US4) circular needle

A

B

C

TENSION

22sts and 31 rows to 10cm (4in) over st st on 4mm (UK8/US6) needles

NOTIONS

4 x 1cm (½in) heart buttons

Stitch holder and spare needle

Large-eyed needle

SPECIAL ABBREVIATIONS

WYIF With yarn in front

WY3 Wrap yarn 3 times around the needle, instead of just once, for each stitch

CLUSTER ST Wyif, [slip next st, dropping extra wraps] x 4 (4:5:5), [bring yarn to back between needles, slip 5sts back to LH needle, bring yarn to front between needles, slip 5sts to RH needle] x 2. When working the cluster stitch be careful not to pull the yarn too tightly when wrapping it around the sts

Back

Using needles A and yarn C, cast on 86 (91:103:109) sts.

K 1 row.

Work daisy patt as follows:

ROW 1 (WS): K.

ROW 2: K1, *[k1 wy3] x 4 (4:5:5), k1; rep from * to end.

ROW 3: K1, *work cluster st over 4 (4:5:5) sts, k1; rep from * to end.

ROWS 4 AND 5: K.

Beg with a k row, work 3 rows of st st then rep rows 1–5 of daisy patt.

Cont to work in st st until the work measures 20 (22:25:27)cm (8 (9:9³⁄₄:10¹⁄₂)in) from cast on edge, ending on a WS row.

DEC ROW (RS): [K2tog, k1] x 3 (6:6:6), k2tog to last 9 (15:15:19) sts, [k1, k2tog] to last 0 (0:0:1) sts, k0 (0:0:1). (46 (51:57:61) sts)

3rd size only

K2tog, k to last 2sts, k2tog. (55sts)

1, 2, and 4 sizes

NEXT ROW (WS): K.

All sizes

Work daisy st from rows 2–5.

Cont working in st st for 6 (6:8:10) rows, ending on a WS row. Shape armhole and back opening.

Right back

ROW 1 (RS): Cast off 2 (2:3:3) sts then k until you have 23 (26:27:30) sts on RH needle, turn, leave rem sts on spare needle and work each side separately.

NEXT ROW (WS): K4, p to end; this sets up 4st buttonband at centre back worked in g st.

Dec 1st at armhole edge on the next 3 rows. (20 (23:24:27) sts)

Cont working without shaping until armhole measures 8 (9:10:11)cm (3 (3¹⁄₂:4:4¹⁄₄)in) from beg of shaping, ending on RS row.

Shape back neck

NEXT ROW (WS): Cast off 12 (13:13:14) sts.

Cont without shaping on rem 8 (10:11:13) sts for a further 6 rows, ending on a WS row.

Cast off.

Left back

With RS facing, rejoin yarn and cast on 4sts (buttonhole band), k to end of row. (25 (27:29:32) sts)

Cast off 2 (2:3:3) sts at beg of WS row, p to last 4sts, k4; this sets up buttonhole band worked in g st as for Right back.

Dec 1st at armhole edge on next 3 rows. (20 (22:23:26) sts)

At beg of next RS row work buttonhole as follows: k1, k2tog, yon.

Work buttonhole in this way on next two following 8th (8th:10th:12th) rows.

Complete to match first side casting off for back neck on RS row.

Front

Work as for the Back until the start of the armhole shaping.

ROW 1 (RS): Cast off 2 (2:3:3) sts at the start of the next 2 rows.

Dec 1st at each edge on next 3 rows. (36 (41:43:49) sts)

Work 13 (13:19:19) rows straight, ending on a WS row.

Shape front neck

NEXT ROW (RS): K across 8 (10:11:13) sts, turn, leave rem sts on a holder and complete each side separately. Cont without shaping until the front matches the back shoulder ending on a WS row. Cast off.

With RS facing, rejoin yarn to rem sts and cast off centre 20 (21:21:23) sts, k to end of row. Complete to match first side.

Sleeves (make 2)

Using needles B and yarn C, cast on 43 (43:47:47) sts.

Work 6 rows of k1, p1 rib.

NEXT ROW (INC ROW): Rib 4, M1, *rib 3, M1; rep from *, end rib 3 (3:4:4). (56 (56:61:61) sts)

Change to needles A and work rows 1–5 of daisy st.

Cont in st st, work 4 (4:6:6) rows, ending on a WS row.

Shape sleeve head

Cast off 3sts at beg of next 2 rows. (50 (50:55:55) sts)

Dec 1st at each end of next 7 (7:5:5) rows. (36 (36:45:45) sts)

Then dec 1st at each end on every foll alt row until 28 (30:29:27) sts remain.

Cast off.

Complete dress

Sew up shoulder seams. Join side seams, being careful to match patt bands.

Using the photograph as a guide, embroider daisies onto the dress and sleeves, adding as many or as few as you like. To create the daisies, use a large-eyed needle and yarn A. Bring the needle from the WS of the knitted fabric to the RS where you wish to position the daisy and insert it back down in the adjacent stitch.

Bring the needle out again three or four stitches away with the original position with the yarn under the needle. Pull gently to make a loop and take a tiny stitch over the yarn to hold it in place. Move onto the next stitch and repeat as required. Work a French knot (see p.120) in the centre of each daisy.

Sew up sleeve seam

Set in sleeves, matching the centre of each sleeve to the shoulder seam and the underarm seam to the side seam of dress.

Neckband

Using needle C, with RS facing and starting at the top of the buttonhole band, pick up and k10 (12:12:12) sts to corner, pick up and k1 from corner, pick up and k16 (18:18:18) sts to front, pick up and k1 from corner, pick up and k18 (19:19:21) sts across front neck, then pick up and k1 from corner, pick up and k16 (18:18:18) sts to back neck, pick up and k1 from corner and finally pick up and k10 (12:12:12) sts to end. (74 (83:83:85) sts)

ROW 1 (WS): K10 (12:12:12), p1, k16 (18:18:18), p1, k18 (19:19:21), p1, k16 (18:18:18), p1, k10 (12:12:12).

ROW 2: K8 (10:10:10), skpo, k1, k2tog, k12 (14:14:14), skpo, k1, k2tog, k14 (15:15:17), skpo, k1, k2tog, k12 (14:14:14), skpo, k1, k2tog, k to end.

ROW 3: K9 (11:11:11), p1, k14 (16:16:16), p1, k16 (17:17:19), p1, k14 (16:16:16), p1, k9 (11:11:11).

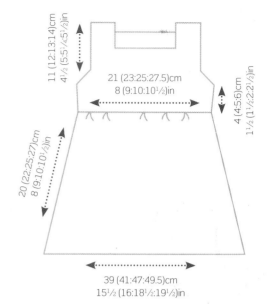

ROW 4: K1, yon, k2tog, k4 (6:6:6), skpo, k1, k2tog, k10 (12:12:12), skpo, k1, k2tog, k12 (13:13:15), skpo, k1, k2tog, k10 (12:12:12) skpo, k1, k2tog, k7 (9:9:9).

ROW 5: K8 (10:10:10), p1, k12 (14:14:14), p1, k14 (15:15:17), p1, k12 (14:14:14), p1, k8 (10:10:10).

ROW 6: Cast off.

Making up

Sew in all loose ends. Attach the four buttons to the neckband and buttonband opposite the buttonholes. Block lightly according to the instructions on the ballband.

TOP TIP *Work the daisy embroidery before you make up the garment.*

Striped beanie

Use the knit two together (k2tog) decreasing technique to shape the top of the beanie and create a tight but elastic ribbed edging by using smaller-sized needles than those required for the rest of the project. For ease, this beanie is knitted flat and then sewn up. Pair it with the Striped tassel-end scarf on p.126.

Essential information

DIFFICULTY Easy

SIZE To fit an adult female

YARN

Rowan Pure Wool DK 50g

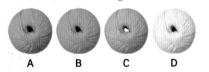

A: 025 Tea rose x 1   **B:** 06 Pier x 1
C: 002 Shale x 1   **D:** 013 Enamel x 1

NEEDLES

A: 1 pair of 3.25mm (UK10/US3) needles
B: 1 pair of 4mm (UK8/US6) needles

A
B

TENSION

22sts and 30 rows to 10cm (4in) over st st on 4mm (UK8/US6) needles

NOTIONS

Large-eyed needle

Brim

Using needles A and yarn A, cast on 122sts.
ROW 1: K2 [p2 k2] to end.
ROW 2: P2 [k2 p2] to end.
Rep these 2 rows x 4, dec 1st at end of last row. (121sts)
Change to needles B and yarn B.
Work in st st for 8 rows, ending with a WS row.
Work 8-row stripes in the following sequence: C, B, A.
To join in the yarn, lay the new yarn over the right needle with the old yarn tail. Knit the first stitch of the new row with both yarns. Drop the old yarn tail and continue with the new. When the knitting is complete, unpick the second thread from the old yarn before darning the ends in with a large-eyed needle.
Change to yarn D and work 4 rows st st.

Shape crown

ROW 1: [K10, k2tog] to last st, k1. (111sts)
ROW 2 AND ALL FOLL ALT ROWS: P.
ROW 3: K.
ROW 5: [K9, k2tog] to last st, k1. (101sts)
ROW 7: [K8, k2tog] to last st, k1. (91sts)
ROW 9: [K7, k2tog] to last st, k1. (81sts)
ROW 11: [K6, k2tog] to last st, k1. (71sts)
ROW 13: [K5, k2tog] to last st, k1. (61sts)

ROW 15: [K4, k2tog] to last st, k1. (51sts)
ROW 17: [K3, k2tog] to last st, k1. (41sts)
ROW 19: [K2, k2tog] to last st, k1. (31sts)
ROW 21: Change to yarn A. [K1, k2tog] to last st, k1. (21sts)
ROW 23: [K2tog] to last st, k1. (11sts)

Making up

Draw yarn through remaining stitches and join side seam using mattress stitch (see p.302).

Slouched garter hat

This relaxed-style hat is created with single rib and garter stitch, and uses variegated silk yarn for a multi-colour effect. Don't worry if the hat comes up smaller in size than you expect as it will stretch during blocking.

Essential information

DIFFICULTY Moderate

SIZE To fit an adult female

YARN

Artesano Manos Del Uruguay Silk Blend DK 100g

4630 Evita x 1

NEEDLES

A: 1 pair of 3.25mm (UK10/US3) needles

B: 4 x 3.75mm (UK9/US5) double-pointed needles, or 40cm (16in), 3.75mm (UK9/US5) circular needle

———————————————— **A**

———————————————— **B**

TENSION

22sts and 40 rows to 10cm (4in) over g st on 3.75mm (UK9/US5) needles

NOTIONS

Stitch markers

Large-eyed needle

Using needles A, cast on 108sts. Join in the round, being careful not to twist sts. Place stitch marker to indicate start of round.

ROUND 1: *K1, p1; rep from * to end.

Rep this round until the brim measures 4.5cm (1³/₄in), then work inc round once as follows:

INC ROUND: K5, kfb; rep from * to end. (126sts) Change to needles B.

Body

ROUND 1: P.

ROUND 2: K.

Rep these 2 rounds until work measures 15cm (6in) from the start of the body section ending with round 2.

Shape crown

ROUND 1: *P2tog; rep from * to end. (54sts)

ROUND 2: K.

ROUND 3: *P2tog; rep from * to end. (27sts)

ROUND 4: K.

ROUND 5: P1, *p2tog; rep from * to end. (14sts)

ROUND 6: K.

ROUND 7: *P2tog; rep from * to end. (7sts)

Break yarn and draw through remaining 7sts, tighten to close.

Making up

Weave in all ends and block (see p.300).

Head size The final circumference of this slouchy hat is 45cm (17³/₄in) before blocking, which will fit a slightly larger head circumference of 47cm (18¹/₂in). Knitting on a slightly larger needle will increase the circumference, but take care not to make the fabric too loose.

Ribbed bobble hat

A fun design that features wide ribs and a knitted bobble. This hat is knitted "in the round" using double-pointed or circular needles (see pp.290–291). It is better suited to an intermediate knitter than a beginner.

Essential information

DIFFICULTY Moderate

SIZE To fit an adult female

YARN

Texere Chunky 100g

1123-0581 Lilac x 1

NEEDLES

4 x 5.5mm double-pointed needles, or 40cm (16in), 5.5mm (UK5/US9) circular needle

TENSION

16sts and 20 rows to 10cm (4in) using st st on 5.5mm (UK5/US9) needles

NOTIONS

Stitch marker

Large-eyed needle

Small amount of polyester toy stuffing for bobble

Brim

Cast on 80sts. Join in the round, being careful not to twist sts. Place stitch marker to indicate start of round.

NEXT ROUND: *P2, k6; rep from * to end.

Rep this round until work measures approx. 18cm (7in).

Shape crown

ROUND 1: *P2, k4, k2tog; rep from * to end. (70sts)

ROUND 2: *P2, k5; rep from * to end.

ROUND 3: *P2, k3, k2tog; rep from * to end. (60sts)

ROUND 4: *P2, k4; rep from * to end.

ROUND 5: *P2, k2, k2tog; rep from * to end. (50sts)

ROUND 6: *P2, k3; rep from * to end.

ROUND 7: *P2, k1, k2tog; rep from * to end. (40sts)

ROUND 8: *P2, k2; rep from * to end.

ROUND 9: *P2, k2tog; rep from * to end. (30sts)

ROUND 10: *P2, k1; rep from * to end.

ROUND 11: *P1, k2tog; rep from * to end. (20sts)

ROUND 12: *P1, k1; rep from * to end.

ROUND 13: *K2tog; rep from * to end. (10sts)

ROUND 14: [K2tog] x 5. (5sts)

Bobble

ROUND 1: *Kfb; rep from * to end. (10sts)

ROUND 2: K.

ROUND 3: *Kfb; rep from * to end. (20sts)

ROUND 4: K.

ROUND 5: *K1, kfb; rep from * to end. (30sts)

ROUND 6: K.

ROUND 7: *K1, k2tog; rep from * to end. (20sts)

ROUND 8: K.

ROUND 9: *K2tog; rep from * to end. (10sts)

ROUND 10: K.

(add bobble stuffing gently at this point)

ROUND 11: *K2tog; rep from * to end. (5sts)

Break yarn with a 20cm (8in) tail. Pull through remaining 5sts, pull tail through to inside of hat and base of bobble, then carefully darn in end to conceal the small hole where the crown joins the bobble.

Making up

Darn in all ends (see p.300). Block.

Classic ladies' beret

This tam, or beret, has a circular detailing on the crown and is worked "in the round" to give a lovely smooth shape and save on sewing up. A ribbed headband adds definition and ensures the hat fits snugly.

Essential information

DIFFICULTY Moderate

SIZES To fit an adult female

YARN

King Cole Merino Blend Aran 50g

009 Scarlet x 2

NEEDLES

4 x 4.5mm double-pointed needles, or 40cm (16in), 4.5mm (US7/UK7) circular needle

TENSION

18sts and 24 rows to 10cm (4in) over patt on 4.5mm (US7/UK7) needles

NOTIONS

Stitch marker

Large-eyed needle

Cast on 84sts.

Join in the round, being careful not to twist sts.

Place stitch marker to indicate start of round.

Brim

ROUND 1: *K1, p1; rep from * to end.

Rep this round until brim measures approx. 3.5cm (1³/₈in) then work increase round once as follows:

INC ROUND: *p1, pfb; rep from * to end. (126sts)

Body

ROUND 1: *K1, p1; rep from * to end.

ROUNDS 2 AND 3: *P1, k1; rep from * to end.

ROUND 4: *K1, p1; rep from * to end.

Rep these 4 rounds until work measures 12cm (5in) from the start of the body section.

Shape crown

NEXT ROUND: *P2tog; rep from * to end. (64sts)

Then work 9 rounds of body stitch patt.

NEXT ROUND: *P2tog; rep from * to end. (32sts)

Then work 5 rounds of body stitch patt.

NEXT ROUND: *P2tog; rep from * to end. (16sts)

Then work 2 rounds of body stitch patt.

NEXT ROUND: *P2tog; rep from * to end. (8sts)

Break yarn and draw through remaining 8sts, tighten to close.

Making up

Darn in all ends with a large-eyed needle.

Block (see p.300).

Ribbed headband For areas that need to fit well, use stretchy rib stitch (see p.274). When blocking, inserting the correct-sized dinner plate into the hat helps to hold the shape, but avoid over-stretching the ribbing.

Floral ear warmer

This classic ribbed band is tapered at the back and embellished with a stylized flower worked as one piece in garter stitch. For an alternative choice of bloom, turn to pp.232–235 where you'll find a selection of five different flower patterns.

Essential information

DIFFICULTY Easy

SIZE To fit an adult female

YARN

King Cole Baby Alpaca DK 50g

A   **B**

A: 513 Lilac x 1   **B:** 501 Fawn x 1

NEEDLES

A: 1 pair of 3.25mm (UK10/US3) needles

B: 1 pair of 3mm (UK11/USn/a) needles

———————————————— A

———————————————— B

NOTIONS

1 x 2.5cm (1½in) button

Large-eyed needle

TENSION

35sts and 30 rows to 10cm (4in) over rib patt on 3.25mm (UK10/US3) needles

SPECIAL ABBREVIATIONS

M1K or **M1P** Make a stitch by picking up bar between sts and knitting or purling into back of it (see pp.278-279)

Headband

With needles A and yarn A, cast on 19sts.

ROW 1 (RS): K1, [p1, k1] to end.

ROW 2: P1, [k1, p1] to end.

These 2 rows form the rib.

Rib 2 rows more.

Shape sides

ROW 1: K1, M1k, rib to last st, M1k, k1.

ROW 2: P2, rib to last 2sts, p2.

ROW 3: K2, rib to last 2sts, k2.

ROW 4: As row 2.

ROW 5: K1, M1p, rib to last st, M1p, k1.

ROWS 6-8: Rib 3 rows straight.

Rep last 8 rows x 2, then work rows 1–5. (35sts)

Cont straight until work measures 40cm (16in) from beg, ending after WS row.

Shape sides

ROW 1: Skpo, rib to last 2sts, k2tog.

ROW 2: P2, rib to last 2sts, p2.

ROW 3: K2, rib to last 2sts, k2.

ROW 4: As row 2.

ROW 5: As row 1.

ROWS 6-8: Rib 3 rows straight.

Rep these 8 rows x 3. (19sts)

Cast off in rib.

Flower

Beg at centre. Using needles B and yarn B, cast on 5sts. K 1 row.

INC ROW: [Kfb] to end.

NEXT ROW: K.

Rep last 2 rows once more. (20sts)

NEXT ROW: [Kfb, k1] to end. (30sts)

K 1 row.

Divide for petals.

*NEXT ROW: K6, turn.

K 4 rows on these 6sts.

NEXT 2 ROWS: K2, k2tog, k2; turn and k5.

NEXT 2 ROWS: K1, k2tog, k2; turn and k4.

NEXT ROW: [K2tog] x 2, then pass second st over first st and fasten off.**

Return to sts on LH needle.*

Rep from * to * x 3, then work from * to **.

Making up

Join first to last petal and neaten edges of flower. Join headband into a ring and sew cast on and cast off edges together. Sew flower in place, then sew button to centre of flower.

Tapered headband Shape the back of this easy-to-knit headband using the M1 increase, and the k2tog and skpo decrease techniques. Cast off in rib effect and sew a flat edge-to-edge seam to form the band.

Men's winter hat

This neatly fitting hat is knitted in textural moss stitch using basic increase and decrease techniques (see pp.277–285). It is worked in a chunky-weight yarn and will, therefore, knit up quickly.

Essential information

DIFFICULTY Moderate

SIZE To fit an adult male

YARN

Texere Chunky 100g

594 Ecru x 2

NEEDLES

4 x 5mm (UK6/US8) double-pointed needles, or 40cm (16in), 5mm (UK6/US8) circular needle

TENSION

15sts and 34 rows to 10cm (4in) over g st on 5mm (UK6/US8) needles

NOTIONS

Stitch marker
Large-eyed needle

Cast on 80sts.
Join in the round, being careful not to twist sts.
Place stitch marker to indicate start of round.
ROUND 1: P all sts.
ROUND 2: K all sts.
Rep these 2 rounds until work measures 5cm (2¼in) ending with round 1.

Body

ROUND 1: *K1, p1; rep from * to end.
ROUND 2: *P1, k1; rep from * to end.
Rep these 2 rounds until work measures approx. 18cm (7in) from cast on edge, ending with round 1.

Shape crown

ROUND 1: *[P1, k1] x 4, k2tog; rep from * to end. (72sts)
ROUND 2: *[K1, p1] x 4, k1; rep from * to end.
ROUND 3: *[P1, k1] x 3, p1, k2tog; rep from * to end. (64sts)
ROUND 4: *[K1, p1] x 3, k2; rep from * to end.

ROUND 5: *[P1, k1] x 3, k2tog; rep from * to end. (56sts)
ROUND 6: *[K1, p1] x 3, k1; rep from * to end.
ROUND 7: *[P1, k1] x 2, p1, k2tog; rep from * to end. (48sts)
ROUND 8: *[K1, p1] x 2, k2; rep from * to end.
ROUND 9: *[P1, k1] x 2, k2tog; rep from * to end. (40sts)
ROUND 10: *[K1, p1] x 2, k1; rep from * to end.
ROUND 11: *P1, k1, p1, k2tog; rep from * to end. (32sts)
ROUND 12: *K1, p1, k2; rep from * to end.
ROUND 13: *P1, k1, k2tog; rep from * to end. (24sts)
ROUND 14: *K1, p1, k1; rep from * to end.
ROUND 15: *P1, k2tog; rep from * to end. (16sts)
ROUND 16: *K1, p1; rep from * to end.
ROUND 17: *K2tog; rep from * to end. (8sts)
Break yarn and draw through remaining 8sts, tighten to close.

Making up

Weave in all ends. Block (see p.300).

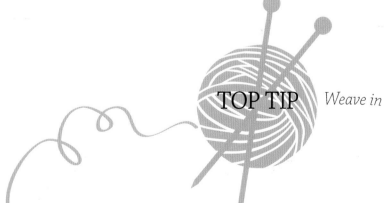

TOP TIP *Weave in the yarn ends vertically through stitches on the wrong side.*

Swirling crown Circling cables create a swirl at the crown of the hat. As you decrease the stitches and the knitting gets smaller, transfer the remaining stitches from your circular needle to double-pointed needles to achieve this affect.

Essential information

DIFFICULTY Difficult

SIZE To fit an adult male

YARN

Rowan Purelife Renew 50g

687 Lorry x 2

NEEDLES

A: 60cm (24in), 5.5mm (UK5/US9) circular needle

B: 60cm (24in), 6mm (UK4/US10) circular needle

C: 4 x 6mm (UK4/US10) double-pointed needles

D: Cable needle

A

B

C

D

TENSION

30sts and 36 rows to 10cm (4in) over patt, when slightly stretched on 6mm (UK4/US10) needles

SPECIAL ABBREVIATIONS

CR4L Place 2sts on cable needle (cn) and leave at front of work, p2, then k2 from cn

CR5L Place 2sts on cn and leave at front of work, p3, then k2 from cn

RIB Work in rib, knitting all presented k sts and purling all presented p sts

RIB2TOG Working in rib, either k2tog, or p2tog as appropriate

Twisted cable hat

The cables on this hat spiral upwards to a dramatic final twist on the crown. It is a challenging project that is worked entirely in right side rows using circular needles. This hat is designed to match the Twisted cable scarf on p.146.

Brim

Using needle A and cable cast on method (see p.265), cast on 96sts.

Join into a round being careful not to twist cast on sts. Place marker at start of round.

ROUND 1: K1, *p2, k2 to last 3sts, p2, k1.

Cont to rep last round until work measures 3.5cm (1³/₈in).

NEXT ROUND: Rib 2, *rib2tog, rib 5, rep from * to end, ending rib 3. (83sts)

Work ridges

ROUNDS 1 AND 2: P.

ROUNDS 3 AND 4: K.

ROUND 5: P.

ROUND 6: P3, *M1p, p6, rep from * to last 2sts, p2. (96sts)

Set cable pattern

Change to needle B and work in cable patt as follows:

PATT ROUND 1: *P2, k2, p2, rep from * to end.

PATT ROUND 2: *Cr4L, p2, rep from * to end.

PATT ROUND 3: *K2, p4, rep from * to end, to last 2sts. Disregard end of round; start next round immediately.

PATT ROUND 4: [Cr4L, p2] x 16.

PATT ROUND 5: *P4, k2, rep from * to end.

PATT ROUND 6: *P2, Cr4L, rep from * to end.

Previous 6 rows set patt. Working in patt as set, rep these 6 rows until work measures 17cm (6³/₄in) from cast on edge, ending with patt row 6.

Shape top

NOTE: As the number of sts reduces, working on a circular needle becomes difficult. At this stage change to double-pointed needles (C).

ROUND 1: *P2tog, k2, p2, rep from * to end of round. (80sts)

ROUND 2: *P1, Cr5L, slip next 2sts on to cable needle and leave at back of work, p2tog then k2 from cable needle, rep from * to end. (72sts)

ROUND 3: [P2, k2, p2, p2tog, p1] x 8. (64sts)

ROUND 4: [P2tog, Cr5L, p1] x 8. (56sts)

ROUND 5: [P1, p2tog, k2, p2] x 8. (48sts)

ROUND 6: [P1, slip next 2sts on to cable needle and leave at front of work, p3, then k2tog tbl from cable needle] x 8. (40sts)

ROUND 7: [P3, k2tog tbl] x 8. (32sts)

Rounds from this point onwards will not finish at actual start point of rounds, but will overlap to form the crown spirals.

ROUND 8: [P1, slip next st on to cable needle, p2tog then k1 tbl] x 8. (24sts)

ROUND 9: [K2tog tbl, p1] x 8. (16sts)

Making up

Draw yarn through rem sts and fasten off. Darn in ends.

Textured quality There is no need to turn the work and no WS rows. Working the cables in one direction, and gradually moving their position creates the travelling cables. This knitted hat can be worn with the brim turned up or down.

Pirate beanie

Follow the chart, below right, to complete the skull-and-crossbones motif that runs around the dome of this child's hat. This project uses just two balls of DK-weight yarn and is knitted circularly on double-pointed needles.

Essential information

DIFFICULTY Moderate

SIZE To fit a child, aged 5–10 years

YARN

Artesano Superwash Merino DK 50g

A   **B**

A: SFN50 Black x 1   **B:** 0157 White x 1

NEEDLES

4 x 4mm (UK8/US6) double-pointed needles

TENSION

22sts and 30 rows to 10cm (4in) over st st on 4mm (UK8/US6) needles

NOTIONS

Large-eyed needle

Brim

Using yarn A, cast on 108sts and join in the round.
Work in k1, p1 rib for 4cm (1^{1}/$_{2}$in).
K 4 rounds.
Join in yarn B, knit every round and follow chart for skull and cross bones from rounds 1–15.
Continue knitting every round in yarn A until work measures 16cm (6^{1}/$_{4}$in) from cast on.

Shape crown

ROUND 1: *K2, k2tog, rep from * to end of round. (81sts)
ROUND 2: K.
ROUND 3: *K1, k2tog, rep from * to end of round. (54sts)
ROUND 4: K.
ROUND 5: *K2tog, rep from * to end of round. (27sts)
ROUND 6: K.
ROUND 7: *K2tog, rep from * to last st, k1.(14sts)
ROUND 8: K.
ROUND 9: *K2tog, rep from * to end of round. (7sts)

Making up

Break yarn and thread through remaining sts, pull up tightly and finish off.

Skull-and-crossbones chart

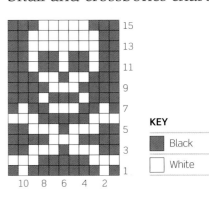

KEY

■ Black
□ White

Tassel head hugger

A simple knitted project that will keep a young child's head warm. We've knitted this cosy hat in 100% extrafine merino wool that is sustainably sourced from villages in Uruguay, but you can use any aran yarn of your choice.

Essential information

DIFFICULTY Easy

SIZE To fit a child, aged 1–3 years

YARN

Manos Del Uruguay Maxima 100g

9644 Chrysanthemum x 1

NEEDLES

1 pair of 5mm (UK6/US8) needles

TENSION

14sts and 26 rows to 10cm (4in) over rib patt on 5mm (UK6/US8) needles

NOTIONS

Large-eyed needle

Cast on 39sts.
ROW 1: P4, *k1 tbl, p4, rep from * to end of row.
ROW 2: K4, *p1 tbl, k4, rep from * to end of row.
Rep rows 1–2 until work measures 20cm (8in).
K 2 rows.
Rep rows 1–2 until work measures 20cm (8in) from k rows.
Cast off loosely.

Making up

Fold hat in half at k rows ridge, and sew up side seams.
Make two tassels (see p.299), 11cm (4¼in) long and stitch them to the corners of the hat with yarn.

Textured ridges It is easy to create a simple textured design using purely knit and purl stitches. Knitting through the back of a knit stitch helps to make a pronounced ridge as it twists the stitch.

TOP TIP   *Don't make the tassels too long or they will dwarf your hat.*

Strawberry eyelet hat

A fun hat for a toddler, with intarsia strawberries that are brought to life by adding tiny embroidered seeds. This beanie also features a picot edging as a pretty alternative to a rib, followed by a raised band of lace holes to add definition.

Essential information

DIFFICULTY Moderate

SIZE To fit a child, aged 6 months–2 years

YARN

Sublime Baby Cashmere Merino Silk DK 50g

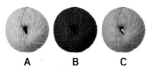

A   **B**   **C**

A: 245 Caterpillar x 1
B: 192 Teddy red x 1
C: 303 Giallo medio x 1

NEEDLES

4 x 4mm (UK8/US6) double-pointed needles

TENSION

22sts and 24 rows to 10cm (4in) over st st on 4mm (UK8/US6) needles

NOTIONS

Large-eyed needle
1 embroidery needle

Brim

Using yarn B, cast on 84sts and join in the round.
K 4 rounds.
NEXT ROUND: K1, * yon, k2tog, rep from * to last st, k1.
K 6 rounds.
Break yarn and join in yarn C.
P 1 round.
K1, * yon, k2tog, rep from * to last st, k1.
P 1 round.
K 1 round.
Break yarn.
Join in yarn A and working every stitch as k st, follow the chart using the intarsia technique (see pp.306–307). Continue knitting every round in yarn A until work measures 14cm (5¹/₂in) from cast on.

Shape crown

*Skpo, k12, rep from * to end of round.
*Skpo, k11, rep from * to end of round.
*Skpo, k10, rep from * to end of round.
Continue decreasing on every round as set, taking 1 less stitch on each round until you have worked skpo, k4.
Break yarn and thread through stitches; pull up tightly and finish off.

Making up

Fold picot edge to inside and slip st in place. Using yarn C and an embroidery needle, embroider seed stitches randomly over each strawberry. To do this, work two backstitches into the same hole to form raised dots.

TOP TIP   *Strand the yarn ends loosely from one strawberry motif to the next.*

Strawberry chart

13
11
9
7
5
3
1

12 10 8   6   4   2

KEY

Teddy red

Caterpillar

Giallo medio

Girl's floral beanie

A pretty hat for a girl, which is knitted with a zigzag eyelet stitch above the rib, and decorated with flowers that feature a French knot in the centre. Worked in cotton yarn, this lightweight hat can be worn in the spring or autumn.

With needles A, cast on 98sts.

Brim
ROWS 1–6: [K1, p1] to end.
Change to needles B.

Zigzag eyelet
ROW 7: K1, [yrn, k2tog, k2] to last st, k1.
ROW 8, 10, AND 12: P to end.
ROW 9: K1, [k2, yrn, k2tog] to last st, k1.
ROW 11: K to end.

Flower design (embroidered knot centre)
ROW 1: [K5, MB, k1, MB] to last 2sts, k2.
ROW 2 AND ALL EVEN ROWS: P to end.
ROW 3: K1, [k3, MB], to last st, k1.
ROW 5: Rep row 1.
ROWS 7: K to end.

Flower design (eyelet centre)
ROW 9: K1, [MB, k1, MB, k5] to last st, k1.
ROW 11: K1, [k1, yrn, k2tog, MB, k3, MB] to last st, k1.
ROW 13: Rep row 9.
ROW 15: K to end.
ROW 17: [K5, MB, k1, MB] to last 2sts, k2.
ROW 19: K1, [k3, MB, k1, yrn, k2tog, MB] to last st, k1.
ROW 21: Rep row 17.
ROW 22: P to end.

Shape crown
ROW 1: [Skpo, k1, k2tog, k3] to last 2sts, k2. (74sts)
ROW 2 AND ALL EVEN ROWS: P to end.
ROW 3: K2, MB, [k3, MB, k1, MB] to last 5sts, k3, MB, k1.
ROW 5: K1, yrn, k2tog, MB, [k1, MB, k1, yrn, k2tog, MB] to last 4sts, k1, MB, k2.
ROW 7: As row 3.
ROW 9: K2, k2tog, [k1, skpo, k1, k2tog] to last 4sts, k1, skpo, k1. (50sts)
ROW 11: K1, [yon, k2tog, k2] to last st, k1.
ROW 13: K1, [k2, yon, k2tog] to last st, k1.
ROW 15: K1, [k2tog, k2] to last st, k1. (38sts)
ROW 17: K1, [k2tog, k1] to last st, k1. (26sts)
ROW 19: K1, [k2tog] to last st, k1. (14sts)
ROW 21: K1, [k2tog] to last st, k1. (8sts)
Cut yarn and thread through rem sts, draw up tightly and secure.

Making up
Embroider a French knot at the centre of each of the first row of flowers in a contrasting yarn. To make a French knot, knot the end of a strand of yarn and bring it out where the knot is wanted. Wrap the thread twice around the needle. Pull the wraps tight against the fabric and insert the needle back next to its starting point. Hold the knot against the fabric and take the thread through to the back. Secure it with a small backstitch. Sew the back seam, 1st in from the edge.

Essential information

DIFFICULTY Moderate

SIZE To fit a child, aged 2-5 years

YARN

Rowan Wool Cotton 50g

951 Tender x 1

Scrap of yarn for French knot (we've used 911 Rich)

NEEDLES

A: 1 pair of 3.25mm (UK10/US3) needles

B: 1 pair of 3.75mm (UK9/US5) needles

A

B

TENSION

22sts and 30 rows to 10cm (4in) over st st on 3.75mm (UK9/US5) needles

NOTIONS

Large-eyed needle

SPECIAL ABBREVIATIONS

MB Make bobble: k1, p1 in the next st. Turn, p2. Turn, skpo

Chullo earflap hat

Keep your child's ears warm during cold days with a hat that includes earflaps. It is knitted in the round using stocking stitch and is totally practical with optional chin ties to stop the hat from being pulled off.

Essential information

DIFFICULTY Moderate

SIZE To fit a child, aged 3–8 years

YARN

Sirdar Crofter Chunky 50g

054 Fair Isle x 2

NEEDLES

4 x 6mm (UK4/US10) double-pointed needles, or 40cm (16in), 6mm (UK4/US10) circular needle

TENSION

14sts and 20 rows to 10cm (4in) over st st on 6mm (UK4/US10) needles

NOTIONS

Stitch markers
1 stitch holder
Large-eyed needle
Crochet hook (optional)

Earflaps (make 2)

Cast on 3sts.
ROW 1 (RS): K1, kfb, k1. (4sts)
ROW 2 (WS): K1, p2, k1.
ROW 3: K1, kfb, kfb, k1. (6sts)
ROW 4: K1, p4, k1.
ROW 5: K1, kfb, k2, kfb, k1. (8sts)
ROW 6: K1, p6, k1.
ROW 7: K1, kfb, k4, kfb, k1. (10sts)
ROW 8: K1, p8, k1.
ROW 9: K1, kfb, k6, kfb, k1. (12 sts)
ROW 10: K1, p10, k1.
ROW 11: K1, kfb, k8, kfb, k1. (14sts)
ROW 12: K1, p12, k1.
ROW 13: K1, kfb, k10, kfb, k1. (16sts)
ROW 14: K1, p to last st, k1.
ROW 15: K all sts.
Break yarn and hold sts on a spare needle or stitch holder ready to join to the body. Work second earflap to match.
With spare needles and yarn, and knitting across both earflaps with RS facing, and using cable cast on method (see p.265), work next round as follows:
Cast on 6sts, k16 from first earflap, cast on 22sts, k16 from second earflap, cast on 6sts then join in the round taking care not to twist the sts. (66sts)

Body

Work st st until work measures 12cm (5in).

Shape crown

ROUND 1: *K9, k2tog; rep from * to end. (60sts)
ROUND 2 AND ALL EVEN ROUNDS: P all sts.
ROUND 3: *K8, k2tog; rep from * to end. (54sts)
ROUND 5: *K7, k2tog; rep from * to end. (48sts)
ROUND 7: *K6, k2tog; rep from * to end. (42sts)
ROUND 9: *K5, k2tog; rep from * to end. (36sts)
ROUND 11: *K4, k2tog; rep from * to end. (30sts)
ROUND 13: *K3, k2tog; rep from * to end. (24sts)
ROUND 15: *K2, k2tog; rep from * to end. (18sts)
ROUND 17: *K1, k2tog; rep from * to end. (12sts)
ROUND 19: *K2tog; rep from * to end. (6sts)
ROUND 21: *K2tog; rep from * to end. (3sts)
Break yarn and draw through remaining 3sts, tighten to close.

Making up

Weave in all ends. Block (see p.300).

Trim (optional)

Work blanket stitch around the lower edge of the hat. Insert a crochet hook into the lowest point of the earflap and work a crochet chain (see p.171) for approx. 10cm (4in) to create a tie cord. Break the yarn and tighten to close. Work a second tie to match the other earflap.

Newborn bonnet

This little hat is quick to knit, and uses DK yarn that is easily adaptable to your choice of colour for a boy or girl. We have chosen a 100% wool yarn that is soft and natural against delicate skin. Knit this bonnet to accompany the Baby booties on p.186.

Essential information

DIFFICULTY Easy

SIZE To fit a newborn baby

YARN

Debbie Bliss Rialto DK 50g

001 White x 1

NEEDLES

1 pair of 3.25mm (UK10/US3) needles

TENSION

25sts and 34 rows to 10cm (4in) over st st on 3.25mm (UK10/US3) needles

SPECIAL ABBREVIATIONS

RIB Work in rib, knitting all presented k sts and purling all presented p sts

RIB2TOG Working in rib, k2tog

Cast on 83sts using the cable cast on method (see p.265).

ROW 1 (RS): *K1, p1, rep from * to last st, k1.

ROW 2: *P1, k1, rep from * to last st, p1.

Rep last 2 rows once more.

ROW 5: [Rib 13, rib2tog] x 5, rib to end. (78sts)

NEXT ROW: P.

NEXT ROW: K.

These 2 rows form st st.

Work in st st for a further 17 rows.

Shape crown

ROW 1 (RS): [K6, k2tog] x 9, k to end. (69sts)

ROW 2 AND EVERY FOLL ALT ROW: P.

ROW 3: K.

ROW 5: [K5, k2tog] x 9, k to end. (60sts)

ROW 7: [K4, k2tog] x 9, k to end. (51sts)

ROW 9: [K3, k2tog] x 10, k to end. (41sts)

ROW 11: [K2, k2tog] x 10, k to end. (31sts)

ROW 13: [K1, k2tog] x 10, k to end. (21sts)

ROW 15: [K2tog] x 10, k1. (11sts)

Break off yarn leaving a long yarn tail and draw this twice through rem sts. Use this end to join row ends with mattress stitch (see p.302). Steam block lightly.

Soft ribbing This tiny bonnet sits against the baby's head, holding its shape with soft ribbing that is just snug enough to retain warmth. By using the same needles throughout the pattern, the ribbing does not end up too tight.

Striped tassel-end scarf

This ice-cream-coloured scarf is knitted in a simple 1x1 rib pattern (also known as knit 1, purl 1 rib), which involves frequent colour changes for a striped result. Add the tassels once you've completed the knitting.

Essential information

DIFFICULTY Easy

SIZE 13cm x 1.8m (5 x 71in)

YARN

Rowan Pure Wool DK 50g

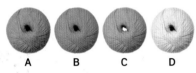

| A | B | C | D |

A: 025 Tea rose x 2   **B:** 006 Pier x 3
C: 002 Shale x 1   **D:** 013 Enamel x 3

NEEDLES

A: 1 pair of 3.25mm (UK10/US3) needles

B: 1 pair of 4mm (UK8/US6) needles

A

B

TENSION

22sts and 30 rows to 10cm (4in) over st st on 4mm (UK8/US6) needles

Using needles A and yarn A, cast on 50sts. Change to needles B and cont as follows:

ROW 1 (RS): S1p, p1, [k1, p1] to end.

ROW 2: S1p, p1, [k1, p1] to end.

These 2 rows form a 1x1 rib with a slipped stitch at beg of each row.

Repeat these 2 rows x 6 (14 rows worked in total), ending with a WS row.

Join in yarn B using a slipknot and work 14 rows of rib.

Work in 14-row stripes of rib in the following yarn sequence: C, B, A, D x 3, A, B. Repeat x 4. To finish the stripe sequence, work 14-row stripes in yarns C, B, then A. Cast off in rib.

Cut yarn B (or your choice of yarn) into lengths approx. 22cm (9in) long. Affix these as tassels along each end of the scarf (see below).

Tassels

To trim your scarf, cut a card template a little wider than the fringe length (approx. 11cm (4¼in)). Wind yarn B repeatedly around the card. Cut along one side of the card, making lengths of yarn double the width of the card. Take several lengths (more make a thicker fringe), fold in half and hold the folded loop in front of the fabric edge. Insert the tip of your needle, or a crochet hook, through the back of the fabric, close to the edge. Catch the folded loop and pull it through to the back. Catch the strands in the hook again and pull through the first loop. Repeat along the edge of the scarf to make eight tassels. Trim the ends evenly with scissors and repeat for the second edge.

Striped colourway A chain selvedge (see p.293) is the best method for creating a neat scarf edge. Each time you change colour, cut the old yarn leaving a 20cm (8in) tail, and join the ends with a slipknot. Once the scarf is completed, undo the slipknots at the edge and darn in the individual tails as described on p300.

Featherweight mantilla

A combination of techniques is used to create this pretty scarf to be worn over the head and shoulders. In the "knit three below" technique, insert the right-hand needle into a stitch worked three rows earlier to lift the gathered loops of yarn into place.

Essential information

DIFFICULTY Difficult

SIZE 28 x 100cm (11 x 39in)

YARN

Rowan Kidsilk Haze 25g

606 Candy girl x 2

NEEDLES

1 pair of 4.5mm (UK7/US7) needles

TENSION

15sts and 16 rows to 10cm (4in) over patt on 4.5mm (UK7/US7) needles

NOTIONS

Large-eyed needle

SPECIAL ABBREVIATIONS

K1B3 As k1b (k one below), but instead of knitting one below, k 3 rows below the next st, allowing above sts to come undone

NOTE: When you read "Drop next yon", be aware that these instructions refer to the yfwd/yrn worked on the previous row and will therefore present on the LH needle. Yarn may have to be teased into shape after rows 5 and 9.

Cast on 43sts using knit on cast on method (see p.264).

ROW 1 (RS): K.

ROW 2 (WS): K1, yfrn, p1, yon, *p1, k1, p1, yrn, p1, yrn, rep from * to last 5sts, p1, k1, p1, yrn, p1, yon, k1. (65sts)

ROW 3: K1, *drop next yrn off LH needle, yrn, k1, drop next yon off LH needle, yrn, k3, rep from * to last 4sts, drop next yon off LH needle, yrn, k1, drop next yon off LH needle, yrn, k1. (65sts)

ROW 4: K1, drop next yon off LH needle, yfrn, p1, drop next yon off LH needle, yrn, *p3, drop next yon off LH needle yrn, p1, drop next yon off LH needle, yon, rep from * to last 7sts, p3, drop next yon off LH needle yrn, p1, drop next yon off LH needle, yon, k1. (65sts)

ROW 5: Dropping all yons from previous row, k1, *yrn, k1b3, yfrn, p3tog tbl, rep from * to last 4sts, yon, k1b3, yrn, k1. (45sts)

ROW 6: K1, p1, k1, p1, *yrn, p1, yrn, p1, k1, p1, rep from * to last st, k1. (65sts)

ROW 7: K1, *k3, drop next yon off LH needle, yrn, k1, drop next yon off LH needle, yrn, rep from * to last 4sts, k4. (65sts)

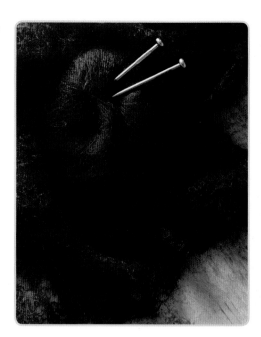

ROW 8: K1, p3, drop next yon off LH needle, yrn, p1, drop next yon off LH needle, yrn, p3, rep from * to last st, k1. (65sts)

ROW 9: Dropping all yons from previous row, k1, *p3tog tbl, yon, k1b3, yfrn, rep from * to last 4sts, p3tog tbl, k1. (43sts)

Rows 2–9 set patt.

Cont working until work measures 100cm (39in), or desired length, ending with a WS row.

NEXT ROW: K.

Cast off. Darn in ends (see p.300).

Rainbow mohair scarf

A luxurious scarf to give as a gift or to knit as a treat for yourself. The colour gradation is achieved by holding two strands of mohair together as you knit, blending the two yarns to create a third in-between shade. Increases and decreases cause the stripes to slant.

Essential information

DIFFICULTY Moderate

SIZE 12.5cm x 2m (5 x 79in)

YARN

Rowan Kidsilk Haze 25g

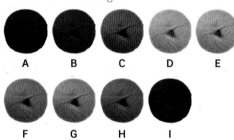

A: 595 Liqueur x 1   **B:** 627 Blood x 1
C: 596 Marmalade x 1   **D:** 644 Ember x 1
E: 597 Jelly x 1   **F:** 629 Fern x 1   **G:** 582 Trance x 1
H: 632 Hurricane x 1   **I:** 641 Blackcurrant x 1

NEEDLES

1 pair of 4mm (UK8/US6) needles

TENSION

22sts and 30 rows to 10cm (4in) over st st with yarn held double on 4mm (UK8/US6) needles

NOTIONS

Large-eyed needle

NOTE: The whole scarf is made by holding two strands of yarn together. For example, the first stripe uses two strands of yarn A, therefore referred to as AA. Yarn AB is one strand of A and one of B, and so on.

Using yarn AA, cast on 50sts.
ROW 1 (WS): [K1, p1] to end.
ROW 2: S1, p1, psso, [k1, p1] to last 2sts, k1, [p1, k1] into next st. (50sts)
ROW 3: [P1, k1] to last 2sts, p2.
ROW 4: Skpo, [p1, k1] to last 2sts, p1, [k1, p1] into next st. (50sts)
Last 4 rows set diagonal patt. Work a further 24 rows as set.
Working in diagonal patt as set, break off one strand of yarn and join in one of yarn B.
Commence stripe patt as set, working 28 rows in each colour pattern. AB, BB, BC, CC, CD, DD, DE, EE, EF, FF, FG, GG, GH, HH, HI, II.
17 stripes worked in total.
Cast off. Darn in all ends (see p.300).

Simple ribbed knitting The pattern for this scarf (1x1 rib) is double-sided and so produces a thick knitted fabric, making the scarf lovely and warm.

Loop-edge scarf

A speedy project that will knit up in no time because it uses large needles and a simple garter stitch pattern for most of the scarf. The decorative looped edges are created by wrapping yarn around your thumb before knitting it.

Essential information

DIFFICULTY Easy

SIZE 13cm x 1.5m (5 x 59in)

YARN

Rowan Big Wool 100g

58 Heather x 3

NEEDLES

1 pair of 10mm (UK000/US15) needles

TENSION

11sts and 20 rows to 10cm (4in) over g st on 10mm (UK000/US15) needles

NOTIONS

1 spare needle or stitch holder
Large-eyed needle

SPECIAL ABBREVIATIONS

ML Make a loop

Cast on 14sts.

ROW 1: K1, ML to last st, k1.

ROW 2: P to end.

Rep rows 1 and 2 x 2, then row 1 once more. Work g st (k every row) until work measures 75cm (30in), ending with a WS row.

Cut yarn and keep sts on a spare needle or stitch holder.

Make another section of scarf in the same way, ending with a RS row, cut yarn leaving a tail four times the width of the knitting. Graft the two pieces together. To graft garter stitch, place stitches from holder onto needle. Hold two needles parallel and pointing in the same direction, so that your knitting is end to end, and the last row of stitches facing you directly below the front needle are purl stitches and those directly below the rear needle are knit stitches. Thread long tail of yarn onto large-eyed sewing needle. Insert sewing needle purlwise into first stitch on front needle, and pull yarn through. Insert needle purlwise into first stitch on rear needle and pull yarn through. *Insert sewing needle into first front stitch knitwise and remove stitch from knitting needle, gently pulling yarn through stitch loop. Insert sewing needle into next front stitch purlwise and pull yarn through. Insert sewing needle into first backstitch knitwise and slip stitch off needle. Pull yarn through stitch. Insert needle into next back stitch purlwise and pull yarn through. *Repeat from * to * until no stitches remain. Sew in end. Alternatively for an easier but more noticeable join, end both pieces on a WS row. Hold both needles in your left hand, WS together and taking one loop from one needle and one from the other, cast off the loops together in twos (see Three needle cast off p.271).

Make a loop (ML)

Knit a stitch without slipping it off the LH needle. Bring yarn between needles to front of work and wrap it around your thumb from left to right. Take yarn between needles to back of work. Keeping your thumb in the loop, knit into the same stitch again this time taking it to the RH needle and letting it drop. Take the yarn over the needle from front to back and pass last 2sts on RH needle over as if casting off. Slide your thumb out of the loop.

TOP TIP   *Gently tug each yarn loop edge to tighten the stitches.*

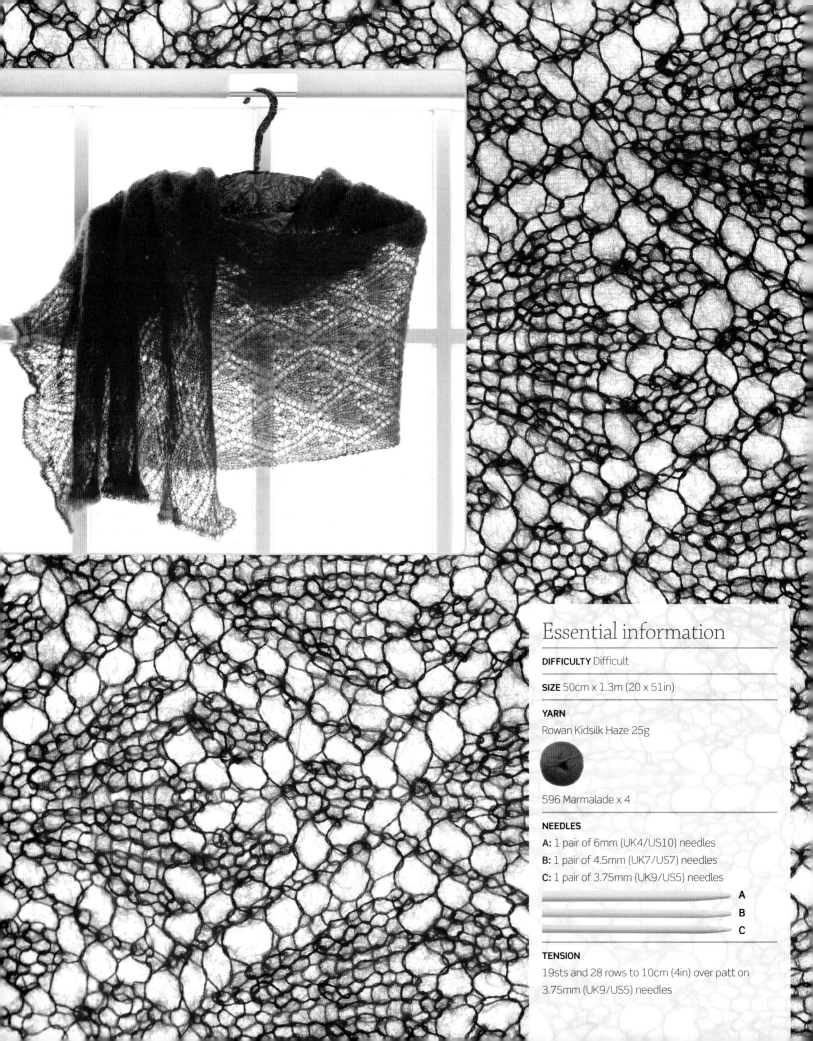

Essential information

DIFFICULTY Difficult

SIZE 50cm x 1.3m (20 x 51in)

YARN

Rowan Kidsilk Haze 25g

596 Marmalade x 4

NEEDLES

A: 1 pair of 6mm (UK4/US10) needles

B: 1 pair of 4.5mm (UK7/US7) needles

C: 1 pair of 3.75mm (UK9/US5) needles

A

B

C

TENSION

19sts and 28 rows to 10cm (4in) over patt on 3.75mm (UK9/US5) needles

Lace evening stole

Creating a beautiful, lace-weight shawl is truly rewarding and wonderful to wear. Filigree diamonds create a geometric pattern by using yarnovers, increases and decreases. Knit and purl stitches also add texture to the umbrella-style lace pattern.

Using the knit on cast on (see p.264) method and needles A, cast on 190sts. Change to needles B and cont as follows:

Work edging

ROW 1 (WS): K.

ROW 2: [K but wrap yarn x 2 around needle, bringing both loops through] to end.

ROW 3: [P into one of two loops in next stitch, knock off other loop] to end.
Change to needles C.

ROW 4: [K2tog] to end. (95sts)

Commence pattern

ROW 1: K3 *[p2, k1] x 2, yon, k2tog, yon, k1, yon, skpo, yon, [k1, p2] x 2, k1; rep from * to last 2sts, k2.

ROW 2: K2, [p1, k2] x 2, p9, *k2, [p1, k2] x 3, p9; rep from * to last 8sts, k2, [p1, k2] x 2.

ROW 3: K3, *[p2, k1] x 2, yon, k2tog, yon, k3, yon, skpo, yon [k1, p2] x 2, k1; rep from * to last 2sts, k2.

ROW 4: K2, [p1, k2] x 2, p11, *k2, [p1, k2] x 3, p11; rep from * to last 8sts, k2, [p1, k2] x 2.

ROW 5: K3, *[p2tog, k1] x 2, yon, k2tog, yon, skpo, k1, k2tog, yon, skpo, yon, [k1, p2tog] x 2, k1; rep from * to last 2sts, k2.

ROW 6: K2, [p1, k1] x 2, p11, *k1, [p1, k1] x 3, p11; rep from * to last 6sts, [k1, p1] x 2, k2.

ROW 7: K3, *[p1, k1] x 2, yon, k2tog, yon, k1 tbl, yon, sk2p, yon, k1 tbl, yon, skpo, yon, [k1, p1] x 2, k1; rep from * to last 2sts, k2.

ROW 8: K2, [p1, k1] x 2, p13, *k1, [p1, k1] x 3, p13; rep from * to last 6sts, [k1, p1] x 2, k2.

ROW 9: K3, *[k2tog] x 2, yon, k2tog, yon, k3, yon, k1, yon, k3, yon, skpo, yon [skpo] x 2, k1; rep from * to last 2sts, k2.

ROW 10: K2, p to last 2sts, k2.

ROW 11: K3, *[k2tog, yon] x 2, skpo, k1, k2tog, yon, k1, yon, skpo, k1, k2tog, [yon, skpo] x 2, k1; rep from * to last 2sts, k2.

ROW 12: As row 10.

ROW 13: K2, [k2tog, yon] x 2, k1 tbl, yon, sk2p, yon, k3, yon, sk2p, yon, k1 tbl, yon, skpo, *yon, sk2p, yon, k2tog, yon, k1 tbl, yon, sk2p, yon, k3, yon, sk2p, yon, k1 tbl, yon, skpo; rep from * to last 4sts, yon, skpo, k2.

ROW 14: As row 10.

ROW 15: K3, *yon, skpo, yon, [k1, p2] x 4, k1, yon, k2tog, yon, k1; rep from * to last 2sts, k2.

ROW 16: K2, p5, [k2, p1] x 3, k2, *p9, [k2, p1] x 3, k2; rep from * to last 7sts, p5, k2.

ROW 17: K4, yon, skpo, yon, [k1, p2] x 4, k1, yon, k2tog, *yon, k3, yon, skpo, yon, [k1, p2] x 4, k1, yon, k2tog; rep from * to last 4sts, yon, k4.

ROW 18: K2, p6, [k2, p1] x 3, k2, *p11, [k2, p1] x 3, k2; rep from * to last 8sts, p6, k2.

ROW 19: K3, *k2tog, yon, skpo, yon, [k1, p2tog] x 4, k1, yon, k2tog, yon, skpo, k1; rep from * to last 2sts, k2.

ROW 20: K2, p6, [k1, p1] x 3, k1, *p11, [k1, p1] x 3, k1; rep from * to last 8sts, p6, k2.

ROW 21: K2, k2tog, yon, k1 tbl, yon, skpo, yon, [k1, p1] x 4, k1, yon, k2tog, yon, k1 tbl, *yon, sk2p, yon, k1 tbl, yon, skpo, yon, [k1, p1] x 4, k1, yon, k2tog, yon, k1 tbl, rep from * to last 4sts, yon, skpo, k2.

ROW 22: K2, p7, [k1, p1] x 3, k1, *p13, [k1, p1] x 3, k1; rep from * to last 9sts, p7, k2.

ROW 23: K3, *yon, k3, yon, skpo, yon, [skpo] x 2, k1, [k2tog] x 2, yon, k2tog, yon, k3, yon, k1; rep from * to last 2sts, k2.

ROW 24: As row 10.

ROW 25: K3, * yon, skpo, k1, k2tog, [yon, skpo] x 2, k1, [k2tog, yon] x 2, skpo, k1, k2tog, yon, k1; rep from * to last 2sts, k2.

ROW 26: As row 10.

ROW 27: K4, yon, sk2p, yon, k1 tbl, yon, skpo, yon, sk2p, yon, k2tog, yon, k1 tbl, yon, sk2p, *yon, k3, yon, sk2p, yon, k1 tbl, yon, skpo, yon, sk2p, yon, k2tog, yon, k1 tbl, yon, sk2p; rep from * to last 4sts, yon, k4.

ROW 28: As row 10.

These 28 rows set lace patt. Rep rows 1–28 x 12, ending with a WS row.

Work top edging

ROW 1 (RS): [(K1, p1) into next st] to end. (190sts)
Change to needles B and work as follows:

ROW 2: [P but wrap yarn x 2 around needle, bringing both loops through] to end.

ROW 3: [K into one of two loops in next stitch, knock off other loop] to end.
Cast off using needles A.

Handwash and wet block the stole, making sure that you stretch the lace pattern out until visible, keeping the edges of the scarf straight.

Essential information

DIFFICULTY Easy

SIZE 15cm x 1.8m (6 x 71in)

YARN

Sirdar Baby Bamboo DK 50g

131 Cream x 3

NEEDLES

1 pair of 4mm (UK8/US6) needles

TENSION

22sts and 28 rows to 10cm (4in) over st st on 4mm
(UK8/US6) needles

NOTIONS

Large-eyed needle

Summer eyelet scarf

This pretty scarf is knitted in bamboo yarn, a blend of 80 per cent natural bamboo and 20 per cent wool, which is lightweight and allows the skin to breathe. The eyelet patterning at each end adds a delicate finish and is moderately easy to create.

Zigzag edge

Cast on 1st.

ROW 1: Kfb.

ROW 2: P1, pfb, p1.

ROW 3: K2, yon, k2.

ROW 4 AND ALL EVEN ROWS: P to last st, M1, p1.

ROW 5: K2, yon, k2tog, yon, k2.

ROW 7: K2, yon, k2tog, yon, k2tog, yon, k2.

ROW 9: K2, yon, k2tog, yon, k2tog, yon, k2tog, yon, k2. (11sts)

Cut yarn and leave sts on needle.

Casting on a new stitch both times, on the empty needle, rep rows 1–9 x 2, keeping the yarn attached on the 3rd zigzag.

ROW 10: P10, p2tog, p9, p2tog, p10. (31sts)

ROW 11: K3, [yon, k2tog] to last 2sts, k2.

ROW 12: P to end.

ROW 13: K2, [yon, k2tog] to last st, k1.

Main pattern

*Work 3 rows of st st starting with a p row.

NEXT ROW: K3, [yon, k2tog] to last 2sts, k2.

Work 3 rows of st st starting with a p row.

ROW 7: K2, [yon, k2tog] to last st, k1.*

Rep from * to * once more.

**Work 3 rows of st st starting with a p row.

NEXT ROW: K3, [yon, k2tog, k2] to end.

Work 3 rows of st st starting with a p row.

NEXT ROW: K5, [yon, k2tog, k2] to last 2sts, k2.**

Rep from ** to ** once more.

Next section

*Work 5 rows of st st starting with a p row.

NEXT ROW: K3, [yon, k2tog, k2] to end.*

Work 5 rows of st st starting with a p row.

NEXT ROW: K5, [yon, k2tog, k2] to last 2sts, k2.

Rep from * to * once more.

Continue in st st, starting and ending with a p row until scarf measures 1.6m (63in).

Next section

*ROW 1: K3, [yon, k2tog, k2] to last st.

Work 5 rows of st st starting with a p row.*

ROW 7: K5, [yon, k2tog, k2] to last 2sts, k2.

Work 5 rows of st st starting with a p row.

ROW 13: Rep from * to * once more.

Next section

**ROW 19: Rep last row 7.

Work 3 rows of st st starting with a p row.

NEXT ROW: Rep last row 1.

Work 3 rows of st st starting with a p row.**

Rep from ** to ** once more.

Next section

ROW 1: K2, [yon, k2tog] to last st, k1.

Work 3 rows of st st starting with a p row.

ROW 5: K3, [yon, k2tog] to last 2sts, k2.

Work 3 rows of st st starting with a p row.

Rep these 8 rows once more.

Next section

ROW 1: K2, [yon, k2tog] to last st, k1.

ROW 2: P to end.

ROW 3: K3, [yon, k2tog] to last 2sts, k2.

ROW 4: P10, pfb, p9, pfb, p10.

Zigzag edge

Work the three zigzags of 11sts separately, while leaving the rest of the sts on the needle.

Over first 11sts.

ROW 5: K2, [yon, k2tog] x 4, k1. (11sts)

ROWS 6, 8, 10, 12, 14: P to end.

ROW 7: K1, k2tog [yon, k2tog] x 3, k2tog. (9sts)

ROW 9: K1, k2tog [yon, k2tog] x 2, k2tog. (7sts)

ROW 11: K1, k2tog, yon, k2tog, k2tog. (5sts)

ROW 13: Skpo, k1, k2tog. (3sts)

ROW 15: P3tog. (1st)

Fasten off final st.

Repeat for next two groups of 11sts.

Carefully darn in ends and block.

Moss stitch scarf

This wide striped scarf can be worn as it is or transformed into a snood by stitching the ends together. Vary the colour widths by working different numbers of moss stitch rows in each yarn. Alternatively, knit the scarf in up to four shades.

Essential information

DIFFICULTY Easy

SIZE 22cm x 1.5m (9 x 59in)

YARN

Debbie Bliss Cotton DK 50g

A　　**B**

A: 02 Ecru x 4　**B:** 19 Taupe x 4

NEEDLES

1 pair of 4mm (UK8/US6) needles

TENSION

20sts and 30 rows to 10cm (4in) over moss st using 4mm (UK8/US6) needles

NOTIONS

Large-eyed needle

Stripe sequence

6 rows in yarn A, 4 rows in yarn B, 4 rows in yarn A, 10 rows in yarn B, 6 rows in yarn A, 4 rows in yarn B.
Rep these 34 rows x 13.

Commence pattern

Using yarn A, cast on 45sts.
ROW 1: K1, [p1, k1] to end.
Cont in moss st and stripe sequence until 442 rows (13 patt reps) have been worked.
Using yarn B, cast off in moss st.

Making up (optional)

Join the cast on edge to the cast off edge using an overcast seam (see p.301). Carefully press the seam flat to avoid a ridge but do not block the scarf or it will lose some of its texture.

Touchable texture Moss stitch gives this scarf a tactile quality, which works particularly well when you use a cotton-rich yarn. For an alternative textured stitch, try broken moss stitch (p.312).

Rosette snood

This ladies' winter knit is worked in a medium-weight yarn spun from the fleece of Peruvian alpacas and sheep, making it both luxurious and thick, but any aran yarn will work just as well. The simple pattern is embellished with knitted rosettes.

Essential information

DIFFICULTY Easy

SIZE 36cm x 1.4m (14¼ x 55in)

YARN

Artesano Alpaca Aran 100g

A   **B**

A: 2200 Laxford x 2   **B:** 5083 Lomond x 1

NEEDLES

A: 1 pair of 10mm (UK000/US15) needles

B: 1 pair of 7.5mm (UK1/USn/a) needles

A

B

TENSION

10sts and 12 rows to 10cm (4in) over patt on 10mm (UK000/US15) needles

NOTIONS

Large-eyed needle

3 x 2cm (¾in) mother-of-pearl buttons

Using needles A and yarn A, cast on 40sts.

ROW 1: K.

ROW 2: K.

ROW 3: *K1, p1, rep from * to end of row.

ROW 4: *K1, p1, rep from * to end of row.

Rep rows 1–4 until work measures 1.4m (55in).

Cast off loosely.

Sew cast on edge to cast off edge.

Block (see p.300).

Rosettes

Using needles B and yarn B, cast on 15sts.

ROW 1: K.

ROW 2: Kfb into every st.

ROW 3: K.

ROW 4: K.

ROW 5: Kfb into every st.

ROW 6: K.

ROW 7: K.

Cast off loosely.

Roll strip into flower shape, stitching as you go.

Attach button to centre of flower and sew flowers to snood.

Knitted rosettes An easy mini project, these pink roses "grow" when you knit into the front and back of each stitch to increase the fabric. They are attached to the snood with mother-of-pearl buttons.

TOP TIP *Add mother-of-pearl buttons for a delicate, shimmering finish.*

Lace patterned wrap

This pretty scarf, worked in lavendar lace stitch on a circular needle, forms a ring to wrap around your neck and shoulders. The ripple pattern is created by a series of yarnover increases and slip, slip, knit (ssk) decreases.

Essential information

DIFFICULTY Moderate

SIZE 36cm x 1.5m (14¼ x 59in)

YARN

Adriafil Soffio Plus Classic 50g

046 Sea green x 2

NEEDLES

80cm (32in), 5mm (UK6/US8) circular needle

TENSION

14sts and 22 rows to 10cm (4in) over lace patt on 5mm (UK6/US8) needles

NOTIONS

Large-eyed needle

Cast on 187sts and join in the round without twisting the yarn.

ROUND 1: *Ssk, k3 tbl, yon, k1, yon, k3 tbl, k2tog, rep from * to end of round.

ROUND 2: K.

ROUND 3: *Ssk, k2 tbl, yon, k1, yon, ssk, yon, k2 tbl, k2tog, rep from * to end of round.

ROUND 4: K.

ROUND 5: *Ssk, k1 tbl, yon, k1, [yon, ssk] x 2, yon, k1 tbl, k2tog, rep from * to end of round.

ROUND 6: K.

ROUND 7: *Ssk, yon, k1, [yon, ssk] x 3, yon, k2tog, rep from * to end of round.

ROUND 8: K.

ROUND 9: *K1, p1, k7, p1, k1, rep from * to end of round.

ROUND 10: *K1, p1, k7, p1, k1, rep from * to end of round.

Rep rows 1–10 x 6.

Cast off loosely.

Sew in ends.

Block carefully (see p.300).

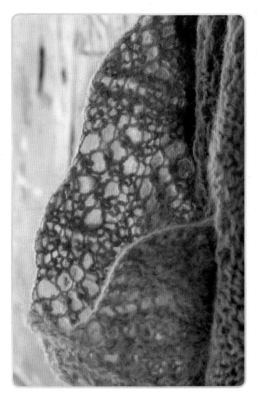

TOP TIP *Stretch the fabric slightly when blocking to see the full effect of the pattern.*

Soft and fine mohair The Italian blended mohair and acrylic yarn we've used for this wrap gives it a breezy, soft feel, and shiny look.

Ribbed scarf

Knitted in seeded rib stitch, this scarf is quick and easy to knit and looks stylish, while the chunky-weight yarn makes the ridges prominent. We've used a 100% organic wool yarn, but an alternative chunky yarn will work just as well.

Essential information·

DIFFICULTY Easy

SIZE 20cm x 1.5m (8 x 59in)

YARN

Rico Eco Chunky 50g

001 Off-white x 4

NEEDLES

1 pair of 7mm (UK2/USn/a) needles

TENSION

14sts and 19 rows to 10cm (4in) over st st on 7mm (UK2/US n/a) needles

Cast on 30sts.
ROW 1: K1 *k3, p1, rep from * to last st, k1.
ROW 2: K1 *k2, p1, k1, rep from * to last st, k1.
These 2 rows form the patt.
Rep until 1.5m (59in) have been worked.
Cast off.
Press lightly according to ballband instructions.

TOP TIP   *Cast on an even number of stitches when knitting the ribs.*

Twisted cable scarf

The long length of this scarf means that it will wrap around your neck at least once and still hang to a reasonable length so everyone can see your handywork.

Essential information

DIFFICULTY Moderate

SIZE 19cm x 2m (7½ x 79in)

YARN

Rowan Purelife Renew 50g

687 Lorry x 6

NEEDLES

A: 1 pair of 6mm (UK4/US10) needles
B: Cable needle

A

B

TENSION

20sts and 19 rows to 10cm (4in) over cable patt using 6mm (UK4/US10) needles

NOTIONS

Large-eyed needle

SPECIAL ABBREVIATIONS

C10F Place 5sts on cable needle (cn) and leave at front of work, k5, then k5 from cn

CR7R Place 2sts on cn and leave at back of work, k5, then p2 from cn

CR7L Place 5sts on cn and leave at front of work, p2, then k5 from cn

Using needles A, cast on 31sts.
Starting with a k row, work 4 rows g st.
ROW 5 (RS): K3, p to last 11sts, k5, p3, k3.
ROW 6: K6, p5, k to end.
ROW 7: As row 5.
ROW 8 (INCREASE ROW): K6, [M1, p1] x 5, k to end. (36sts)
ROW 9: K3, p17, k10, p3, k3.
ROW 10: K6, p10, k to end.

Set cable panel

When working the chart, read as all RS (odd) rows from R to L and all WS (even) rows from L to R.
NEXT ROW (RS): K3, work next 30sts as row 1 of cable chart, k3.
NEXT ROW: K3, work next 30sts as row 2 of cable chart, k3.
These 2 rows set sts.
Continue repeating the 88-row pattern repeat from chart until work measures 1.98m (78in), or desired length, ending after chart row 1.
DECREASE ROW (WS): K6, [p2tog] x 5, k to end. (31sts)
ROW 1: K3, p17, k5, p3, k3.
ROW 2: K6, p5, k to end.
ROW 3: As row 1.
Work 5 rows g st.
Cast off on WS.
Darn in all ends and block lightly under a damp cloth, being careful not to squash the cables.

KEY

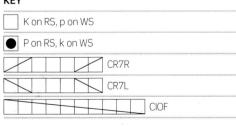

	K on RS, p on WS
	● P on RS, k on WS
	CR7R
	CR7L
	C10F

Cable chart

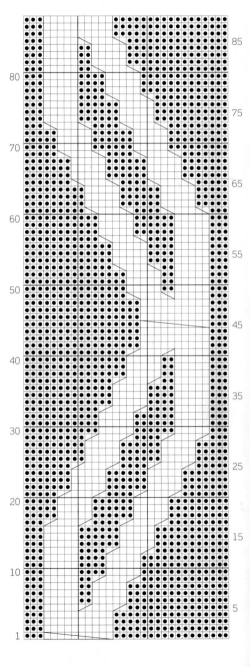

Cable twists and turns The travelling nature of this helix cable pattern, which moves every four rows, makes it easy to identify where the next cable will start. After a few pattern repeats, you may not need to be constantly consulting the chart, below left. This scarf matches the Twisted cable hat on p.112.

Two-way textured muffler

This short-length scarf is knitted in a warm aran wool. Its texture is created by working an eyelet pattern throughout using the yarnover technique (see pp.280–281 for help with this). The muffler ends naturally shape at an angle, so you can sew it up into a snood, should you wish.

Essential information

DIFFICULTY Moderate

SIZE 17cm x 1.8m (6¾ x 71in)

YARN

Artesano Aran Alpaca 100g

C853 Pine x 2

NEEDLES

1 pair of 5mm (UK6/US8) needles

TENSION

20sts and 16 rows to 10cm (4in) over eyelet patt on 5mm (UK6/US8) needles

NOTIONS

Large-eyed needle

Cast on 32sts.
ROW 1: K.
ROW 2: K2, *sk2p, yon, k1, yon, rep from * to last 2sts, k2.
Rep rows 1–2 until work measures 1.8m (71in), or length required.
K 2 rows.
Cast off loosely.
Darn in ends.
Block carefully (see p.300).

 TOP TIP   *Block the scarf to correct a slight bias as the knitting forms.*

Two-tone scarf

The double-sided effect of this project is achieved when you simultaneously work backwards and forwards across two pieces of knitted fabric in different colours.

Essential information

DIFFICULTY Difficult

SIZE 15cm x 1.5m (6 x 59in)

YARN

Rowan Wool Cotton DK 50g

A   **B**

A: 900 Antique x 3   **B:** 946 Elf x 3

NEEDLES

40cm (16in) long, 3.75mm (UK9/US5) circular needle

TENSION

23sts and 31 rows to 10cm (4in) over st st on 3.75mm (UK9/US5) needles

NOTIONS

Large-eyed needle

Using yarn A and tubular cast on (see p.268), cast on 70sts. Do not join.

ROW 1: Using yarn A, *k1, s1 wyif, rep from * to end. Without turning your work, push sts up to tip of circular needle in your left hand, to be reworked. This will be where you worked the beginning of the last row.

ROW 2: Using yarn B, *s1 wyib, p1, rep from * to end of row. Turn work over, to now go in the opposite direction. Twist yarns together once to prevent holes from forming.

ROW 3: Using yarn B, work as row 1.

ROW 4: Using yarn A, work as row 2. Turn work over and work in opposite direction.

Twist yarns together once.

These last 4 rows form the patt.

Cont repeating last 4 rows until work measures 1.5m (59in), ending with patt row 4.

Cast off, using tubular cast off (see p.272), in yarn B.

Darn in ends (see p.300). Block lightly with a warm iron under a damp cloth.

Double-sided knitting It looks as if the knitted fabric in this project has been folded or grafted to create a seamless edge all the way round the scarf. Turn to p.268 and p.272 for step-by-step instructions on tubular cast on and cast off methods.

TOP TIP *Twist yarns over each other where the colours meet at the edges.*

Striped snake scarf

This child's scarf, worked in moss stitch, is a simple project for a beginner. The cotton yarn is a joy to work with and the stocking stitch pattern is quick to complete. Finish your creation with a pom-pom tail.

Essential information

DIFFICULTY Easy

SIZE 15cm x 1.5m (6 x 59in)

YARN

Debbie Bliss DK Cotton 50g

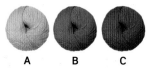

A   **B**   **C**

A: 20 Green x 2   **B:** 62 Blue x 2   **C:** 47 Red x 1

NEEDLES

1 pair of 4mm (UK8/US6) needles

TENSION

20sts by 30 rows to 10cm (4in) over st st on 4mm (UK8/US6) needles

NOTIONS

Large-eyed needle

SPECIAL ABBREVIATIONS

MB Make a bobble

Striped pattern

Using yarn A, k 10 rows.
Using yarn B, k 6 rows.
Rep throughout, until row 188, then cont in yarn B only.

Body

In yarn A cast on 2sts.
ROW 1: *K1, p1.
ROW 2: P1, k1.
Rep from *.
Cont in moss st as above and inc (kfb or pfb) into the first and last st every 4th row. Cont stripe as stated until you are left with 36sts and have 68 rows.
Cont knitting straight in moss st and foll the stripe layout until 177 rows have been knitted.
ROWS 178–188: Cont in moss st, dec 1st (k2tog or p2tog) at beg and end of row 178, row 182, and row 188. (30sts)
ROWS 189–200: Cont in moss st for 12 rows inc into first and last stitch every 2 rows. (42sts)
ROWS 201–225: Cont in moss st straight.
ROW 226: Cont in moss st. Dec 1st at beg and end of each row. At sts 17 and 23 MB, (using yarn A, k into front, back, front, back of st, turn, p4, turn, k4, turn, p4, k2, k2tog, then pass third and fourth sts over first st).
ROWS 227–242: Cont in moss st. Dec 1st at beginning and end of each row.
ROW 243: Change to yarn C. (8sts)
Cont knitting in moss st for 15 rows.

Forked tongue

ROW 259: *K1, p1, k1, p1, turn.
ROW 260: P1, k1, p1, k1, turn.
ROW 261: K1, p1, k1, p1, turn.
ROW 262: P1, k1, p1, k1, turn.
ROW 263: K1, p1, k1, p1, turn.
Break yarn and cast off these 4sts.
Reattach yarn to rem 4sts and rep from *.
Cast off.

Pom-pom

Cut two circles of card (6cm (2¹/₂in) diameter); cut a smaller circle out of the centre. Place two circles on top of each other. Wrap yarn C around the circle until there is no hole left in the centre (it is easier to wrap with small bundles of yarn). Using scissors, cut all the way around the edge of the circle, take a separate piece of yarn and wrap it around the middle of the pom-pom, making sure to go between the two pieces of circular card; secure tightly. Remove the card circles and puff up the pom-pom. Sew the pom-pom onto the bottom of the snake as a tail. For more information about making a pom-pom, turn to p.299.

Women's cosy gloves

You can make these gloves a perfect fit for longer or shorter fingers by increasing or decreasing the number of rows knitted for each finger.

Essential information

DIFFICULTY Moderate

SIZE To fit an adult female

YARN

Artesano Alpaca DK 50g

A   **B**

A: C704 Violet x 2   **B:** C743 Fern x 1

NEEDLES

A: 1 pair of 3.25mm (UK10/US3) needles

B: 1 pair of 3.75mm (UK9/US5) needles

——————————————————————— A
——————————————————————— B

TENSION

24sts and 32 rows to 10cm (4in) over st st using 3.75mm (UK9/US5) needles

NOTIONS

Large-eyed needle

Right hand

**With needles A and yarn B, cast on 44sts. Work 1 row k2, p2 rib.
Change to yarn A.
ROW 1: *K2, p2, rep from * to end. Rep this row until work measures 5cm (21/4in) from cast on edge, inc 2sts on last row. (46sts)
Change to needles B and work 8 rows st st.**

Shape thumb

ROW 1: K23, M1, k3, M1, k20. (48sts)
Work 3 rows st st.
ROW 5: K23, M1, k5, M1, k20. (50sts)

ROW 6 AND EVERY FOLL ALT ROW: P.
ROW 7: K23, M1, k7, M1, k20. (52sts)
ROWS 8–13: Cont to inc 2sts as set on every RS row to 58sts.
ROW 14: P.
Divide for thumb.
NEXT ROW: K38, turn.
***NEXT ROW:** P15, turn. Cast on 2sts. (17sts)
Work 12 rows st st on these 17sts.
NEXT ROW: K1 [k2tog, k1] x 5, k1. (12sts)
P 1 row.
K2tog to end of row. (6sts)
Break yarn and draw through sts.
Join thumb seam.
With RS facing, join yarn to base of thumb and k to end. (43sts)
Work 11 rows st st ending with a p row, adjusting length here if required.

First finger

NEXT ROW: K28, turn.
NEXT ROW: P13, cast on 2sts. (15sts)
Work 16 rows st st over these 15sts.
NEXT ROW: [K2, k2tog] x 3, k2tog, k1. (11sts)
P 1 row.
NEXT ROW: [K1, k2tog] x 3, k2tog. (7sts)
Break yarn and draw through sts.
Join seam.

Second finger

With RS facing, pick up and k2 from base of first finger, k5, turn.
NEXT ROW: P12, turn, cast on 2sts. (14sts)
Work 18 rows st st on these 14sts.
NEXT ROW: [K2, k2tog] x 3, k2. (11sts)
P 1 row.
NEXT ROW: [K2tog, k1] x 3, K2tog. (7sts)
Complete as for First finger.

Third finger

With RS facing, pick up and k2 at base of second finger, k5, turn.
NEXT ROW: P12, turn, cast on 2sts. (14sts)
Work 14 rows st st on these 14sts. Complete as for First finger.

Fourth finger

With RS facing, pick up and k2 from base of third finger, k5, turn.
NEXT ROW: P to end. (12sts)
Work 12 rows st st on these 12sts.
NEXT ROW: [K2, k2tog] x 3. (9sts)
P 1 row.
NEXT ROW: [K1, k2tog] x 3. (6sts)
Complete as for First finger.

Left hand

Work as for Right hand, from ** to **
Shape thumb.
ROW 1: K20, M1, k3, M1, k23. (48sts)
Work 3 rows st st.
ROW 5: K20, M1, k5, M1, k23. (50sts)
ROW 6 AND EVERY FOLL ALT ROW: P.
ROW 7: K20, M1, k7, M1, k23. (52sts)
ROWS 8–13: Cont to inc 2sts on every RS row to 58sts.
ROW 14: P.
Divide for thumb.
NEXT ROW: K35, turn, complete as for Right glove from *** to finish.

Making up

Join the side seams (see Edge-to-edge seam on p.300).

Mohair lace armwarmers

A pattern of stable holes and loops, created using increase and decrease techniques (see pp.281–282), form a luxurious lace fabric in mohair yarn. An easy and quick project, these armwarmers are knitted as a tube and require very little shaping.

Essential information

DIFFICULTY Easy

SIZE To fit an adult female

YARN
Debbie Bliss Angel 25g

017 Plum x 1

NEEDLES
4 x 4mm (UK8/US6) double-pointed needles

TENSION
24sts and 32 rows to 10cm (4in) over lace patt on 4mm (UK8/US6) needles

NOTIONS
Large-eyed needle

Cast on 36sts and join in the round without twisting the yarn (see Top Tip, below).
ROUND 1: K.
ROUND 2: P.
ROUND 3: *Yrn, k2tog, rep from * to end of round.
ROUND 4: P.
K 4 rounds.
Rep rounds 3–8 x 14, then work round 3–4 once more.

Shape thumbhole
Work the following rows backwards and forwards (not in the round).
Work 4 rows in st st.
NEXT ROW: *Yrn, k2tog, rep from * to end of round.
NEXT ROW: K.

NEXT ROW: K then cont to join in the round.
K 3 rounds.
Work rounds 3–8 once more.
NEXT ROUND: *Yrn, k2tog, rep from * to end of round.
K 4 rounds.
Cast off loosely.

Making up
Fold over cast off edge to form picot edge and stitch in place.
Sew in ends.
Block carefully.

TOP TIP *The loops of the stitches should run along the top of the needle.*

Men's winter gloves

This project will help you practise M1 increases (see pp.278–279), dividing stitches, and working on part of a row at a time to form long strips for the fingers. There is no need to block the gloves as this will loosen the fabric and make it baggy.

Essential information

DIFFICULTY Moderate

SIZE To fit an adult male

YARN

Artesano Superwash Merino DK 50g

SFN50 Black x 2

NEEDLES

A: 1 pair of 3.25mm (UK10/US3) needles
B: 1 pair of 3.75mm (UK9/US5) needles

A
B

TENSION

24sts and 30 rows to 10cm (4in) over st st on 3.75mm (UK9/US5) needles

NOTIONS

Large-eyed needle

Left hand

Using needles A and double cast on method (see p.266), cast on 45sts.

ROW 1 (RS): K1, *p1, k1 tbl, rep from * to last st, p1 tbl.

ROW 2: *P1 tbl, k1, rep from * to end.

These two rows set twisted rib.

Rep last 2 rows until work measures 6.5cm (2¹/₂in), ending with a RS row.

NEXT ROW (WS): Rib 7, M1, [rib 8, M1] x 4, patt to end. (50sts)

Change to needles B and work in st st for 6 rows, ending on a WS row.

Thumb

ROW 1 (RS): K22, M1, k3, M1, k to end. (52sts)

Starting with a p row, work 3 rows st st.

ROW 5: K22, M1, k5, M1, k to end. (54sts)

ROW 6 AND ALL FOLL ALT ROWS: P.

ROW 7: K22, M1, k7, M1, k to end. (56sts)

ROW 9: K22, M1, k9, M1, k to end. (58sts)

ROW 11: K22, M1, k11, M1, k to end. (60sts)

ROW 13: K22, M1, k13, M1, k to end. (62sts)

ROW 15: K22, M1, k15, M1, k to end. (64sts)

ROW 16: P.

ROW 17: K39. Turn.

ROW 18: P17. Turn.

Working on these 17sts only, work 19 rows st st ending with a RS row.

**NEXT ROW: P1, [p2tog] x 8. (9sts)

Leaving a long tail, break yarn and thread through rem sts.

Rejoin yarn at base of thumb and k to end. Starting with a p row, work 13 rows st st without shaping.

First finger

NEXT ROW: K30. Turn.

NEXT ROW: P13. Turn, cast on 2sts. (15sts for finger)

Working on these 15sts only, work 24 rows st st.

NEXT ROW: K1, [k2tog] x 7. (8sts)

Leaving a long tail, break yarn and thread through rem sts.

Second finger

With RS facing, pick up and k2 from base of first finger, k6. Turn.

NEXT ROW: P14. Turn and cast on 2sts. (16sts for second finger)

Working on these 16sts only, work 24 rows st st.

NEXT ROW: [K2tog] x 8.

Leaving a long tail, break yarn and thread through rem sts.

TOP TIP   *When sewing up, draw the yarn through the stitching to create rounded fingertips.*

Third finger

With RS facing, pick up and k2 from base of first finger, k6. Turn.
NEXT ROW: P14. Turn and cast on 2sts. (16sts for third finger)
Working on these 16sts only, work 22 rows st st.
NEXT ROW: [K2tog] x 8.
Leaving a long tail, break yarn and thread through rem sts.

Fourth finger

With RS facing, pick up and k2 from base of first finger, k5. Turn.
NEXT ROW: P12. Turn and cast on 2sts. (14sts for fourth finger)
Working on these 14sts only, work 15 rows st st.
NEXT ROW (WS): [P2tog] x 7.
Leaving a long tail, break yarn and thread through rem sts.
Use all long tails of yarn to sew up corresponding finger using mattress stitch, being especially careful to run as fine a seam as possible. Continue fourth finger seam to cuff.

Right hand

Work as for Left hand up to Thumb.

Thumb

ROW 1 (RS): K25, M1, k3, M1, k to end. (52sts)
Starting with a p row, work 3 rows st st.
ROW 5: K25, M1, k5, M1, k to end. (54sts)
ROW 6 AND ALL FOLL ALT ROWS: P.
ROW 7: K25, M1, k7, M1, k to end. (56sts)
ROW 9: K25, M1, k9, M1, k to end. (58sts)
ROW 11: K25, M1, k11, M1, k to end. (60sts)
ROW 13: K25, M1, k13, M1, k to end. (62sts)
ROW 15: K25, M1, k15, M1, k to end. (64sts)
ROW 16: P.
ROW 17: K39. Turn.
ROW 18: P17. Turn.
Working on these 17sts only, work 19 rows st st ending with a RS row.
Work from ** to end of instructions for the Left hand.

Striped armwarmers

Using simple stocking stitch the stripes are easily and neatly worked by carrying yarn up the side of the armwarmers. Check your tension regularly to ensure a firm-knit fabric. The tips of the thumbs can be turned down, see left, if desired.

Essential information

DIFFICULTY Easy

SIZE To fit an adult female

YARN

Artesano Superwash Merino DK 50g

A **B**

A: 8141 Hot pink x 1 **B:** 7254 Sand yellow x 1

NEEDLES

A: 1 pair of 3.75mm (UK9/US5) needles

B: 1 pair of 4.5mm (UK7/US7) needles

———————————————— A

———————————————— B

TENSION

23sts and 33 rows to 10cm (4in) over st st on 4.5mm (UK7/US7) needles

NOTIONS

Stitch holders (optional)

Large-eyed needle

Left armwarmer

Using needles A and yarn A, cast on 46sts. Use the single cast on method (see p.264) and starting with a k row, work 10 rows in st st ending with a WS row.

Change to needles B and work a further 6 rows in st st, ending with a WS row. Join in yarn B.

NEXT ROW (RS): Using yarn B, k1, skpo, k to last 3sts, k2tog, k1. (44sts)

Work 9 rows without shaping.

Work 10 rows in yarn A without shaping.

Last 20 rows set stripe patt: 10 rows yarn B, 10 rows yarn A. **Cont working stripe patt throughout, at same time dec as set on next and foll 20th row. (40sts)**

Work 9 rows without shaping, ending with a WS row. **

Thumb gusset

ROW 1: Using yarn A, [k4, M1] x 3, k to end. (43sts)

ROW 2 AND ALL FOLL ALT ROWS: P.

ROW 3: K5, M1, k to end. (44sts)

ROW 5: K5, M1, k4, M1, k6, M1, k to end. (47sts)

ROW 7: K9, M1, k8, M1, k to end. (49sts)

ROW 9: K9, M1, k10, M1, k to end. (51sts)

ROW 11: Using yarn B, k21 and turn, leaving rem sts unworked. Leaving yarn B hanging, join in yarn A, cast on 2sts and p12. Leave the unworked sts on stitch holders if desired. (14 live sts remain)

Thumb

Working on these 14sts only, and starting with a k row, work 8 rows st st.

Change to needles A and using yarn A, work a further 7 rows st st. Cast off loosely using needles B on WS.

Using yarn B, which is still attached at base of thumb, and needles B, with RS facing, pick up and k2 from thumb cast on. K to end of row. (41sts)

NEXT ROW: P.

Work 10 rows without shaping (8 rows B, 2 rows A).

Change to needles A and using yarn A, starting with a k row, work 10 rows st st.

Cast off using needles B, leaving a long yarn tail for sewing up.

Darn in all ends and join row ends and thumb seams using mattress stitch (see p.302).

Right armwarmer

Work as given for Left armwarmer to **.

Thumb gusset

ROW 1: Using yarn A, k29, [M1, k4] x 2, M1, k to end. (43sts)

ROW 2 AND ALL FOLL ALT ROWS: P.

ROW 3: K38, M1, k to end. (44sts)

ROW 5: K29, M1, k6, M1, k4, M1, k to end. (47sts)

ROW 7: K29, M1, k8, M1, k to end. (49sts)

ROW 9: K29, M1, k10, M1, k to end. (51sts)

ROW 13: Using yarn B, k41 and turn, leaving rem sts unworked. Leave yarn B hanging, join in yarn A, cast on 2sts and p12.

Complete as given for Left armwarmer from Thumb.

Essential information

DIFFICULTY Moderate

SIZE To fit a child, aged 10-15 years

YARN
Debbie Bliss Rialto 4-ply 50g

A: 04 Grey x 1   **B:** 27 Chamois x 1

NEEDLES
A: 1 pair of 2.75mm (UK12/US2) needles
B: 1 pair of 3.25mm (UK10/US3) needles

TENSION
28sts and 36 rows to 10cm (4in) over st st on
3.25mm (UK10/US3) needles

NOTIONS
Large-eyed needle

Child's fingerless gloves

These gloves, with a stretchy, double-twisted rib, keep hands warm and fingertips free. For a professional finish, shape a vertical line around the base of each thumb by increasing with the subtle M1 technique (see pp.278–279).

Left hand

Using needles A and double cast on method (see p.266), cast on 45sts in yarn A.

ROW 1 (RS): K1, *p1, k1 tbl, rep from * to end.

ROW 2: *P1 tbl, k1, rep from * to last st, p1.

These 2 rows set twisted rib.

Rep last 2 rows until work measures 9cm (3½in), ending with a RS row.

NEXT ROW (WS): Rib 7, M1, [rib 8, M1] x 4, patt to end. Break off yarn A. (50sts)

Change to needles B and working in yarn B, starting with a k row, work in st st for 8 rows, ending with a WS row. **

Thumb gusset

ROW 1 (RS): K22, M1, k3, M1, k to end. (52sts)

Starting with a p row, work 3 rows st st.

ROW 5: K22, M1, k5, M1, k to end. (54sts)

ROW 6 AND ALL FOLL ALT ROWS: P.

ROW 7: K22, M1, k7, M1, k to end. (56sts)

ROW 9: K22, M1, k9, M1, k to end. (58sts)

ROW 11: K22, M1, k11, M1, k to end. (60sts)

ROW 13: K22, M1, k13, M1, k to end. (62sts)

ROW 15: K22, M1, k15, M1, k to end. (64sts)

ROW 16: P.

ROW 17: K40. Turn. Break off yarn B and join in yarn A.

ROW 18: P17. Turn.

Working on these 17sts only, work 8 rows as given for twisted rib. Cast off.

Using yarn B, rejoin yarn at base of thumb and k to end.

Starting with a WS row (purlwise), work 15 rows st st without shaping.

First finger

NEXT ROW: K30. Turn. Break off yarn B, join in A.

NEXT ROW (WS): P13. Turn. Cast on 2sts. (15sts for finger)

Working on these 15sts only, work 8 rows as given for twisted rib. Cast off in rib leaving a 15cm (6in) yarn tail.

Second finger

With RS facing and using yarn A, pick up and k2 from base of first finger, k6. Turn.

NEXT ROW (WS): P14. Turn and cast on 2sts. (16sts for second finger)

Working on these 16sts only, work 8 rows as given for twisted rib. Cast off in rib leaving a 15cm (6in) yarn tail.

Third finger

With RS facing and using yarn A, pick up and k2 from base of first finger, k5. Turn.

NEXT ROW (WS): P14. Turn and cast on 2sts. (16sts for third finger)

Working on these 16sts only, work 8 rows as given for twisted rib. Cast off in rib leaving a 15cm (6in) yarn tail.

Fourth finger

With RS facing and using yarn A, pick up and k2 from base of first finger, k5. Turn.

NEXT ROW: P12. Turn and cast on 2sts. (14sts for fourth finger)

Working on these 14sts only, work 6 rows as given for twisted rib. Cast off in rib leaving a long yarn tail.

Use all long yarn tails to sew up corresponding fingers using mattress stitch (see p.302), being especially careful to run as fine a seam as possible. Continue fourth finger seam to cuff. Contrasting coloured yarn should not show if mattress stitch is being worked correctly. Block according to ballband instructions, but do not block rib areas.

Right hand

Work as given for Left hand to **.

Thumb

ROW 1 (RS): K25, M1, k3, M1, k to end. (52sts)

Starting with a p row, work 3 rows st st.

ROW 5: K25, M1, k5, M1, k to end. (54sts)

ROW 6 AND ALL FOLL ALT ROWS: P.

ROW 7: K25, M1, k7, M1, k to end. (56sts)

ROW 9: K25, M1, k9, M1, k to end. (58sts)

ROW 11: K25, M1, k11, M1, k to end. (60sts)

ROW 13: K25, M1, k13, M1, k to end. (62sts)

ROW 15: K25, M1, k15, M1, k to end. (64sts)

ROW 16: P.

ROW 17: K43. Turn.

ROW 18: P17. Turn. Break off yarn B and join in yarn A.

Complete as given for Left hand.

Essential information

DIFFICULTY Moderate

SIZE To fit a child, aged 3-5 years

YARN

Rowan British Sheep Breed DK Undyed 50g

780 Bluefaced Leicester x 1

NEEDLES

1 pair of 3.75mm (UK9/US5) needles

TENSION

22sts and 28 rows to 10cm (4in) over patt on 3.75mm (UK9/US5) needles

NOTIONS

Large-eyed needle

2 x 1cm (½in) red buttons

SPECIAL ABBREVIATIONS

S1 WYIB Slip 1st with yarn in back

S1 WYIF Slip 1st with yarn in front

Child's convertible mittens

Always handy for keeping fingers warm, these mittens can also be worn as fingerless gloves to enable a young child to pick up toys. Use this project to practise your shaping skills and for learning how to knit a button loop.

Mitten (make 2)

Cast on 26sts.

ROW 1: [K2, p2] x 6, k2.

ROW 2: [P2, k2] x 6, p2.

Rep rows 1–2 x 7.

ROW 15: K13, M1 (see pp.278–279), k13. (27sts)
Continue in st st from now on shaping as described in rows below.

ROW 17: K1, M1, k11, [M1, k1] x 3, M1, k11, M1, k1. (33sts)

ROW 20: P1, M1, p14, M1, p3, M1, p14, M1, p1. (37sts)

ROW 23: K1, M1, k14, M1, k1, M1, k5, M1, k1, M1, k14, M1, k1. (43sts)

ROW 26: P1, M1, p17, M1, p7, M1, p17, M1, p1. (47sts)

ROW 29: K19, M1, k9, M1, k19. (49sts)

ROW 30: P30 turn piece (start of thumb).

ROW 31: K11.

ROWS 32-36: Working only these 11sts, st st.

ROW 37: K2tog, k2, s1 wyib, k2tog, psso, k2, k2tog. (7sts)

ROW 38: P2tog, s1 wyif, p2tog, psso, p2tog. (3sts)

ROW 39: K3tog and pull thread through. Back to the hand.

Introduce a new ball of yarn and finish the second half of row 30, p19.

ROW 31: K38 working across whole row in one go.

ROWS 32–40: St st.

ROW 41: [K2, p2] x 9, k2.

ROW 42: [P2, k2] x 9, p2.

ROW 43: As row 41.

ROW 44: As row 42.

Cast off following the rib.

With WS facing, sew up the thumb seam and the side of the hand using a neat overstitch so the seam sits flat.

Cap (make 2)

Cast on 38sts.

ROW 1: K2, [p2, k2] x 6.

ROW 2: P2, [k2, p2] x 6.

ROWS 3-4: As rows 1 and 2.

Continue in st st shaping as shown in rows below.

ROW 5: K2tog, k34, k2tog. (36sts)

ROW 6: P16, p2tog, p2tog, p16. (34sts)

ROW 7: K2tog, k30, k2tog. (32sts)

ROW 9: [K2tog, k12, k2tog] x 2. (28sts)

ROW 11: [K2tog, k10, k2tog] x 2. (24sts)

ROW 13: [K2tog, k8, k2tog] x 2. (20sts)

ROW 14: [P2tog] x 2, p2, [p2tog] x 4, p2, [p2tog] x 2. (12sts)

ROW 15: [S1 wyib, k2tog, psso] x 4. (4sts)

ROW 16: P4tog and pull yarn through.

With WS facing, sew up the side seam of the cap from the top down with a neat overstitch (see p.301) and leave the yarn tails long for sewing it to the mitten.

Button loops (make 2)

Cast on 7sts and immediately cast them off again – leave the yarn tails long for sewing.

Making up

Turn your mitten and cap so they are RS out. Place the cap onto the mitten so the cast on rib of the cap sits 4 st st below the rib of the hand. The cap should be upside down in this position and sitting so the seam edge is next to the seam of the hand. From this side sew the cap to the hand, matching stitch-to-stitch along the row using a neat overstitch. Sew in the ends. Then take your button loop and sew each end onto the top of the cap and tie both ends in a knot on the WS and sew the ends in. Now your cap should open and close over the hand and you can see where to place the button.

Chunky mittens

This is a versatile pattern for a pair of child's mittens. It is a relatively easy project that features shaping, simple stocking stitch, M1 increases, and 2x2 ribbing at the cuffs. It is an ideal project for a newcomer to shaped knitting.

Essential information

DIFFICULTY Moderate

SIZE To fit a child, aged 8-10 years

YARN

Debbie Bliss Rialto Chunky 50g

A   **B**

A: 11 Denim x 1

B: 03 Ecru x 1

NEEDLES

1 pair of 6.5 mm (UK3/US10½) needles

TENSION

15sts and 20 rows to 10cm (4in) over patt on 6.5mm (UK3/US10½) needles

Mitten (make 2)

Using yarn A, cast on 18sts.

ROW 1: [K2, p2] x 4, k2.

ROW 2: P2, [k2, p2] x 4.

ROWS 3–10: Rep rows 1–2.

ROW 11: K9, M1 (See pp.278–279), k9. (19sts)

ROW 12: P9, M1, p1, M1, p9. (21sts)

ROW 13: K.

ROW 14: P1, M1, p7, M1, p5, M1, p7, M1, p1. (25sts)

ROW 15: K.

ROW 16: Using yarn B, p11, M1, p3, M1, p11. (27sts)

ROW 17: K.

ROW 18: Using yarn A, p1, M1, p9, M1, p7, M1, p9, M1, p1. (31sts)

ROW 19: K.

ROW 20: P13, M1, p5, M1, p13. (33sts)

ROW 21: K.

ROW 22: P20 turn piece – this is the start of the thumb.

ROW 23: K7.

ROWS 24–27: St st over 7sts.

ROW 28: [P2tog] x 3, p1.

ROW 29: K4 tog and pull yarn through.

Back to the hand

Taking your yarn, continue with the second half of row 22, p13.

ROW 23: K26 working across whole row in one go.

ROWS 24–30: St st using yarn B.

ROWS 31–32: St st using yarn A.

ROW 33: [K2tog, k9, k2tog] x 2. (22sts)

ROW 34: [P2tog, p7, p2tog] x 2. (18sts)

ROW 35: [K2tog, k5, k2tog] x 2. (14sts)

ROW 36: [S1 wyif, p2tog, psso] x 4, p2tog.

ROW 37: K5tog and pull yarn through.

Making up

With WS facing, oversew down the thumb seam and the side seam then sew in the ends.

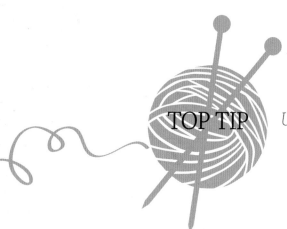

TOP TIP   *Use M1 rather than other increases around the thumb to avoid leaving holes.*

Newborn mittens

Keep a newborn baby warm with these thumbless mittens knitted in stocking stitch. Worked in lightweight 4-ply yarn, the mittens are knitted in 100 per cent pure wool so they don't irritate delicate skin. An optional crocheted cord keeps the mittens together so they won't get lost if one falls off.

Essential information

DIFFICULTY Easy

SIZE To fit a newborn baby

YARN

Patons Fairytale Dreamtime 4-ply 50g

A   **B**

A: 333 Sweet pink x 1
B: 2934 Pastel blue x 1

NEEDLES

A: 1 pair of 2.75mm (UK12/US2) needles
B: 1 pair of 3.75mm (UK9/US5) needles
C: Crochet hook (optional)

A
B
C

TENSION

28st and 36 rows to 10cm (4in) over st st on 3.75mm (UK9/US5) needles

NOTIONS

Large-eyed needle

Mitten (make 2)

Using needles A and yarn A, cast on 30sts.
Beg k, st st 4 rows.
NEXT ROW (RS): Join in yarn B. K1B, [k1A, k2B] to last 2sts, k1A, k1B.
Cont in patt, carrying yarn not in use across WS of work:
ROW 1 (WS): *K1B, [p1A, k2B] to last 2sts, p1A, k1B.
ROW 2: P1B, [k1A, p2B] to last 2sts, k1A, p1B.*
Rep * to * x 2.
ROW 3: As row 1.
Break off B. Change to needles B and beg k row, cont in st st until work measures 8cm (3in) from beg, ending after p row.

Shape top

ROW 1: K1, [k2tog, k3] to last 4sts, k2tog, k2. (24sts)
ROW 2: P.
ROW 3: K1, [k2tog, k2] to last 3sts, k2tog, k1. (18sts)
ROW 4: [P2tog] x 9. (9sts)
ROW 5: [K2tog] x 2, k1, [k2tog] x 2. (5sts)
Break yarn, thread end through rem sts, gather up tightly and fasten off.

Making up

Join side seams. If making the cord, use a crochet hook and yarns A and B tog to make a chain and sew one end to inside of each mitten.

TOP TIP *Two-coloured wristbands add a simple design detail.*

Crocheting a cord Make a slip knot and slide it onto a crochet hook. With your yarn hand forefinger, yarnover the hook from back to front (see p.281). Slide the yarn from the yarnover into the inner bend of the hook. Pull the hook carrying the wrapped strand of yarn through the loop on your hook. Repeat to create a chain as a cord.

Self-striping socks

These colourful socks are quick to knit and have a reinforced heel for a good fit. The luxurious Japanese silk yarn creates its own striped pattern as the socks grow and has enough strength to make hard-wearing socks.

Essential information

DIFFICULTY Moderate

SIZE To fit an adult female, shoe size UK 5-8

YARN

Noro Silk Garden Sock 100g

289 x 2

NEEDLES

4 x 4.5mm (UK7/US7) double-pointed needles

TENSION

19sts and 25 rows to 10cm (4in) over st st on 4.5mm (UK7/US7) needles

NOTIONS

Large-eyed needle

Cuff edging

Using the double cast on method (see p.266), cast on 40sts.
Divide sts between three needles and arrange as follows:
Needle 1: 10 heel sts.
Needle 2: 20 instep sts.
Needle 3: 10 heel sts.
NEXT ROUND: [K1 tbl, p1] to end of round.
Last row sets twisted rib. Work in this patt as set for a further 9 rows.

Leg

Work in st st (k every round) until work measures 13cm (5¼in).

Divide for heel

K10, turn.
S1 purlwise, p19 onto same double-pointed needle. Divide remaining 20sts between two needles.
With RS facing, work back and forth as follows:
ROW 1: *S1p, k1. Rep from * to end.
ROW 2: S1p, p to end.
Rep these 2 rows x 3 (8 rows in total).

Turn heel

ROW 1 (RS): K11, skpo, k1. Turn.
ROW 2 (WS): S1, p4, p2tog, p1. Turn.
ROW 3: S1, k5, skpo, k1. Turn.
ROW 4: S1, p6, p2tog, p1. Turn.
ROW 5: S1, k7, skpo, k1. Turn.
ROW 6: S1, p8, p2tog, p1. Turn.
ROW 7: S1, k9, skpo, k1. Turn.
ROW 8: S1, p10, p2tog. Turn.
12sts remain. K6.

Heel gusset

Rearrange sts on needles 2 and 3 so they now sit on the same needle. One needle is now spare. Use this spare needle to knit across the remaining 6 heel sts.
Continuing with the same needle, pick up 6sts along the side of the heel, pick up a loop of yarn to M1 from between instep and heel sts (needle 1 has 13sts in total).
On next needle, k across 20 instep sts (needle 2). With free needle, pick up and knit from row below the first heel st to M1. With same needle, pick up 6sts along side of the heel and work across remaining heel sts (needle 3 has 13sts in total).

Shape gusset

ROUND 1: (Dec round).
Needle 1: K to 3sts from end. K2tog, k1.
Needle 2: (Instep.) Work even.
Needle 3: K1, skpo, work to end.
ROUND 2: K.
Repeat rounds 1 and 2 x 2. (40sts)

Foot

Continue working in rounds until foot measures 20cm (8in) from base of heel.

Shape toe

ROUND 1: Work to last 3sts on needle 1, k2tog, k1. Needle 2, k1, ssk, work to last 3sts, k2tog, k1.
Needle 3, k1, ssk, complete round.
ROUND 2: Work even.
Rep rounds 1 and 2 until 28sts remain in total. Work round 1 only until 12sts remain (6 instep sts, 6 sole sts).

Making up

K across sts on needle 1. Turn sock inside out through the middle of the needles. Slip sts from needle 3 to opposite end of needle 1. Holding two needles together, and with WS facing, cast off using three needle cast off (see p.271). Darn in ends. Work second sock.

Luxury bed socks

These chunky-yarn slipper socks are knitted flat, not in the round. Cable designs are created by moving knit stitches to the left or right of the stitches next to them using a cable needle. Refer to the Special abbreviations, below, for how many stitches to cable.

Essential information

DIFFICULTY Difficult

SIZE To fit an adult woman, shoe size UK 4–6

YARN

Debbie Bliss Rialto Chunky 50g

016 Pink x 2

NEEDLES

A: 1 pair of 6mm (UK4/US10) needles

B: Cable needle

TENSION

15sts and 20 rows to 10cm (4in) over patt on 6mm (UK4/US10) needles

NOTIONS

1 stitch holder

Large-eyed needle

SPECIAL ABBREVIATIONS

C2F Cross 2 front: slip next st to cable needle (cn) and hold at front of work, k next st from LH needle then k st from cn

C2B Cross 2 back: slip next st to cn and hold at the back of work, knit next st from LH needle then k st from cn

S1 WYIF Slip 1st with yarn in front

S1 WYIB Slip 1st with yarn in back

Right foot

Using needles A cast on 37sts.

ROW 1: [K2, p2] x 9, k1.

ROW 2: P1, [k2, p2] x 9.

ROW 3–8: As rows 1–2.

ROW 9: K1, p14, [k1, C2F] x 2, k8, [C2B] x 2, k1.

ROW 10: P22, k14, p1.

ROW 11: K1, p14, k1, [k1, C2F] x 2, C4F, C4B, [C2B, k1] x 2, k1.

ROW 12: As row 10.

ROW 13: As row 9.

ROW 14: P.

ROW 15: K5 make a heel over next 7sts.

Making a heel

K7, turn your piece, p7. K another 5 rows of st st over these 7sts.

Before doing your next p row use a stitch holder to go through each of the edge stitches of the previous 6 rows you completed. Slip one of these onto the needle with the heel stitches. P this then p7. Insert a stitch holder on this edge, too, p the last of these sts from the holder.

Turn your piece

Slip the next stitch from the stitch holder, k9, then k the next stitch from the holder on this side of your knitting. Turn your piece, slip the next stitch from the holder, p11 then p the next stitch from the holder.

Continue like this until your heel has 19sts in it, all the held stitches are used, and you can finish the second half of row 15.

K5, C2F, k1, C2F, C4F, C4B, [C2B, k1] x 2, k1.

ROW 16: P24, p2tog, p17, p2tog, p4. (47sts)

ROW 17: K3, k2tog, k17, k2tog, k3, C2F, k1, C2F, k8, [C2B, k1] x 2, k1. (45sts)

ROW 18: P.

ROW 19: K25, C2F, k1, C2F, C4F, C4B, C2B, k1, C2B, k2.

ROW 20: P21, p2tog, p19, p2tog, p1. (43sts)

ROW 21: K1, k2tog, k17, k2tog, k1, C2F, k1, C2F, k8, C2B, k1, C2B, k2. (41sts)

ROW 22: P21, p2tog, p15, p2tog, p1. (39sts)

ROW 23: K1, k2tog, k13, k2tog, k1, C2F, k1, C2F, C4F, C4B, C2B, k1, C2B, k2. (37sts)

ROW 24: P22, k13, p2.

ROW 25: K2, p13, k2, C2F, k1, C2F, k8, [C2B, k1] x 2, k1.

ROW 26: As row 24.

Follow cable pattern as set until row 45.

ROW 46: P.

ROW 47: K.

ROW 48: P2tog, p15, s1 wyif, p2tog psso, p15, p2tog.

ROW 49: K2tog, k13, s1 wyib, k2tog psso, k13, k2tog.

ROW 50: P2tog, p11, s1 wyif, p2tog psso, p11, p2tog.

ROW 51: K2tog, k9, s1 wyib, k2tog psso, k9, k2tog.

ROW 52: P2tog, p7, s1 wyif, p2tog psso, p7, p2tog.

ROW 53: K2tog x 8, k1.

ROW 54: [S1 wyif, p2tog psso] x 3.

ROW 55: K3tog.

Left foot

Cast on 37sts.

ROW 1: K1, [p2, k2] x 9.

ROW 2: [P2, k2] x 9, p1.

ROW 3–8: As rows 1–2.

ROW 9: K1, [k1, C2F] x 2, k8, [C2B, k1] x 2, k1, p14, k1.

ROW 10: P1, k14, p22.

ROW 11: K1, [k1, C2F] x 2, C4F, C4B, [C2B, k1] x 2, k1, p14, k1.

ROW 12: As row 10.

ROW 13: As row 9.

ROW 14: P.

ROW 15: K1, [k1, C2F] x 2, C4F, C4B, C2B, k1, C2B, k5.

Make heel over next 7sts, k5. (49sts)

ROW 16: P4, p2tog, p17, p2tog, p24. (47sts)

ROW 17: K1, [k1, C2F] x 2, k8, C2B, k1, C2B, k3, k2tog, k17, k2tog, k3. (45sts)

ROW 18: P.

ROW 19: K1, [k1, C2F] x 2, C4F, C4B, C2B, k1, C2B, k25.

ROW 20: P1, p2tog, p19, p2tog, p21. (43sts)

ROW 21: K1, [k1, C2F] x 2, k8, C2B, k1, C2B, k1, k2tog, k17, k2tog, k1. (41sts)

ROW 22: P1, p2tog, p15, p2tog, p21. (39sts)

ROW 23: K1, [k1, C2F] x 2, C4F, C4B, C2B, k1, C2B, k1, k2tog, k13, k2tog, k1. (37sts)

ROW 24: P2, k13, p22.

ROW 25: K1, [k1, C2F] x 2, k8, C2B, k1, C2B, k2, p13, k2.

Continue on following cable pattern as set until you reach row 45. Repeat rows 46–55 as for Right foot.

Making up

Pull through a long piece of yarn, and with RS facing, use it to sew up the side seam with a neat overstitch matching the rows together.

Slouchy wellie warmers

These ribbed boot socks are worked on two needles with a seam up the side.

Essential information

DIFFICULTY Moderate

SIZE To fit an adult female, shoe size UK 4-6

YARN

Hayfield Bonus Chunky 100g

817 Mill blue x 2

NEEDLES

A: 1 pair of 6mm (UK4/US10) needles

B: Cable needle

TENSION 13sts and 18 rows to 10cm (4in) over st st on 6mm (UK4/US10) needles

NOTIONS

2 stitch holders

Large-eyed needle

SPECIAL ABBREVIATIONS

CN Cable needle

C4B Slip next 2sts to cn and hold at back, k next 2sts from LH needle then k2 from cn

C4(6)F Slip next 2(3)sts to cn and hold at front, k next 2(3)sts from LH needle then k2(3) from cn

S1 WYIB Slip 1st with yarn in back

S1 WYIF Slip 1st with yarn in front

Right foot

Cast on 47sts.

ROW 1: K1, [p2, k2] x 11, p1, k1.

ROW 2: P1, k1, [p2, k2] x 11, p1.

For all rows not listed, k all k sts, p all p sts.

ROWS 3–6: As rows 1–2.

ROW 7: K1, p2tog, k2, [p2, k2] x 10, p1, k1. (46sts)

ROW 13: K1, p1, k2, p2tog, k2, [p2, k2] x 9, k1. (45sts)

ROW 17: K1, [p1, k2] x 2, p2tog, k2, [p2, k2] x 8, p1, k1. (44sts)

ROW 23: K1, [p1, k2] x 3, p2tog, k2, [p2, k2] x 7, p1, k1. (43sts)

ROW 27: K1, [p1, k2] x 4, p2tog, k2, [p2, k2] x 6, p1, k1. (42sts)

ROW 33: K1, [p1, k2] x 5, p2tog, k2, [p2, k2] x 5, p1, k1. (41sts)

ROW 37: K1, [p1, k2] x 6, p2tog, k2, [p2, k2] x 4, p1, k1. (40sts)

ROW 43: K1, [p1, k2] x 7, p2tog, k2, [p2, k2] x 3, p1, k1. (39sts)

ROW 47: K1, [p1, k2] x 8, p2tog, k2, [p2, k2] x 2, p1, k1. (38sts)

ROW 53: K1, [p1, k2] x 9, [p2tog, k2] x 2, p1, k1. (36sts)

ROW 58: P5, k2tog, p6, k2tog, p4, p2tog, p15. (33sts)

ROW 59: K20, p1, k6, p1, k5.

ROW 60: P5, k1, p6, k1, p20.

ROW 61: K16, C4B, p1, C6F, p1, C4B, k1.

ROW 62: As row 60.

ROW 63: As row 59.

ROW 64: P5, k1, p6, k1, p9 make a heel.

Making a heel

P7 turn, k the same 7sts. K 4 rows of st st. Use two holders to pick up the edge st (on both sides) of each of first 5 rows. Make sure opening end of the holders are at top of piece. Before you p next row, s1 off holder and p, p7, then p first stitch off next stitch holder. Before knitting next row, slip next st from holder and k, k9, k next stitch off holder. Repeat until all stitches on holders are used. Finish the rest of row 64 with p4. (43sts)

ROW 65: K3, k2tog, k15, k2tog, k4, C4B, p1, k6, p1, C4B, k1. (41sts)

ROW 66: P5, k1, p6, k1, p7, p2tog, p15, p2tog, p2. (39sts)

ROW 67: K26, p1, C6F, p1, k5.

ROW 68: P5, k1, p6, k1, p26.

ROW 69: K1, k2tog, k17, k2tog, C4B, p1, k6, C4B, k1. (37sts)

ROW 70: P5, k1, p6, k1, p4, p2tog, p15, p2tog, p1. (35sts)

ROW 71: K1, k2tog, k13, k2tog, k4, p1, k6, p1, k5. (33sts)

ROW 72: P5, k1, p6, k1, p20.

ROW 73: K16, C4B, p1, C6F, p1, C4B, k1.

ROW 74 AND ALL OTHER EVEN ROWS UNTIL STATED: As row 72.

ROW 75: K20, p1, k6, p1, k5.

ROW 77: K16, C4B, p1, k6, p1, C4B, k1.

ROW 79: K20, p1, C6F, p1, k5.

ROW 81: As row 77.

ROW 83: As row 75.

ROW 85: As row 73.

ROW 87: As row 75.

ROW 89: As row 77.

ROW 91: As row 79.

ROW 92: P.

ROW 93: K.

ROW 94: P2tog, p13, s1 wyif, p2tog, psso, p13, p2tog. (29sts)

ROW 95: K2tog, k11, s1 wyib, k2tog, psso, k11, k2tog. (25sts)

ROW 96: P2tog, p9, s1 wyif, p2tog, psso, p9, p2tog. (21sts)

ROW 97: K2tog, k7, s1 wyib, k2tog, psso, k7, k2tog. (17sts)

ROW 98: P2tog, p5, s1 wyif, p2tog, psso, p5, p2tog. (13sts)

ROW 99: K2tog, [s1 wyib, k2tog, psso] x 3, k2tog. (5sts)

ROW 100: P5 tog.

Left foot

Cast on 47sts.

ROW 1: K1, p1, [k2, p2] x 11, k1.

ROW 2: P1, [k2, p2] x 11, k1, p1.

ROWS 3-6: As rows 1–2.

ROW 7: K1, p1, [k2, p2] x 10, k2, p2tog, k1. (46sts)
Cont to follow the stitch layout in the previous row as before dec in the next rib along in the following rows: 13, 17, 23, 27, 33, 37, 43, 47. Dec both last rem ribs as you did for Right foot in row 53.

ROW 58: P15, p2tog, p4, k2tog, p6, k2tog, p5. (33sts)

ROW 59: K5, p1, k6, p1, k20.

ROW 60: P20, k1, p6, k1, p5.

ROW 61: K1, C4F, p1, C6B, p1, C4F, k16.

ROW 62: As row 60.

ROW 63: As row 59.

ROW 64: P4 make heel as for Left foot. Finish row 64 p9, k1, p6, k1, p5. (43sts)

ROW 65: K1, C4F, p1, k6, p1, C4F, k4, k2tog, k15, k2tog, k3. (41sts)

ROW 66: P2, p2tog, p15, p2tog, p3, p4, k1, p6, k1, p5.

ROW 67: K5, p1, C6B, p1, k22.
Cont making cables as set until row 91.

ROWS 92-100: Rep rows 92–100 of Right foot.

Making up

Sew up the side seam. With RS facing, overstitch matching up stitch to stitch so the seam sits flat.

Essential information

DIFFICULTY Difficult

SIZE To fit an adult male, shoe size UK 9–12

YARN

Rowan Felted Tweed DK 50g

157 Camel x 2

NEEDLES

A: 4 x 3mm (UK11/US n/a) double-pointed needles
B: Cable needle

A

B

TENSION

30sts and 36 rows to 10cm (4in) over patt, when slightly stretched on 3mm (UK11/US n/a) needles

NOTIONS

Large-eyed needle

SPECIAL ABBREVIATIONS

C2F Cross 2 front: Slip 1st on to cable needle (cn) and leave at front of work, k1, then k1 from cn
C2B Cross 2 back: Slip 1st on to cn and leave at back of work, k1, then k1 from cn
T3F Twist 3 front: Slip 2sts on to cn and leave at front of work, k1, then k2 from cn

Cabled ankle socks

Hard-wearing at both toe point and heel, these tweed socks are finished with a strong inner toe seam for durability. The cable pattern is not difficult to work, but take your time when using cable needles alongside double-pointed needles.

Using only two double-pointed needles, cast on 68sts using double cast on method (see p.266). Rearrange sts over three needles so that there are 22, 22, and 24sts.

Cuff edging

ROUND 1: K1, *p2, k2, to last 3sts, p2, k1.
Rep last round x 17 (18 rounds worked in total).
SET-UP ROUND: *C2B, C2F, rep from * to end.
NEXT ROUND: *P1, k2, p1, rep from * to end.
INC ROUND: *P1, k1, M1, k1, p1, rep from * to end. (85sts)

Leg

Commence Patt:
PATT ROUND 1: *P1, k3, p1, rep from * to end.
PATT ROUND 2: *P1, T3F, p1, rep from * to end.
PATT ROUNDS 3 AND 4: As round 1.
Rep patt rounds 1–4 until work measures 16cm (6¼in), ending with round 3.

Divide for heel

ROW 1: [P1, k2tog, k1, p1] x 4. Turn.
ROW 2: S1p, p16, [p2tog, p3] x 3, p2tog, p2. Turn. (77sts)
These 32sts set heel. Divide rem 45sts between two double-pointed needles and work heel flap as follows:
ROW 1 (RS): S1, k31. Turn.
ROW 2: S1, p31. Turn.
Rep last 2 rows x 13, ending with a WS row (28 rows worked in total).

Turn heel

SET-UP ROW: S1, k19, skpo, k1. Turn.
ROW 1: S1k, p9, p2tog, p1. Turn.
ROW 2: S1k, k10, skpo, k1. Turn.
ROW 3: S1k, p11, p2tog, p1. Turn.
ROW 4: S1k, k12, skpo, k1. Turn.
Cont shaping in this way, taking 1st more into heel shaping on every row until row "s1k p17, p2tog, p1, turn" has been worked.
NEXT ROW: S1k, k18, skpo. Turn.
NEXT ROW: S1k, p18, p2tog. Turn (20 live sts remain). K across these 20sts, pick up and k16 down LH side of heel flap, work in patt across 45 instep sts, pick up and k16 up RH side of heel flap, k10. This point marks end of round. (97sts)
Rearrange sts so that 26sts lie on needles 1 and 3 and 45 instep sts sit separately on needle 2.
NEXT ROUND: K10, k16 tbl, work in patt across 45 instep sts, k16 tbl, k10.
INSTEP-SHAPING ROUND: K to last 3sts on needle 1, k2tog, k1, work in patt across 45 instep sts, k1, skpo, k to end.
NEXT ROUND: K to instep, work in patt across 45 instep sts, k to end.
Rep last 2 rounds until 77sts remain (16sts on needles 1 and 3, 45sts on needle 2).
Cont in patt with st st on sole, and instep in patt until work measures 20cm (8in) from start of heel shaping.

Shape toe

DEC ROUND: K16, [p1, k2tog, k1, p1] x 9, k to end. (68sts)
Rearrange sts so that there are 17sts on needles 1 and 3, and 34sts on needle 2.
NEXT ROUND: K.
TOE-SHAPING ROUND: K to last 3sts on needle 1, k2tog, k1. On needle 2, k1, skpo, k to last 3sts on needle, k2tog, k1. On needle 3, k1, skpo, k to end. (64sts)
K 3 rounds without shaping.
Dec as set by toe-shaping round, dec on next and following third round, then on 2 foll alt rounds and every foll round until 20sts remain.
NEXT ROUND: K across 5 rem sts on needle 1, turn work inside out through the centre of the double-pointed needles. Slide 5sts from needle 3 to needle 1 (10sts on each needle). Cast off using three needle cast off (see p.271).
Darn in ends. Work second sock.
To wash the socks, hand wash in warm water, reshape and dry flat.

Essential information

DIFFICULTY Moderate

SIZE To fit an adult female, shoe size UK 4-6

YARN

Debbie Bliss Baby Cashmerino 50g

A: 027 Denim x 3
B: 006 Candy pink x 2
C: 002 Apple x 2

NEEDLES

1 pair of 3.75mm (UK9/US5) needles

TENSION

25sts and 34 rows to 10cm (4in) over st st on 3.75mm (UK9/US5) needles

NOTIONS

1 stitch holder and spare needle
Stitch markers
Large-eyed needle

Striped knee-high socks

Adjust the length by knitting fewer or more rows after you shape the heel. Measure your legs first and work out the number of rows needed before you cast on.

Socks (make 2)

With yarn A, cast on 66sts.
ROW 1: K1, *k2, p2. Rep from * to last st, k1.
Rep until your work measures 3.5cm (1³⁄₈in).
ROWS 1–4: Join in yarn B and work 4 rows st st.
ROWS 5–8: Join in yarn C and work 4 rows st st.
ROWS 9–14: With yarn A, work 6 rows st st.
Cont to work 14 rows stripe sequence, until your work measures 45cm (17³⁄₄in) from cast on edge, finishing with a RS row.
NEXT ROW: P4, [p2tog, p5] x 8, p2tog, p4. (57sts)
Cont in stripe as set until work measures 61cm (23¹⁄₂in) from cast on edge.
Break off yarn.

Divide for heel

With RS facing, slip first 14sts onto RH needle, slip next 29sts onto a stitch holder for instep, slip rem 14sts onto a spare needle.
With WS facing, join yarn A to instep edge of 14sts on RH needle from previous row, p to end, turn spare needle around and p14 on spare needle. (28sts)
With yarn A, cont as follows:
NEXT ROW: K1, *k1, s1p, rep from * to last st, k1.
NEXT AND EVERY FOLL ALT ROW: P.
Rep these 2 rows x 9.

Turn heel

ROW 1: K15, skpo, k1, turn.
ROW 2: P4, p2tog, p1, turn.
ROW 3: K5, skpo, k1, turn.
ROW 4: P6, p2tog, p1, turn.
ROW 5: K7, skpo, k1, turn.
ROW 6: P8, p2tog, p1, turn.
ROW 7: K9, skpo, k1, turn.
ROW 8: P10, p2tog, p1, turn.

ROW 9: K11, skpo, k1, turn.
ROW 10: P12, p2tog, p1, turn.
ROW 11: K13, skpo, k1, turn.
ROW 12: P14, p2tog, p1. (16sts)
Break off yarn.
With RS facing, join yarn A to instep edge, pick up and k11 evenly along side edge of heel, k across 16sts of heel, then pick up and k11 along other side of heel. (38sts)
P 1 row.
ROW 1: K1, skpo, k to last 3sts, k2tog, k1. (36sts)
ROW 2 AND EVERY FOLL ALT ROW: P.
ROW 3: K.
ROW 4: As row 2.
Rep these 4 rows x 4. (28sts)
Cont in st st until work measures 18cm (7in) from back of heel, finishing with RS facing. (Length can be adjusted here, allowing 3.5cm (1³⁄₈in) for the toe shaping.)

**Shape toe

ROW 1: K1, skpo, k2, *p2, k2, rep from * to last 3sts, k2tog, k1. (26sts)
ROW 2: P2, *p2, k2, rep from * to last 4sts, p4.
ROW 3: K1, skpo, k1, *p2, k2, rep from * to last 6sts, p2, k1, k2tog, k1. (24sts)
ROW 4: P3, *k2, p2, rep from * to last 5sts, k2, p3.
Keeping continuity of rib as set, cont to dec 1st at each end of next and foll 4 alt rows. (14sts)
NEXT ROW: P2, *k2, p2, rep from * to end. **
Break off yarn and leave these 14sts on a spare needle.

Instep (RS facing)

Keeping continuity of stripes, k across 29sts on stitch holder, dec 1st at centre (28sts). (Place markers at each end of this row.)

Starting with a p row, work in st st and stripes as set until work measures the same as sole to toe shaping from markers.

Shape toe

With yarn A, work as for lower foot from ** to **.
Placing RS of upper foot facing, cast off as follows: P2tog 1st from upper and lower foot, across all sts, casting off as each st is worked.

Making up

Join the upper and lower foot seams and back seam (see pp.300–302).

Leg warmers

Worked in knit one, purl one rib, instructions are given here for both seamless legwarmers knitted in the round on four double-pointed needles, and for ones that can be knitted on two regular needles and seamed afterwards. The choice is yours.

Essential information

DIFFICULTY Easy

SIZE One size fits all, 55cm (22in) long

YARN

King Cole Merino Blend DK 50g

791 Denim x 4

NEEDLES

A: 4 x 3.75mm (UK9/US5) double-pointed needles, or 1 pair of 3.75mm (UK9/US5) needles
B: 4 x 4mm (UK8/US6) double-pointed needles, or 1 pair of 4mm (UK8/US6) needles

A

B

TENSION

22sts and 30 rows to 10cm (4in) over st st on 4mm (UK8/US6) needles

NOTIONS

Large-eyed needle

In the round (make 2)

With double-pointed needles A, cast on 60sts and distribute them evenly on 3 needles.
Work in rounds of k1, p1 rib for 5cm (2¼in).
Change to double-pointed needles B and cont in rib until your work measures 50cm (20in) from beg. Change to needles A and rib a further 5cm (2¼in). Cast off in rib.

With seam (make 2)

With straight needles A, cast on 60sts.
Work in k1, p1 rib for 5cm (2¼in).
Change to straight needles B and cont in rib until work measures 50cm (20in) from beg.
Change to straight needles A, and rib a further 5cm (2¼in).
Cast off in rib.
Join back leg seam (see pp.300–302).

TOP TIP   *Continue the rib pattern to increase the height of the leg warmers.*

Essential information

DIFFICULTY Moderate

SIZE To fit a child, aged 2-3 (4-5, 6-7) years

YARN

Sublime Baby Cashmere Merino Silk 4-ply 50g

A   **B**   **C**

A: 03 Vanilla x 1   **B:** 04 Gooseberry x 1
C: 100 Paddle x 1

NEEDLES

1 pair of 3.25mm (UK10/US3) needles

NOTIONS

2 stitch holders or spare needles
Large-eyed needle

TENSION

30sts and 40 rows over 10cm (4in) in st st using
3.25mm (UK10/US3) needles

Child's stripey socks

Knit these striped patterned socks to fit a child aged between two and seven years. The shaped ribbed heels add strength and durability to the socks while the stretchy ribbed cuffs and toes create extra comfort for little feet.

Socks (make 2)

With yarn A, cast on 46 (50:54) sts.

RIB ROW: K1, *k2, p2, rep from * to last st, k1.

Rep this row x 3.

Working in st st, k stripes as follows:

ROWS 1–4: Yarn A.

ROWS 5–8: Yarn B.

ROWS 9–12: Yarn A.

ROWS 13–16: Yarn C.

Rep these 16 rows once more, then rows 1–4 (1–8:1–12) once more, dec 1st at centre of last row. (45 (49:53) sts)

Break off yarn.

Divide for heel

NEXT ROW: Slip first 11 (12:13) sts onto RH needle, slip next 23 (25:27) sts onto holder, slip remaining 11 (12:13) sts onto spare needle, turn. With WS facing, join yarn A to instep edge of 11 (12:13) sts on the previous RH needle and p to end, turn spare needle around and p across 11 (12:13) sts on spare needle. (22 (24:26) sts)

NEXT ROW: K1, *k1, s1p, rep from * to last st, k1.

NEXT ROW: P.

Rep these 2 rows x 5 (6:7).

Turn heel

ROW 1: K12 (13:15), skpo, k1, turn.

ROW 2: P4 (4:6), p2tog, p1, turn.

ROW 3: K5 (5:7), skpo, k1, turn.

ROW 4: P6 (6:8), p2tog, p1, turn.

ROW 5: K7 (7:9), skpo, k1, turn.

ROW 6: P8 (8:0), p2tog, p1, turn.

ROW 7: K9 (9:0), skpo, k1, turn.

ROW 8: P10 (10:0), p2tog, p1, turn.

ROW 9: K11 (11:0), skpo, [skpo, k1], turn.

ROW 10: P11 (12:14), p2tog, [p2tog, p1], turn. (12 (14:16) sts)

Break off yarn.

With yarn A and RS facing, join yarn to instep. Pick up and k8 (9:10) sts along side edge of heel, k across 12 (14:16) sts of heel, pick up and k8 (9:10) sts along other side of heel. (28 (32:36) sts)

P 1 row.

ROW 1: K.

ROW 2: P.

ROW 3: K1, skpo, k to last 3sts, k2tog, k1. (26 (30:34) sts)

ROW 4: P.

Rep these 4 rows x 3. (20 (24:28) sts)

Work a further 24 (28:32) rows st st, finishing with a WS row.

Length of foot can be adjusted here.

Shape toes (all sizes)

ROW 1: K1, skpo, *p2, k2, rep from * to last 5sts, p2, k2tog, k1. (18 (22:26) sts)

ROW 2: P1, p2tog, k1, *p2, k2, rep from * to last 6sts, p2, k1, p2tog tbl, p1. (16 (20:24) sts)

ROW 3: K1, skpo, *k2, p2, rep from * to last 5sts, k2, k2tog, k1. (14 (18:22) sts)

ROW 4: P1, p2tog, p1, *k2, p2, rep from * to last 6sts, k2, p1, p2tog tbl, p1. (12 (16:20) sts)

ROW 5: As row 1. (10 (14:18) sts)

Leave remaining sts on spare needle.

2nd and 3rd sizes

ROW 6: P2, *k2, p2, rep from * to end.

ROW 7: K1, skpo, p1, *k2, p2, rep from * to last 6sts, k2, p1, k2tog, k1 (12:16) st.

2nd size only

Leave 12sts on spare needle.

3rd size only

ROW 8: P2, k1, *p2, k2, rep from * to last 5sts, p2, k1, p2.

ROW 9: As row 3. (14sts)

Leave these 14sts on spare needle. Join yarn B (yarn A:yarn C) to sts left on st holder for upper foot. Cont working in stripes as set for 36 (40:44) rows, dec 3sts (1st) on last row for first and second sizes, and inc 1st at centre of last row for third size. (20 (24:28) sts)

With yarn A only, complete toe shaping as for lower foot. Join back seam and foot seams (see pp.300–302).

Baby booties

These tiny booties curve to follow the shape of a baby's foot, providing plenty of room for growth. Increases and decreases curve the booties as you knit. We've chosen a soft DK yarn and used smaller than usually recommended needles to achieve a taut, firm fabric suitable for tiny toes.

Essential information

DIFFICULTY Moderate

SIZE To fit a newborn baby

YARN

Debbie Bliss Rialto DK 50g

01 White x 1

NEEDLES

A: 1 pair of 3mm (UK11/US n/a) needles
B: 1 pair of 2.75mm (UK12/US2) needles

———————————————————— A
———————————————————— B

TENSION

25sts and 46 rows to 10cm (4in) over g st on 3mm (UK11/US n/a) needles

NOTIONS

70cm (27½in) co-ordinating ribbon, 5-7mm (¼-⅜in) wide
Large-eyed needle

Booties (make 2)

Using needle A, cast on 37sts.
ROW 1 (WS): K.
ROW 2: Inc in next st, k15, inc in next st, k3, inc in next st, k15, inc in last st. (41sts)
ROWS 3, 5 AND 7: K.
ROW 4: Inc in next st, k17, inc in next st, k3, inc in next st, k17, inc in last st. (45sts)
ROW 6: Inc in next st, k19, inc in next st, k3, inc in next st, k19, inc in last st. (49sts)
K 16 rows, ending with a WS row.

Shape for toe

ROW 1 (RS): K17, skpo, k11, k2tog, k17. (47sts)
ROW 2: K17, skpo, k9, k2tog, k17. (45sts)
ROW 3: K17, skpo, k7, k2tog, k17. (43sts)
ROW 4: K17, skpo, k5, k2tog, k17. (41sts)
ROW 5: K17, skpo, k3, k2tog, k17. (39sts)
ROW 6: K17, skpo, k1, k2tog, k17. (37sts)
ROW 7: K17, sk2p, k17. (35sts)

Shape for ankle

Change to needle B and work as follows:
NEXT ROW (RS): K1, *p1, k1, rep from * to end.
NEXT ROW: P1, *k1, p1, rep from * to end.
Rep last 2 rows x 2.
EYELET ROW: K1, *yon, k2tog, rep from * to end.
NEXT ROW: P1, *k1, p1, rep from * to end.

Work edging

NEXT ROW: (Casting off) *k2, pass first st over second so that 1st rem on RH needle as if casting off, place this 1st back on LH needle, rep from * until 1st remains.

Making up

Fasten off, leaving a long yarn tail. Join row ends with mattress stitch using the yarn tail from cast off edge. Fold over ribbed edging and catch to main bootie with a long running stitch. Thread ribbon through eyelets and tie in a bow.

TOP TIP *The mattress stitch seam makes the knitting appear continuous.*

Projects:
Home and accessories

New baby's blanket

Knitted in 100 per cent natural wool yarn, this blanket will make an ideal gift for a newborn. A textured moss stitch is used for the border, which prevents the edges from curling. The main part of the blanket has a diamond design, created using basic knit and purl stitches.

Essential information

DIFFICULTY Easy

SIZE 62 x 87cm (24½ x 34¼in)

YARN

Debbie Bliss Rialto DK 50g

01 White x 7

NEEDLES

1 pair of 4mm (UK8/US6) needles

TENSION

22sts and 30 rows to 10cm (4in) over patt on 4mm (UK8/US6) needles

NOTIONS

Large-eyed needle

Bottom border design

Cast on 137sts.

MOSS ST ROW: [K1, p1] to last st, k1.

This row forms moss st.

Rep this row x 5.

Commence pattern

ROW 1 (RS): [K1, p1] x 2, k4, *p1, k7, rep from * to last 9sts, p1, k4, [p1, k1] x 2.

ROWS 2 AND 8: [K1, p1] x 2, p3, *k1, p1, k1, p5, rep from * to last 10sts, k1, p1, k1, p3, [p1, k1] x 2.

ROWS 3 AND 7: [K1, p1] x 2, k2, *p1, k3, rep from * to last 7sts, p1, k2, [p1, k1] x 2.

ROWS 4 AND 6: [K1, p1] x 2, p1, *k1, p5, k1, p1, rep from * to last 4sts, [p1, k1] x 2.

ROW 5: [K1, p1] x 2, *p1, k7, rep from * to last 5sts, p1, [p1, k1] x 2.

Rep rows 1–8 until work measures 84cm (33in) from cast on edge, ending with row 8.

Top border design

MOSS ST ROW: [K1, p1] to last st, k1.

This row forms moss st.

Rep this row x 5.

Cast off in patt.

Darn in ends on WS and block according to the ballband instructions.

TOP TIP   *It is good practice to complete a row before putting your work down.*

Chequered cot blanket

A hand-knitted cot blanket is one of the most cherished items in a child's early years. This blanket is worked using little check stitch (see p.310) on a ground of garter stitch. The ruffled border is worked in stocking stitch to complete the project.

Essential information

DIFFICULTY Easy

SIZE 72.5cm x 1m (28½ x 39in)

YARN

Sublime Extra Fine Merino Wool DK 50g

307 Julep x 11

NEEDLES

1 pair of 4mm (UK8/US6) needles

TENSION

22sts and 28 rows to 10cm (4in) over little check stitch patt on 4mm (UK8/US6) needles

NOTIONS

Large-eyed needle

Cast on 169sts.

ROW 1 (RS): P.

ROW 2: P.

ROW 3: P2, s1 p1 psso, p to last 4sts, p2tog, p2. (167sts)

ROW 4: P.

ROW 5 AND EVERY ALT ROW: K2, sk2p, k to last 5sts, k3tog tbl, k2.

ROW 6 AND EVERY ALT ROW: P.

Rep rows 5 and 6 until 127sts remain.

ROW 25: S1 [25sts from little check stitch patt (see p.310), k25] x 2, 25sts from little check stitch patt, k1.

ROW 26: S1, [p25, k25] x 2, p26.

ROWS 27–30: Rep rows 25 and 26 twice.

ROW 31: As row 25.

ROW 32: S1, [25sts from little check stitch patt, k25] x 2, 25sts from little check stitch patt, k1.

ROW 33: S1, k to end.

ROWS 34–37: Rep rows 32 and 33 twice.

ROW 38: As row 33.

ROWS 39–52: Rep rows 25–38.

ROW 53: S1, [k25, 25sts from little check stitch patt] x 2, k26.

Cont to work with the patt blocks set in this way until you have made 11 reps of the squares.

ROW 333 AND EVERY FOLL ALT ROW: S1, k1, inc 2sts in next st, inc 1st in next st, k to last 4sts, inc 1st in next st, inc 2sts in next st, k2.

ROW 334 AND EVERY FOLL ALT ROW: S1, p2 pass second st on LH needle over first st, p to last 5sts, put point of RH needle through first st on LH needle and p second st, passing both loops off needle together, p3.

ROW 352: S1, p1, inc in next st, pass second st on LH needle over first st, p to last 5sts, put point of RH needle through first st on LH needle and p second st, passing both loops off needle together, inc in next st, p2.

ROWS 353–355: P.

Cast off.

Side panels

With RS facing, pick up and k294 evenly along straight side edge.

ROW 1 (WS): P.

ROW 2: As row 333.

ROW 3: As row 334.

ROWS 4–21: Rep rows 2 and 3.

ROWS 22–24: P.

Cast off.

Rep on opposite straight edge.

Making up

Neatly sew up the corner shaping and then sew in all of the yarn tails. Press gently, encouraging the border to ruffle (refer to p.300 for information about blocking).

Cabled throw

The cables in this sumptuous throw join up to form little arches, which then create a pattern across the knitted fabric. Worked in a warm, chunky-weight yarn the 6-stitch cable pattern is interspersed with rows of garter stitch.

Essential information

DIFFICULTY Easy

SIZE 1 x 1.3m (39 x 51in)

YARN

Patons Silenzio Chunky 50g

90 Stone x 20

NEEDLES

A: 1 pair of 6.5mm (UK3/US10½) needles

B: Cable needle

TENSION

15sts and 22 rows to 10cm (4in) over g st on 6.5mm (UK3/US10½) needles

SPECIAL ABBREVIATIONS

C6F Cable 6 front: slip next 3sts to cable needle (cn) and hold at front, k3 from LH needle then k3 from cn

C6B Cable 6 back: slip next 3sts to cn and hold at back, k3 from LH needle then k3 from cn

Cast on 150sts using needles A.

Bottom border

Work 6 rows: K to end in g st.

Cable design

ROW 1: *K to end.

ROW 2: K4, p6, [k2, p6] to last 4sts, k4.

Rep from * x 3.

ROW 9: K4, C6F, [k2, C6F] to last 4sts, k4.

ROWS 10–14: K to end.

Now rep these 14 rows of cable design once more but on row 15 C6B instead of C6F.

These 28 rows form the design repeat.

Work these 28 rows x 10.

Top border

Work 6 rows of g st.

Cast off.

Cables and garter stitch Breaking the cables with rows of garter stitch creates deep, cosy texture across the throw and makes this project quicker to knit than a solid cable pattern.

TOP TIP *Cabling is when one group of stitches cross over another group.*

Wave and shell throw

Yarnovers and decreases give this throw its wavy pattern (see pp.277–285 for details about increases and decreases), while the lace eyelets (see p.289) create a light and airy feel to the finished project.

Essential information

DIFFICULTY Moderate

SIZE 1 x 1.3m (39 x 51in)

YARN

Rowan Wool Cotton 50g

A   **B**

A: 963 Smalt x 1
B: 900 Antique x 15

NEEDLES

1 pair of 4mm (UK8/US6) needles

TENSION

24sts and 32 rows to 10cm (4in) over st st on 4mm (UK8/US6) needles

NOTIONS

Large-eyed needle

NOTE: Cast on and work rows 1 and 2 in yarn A, for the first time only, then work in yarn B until the final 2 rows and casting off the throw.

Border design

Cast on 254sts in yarn B.
ROW 1: K1, *p2tog x 3, [k1, yon] x 6, p2tog x 3*, rep * to * to last st, k1.
Rep from * to * to last st, k1.
ROWS 2, 4, AND 6: P to end.
ROWS 3 AND 5: K to end.
These 6 rows form the border design.
Work 5 times.

Main section

Commence patt.
ROW 1: K6 *k2tog, k1, yon, k1, yon, k1, skpo, k2*, rep from * to * to last 5sts, k5.
ROWS 2–6: Work st st starting with a p row.
These 6 rows form the main design. Work until your throw measures approx. 1.2m (48in).
Work border design x 4 changing to yarn A for final row.
Using yarn A, work row 1 of the border design once more.
Cast off in yarn A.

Shells

In yarn A, cast on 12sts using the finger loop method (see p.265). K1, k1 and pass back to LH needle. With RH needle lift remaining 10sts over this st and off the needle. Pass st from RH needle to LH needle and lift second st over first st and off the needle. Make a crochet chain (see p.171, but use the stitch from making the shell rather than starting with a slip knot) in the remaining stitch 4sts long, then secure the end leaving enough yarn to sew into the throw. Make 58 shells.
Stitch the shells in place along the edge of the throw.

Home-style blanket

This blanket uses stocking stitch and the intarsia technique (see pp.306–307) to create inlaid colour motifs in individual blocks that are then sewn together. There are three motifs, but you could use just one, or a mixture, if you prefer.

Essential information

DIFFICULTY Moderate

SIZE 1.3 x 1m (51 x 39in)

YARN

Debbie Bliss Donegal Luxury Aran Tweed 50g

A   B   C   D   E

A: 34 Royal purple x 4   **B:** 09 Slate x 3
C: 32 Aqua x 3   **D:** 10 Grey x 6
E: 07 Oatmeal x 4

NEEDLES

A: 1 pair of 5mm (UK6/US8) needles

B: 1.2m (48in), 4.5mm (UK7/US7) circular needle

———————————————— **A**
———————————————— **B**

TENSION

19sts and 25 rows to 10cm (4in) over st st on 5mm (UK6/US8) needles

NOTIONS

Yarn bobbins (optional)
Large-eyed needle

Bordered square (make 10)

Using needles A and yarn B, cast on 48sts. Work as given for Bordered square chart (see p.201) for 68 rows, then cast off.

Heart square (make 5)

Using needles A and yarn E, cast on 48sts. Work as given for Heart square chart (see p.201) for 68 rows, then cast off.

Star square A (make 2)

Using needles A and yarn A, cast on 48sts. Work as given for the Star square A chart (see p.201) for 68 rows, then cast off.

Star square B (make 3)

Using needles A and yarn E, cast on 48sts. Work as given for the Star square B chart (see p.201) for 68 rows, then cast off.

Block all squares according to the ballband instructions and arrange the squares into a 4 x 5 pattern of your choice. Use matress stitch to join all squares together, or try oversewing if preferred.

Bottom and top borders

Using needles B and yarn B, and with RS facing, pick up and k192 across the bottom edge of the blanket (cast on edge of squares). Work 10 rows g st and cast off. Rep for the top edge of the blanket.

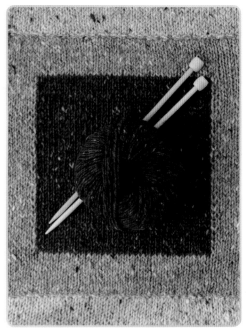

Mattress stitch The best way to sew up seams that appear as if they are knitted together in the first place is by using mattress stitch. See p.302 for a detailed description of how to work this method of making up.

Side borders

Using needles B and yarn B, pick up and k5 from right bottom border edge, 210sts along blanket squares, and 5sts from top border edge. Work 10 rows in g st and cast off. Rep for left border. Darn in the ends and steam the entire blanket lightly under a damp cloth (see p.300).

Bordered square

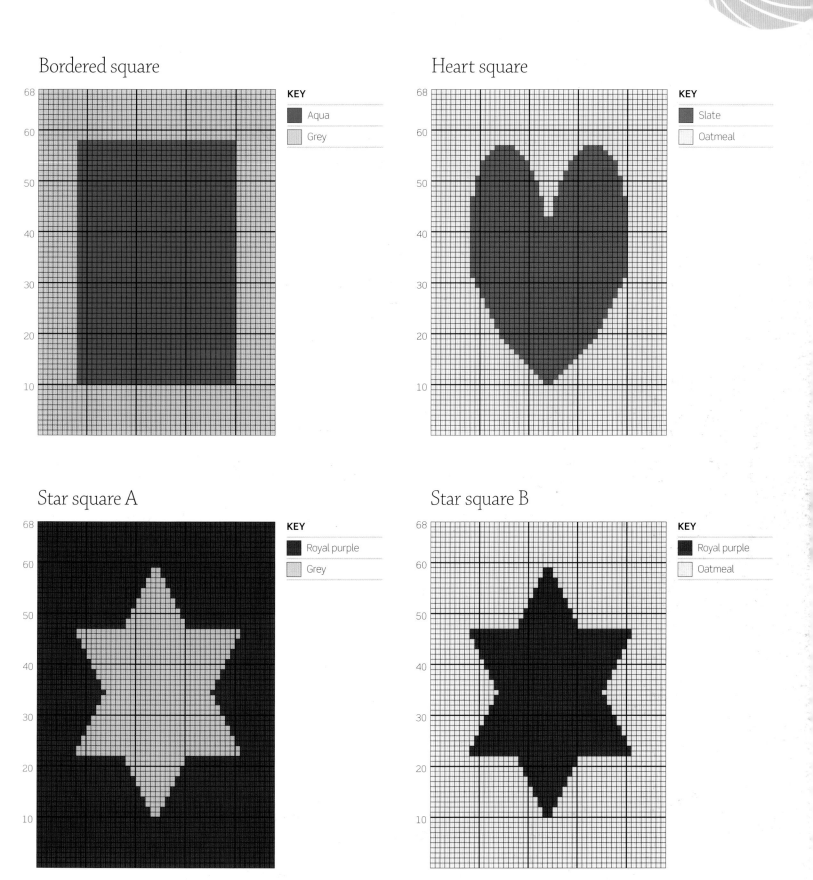

KEY
- ■ Aqua
- ▨ Grey

Heart square

KEY
- ■ Slate
- ▨ Oatmeal

Star square A

KEY
- ■ Royal purple
- ▨ Grey

Star square B

KEY
- ■ Royal purple
- ▨ Oatmeal

Elephant cushion

A cute knitted project to give to a child, this elephant-motif cushion is created using the intarsia technique (see pp.306–307). The elephant's ear is knitted separately and sewn on afterwards together with a three-dimensional stranded tail.

Essential information

DIFFICULTY Moderate

SIZE 40cm (16in) square

YARN

Debbie Bliss Cotton DK 50g

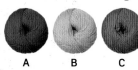

A   **B**   **C**

A: 62 Blue x 4   **B:** 20 Green x 2   **C:** 64 Salmon x1

NEEDLES

1 pair of 4mm (UK8/US6) needles

TENSION

20sts and 30 rows to 10cm (4in) over patt on 4mm (UK8/US6) needles

NOTIONS

Yarn bobbins

Large-eyed needle

Crochet hook (optional)

40cm (16in) square cushion pad

Front

Cast on 80sts in yarn A.

ROW 1 (RS): K to end.

ROW 2: P to end.

Rep rows 1 and 2 until 28 rows worked.

ROW 29: Follow the Elephant chart (see p.205) until patt knitted.

ROW 77: K to end.

ROW 78: P to end.

Rep row 77 and 78 and cont until 28 rows are knitted.

Cast off.

Back (make 2)

Cast on 80sts in yarn A and cont as follows:

ROW 1 (RS): *K to end.

ROW 2: P to end.

ROW 3: Rep from * until 46 rows are knitted.

ROW 47: *Change to yarn B and k to end.

ROW 48: K.

ROW 49: Change to yarn C and k to end.

ROW 50: K.

Rep from * until 20 rows knitted in total.

Ear piece

Cast on 27sts in yarn B.

ROW 1 (RS): K to end.

ROW 2: K to end.

ROW 3: K to st 27 then inc 1st. (28sts)

ROWS 4–6: K to end.

ROW 7: K to st 28 then inc 1st. (29sts)

ROWS 8–11: K to end.

ROW 12: K to st 27 then k2tog. (28sts)

ROW 13: K to end.

ROW 14: K2tog, k to st 24 then k2tog. (26sts)

ROW 15: K to end.

ROW 16: K2tog, k2tog, k to st 22, k2tog. (23sts)

ROW 17: K2tog, k to end. (22sts)

ROW 18: K2tog, k to st 22, k2tog. (20sts)

ROW 19: K2tog, k to end. (19sts)

ROW 20: K2tog, k to st 19, k2tog. (17sts)

ROW 21: K2tog, k to end. (16sts)

ROW 22: K2tog, k2tog, k to st 12, k2tog. (13sts)

ROW 23: K2tog, k to st 10 then k2tog. (11sts)

ROW 24: K2tog, k to st 5, k2tog, k2tog. (8sts)

ROW 25: K to end.

Cast off.

TOP TIP *Use small pieces of card if you don't have any yarn bobbins.*

Yarn bobbins When working the intarsia method of colourwork used for the elephant, cut short lengths of yarn from the main balls and wind them onto yarn bobbins to prevent tangles. When changing colours, twist the yarn around each other to avoid holes in your elephant.

Striped border Insert your cushion pad inside the knitted cover, then overlap the striped edges to close. Alternatively, sew a strip of hook-and-loop fastening tape to the inside of each edge.

KEY

$\boxed{I}$	Stocking st (k1r, p1r)
$\boxed{-}$	Garter st (k every row)
▨	Blue
▨	Green
▨	Salmon

Elephant chart

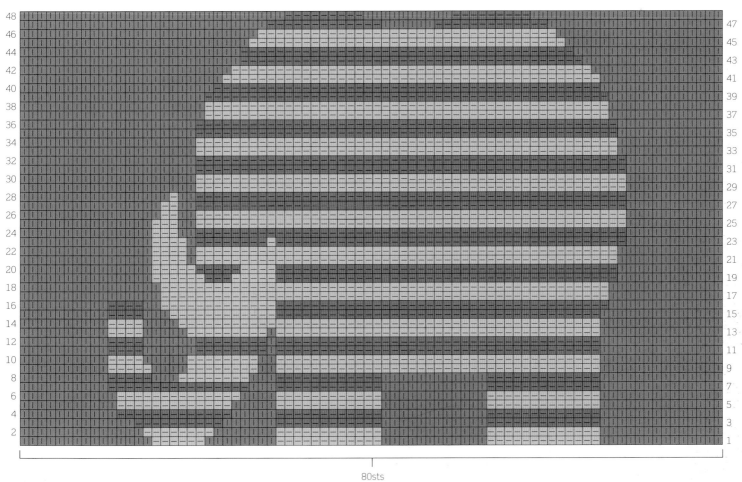

80sts

Making up

Lay all pieces flat RS together and check that each side measures 40cm (16in). For the two back panel pieces, overlap the striped edges and backstitch around the edges (see p.301).

Attach the ear

Place the cast on edge on the diagonal from the edge of the tusk to the top of the head. Use mattress stitch (see p.302) to attach the ear along the underneath of the cast on edge so the stitches are invisible.

Tassel

Cut 20cm (8in) lengths of yarns B and C, fold them in half and, using a crochet hook or the tip of your needle, pull the folded section through from the back to the front where you want the tail to be positioned. Do the same with the bottom of the tail a few rows below. Pull the bottom of the tail through the loop. Insert the cushion pad.

Essential information

DIFFICULTY Moderate

SIZE 40cm (16in) square

YARN

Sirdar Sublime Egyptian Cotton DK 50g

321 Frothy x 5

NEEDLES

A: 1 pair of 4mm (UK8/US6) needles

B: 1 pair of 3.25mm (UK10/US3) needles

A

B

TENSION

22sts and 28 rows to 10cm (4in) over st st on 4mm (UK8/US6) needles

NOTIONS

1 x 1.5cm (4¾in) mother-of-pearl button for centre of flower

3 x 2cm (¾in) mother-of-pearl buttons for back

Large-eyed needle

40cm (16in) square cushion pad

Daisy cushion

A delicate project knitted in 100 per cent cotton yarn, this cushion is formed of knitted daisies and embellished with a flower and scallop shell lace edging.

Front

With needles A, cast on 89sts.
Work 4 rows st st starting with a k row.
ROWS 1 AND 3: K to end.
ROWS 2 AND 4: P to end.
ROW 5: K2, [*k1, count 2sts ahead on the LH needle and 4 rows down, then put the point of the RH needle into the centre of this stitch from front to back and draw a loop through to the front and put it on the RH needle, k2, draw a 2nd loop through the same st, k2, make a 3rd loop into same st*, k5] x 8, rep from * to * once more, k2.
ROW 6: P2 [*p loop and next st tog, p1, p loop and next st tog, p1, p loop and next st tog*, p5] x 8, rep from * to * once more, p2.
ROWS 7 AND 9: K to end.
ROWS 8 AND 10: P to end.
ROW 11: K2, [k5, count 2sts ahead on the LH needle and 4 rows down, then put the point of the RH needle into the centre of this stitch from front to back and draw a loop through to the front and put it on the RH needle, k2, draw a 2nd loop through the same st, k2, make a 3rd loop into same stitch] x 8, k7.
ROW 12: P2 [p5, p loop and next st tog, p1, p loop and next st tog, p1, p loop and next st tog*] x 8, p7.
Rep rows 1–12 x 8 then rows 1–6 once more.
Work 4 rows st st starting with a k row.
Cast off.

Back (make 2)

With needles A, cast on 89sts.
Work 54 rows st st, starting with a k row.
Change to needles B.
ROW 1 AND 3: [K1, p1] to last st, k1.

ROW 2: [P1, k1] to last st, p1.
ROW 4: [P1, k1] x 10, p1, yon, p2tog, [k1, p1] x 10, k1, yon, k2tog, [p1, k1] x 10, p1, yon, p2tog, [k1, p1] x 10.
ROWS 5 AND 7: As row 1.
ROW 6: As row 2.
Cast off in stitch.
Work two pieces, replacing row 4 on the second piece with a repeat of row 2.

Scallop shell lace (make 2)

With needles A, cast on 107sts using finger loop method (see p.265).
ROW 1: K1, yon, *k5, 1 at a time lift 2nd, 3rd, 4th, and 5th sts just worked over the 1st st and off needle, yon* rep from * to * to last st, k1.
ROW 2: P1, *[p1, yon, k1 tbl] into next st, p1*, rep from * to * to end.
ROW 3: K2, k1 tbl, *k3, k1 tbl*, rep from * to * to last 2sts, k2.
Work 3 rows g st.
Cast off.

Flower

With needles A, cast on 57sts.
ROW 1: P to end.
ROW 2: K2, *k1, slip this st back to LH needle, lift next 8sts on LH needle over this st and off needle, yon twice, knit first st again, k2*. Rep from * to * to end. (27sts)
ROW 3: P1, *p2tog, drop 1 yon loop, [kfb] x 2 in rem yon of previous row, p1*. Rep from * to * to last st, p1. (32sts)
ROW 4: K1, [k3tog] x 10, k1. (12sts)
ROW 5: (P2tog) to end. (6sts)
Slip 2nd, 3rd, 4th, 5th, and 6th st over first st. Fasten off.

Making up

Steam and block the front and back pieces. Lay out the cover front, RS up. Pin the lace strips, RS facing, to the edges of the front pieces, with the cast off edge of the lace lined up with the outer edge of the front. Lay the back piece with buttonholes on top, RS down and with the cast on edge over the cast off edge of the front piece. Lay the second back piece on top, RS down, with the cast on edge over the cast on edge of the front piece, overlapping the two back pieces in the centre. Pin, then backstitch the pieces together around all four edges. Turn the cover RS out and sew the flower to the cushion cover with the button in centre. Sew three buttons along the cast off edge on the back, aligning each one with the buttonholes. Insert a cushion pad and button up to close.

Essential information

DIFFICULTY Easy

SIZE 40cm (16in) square

YARN

Sirdar Simply Recycled Aran 50g

A   B   C

A: 034 Raffia x 3   **B:** 032 Dusk x 2
C: 031 Cyprus x 2

NEEDLES

1 pair of 5mm (UK6/US8) needles

TENSION

18sts and 25 rows to 10cm (4in) over patt on 5mm
(UK6/US8) needles

NOTIONS

35cm (14in) cream zip
Sewing needle
Sewing thread (to match yarn A)
Large-eyed needle
40cm (16in) square cushion pad

Striped cushion

This pattern makes a cover that is slightly smaller than the recommended inner pad, which means that the cushion will be nice and plump. If you want to make longer or thicker tassels, allow one more ball of yarn A.

Back

Using yarn A, cast on 65sts.

ROW 1: K.

ROWS 2 AND 3: K.

ROW 4: P.

ROW 5: Change to yarn B. K2, slip next stitch purlwise,*k5, s1*. Rep from * to 2sts before end, k2 at end of row.

ROW 6: P, slipping each stitch which is still in yarn A.

ROWS 7–9: Work 3 rows in st st starting and ending with a k row.

ROWS 10 AND 11: K.

ROW 12: P.

ROW 13: Change to yarn A. K5, slip next stitch purlwise,*k5, s1*. Rep from * to 5sts from end, k5 at end of row.

ROW 14: P, slipping each stitch which is still in yarn B.

ROWS 15–17: Work 3 rows in st st starting and ending with a k row.

ROWS 18 AND 19: K.

ROW 20: P.

ROW 21: Change to yarn C. K2, slip next stitch purlwise, *k5, s1*. Rep from * to 2sts before end, k2 at end of row.

ROW 22: P, slipping each stitch that is still in yarn A.

ROWS 23–25: Work 3 rows in st st starting and ending with a k row.

ROWS 26 AND 27: K.

ROW 28: P.

ROW 29: Change to yarn A. K5, slip next stitch purlwise, *k5, s1*. Rep from * to 5sts before end, k5 to end of row.

ROW 30: P, slipping each stitch which is still in yarn C.

ROWS 31–33: Starting with a k row, work 3 rows in st st.

Rep rows 2–33 x 2. (97 rows of patt).

ROW 98: P.

Cast off.

Repeat for the front panel.

Making up

Lay both pieces flat, RS facing with cast off edges together (if the cast on is neater, then use those edges instead), and pin the zip centrally between the edges. Using a sharp sewing needle and sewing thread that matches yarn A, sew a zip neatly in place close to the cast on/off edge (see p.295). Sew together any of the seam that is still open at each end of the zip. Turn the cushion inside out and, carefully matching the stripes, backstitch all remaining seams (see p.301).

Tassels

Cut a 9cm (3¹⁄₂in) square of card and wind a long length of yarn A forty times around the card. Take a 20cm (8in) length of yarn A, thread it through the wound yarn at one end of the card and tie a tight knot leaving the ends free. Cut through the wound yarn at the opposite

end from the knot, and slide the card out without disturbing the folded threads. Take another 20cm (8in) length of yarn A and knot it very tightly around the tassel, about 2cm (³⁄₄in) below the first knot. Thread the ends onto a large-eyed needle and sew them through the tassel to secure. Trim the ends of the tassel to a uniform length, about 8cm (3in) long. Thread the knotted yarn ends into a large-eyed needle and sew the tassel securely to a corner of the cushion. Repeat for each corner.

Essential information

DIFFICULTY Moderate

SIZE 40 x 45cm (16 x 17¾in)

YARN

Artesano Superwash Merino 50g

A B C D E

A: SFN41 Grey x 3
B: 3083 Red x 1
C: 7254 Sand yellow x 1
D: 6315 Lime green x 1
E: SFN21 Biscuit x 1

NEEDLES

1 pair of 4mm (UK8/US6) needles

TENSION

20sts and 28 rows to 10cm (4in) over st st on 4mm
(UK8/US6) needles

NOTIONS

Yarn bobbins
Large-eyed needle
7 x 22mm (¾in) buttons
Sewing needle and matching sewing thread
40 x 45cm (16 x 17¾in) cushion pad

Hen cushion

This cushion is knitted in stocking stitch and has a row of intarsia hens nestling along the base. The reverse side is patterned in stripes with a picot edged opening.

Front

Using yarn A, cast on 91sts.
Work 4 rows in st st.
Cont in st st and follow the Hen chart from rows 1–34.
On each row work the first 2sts and the last 2sts in yarn A before following the chart.
Cont in st st using yarn A until the work measures 40cm (16in).
Cast off.

Lower back

Using yarn B with RS facing, pick up and k91 along cast on edge.
K 1 row.
Work 2 rows in st st.
Cont in st st, following stripe sequence:
ROWS 1-4: Yarn C.
ROWS 5-8: Yarn D.
ROWS 9-14: Yarn A.
ROWS 15-18: Yarn B.
Rep stripe sequence once more, then work:
ROWS 37-40: Yarn C.
ROWS 41-44: Yarn D. ***
ROWS 45-50: Yarn A.
NEXT ROW: Cont in yarn A.
K2, *yon, k2tog, rep from * to last 2sts, k1.
NEXT ROW: P.
Work 3 rows in st st.
Cast off loosely.
Fold picot edge over and slip stitch in place.

Upper back

Using yarn B with RS facing, pick up and k91 along cast off edge.
Cont as for Lower Back to ***.
NEXT ROW: Cont in yarn A.
Work 2 rows in st st.
NEXT ROW: K3, *k2tog, yon, k12, rep from * to last 6sts, k2tog, yon, k2.
NEXT ROW: P.
Work 2 rows in st st.
NEXT ROW: K2tog, *yon, k2tog, rep from * to last 2sts, k1.
NEXT ROW: P.
Work 2 rows in st st.
NEXT ROW: K3, *k2tog, yon, k12, rep from * to last 6sts, k2tog, yon, k2.
NEXT ROW: P.
K 1 row.
Cast off loosely.
Fold picot edge over and stitch in place.

Making up

Sew up the side seams (see pp.300–302), overlapping the upper back and lower back. Make sure the buttonhole band is on the top. Sew on the buttons to correspond with the buttonholes. Embroider a French knot (see p.120) for each eye using yarn A as marked on the chart, above right. Embroider the beaks in yarn C as marked on the chart, making three small backstitches for each beak.
Darn in ends (see p.300) and block. Insert a cushion pad and button the cover closed.

Hen chart

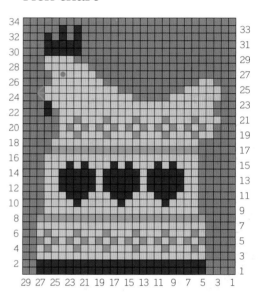

KEY

■	Grey
■	Red
■	Sand yellow
■	Lime green
▥	Biscuit
●	French knot for eye
—	Backstitches for beak

Cable cushion

Two squares of cabled knitting are sewn together to form a textured cushion. The garter stitch and cables result in a thicker fabric than that made by stocking stitch, so it forms a very strong, machine-washable cushion cover.

Essential information

DIFFICULTY Moderate

SIZE 40cm (16in) square

YARN

Debbie Bliss Rialto Aran 50g

01 Beige x 4

NEEDLES

A: 1 pair of 5mm (UK6/US8) needles
B: Cable needle

TENSION

18sts and 21 rows to 10cm (4in) over patt on 5mm (UK6/US8) needles

NOTIONS

Large-eyed needle
35cm or 40cm (14in or 16in) matching zip
Sewing thread (to match yarn colour)
Sewing needle
40cm (16in) square cushion pad

SPECIAL ABBREVIATIONS

C8F (on RS) Slip 4sts to cable needle (cn), hold in front, k4, k4 from cn
C8B (on RS) Slip 4sts to cn, hold in back, k4, k4 from cn

Cushion side (make 2)

Cast on 66sts using cable cast on method (see p.265).
ROW 1 (RS): K11, [inc in next st, k4, inc in next st, k15] x 2, inc in next st, k4, inc in next st, k to end. (72sts)
ROW 2 (WS): K9 [p12, k9] to end.

Commence pattern

Work all RS (odd) rows from right to left and all WS (even) rows from left to right.
ROW 1 (RS): K9, [work next 21sts as given for chart] x 3.
ROW 2 (WS): [Work next 21sts as given for chart] x 3, k9.
Cont working last 2 rows in patt as set, rep 12 rows of chart until work measures 40cm (16in), ending with a RS row.
DEC ROW: K9, [p3, p2tog, p2, p2tog, p3, k9] x 3. (66sts)
Cast off.

Making up

There should not be any need to block this cushion. Sew along three sides, sew in a zip along the bottom seam edge (see p.295) and insert a cushion pad.

Cable chart

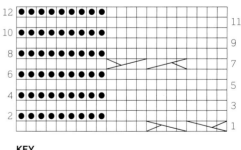

KEY

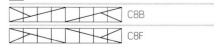

K on RS rows, p on WS rows

● P on RS rows, k on WS rows

C8B

C8F

Colour-block cushion

A large buffer that can double as a pillow, this bold pattern is knitted in stocking stitch with a Fair Isle patterned border and intarsia colour blocks. The intricate pattern is inspired by an antique textile throw.

Essential information

DIFFICULTY Easy

SIZE 30 x 45cm (12 x 17¾in)

YARN

King Cole Merino Blend DK 50g

| A | B | C | D |

A: 702 Graphite x 2 **B:** 790 Caramel x 1
C: 069 Olive x 1 **D:** 906 Emperor purple x 1

NEEDLES

1 pair of 4mm (UK8/US6) needles

TENSION

22sts and 28 rows to 10cm (4in) over st st on 4mm (UK8/US6) needles

NOTIONS

Yarn bobbins (optional)
2 x 2cm (¾in) buttons
30 x 45cm (12 x 17¾in) cushion pad
Large-eyed needle

Front

Using yarn A, cast on 96sts.
Work 86 rows from the chart (see p.217) using stranded Fair Isle for small areas of pattern and intarsia, crossing colours where they meet, for larger blocks of colour.
The design is worked in st st, k all sts on odd rows, p all sts on even rows.
Cast off in yarn A.

Lower back

Using yarn A, cast on 53sts.
ROW 1: K.
ROW 2: P to last 7sts, k7.
Rep rows 1 and 2 x 14; (28 rows).
BUTTONHOLE ROW: K3, yon, k2tog, k to end.
NEXT ROW: As row 2.
Rep rows 1 and 2 x 13.
Rep buttonhole row.
Rep row 2.
Rep rows 1 and 2 x 13.
Cast off.

Upper back

Using yarn A, cast on 52sts.
ROW 1: K to end.
ROW 2: K7, p to end.
Rep rows 1 and 2 x 42; (84 rows).
Cast off.

Making up

Lay out the cover front, RS facing upwards. Lay the lower back piece with buttonholes on top, RS together and with the cast on edge on top of the cast on edge of the front piece, lining them up to the right side. Lay the upper back piece on top, RS together, with the cast on edge on top of the cast on edge underneath and overlapping the two back pieces in the centre for the buttons and buttonholes, and lining them up on the left side. Pin, then backstitch the pieces together around all four edges. Turn the cover RS out and sew buttons on the underside of the back to match the buttonholes. Insert a cushion pad and button the cover closed.

TOP TIP *Refer to pp.294–295 for information about buttonholes.*

KEY

- ■ Graphite
- ▢ Caramel
- ▢ Olive
- ■ Emperor purple

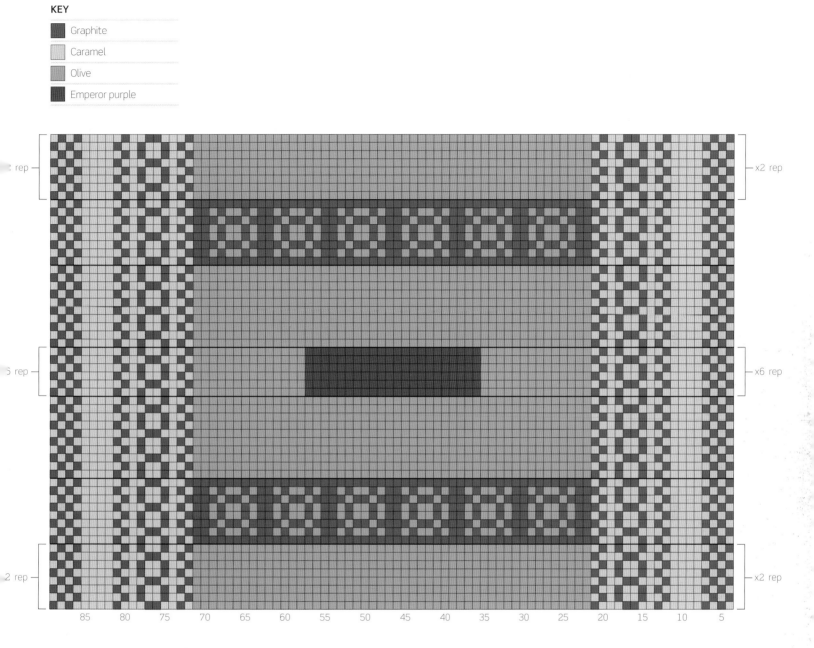

Colour-block chart

Follow this chart to create the colour-block cushion. Each square represents one garter stitch. Refer to the key to position the colours. Start at the bottom right-hand corner of the chart and work across, reading from the right for knit rows and from the left for purl rows. Make sure that you repeat the rows as indicated. Check your knitting regularly to ensure that the pattern grows as it should. The geometric design will make it easy to spot a mistake, in which case unravel your knitting, correct the mistake, and continue as before.

Anytime shoulder bag

This bag is incredibly easy to knit because it is made up of one rectangle of knitted fabric worked in stocking stitch. We've included two options for the strap size, so you can wear it over your shoulder or across the body.

Essential information

DIFFICULTY Easy

SIZE 22 x 18cm (9 x 7in)

YARN

Rowan Belle Organic DK 50g

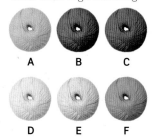

A   B   C

D   E   F

A: 026 Marina x 2   **B:** 021 Garnet x 2
C: 029 Dahlia x 1   **D:** 013 Moonflower x 1
E: 016 Cilantro x 1   **F:** 023 Bluebell x 1
Oddments of two different coloured yarns for marking (we've used red and black)

NEEDLES

A: 1 pair of 4.5mm (UK7/US7) needles
B: 1 pair of 5mm (UK6/US8) needles
C: 80cm (32in), 4.5mm (UK7/US7)
circular needle

A

B

C

TENSION

16sts and 23 rows to 10cm (4in) over st st using 5mm (UK6/US8) needles

NOTIONS

Large-eyed needle

Stripe pattern

6 rows in yarn F, 4 rows in A, 4 rows in C, 6 rows in B, 4 rows in A, 6 rows in F, 4 rows in A, 6 rows in D, 6 rows in E, 4 rows in yarn A. (50 rows in total)

Bag

Using needles A and yarn A, cast on 34sts. Starting with a k row, work 4 rows g st, ending with a WS row.

Set border and stripe patt

Change to needles B. Working as given for stripe patt (above), set border as follows:

ROW 1 (RS): K.

ROW 2: K3, p to last 3sts, k3.

Last 2 rows set border. Rep last 2 rows throughout. At same time, place black markers at each end of rows 56 and 65, and red markers at each end of rows 121 and 130. Cont in patt until work measures 80cm (31$\frac{1}{2}$in) from cast on edge, ending with a RS row.

Change to needles A; join in yarn A. Starting with a k row, work 3 rows g st. Cast off.

Darn in all ends and block as given on ballband.

Strap

Using needles C and yarn B, cast on 200sts for a short strap or child's bag, or 300sts for a long strap or adult's bag, placing black markers at 44th and 156th sts (or 256th st for longer strap). Starting with a k row (RS), work 4 rows g st. Break off B, join in C and work a further 4 rows g st. Cast off, placing black markers at 44th and 156th sts (256th st for longer strap). Darn in ends.

Making up

Lay main piece of bag flat with WS facing, align row ends of strap with bag row ends between red markers. Sew in place using backstitch (see p.301). Fold main bag piece around strap so that black markers on both pieces meet. Pin in place along bag row ends and strap cast on/cast off edges. Sew these side seams using backstitch. Darn in ends (see p.300).

Knitted gift bag

A shiny yarn highlights the texture and pattern on this luxury gift bag. The rows of eyelets make a decorative zigzag shape using increases and decreases, which influence the shape of the rows as they are knitted.

Essential information

DIFFICULTY Moderate

SIZE 20cm (8in) tall

YARN

Gedifra Amara 50g

3716 Silver x 1

NEEDLES

1 pair of 4.5mm (UK7/US7) needles

TENSION

19sts and 24 rows to 10cm (4in) over st st on 4.5mm (UK7/US7) needles

NOTIONS

Large-eyed needle

60cm (23½in) co-ordinated ribbon, 7mm–2cm (⅜–¾in) wide

Decorative beads (optional)

SPECIAL ABBREVIATIONS

P2SSO/P3SSO Pass 2/pass 3 slipped sts over. Please note that all slipped sts are worked knitwise throughout

Bag (all one piece)

Cast on 57sts.

Work 3 rows g st (knit every row), ending with a WS row.

ROW 1 (RS): *K2tog, yon, rep from * to last st, k1.

ROW 2: P.

Commence patt

ROW 1: K1, [M1, k5, s2 k1 p2sso, k5, M1, k1] x 4.

ROW 2 AND ALL FOLL ALT ROWS: P.

Last 2 rows set chevron patt. Work 4 more rows in patt.

Ribbon eyelets

ROW 1: K1, [yon, k5, s2 k1 p2sso, k5, yon, k1] x 4.

ROW 2 AND ALL FOLL ALT ROWS: P.

ROW 3: K1, M1, k5, *yon, s2 k1 p2sso, yon, k5, M1, k1, M1, k5, rep from * to last 9sts, yon, s2 k1 p2sso, yon, k5, M1, k1. (65sts)

ROW 5: K1, [yon, k6, s2 k1 p2sso, k6, yon, k1] x 4.

ROW 7: K1 [M1, k6, s2 k1 p2sso, k6, M1, k1] x 4.

Cont working in chevron patt (rows 7 and 8) until work measures 15cm (6in) from cast on edge at protruding chevron points, ending with a WS row.

NEXT ROW (RS): *K2tog, yon, rep from * to last st, k1.

Cont working in chevron patt until work measures 20cm (8in) from cast on edge at protruding chevron points, ending with a WS row.

Shape base

ROW 1 (RS): K1, [M1, k5, s3, k2tog, p3sso, k5, M1, k1] x 4. (57sts)

ROW 2 AND ALL FOLL ALT ROWS: P.

ROW 3: K1, [M1, k5, s2 k1 p2sso, k5, M1, k1] x 4.

ROW 5: K1, [M1, k4, s3, k2tog, p3sso, k4, M1, k1] x 4. (49sts)

ROW 7: K1, [M1, k3, s3, k2tog, p3sso, k3, M1, k1] x 4. (41sts)

ROW 9: K1, [M1, k2, s3, k2tog, p3sso, k2, M1, k1] x 4. (33sts)

ROW 11: S1 k1 psso, k1, *s2 k1 p2sso, k1, rep from * to last 2sts, k2tog. (17sts)

ROW 13: *S1 k1 psso, rep from * to last 3sts, s2 k1 p2sso. (8sts)

Break off yarn leaving a long tail, draw it through rem sts and pull tight. Block lightly if desired and join row ends, with RS facing, using mattress stitch (see p.302). Thread ribbon through ribbon eyelets and add decorative beads if desired.

Beaded party clutch

Embellished with knitted-in beads (see pp.296–298), this glittery evening bag is stunning! Follow the chart below to position each bead. Line your party clutch with matching fabric and a zip.

Essential information

DIFFICULTY Moderate

SIZE 18 x 13cm (7 x 5¼in)

YARN

Rowan Cotton Glace 50g

727 Black x 1

NEEDLES

1 pair of 3.5mm (UK n/a/US4) needles

TENSION

22sts and 32 rows to 10cm (4in) over st st using 3.5mm (UK n/a/US4) needles

NOTIONS

18cm (7in) zip

450 x 3mm (⅛in) glass knitting beads

23 x 33cm (8½ x 13in) strong lining fabric

Sewing needle and black sewing thread

Matching ribbon, 3mm (⅛in) wide (optional)

Beads for wrist strap (optional)

Bag (make 2)

Cast on 42sts using the knit on cast on method (see p.264). Work 2 rows st st, ending with a WS row.

Place chart

ROW 1: K1, [work next 8sts as given for row 1 of chart] x 5, k1.

ROW 2: P1, [work next 8sts as given for row 2 of chart] x 5, p1.

These two rows set position of chart. Cont working from chart until piece measures 11.5cm (4¾in) repeating the 12 row patt and ending on a patt row 12.

Beginning with a k row, work 2 rows st st. Cast off.

Making up

With WS facing, sew row ends and cast on edges together using backstitch (see p.301). Turn work inside out and block lightly. Sew the assembled bag pieces to the zip. Make the lining by folding the fabric in half along the long edge, RS together. Trim to size: it should be slightly larger than the side of the bag, and have a 1cm (½in) seam allowance on each side edge and the top edge. Stitch the side seams and turn RS out. With the bag WS out, insert the lining. Catch the corners of the fabric to the corners of the bag to prevent the lining floating about. Fold the top edges over, and oversew to the bag. To make a wrist strap, thread 40cm (16in) strands of ribbon through the zip pull, and knot. Thread beads onto the ends of the ribbon, trim, and knot the end of each beaded strand.

Bead chart

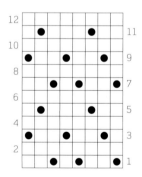

KEY

☐ K on RS rows, p on WS rows

● Place bead

Essential information

DIFFICULTY Easy

SIZE 32 x 38cm (12½ x 15in)

YARN

Rowan Colourscape Chunky 100g

447 Jungle x 2

NEEDLES

1 pair of 7mm (UK2/US n/a) needles

TENSION

(Before felting) 14sts and 28 rows to 10cm (4in)
over st st on 7mm (UK2/US n/a) needles

NOTIONS

20 (approx.) rhinestone studs

Felted tote bag

A roomy bag ideal for storing your yarn and needles, this project is worked in stocking stitch, then felted, and embellished with rhinestone studs. Refer to the felting instructions here, or follow the manufacturer's information on your ballband.

Cast on 50sts.

Starting with a k row, and working in st st, inc at both ends of 5th row. Work 9 rows without shaping. (52sts)

ROW 15 (RS): Inc in first st, k15, cast off 20sts, k15, inc in last st. (54sts)

ROW 16: P17, cast on 20sts, p to end.

Cont working in st st, inc at each end on 8th and every foll 10th row, until there are 66sts. Work 19 rows without shaping.

Dec at each end of next and every foll 10th row until 54sts remain.

Work 8 rows without shaping.

NEXT ROW (WS): P17, cast off 20sts, p to end.

NEXT ROW: S1 k1 psso, k15, cast on 20sts, k to last 2sts, k2tog. (52sts)

Cont working in st st, dec on foll 10th row. Work 5 more rows without shaping. Cast off. Fold work with WS facing you so that cast on and cast off edges meet. Join row ends using a long backstitch (see p.301), and felt the bag in the washing machine at 60°C (140°F), (see right). Stuff the felted bag with clean plastic bags to hold it in its pear shape and leave to dry. Add rhinestone studs on the bag, using the photograph as a guide.

How to felt your knitting

First, hand test the yarn to see if it will felt. Roll a 90cm (36in) long strand into a ball. Add a drop of detergent and rub it together for 2 minutes under hot running water. If the yarn clumps and is difficult to pull apart, it is a good candidate for test-felting. Next, knit and block a 10cm (4in) swatch. Submerge it in soapy hand-hot water. Squeeze and knead it gently, adding more hot water as required for up to 30 minutes. Rinse and squeeze out the water (do not wring) and roll in a towel. Pat the felt, right-side up, into a rectangle and leave to dry overnight. If the yarn has felted successfully, test a bigger swatch in a washing machine.

Preparing for test-felting

By test-felting a swatch of your yarn you can determine how much it will shrink, although felting is not an exact science. Washing machine agitation, water temperature, detergent type, and yarn fibre content, spin, and colour all vary.

Knit a swatch of stocking stitch at least 20cm (8in) square (accurate shrinkage measurements cannot be obtained with smaller swatches). Block the swatch carefully. If unblocked, the side edges will felt too thickly due to the curling.

Machine felting

Put a swatch in the washing machine along with a large towel (this increases the agitation). Add half the amount of detergent used for a full load. Wash at 40°C (104°F) for yarn that contains mohair, and 60°C (140°F) for 100 per cent wool yarns, using the full washing and spin cycle. Tug the washed swatch gently in both directions, lay it right-side up and pat into a rectangle. Leave to dry completely. If necessary, do more tests with new swatches, altering the temperature or the length of the wash cycle. Keep detailed records of tension, needle size, sizes of pre-felted and felted swatches, wash settings, and type and amount of detergent used.

Tips for felting

If you are trying felting for the first time, make several test swatches in different weights of yarn and felt them together in the same load. This way you can get a feel for the different thicknesses of knitted felt. When using highly contrasting colours, put a colour catcher sheet in the machine to absorb loose dye and prevent colours from running. Wool will fade slightly when felted, due to the high temperatures and the detergent, but this adds an attractive quality to the felt. Clean your washing machine after a felting load by wiping it out with a damp cloth to remove any stray fibres.

Essential information

DIFFICULTY Easy

SIZE 24cm (9½in) widening to 18 x 28cm
(7 x 11in)

YARN

Rowan Handknit Cotton 50g

251 Ecru x 3

NEEDLES

A: 1 pair of 4mm (UK8/US6) needles
B: 1 pair of 3.25mm (UK10/US3) needles

——————————————————————— A
——————————————————————— B

TENSION

19sts and 28 rows to 10cm (4in) over patt on 4mm
(UK8/US6) needles

NOTIONS

1 spare needle
Large-eyed needle
2 pieces of lining fabric, 26 x 30cm (10 x 12in)
Sewing needle and cream sewing thread

Ruffle and frill bag

This tapered shoulder bag is decorated with a turned-down frilly cuff and has a diamond openwork eyelet pattern running vertically down the centre. Line the bag with co-ordinated fabric to make your knitting more substantial.

Ruffle (make 2)

With needles A, cast on 74sts.
Work 5 rows st st, starting with a k row.
NEXT ROW: P2tog to end. (37sts)
Transfer sts to a spare needle.

Bag (make 2)

With needles A, cast on 51sts.
ROW 1: K.
ROW 2 AND ALL EVEN ROWS: P to end.
Mark central 9sts.
ROW 3: K to central 9sts (21sts reducing to 15sts for the final half rep), k4, yon, k2tog, k3, K to end.
ROW 5: K to central 9sts, k3, yon, k2tog, yon, k2tog, k2, k to end.
ROW 7: Rep row 3.
ROW 9: K to central 9sts, k1, yon, k2tog, k4, yon, k2tog, k to end.
ROW 11: K1, skpo, k to central 9sts, yon, k2tog, yon, k2tog, k2, yon, k2tog, yon, k2tog, k to last 3sts, k2tog, k1.
ROW 13: Rep row 9.
ROW 15: Rep row 3.
ROW 17: Rep row 5.
ROW 19: Rep row 3.
ROW 21: K1, skpo, k to last 3sts, k2tog, k1
ROW 22: P to end.
Rep rows 3–22 x 2.
Rep rows 3–10 once more.

NEXT ROW: K to central 9sts, yon, k2tog, yon, k2tog, k2, yon, k2tog, yon, k2tog, k to end. (39sts)
Work 3 rows of st st, starting with a p row.
Hold the needle with the bag on it behind one of the needles with the ruffle on it.
NEXT ROW: K1, k through 1st from the ruffle and 1st from the bag, drawing a single st through both and continue likewise on every st to last st, k1.
Change to needles B.
RIB ROW 1: K1, [p1, k1] to end.
RIB ROW 2: P1, [k1, p1] to end.
Rep rib rows 1 and 2 twice more then rib row 1 once again.
Cast off in rib (see p.270).

Strap

Using needles B, cast on 9sts.
ROW 1: K1, [p1, k1] to end.
ROW 2: P1, [k1, p1] to end.
Work until strap measures 80cm (31$^{1}/_{2}$in).
Cast off.

Bow

Using needles A, cast on 5sts.
K every st on every row until piece measures 14cm (5$^{1}/_{2}$in).
Cast off leaving a long yarn tail.
Stitch ends of strip together to form a loop then bind with yarn at centre to form a bow shape.

Making up

With RS facing, stitch sides and base of two bag pieces together, 1st from edge and not including the ruffle in the seams.
Turn through and sew the ruffles together, edge-to-edge, at side seams.
Stitch the strap in place on rib at side seams.
Using the bag WS out as a guide, cut two pieces of lining fabric adding a 1cm ($^{1}/_{2}$in) seam allowance to the sides and base. Stitch sides and base of two lining pieces together. Fold 2.5cm (1in) of fabric to the WS along the top edge of the lining. Put the lining "bag" inside the knitted bag with WS together. Attach the top of the lining to the knitted bag at the bottom of the rib using small, invisible stitches.
Attach bow to front rib.

Mobile phone sock

Protect your phone with a knitted cover in a choice of three different colourways. Knitted in single rib, the sock includes a slim pocket to store a memory card or earphones. An ideal project for a beginner.

Essential information

DIFFICULTY Easy

SIZE 7 x 15cm (2¾ x 6in)

YARN

Patons Diploma Gold DK 50g

| A | B | C | D |

A: 6220 Blue x 1 or **B:** 6245 Plum x 1 or
C: 6125 Apple green x 1   **D:** White 6142 x 1

NEEDLES

1 pair of 3.25mm (UK10/US3) needles

TENSION

30sts and 30 rows to 10cm (4in) over 1x1 rib on 3.25mm (UK10/US3) needles

NOTIONS

Large-eyed needle

Front and back (make 2)

In the colour of your choice (A, B, or C) cast on 21sts.

ROW 1: K1, [p1, k1] to end.

ROW 2: P1, [k1, p1] to end.

Rep these 2 rows to form 1x1 rib until your work measures 12cm (5in).

Work 1x1 rib, as above, 1 row in yarn D and 1 row in yarn A, B, or C x 4.

To halve the number of yarn ends when knitting single rows, cut off a piece of yarn about eight times the width of the work and knit the first row, starting from the middle of the strand. Do this again for the next colour, and then pick up the tail of the first yarn to knit the 3rd row. Continue in this way with a new strand of yarn introduced for every 2 rows of a colour instead of every row.

Cast off in stitch using yarn D.

Pocket

In yarn A, B, or C cast on 21sts.

ROW 1: K1, [p1, k1] to end.

ROW 2: P1, [k1, p1] to end.

Rep these 2 rows until your work measures 5cm (2in).

Work 1 row of 1x1 rib in yarn D and 1 row in yarn A, B, or C x 4.

Cast off in stitch using yarn D.

Making up

Lay the back piece RS up. Lay the pocket on top, RS down, lining up the cast on edges. Lay front piece on top with RS down, lining up the cast on edges. Backstitch (see p.301) down sides and across bottom. Turn through.

Protective cover This stitch is stretchy so the sock will fit most phones. Refer to p.274 for information on how to knit single ribbing. Turn to p.270 for casting off in rib effect, which will help you to maintain the rib pattern throughout your project.

Essential information

DIFFICULTY Easy

SIZE 12 x 12cm (5 x 5in)

YARN

Debbie Bliss Rialto DK 50g

A   B   C

A: 12 Scarlet x 1
B: 01 White x 1
C: 42 Pink x 1

NEEDLES

1 pair of 3.75mm (UK9/US5) needles

TENSION

26sts and 30 rows to 10cm (4in) over st st on 3.75mm (UK9/US5) needles

NOTIONS

Large-eyed needle
Polyester toy stuffing
90cm (35in) x 6mm (¼in)-wide red ribbon
Sewing needle and red sewing thread
3 x 1cm (½in) mother-of-pearl buttons

Heart sachets

A trio of hanging hearts that sport knitted and embroidered motifs.

Red heart (make 2)

With yarn A, cast on 3sts.
K 1 row and p 1 row.
Now shape sides as follows:
ROW 1: K1, yon, k1, yon, k1.
ROW 2: P1, yrn, p into back of yon on previous row, p1, p into back of yon on previous row, yrn, p1.
ROW 3: K1, yon, k into back of yrn on previous row, k3, k into back of yrn on previous row, yon, k1.
ROW 4: P1, yrn, p into back of yon on previous row, p5, p into back of yon on previous row, yrn, p1.
ROW 5: K1, yon, k into back of yrn on previous row, k to last 2sts, k into back of yrn on previous row, yon, k1.
ROW 6: P1, yrn, p into back of yon on previous row, p to last 2sts, p into back of yon on previous row, yrn, p1.
Rep the last 2 rows until there are 35sts, ending with a p row. *

Cont in st st, beg with a k row, work 20 rows straight.
**Shape top.
NEXT ROW: K17, turn and cont on these sts only for first side.
Now dec 1st at both ends of next 5 rows. (7sts)
Cast off.
With RS of work facing, rejoin yarn to rem sts.
K2tog and then k to end.
Dec 1st at both ends of next 5 rows. (7sts)
Cast off.
Following Chart 1, below left, and using yarn B, cross-stitch a heart in the centre of both sides.

Pink heart (make 2)

Using yarn C, work as for Red Heart until there are 31sts, ending with a p row. **Cont to shape sides as set until there are 35sts, at the same time now work in patt from Chart 2, below centre.** Odd numbers are RS rows and read from right to left, even numbered rows are WS rows and read from left to right. Use a separate ball of yarn for each area of colour, twisting yarns tog when joining colours to avoid a hole from forming. When chart is complete, work a further 6 rows st st using yarn C only.
Complete as given for Red Heart from ** to end.

White heart (make 2)

Using yarn B, work as for Red Heart to *.
Following Chart 3, below right, work 14 rows in Fair Isle patt (see pp.306–307).
When chart is complete, work a further 6 rows st st using yarn B only.
Complete as given for Red Heart from ** to end.

Making up

Place front and back together with RS facing and stitch around outer edges, leaving a small opening in one straight edge. Turn RS out. Stuff the hearts and stitch closed. Cut a length of ribbon 30cm (12in) long and sew it to the top of the front with matching thread. Sew on one button to cover the raw ends of the ribbon.

Chart 1

Chart 2

Chart 3

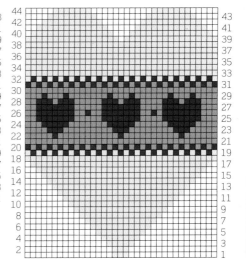

KEY

- Scarlet
- White
- Pink

Floral embellishments

Fabulous decoration for perking up plain knitwear, these five flowers and one leaf can be sewn onto a dress as a corsage, to liven up a hat, or as a row of blooms along a scarf edge. The patterns are easy to make using increase and decrease techniques.

Essential information

DIFFICULTY Moderate

SIZE 8cm (3in) diameter approx.

YARN
Yarn and colour of your choice (we've used Sirdar Flirt DK 50g and Sirdar Country Style DK 50g)

NEEDLES
A: 1 pair of 4mm (UK8/US6) needles
B: 4 x 4mm (UK8/US6) double-pointed needles (for the leaf)

—————————————————— **A**
—————————————————— **B**

TENSION
22sts and 28 rows to 10cm (4in) over patt on 4mm (UK8/US6) needles

NOTIONS
Large-eyed needle

Twelve-petal flower (left)

Using knit on cast on method (see p.264), cast on 12sts, leaving a yarn tail at least 25cm (9³/₄in) long.

ROW 1 (RS): Cast off 10sts knitwise and slip st on RH needle back on to LH needle. (2sts)

NOTE: Do not turn work when working petals, but keep RS facing.

ROW 2 (RS): Cast on 12sts on LH needle using knit on cast on method, then cast off 10sts knitwise and slip st on RH needle back on LH needle. (4sts)

ROWS 3–12: [Rep row 2] x 10 to make a total of 12 petals (24sts – 2sts at base of each petal). Cut off yarn.

Using a second yarn and working across all 24sts, cont in usual rows for flower centre as follows:

ROW 13 (RS): [K2tog] x 12. (12sts)

ROW 14 (WS): K.

ROW 15 (RS): K.

**Slip all sts back on to LH needle. Then cut off yarn, leaving a yarn tail at least 25cm (10in) long. Thread yarn tail through a large-eyed needle. With RS facing, thread yarn through rem sts, slipping them off knitting needle as you proceed. Pull yarn tightly to gather sts firmly. With WS facing and still using large-eyed needle, oversew row ends of flower centre together, working from centre to beginning of petal yarn. Knot ends of matching yarn together, close to work on WS, then knot all yarn ends together close to WS.
To form a stem, plait together yarn ends, holding two ends of the first yarn together and using strands of the second yarn singly for

three strands of plait. Knot end of stem and trim yarn ends. ******
Do not press.

Anemone (see p.235)

NOTE: Slip all slipped sts purlwise with yarn at WS of work. Using double cast on method (see p.266), cast on 41sts, leaving a yarn tail at least 25cm (10in) long.

ROW 1 (RS): *S1, k7, rep from * to last st, p1.

ROW 2: *S1, k to end.

ROW 3: As row 1.

ROW 4: *S1, p7, *s1, take yarn to back of work between two needles then around knitting over cast on edge, over top of knitting between two needles and around cast on edge again, so ending at front of work, pull yarn to gather knitting tightly, p7, rep from * to last st, k1. Cut off yarn and change to second yarn.

ROW 5: *K2tog, rep from * to last 3sts, sk2p. (20sts)

ROW 6: K.
Cut off yarn and change to third yarn.

ROW 7: [K2tog] x 10. (10sts)
Finish as for Twelve-petal flower from ** to **, but also using first yarn to sew short petal seam (leaving part of seam unworked to create indent between petals as between other petals) and making a plait with two strands each of the first, second, and third yarn. Do not press.

Green and red flower (see p.235)

Using double cast on method, cast on 90sts, leaving a yarn tail at least 25cm (9³/₄in) long.

ROW 1 (WS): K6, sk2p, *k12, sk2p, rep from * to last 6sts, k6. (78sts)

Cut off yarn and change to second yarn.

ROW 2 (RS): *K1, cast off next 11sts knitwise, rep from *. (6sts)

Cut off yarn and change to third yarn.

ROW 3: P.

ROW 4: *K2tog, k1, rep from *. (4sts)

Finish as for Twelve-petal flower from ** to **, but also using first yarn to sew beginning and end of cast on sts together and making plait with two strands each of the first, second, and third yarn. Do not press.

Two-tone pink flower (centre)

NOTE: This pattern is also knitted in a pink and purple colourway, bottom right.

Using double cast on method, cast on 72sts, leaving a yarn tail at least 25cm (9³/₄in) long.

Cut off yarn and change to second yarn.

ROW 1 (RS): K.

ROW 2: *Kfb, cast off next 8sts knitwise, rep from * to end. (16sts)

Cut off yarn and change to third yarn.

ROW 3: K.

ROW 4: *K2, k2tog, rep from * to end. (12sts)

ROW 5: K.

ROW 6: P.

ROW 7: *K2, k2tog, rep from * to end. (9sts)

Finish as for Twelve-Petal Flower from ** to **, but also using first yarn to sew beginning and end of cast on sts together and making plait with two strands each of the first, second, and third yarn. Do not press. Decorate centre with small button if desired.

Blue flower (top right)

Using knit on cast on method, cast on 10sts, leaving a yarn tail at least 25cm (9³/₄in) long.

ROW 1 (RS): K8 and turn, leaving rem sts unworked.

ROW 2 (WS): K to end.

ROWS 3 AND 4: Rep rows 1 and 2.

ROW 5 (RS): Cast off 8sts loosely knitwise, slip st on RH needle back on to LH needle. (2sts)

NOTE: Do not turn work after last row of each petal (cast off row), but keep RS facing for next row.

ROW 6 (RS): Cast on 10sts on LH needle using knit on cast on method, k8 and turn.

ROWS 7, 8, 9, AND 10: Rep rows 2–5 of first petal. (4sts)

[Rep rows 6–10] x 5 to make a total of 7 petals; (14sts – 2sts at base of each petal).

Cut off yarn.

Using second yarn and working across all 14sts, cont in usual rows for flower centre as follows:

K 3 rows.

P 1 row.

K 1 row, so ending with a RS row.

Finish as for Twelve-petal flower from ** to **.

Do not press.

Decorate centre with small button if desired.

Green leaf (bottom left)

NOTE: Although the stem is worked on two double-pointed needles, you can change to ordinary needles after row 1. Cast on 3sts on a double-pointed needle and k 1 row (this is RS).

CORD ROW (RS): With RS still facing, slide sts to opposite end of needle, then take yarn across WS of work, pull yarn tightly and k to end. Rep cord row until stem is the desired length.

ROW 1 (RS): With RS of work still facing, slide sts to opposite end of needle, then take yarn across WS of work, pull yarn tightly and work k1, [yfwd, k1] x 2. (5sts)

Cont in rows, turning work in usual way.

ROW 2 (WS): K2, p1, k2.

ROW 3: K2, yfwd, k1, yfwd, k2. (7sts)

ROW 4 (WS): Cast on 1st on LH needle (using knit on cast on method), cast off 1st (knitwise), k to centre st, p centre st, k to end. (7sts)

ROW 5: Cast on 1st on LH needle, cast off 1st, k to centre st, yfwd, k centre st, yfwd, k to end. (9sts)

ROWS 6–9: [Rep rows 4 and 5] x 2. (13sts)

ROW 10: As row 4. (13sts)

ROW 11: Cast on 1st on LH needle, cast off 1st, k to end. (13sts)

ROW 12: As row 4. (13sts)

ROW 13: Cast on 1st on LH needle, cast off 1st, k to 2sts before centre st, k2tog, k centre st, ssk, k to end. (11sts)

ROWS 14–19: [Rep rows 4 and 13] x 3. (5sts)

ROW 20: K2, p1, k2.

ROW 21: K2tog, k1, ssk. (3sts)

ROW 22: K1, p1, k1.

ROW 23: Sk2p and fasten off. Darn in yarn ends. Do not press.

TOP TIP *Each flower is worked in one piece with little or no sewing-up required.*

Buttons galore

When you've taken the time to knit a cardigan or sweater, it's great to be able to add matching buttons. Use this pattern to knit a selection of covered buttons.

Essential information

DIFFICULTY Easy

SIZE Variable

YARN
Yarn of your choice x 1 (we've used DK weight)

NEEDLES
One size smaller than ballband instructions (we've used 1 pair of 4mm (UK8/US6) needles

TENSION
To match ballband instructions

NOTIONS
Plastic buttons
Large-eyed needle

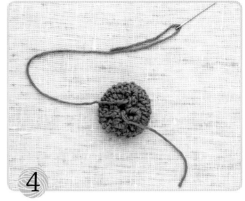

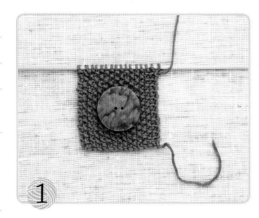

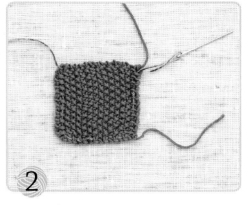

STEP 1: On smaller needles than the suggested size for your yarn, knit a square that is at least one and a half times as big as the button front. These buttons use moss stitch, but use whatever stitch matches your knitted garment.

STEP 2: Cut the yarn with a 20cm (8in) tail, thread a large-eyed needle with the tail and thread back through stitches as they are removed from the needle. Sew small running stitches (see p.303) around the three edges of the knitting, leave the thread end loose. (A contrast thread has been used here for clarity.)

STEP 3: Gently draw the knitting up into a shallow bag. Insert the button into the bag and draw the threads tight.

STEP 4: Sew the knitted fabric closed with the yarn tail. Sew the button to the garment with knitting yarn or matching thread. To secure big buttons, try sewing through a small plastic button at the back of the knitting at the same time. To prevent the button showing through from inside the stretched stitches you can insert a layer of fine woven fabric, such as muslin or calico, under the knitting if you wish.

Cuddly baby toys

Suitable for newborns to older babies, these stylized tiny cot toys are quick to knit.
The patterns include stocking stitch and garter stitch with embroidered detailing.

Essential information

DIFFICULTY Easy

SIZE 14.5 x 6.5cm (6 x 2½in) approx.

YARN

Sublime Baby Cashmere Merino Silk DK 50g

A   **B**   **C**

A: 278 Muffin x 1 **B:** 03 Vanilla x 1
C: 124 Splash x 1
Scrap of yarn for embroidery (we've used 051 Button)

NEEDLES

A: 1 pair of 3.25mm (UK10/US3) needles
B: 1 pair of 4mm (UK8/US6) needles

A
B

TENSION

22sts and 28 rows to 10cm (4in) over st st on 4mm
(UK8/US6) needles

NOTIONS

Large-eyed needle
Polyester toy filling
Water-soluble pen
Spray bottle (optional)

Knitted lamb toy

The body and head are knitted together from
the base to the top of the head.

Body and head (make 2)

Using needles A and yarn A, cast on 18sts.
K 34 rows.
Break yarn and join yarn B.
Work 10 rows in st st.
NEXT ROW: K2, k2tog, k to last 4sts, ssk, k2.
(16sts)
NEXT ROW: P2tog, p to last 2sts, p2tog. (14sts)
Rep last 2 rows once more. (10sts)
Cast off.

Ears (make 2)

Using needles A and yarn B, cast on 10sts.
ROW 1: P.
ROW 2: K1, k2tog, k4, ssk, k1. (8sts)
ROW 3: P2tog, p4, p2tog. (6sts)
ROW 4: K1, k2tog, ssk, k1. (4sts)
ROW 5: [P2tog] x 2. (2sts)
ROW 6: K2tog. (1st)
Break yarn and pull through rem st.

Forelock

Using needles B and yarn A, cast on 5sts.
ROW 1: Inc 1st, k2, inc 1st, k1. (7sts)
K 2 rows.
NEXT ROW: K2tog, k3, ssk. (5sts)
Cast off.

Making up

Join the side seams and top seam of the lamb
using mattress stitch (see p.302) and matching
yarns. Make sure all yarn tails are secure and on
the inside of your toy. Stuff fairly lightly with
toy filling. Sew the lower edge using mattress
stitch. Fold the ears in half lengthways with RS
on the outside. Oversew the seam close to the
edge. Oversew the ears in place so that the
seams are at the front. Secure the forelock in
place by working a circle of running stitch (see
p.303) around the edge. Using the photograph
as a guide, draw on the lamb's features using the
water-soluble pen. Work French knots for the
eyes (see p.120), using an oddment of yarn and
a large-eyed needle. Embroider three straight
stitches in a "Y" shape for the nose and mouth.
Spray the toy lightly with water to remove the
pen marks and leave to dry.

TOP TIP *Give the toys different expressions by varying your embroidery.*

Knitted kitten toy

The body and head are knitted together from the base to the top of the head.

Body and head (make 2)

Cast on 18sts in yarn C.

K 34 rows.

Break yarn and join yarn A.

Work 12 rows in st st.

ROW 47: K8, cast off 2sts, k to end.

ROW 48: P8, turn and work on these 8sts only, leaving rem sts on needle.

ROW 49: K1, k2tog, k to end. (7sts)

ROW 50: P.

Rep last 2 rows x 2. (5sts)

ROW 55: K1, k2tog, k2. (4sts)

ROW 56: [P2tog] x 2. (2sts)

ROW 57: K2tog. (1st)

Break yarn and pull through rem st.

Rejoin yarn to rem sts on WS of work.

ROW 58: P.

ROW 59: K to last 3sts, ssk, k1. (7sts)

ROW 60: P.

Rep last 2 rows x 2. (5sts)

ROW 65: K2, ssk, k1. (4sts)

ROW 66: [P2tog] x 2. (2sts)

ROW 67: Ssk. (1st)

Break yarn and pull through rem st.

Making up

Join the side seams using mattress stitch (see p.302) and matching yarns. Turn the kitten inside out and oversew round the ears. Turn the kitten RS out again. Make sure all yarn tails are secure and on the inside of your toy. Stuff with polyester toy filling. Sew the lower edge closed. Using the photograph as a guide, draw on the kitten's features using the water-soluble pen. Embroider the features in backstitch (see p.301), using an oddment of yarn and a large-eyed needle. Spray the toy lightly with water to remove the pen marks and leave to dry.

Cheeky monkey

If you have never knitted a toy before, try this easy monkey and you'll be a fan for life. Refer to pp.304–305 for more information on how to knit and assemble your toy. It is important not to overstuff your finished character as this will stretch the knitted fabric and give the toy an odd shape.

Essential information

DIFFICULTY Moderate

SIZE 35 x 12.5cm (14 x 5in)

YARN

King Cole Merino Blend DK 50g

A   B

A: 857 Bark x 2   **B:** 790 Caramel x 1

NEEDLES

1 pair of 4mm (UK8/US6) needles

TENSION

22sts and 28 rows to 10cm (4in) over st st on 4mm (UK8/US6) needles

NOTIONS

6-stranded embroidery thread in black and white
Polyester toy filling
Large-eyed needle

Body and head

The body and head are worked in one piece, starting at the lower end of the body.
Using yarn A, cast on 20sts, leaving a long loose end for back seam.

ROW 1 (RS): [Kfb, k1] x 10. (30sts)

ROW 2: P.

ROW 3: K1, [M1, k3] x 9, M1, k2. (40sts)

ROW 4: P.

ROW 5: K2, [M1, k4] x 9, M1, k2. (50sts)

Cont in st st for 13 rows more, ending with RS facing for next row.

Cont in st st throughout as follows:

NEXT ROW (RS): K6, [k2tog, k10] x 3, k2tog, k6. (46sts)

P 1 row.

NEXT ROW: K1, [k2tog, k4] x 7, k2tog, k1. (38sts)

P 1 row.

NEXT ROW: K3, [k2tog, k8] x 3, k2tog, k3. (34sts)

P 1 row.

NEXT ROW: K4, [k2tog, k3] x 6. (28sts)

Work 9 rows without shaping, ending with RS facing for next row.

Shape shoulders

NEXT ROW (RS): K6, k2tog, k12, k2tog, k6. (26sts)

P 1 row.

NEXT ROW: K5, s1 k2tog psso, k10, s1 k2tog psso, k5. (22sts)

P 1 row.

NEXT ROW: K4, s1 k2tog psso, k8, s1 k2tog psso, k4. (18sts)

P 1 row.

Head

NEXT ROW (RS): K2, [kfb, k1] x 8. (26sts)

P 1 row.

NEXT ROW: K2, [M1, k3] x 8. (34sts)

P 1 row.

NEXT ROW: K4, [M1, k5] x 6. (40sts)

Work 17 rows without shaping, ending with RS facing for next row.

NEXT ROW: K2, [k2tog, k3] x 7, k2tog, k1. (32sts)

P 1 row.

NEXT ROW: K1, [k2tog, k2] x 7, k2tog, k1. (24sts)

P 1 row.

NEXT ROW: [K2tog, k1] x 8. (16sts)

TOP TIP   *Make your monkey appealling with a smiley mouth.*

Knit the body Starting at the base of the body and head piece, cast on loosely and knit the fabric as instructed, shaping the knitting with kfb and then M1 increases (see pp.278–279).

Assemble the pieces Position the top of the arms just below the start of the shoulder shape. Ensure that the diagonal top edge is the correct way up so the arm seam faces the body.

P 1 row.

NEXT ROW: [K2tog] x 8. (8sts)

NEXT ROW: [P2tog] x 4. (4sts)

Cut off yarn, leaving a long loose tail. Thread end onto a blunt-ended yarn needle and pass needle through 4 rem sts as they are dropped from needle. Pull yarn to gather stitches and secure with a few stitches.

Legs (make 2)

Each leg is started at the foot end.

Using yarn B, cast on 6sts using the single cast on method (see p.264) and leaving a long loose yarn tail.

ROW 1 (RS): [Kfb] x 5, k1. (11sts)

ROW 2: P.

ROW 3: K1, [M1, k1] x 10. (21sts)

Beg with a p row, work 9 rows in st st, ending with RS facing for next row.

ROW 13 (RS): K2, [k2tog, k3] x 3, k2tog, k2. (17sts)

ROW 14: P.

Cut off yarn B.

Cont in st st in yarn A throughout as follows:

Work 10 rows without shaping, ending with RS facing for next row.

NEXT ROW (RS): K4, k2tog, k6, k2tog, k3. (15sts)

Work 15 rows without shaping.

NEXT ROW (RS): K3, [k2tog, k2] x 2, k2tog, k2. (12sts) **

Work 11 rows without shaping.

Cast off knitwise.

Arms (make 2)

Each arm is started at the hand end.

Work as for Legs to **.

Work 7 rows without shaping.

Cast off 2sts at beg of next 4 rows.

Cast off rem 4sts, leaving a long loose end for sewing arm to body.

Muzzle

Using yarn B, cast on 6sts, using single cast on method and leaving a long loose yarn tail.

ROW 1 (RS): [Kfb] x 5, k1. (11sts)

ROW 2: P.

ROW 3: K1, [M1, k1] x 10. (21sts)

ROW 4: P.

ROW 5: K1, [M1, k2] x 10. (31sts)

Beg with a p row, work 5 rows in st st.

Cast off knitwise, leaving a long loose yarn tail for sewing muzzle to body.

Ears (make 2)

Using yarn B, cast on 3sts.

ROW 1 (WS): [Kfb] x 2, k1. (5sts)

NOTE: Work the remaining increases as yarnovers, ensuring that each yarnover is crossed when it is knit in the following row to close the hole by knitting it through the back of the loop.

ROW 2 (RS): [K1, yrn] x 4, k1. (9sts)

ROW 3: K to end, knitting each yrn through back loop.

ROW 4: [K2, yrn] x 4, k1. (13sts)

ROW 5: Rep row 3.

ROW 6: K.

K 2 rows.

Cast off loosely knitwise, leaving a long loose end for gathering ear into cupped shape and sewing to head.

Tail

Using yarn B, cast on 3sts, leaving a long loose end for sewing tail to body.

Work in g st (k every row) until tail is a little longer than leg (or desired length).

NEXT ROW: S1 k2tog psso, then fasten off.

Tail will swirl naturally – do not press out this swirl.

Making up

Assemble the monkey and sew up the seams following the instructions on p.305.

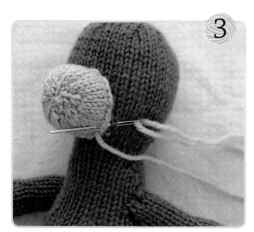

Sew on the muzzle Stuff the knitted muzzle firmly and evenly with polyester toy filling. Sew on the muzzle using yarn B, making tiny stitches that will not be obvious against the dark brown head.

Embroidering the facial features Use all six strands of embroidery thread, or even try off-cuts of black and white DK yarn if you have them. Refer to p.303 for information about embroidery stitches.

Attaching the tail Add the tail using yarn B and a sufficiently large-eyed needle. Knot the end and start taking the needle through the underside of the tail so it does not show.

Essential information

DIFFICULTY Moderate

SIZE 12cm (5in) tall

YARN

Blue colourway King Cole Bamboo Cotton DK 100g

A   **B**   **C**

A: 525 Cobalt x 1   **B:** 538 Cream x 1   **C:** 534 Black x 1

Pink colourway King Cole Bamboo Cotton DK 100g

A   **B**   **C**

A: 528 Rose x 1   **B:** 538 Cream x 1   **C:** 534 Black x 1

NEEDLES

1 pair of 3mm (UK11/US n/a) needles

TENSION 30sts and 37 rows to 10cm (4in) over st st
on 3mm (UK11/US n/a) needles

NOTIONS

Stitch marker

Polyester toy stuffing

Dried chickpeas for stuffing

Large-eyed needle

Knitted bunnies

A gorgeous gift for a baby or young child, and a fun way to improve your increase and decrease skills. Embroidery stitches create the facial features and pom-poms form neat, fluffy tails.

Body

Cast on 16sts in yarn A, placing marker at centre of cast on edge.

ROW 1: Inc into every st to end. (32sts)

ROW 2 AND ALL FOLL ALT ROWS: P.

ROW 3: [K1, inc in next st] to end. (48sts)

ROW 5: [K2, inc in next st] x 3, k to last 7sts, [inc in next st, k2] x 2, inc in last st. (54sts)

ROW 7: K.

ROW 9: [K3, inc in next st] x 3, [k2, inc in next st] to last 12sts, [inc in next st, k3] to end. (70sts)

ROW 11: K.

ROW 13: [K4, inc in next st] x 3, k to last 11sts, [inc in next st, k4] x 2, inc in last st. (76sts)

Work 13 rows without shaping.

Shape back

ROW 1: [K3, k2tog] x 6, k to last 27sts, [k2tog, k3] x 5, k2tog. (64sts)

Work 3 rows without shaping.

ROW 5: [K2, k2tog] x 6, k to last 22sts, [k2tog, k2] x 5, k2tog. (52sts)

NEXT AND ALL FOLL ALT ROWS: P.

ROW 7: [K1, k2tog] x 4, k to last 11sts, [k2tog, k1] x 3, k2tog. (44sts)

ROW 9: K12, k2tog, k2, k2tog, k8, k2tog, k2, k2tog, k to end. (40sts)

ROW 11: K1, k2tog, k to last 3sts, k2tog, k1. (38sts)

ROW 13: K10, k2tog, k2, k2tog, k6, k2tog, k2, k2tog, k to end. (34sts)

ROW 15: K1, k2tog, k to last 3sts, k2tog, k1. (32sts)

Work 7 rows without shaping.

Shape head

ROW 1: *K2, k2tog, rep from * to end. (24sts)

ROW 2 AND ALL FOLL ALT ROWS: P.

ROW 3: [K1, k2tog] to end. (16sts)

ROW 5: [K2tog] to end. (8sts)

Using a darning needle, draw yarn through rem sts twice. Join row ends to form back seam, using mattress stitch (see p.302) and leaving bottom open. Stuff firmly with toy stuffing, inserting a layer of chickpeas at the base of the bunny. Line up back seam with marker at bunny's front and squash flat. Oversew (see p.301) this seam together. Make a 3cm (1¼in) pom-pom (see p.299) in just one colour or a mix of yarn colours. Sew the pom-pom to the bottom of the bunny.

Spots (make 3)

Using yarn B, cast on 3sts.

ROW 1: K.

ROW 2: Inc in first st, p1, inc in last st. (5sts)

ROW 3: K.

ROW 4: P.

ROW 5: K.

ROW 6: P2tog, p1, p2tog. (3sts)

ROW 7: K.

Cast off, leaving a long tail of yarn. Arrange spots randomly on the bunny and, using long yarn tail and running stitch (see p.303), sew in place.

Feet (make 2)

Using yarn A, cast on 6sts.

ROW 1: K.

ROW 2: P.

Rep last 2 rows five times more. Cast off. With RS facing, oversew cast on and cast off edge together. This seam forms the back of the foot. Using picture as a guide, pin in place and oversew to underside of body.

Ears (make 2)

Using yarn A, cast on 6sts and work 10 rows st st.

NEXT ROW (RS): K1, skpo, k2tog, k1. (4sts)

NEXT ROW: P.

Change to yarn B.

NEXT ROW: K2, M1, k2. (5sts)

Beginning with a p row, work 9 rows st st. Cast off.

Fold ear piece in half to match cast on to cast off edge. Join row ends and stitch in position; catch the right ear down with a single stitch to affix to bunny's head.

Using yarn B and C, embroider the eyes and nose in satin stitch (see p.303).

Repeat to make a pair of bunnies.

Basic equipment and techniques

Yarns

A yarn is the long, stranded, spun fibre that we knit with. There are many types of yarns, allowing knitters to enjoy a variety of sensory experiences as they express themselves through the medium. Yarns may be made of different fibres and have a range of textures. Their possibilities are exciting: you can, in theory, knit with anything – from a skein of supple silk sock yarn to the plastic bag that you brought it home in. Choose from a colour palette that sweeps from subtle, muted tones to eye-popping brights.

Wool

Merino wool

Alpaca

Wool The hair, or wool, of a variety of breeds of sheep, such as the Shetland Moorit or Bluefaced Leicester, is made into pure wool yarns, or blended with other fibres. It is very warm and hard-wearing, and great for winter wear such as jackets, cardigans, hats, and gloves. Some wool is rough, but it will soften with wear and washing. Wool sold as "organic" often contains a high proportion of lanolin, making a strong, waterproof yarn.

Merino wool This is wool from the merino sheep, which is said to have one of the softest wools of any sheep breed. The bouncy, smooth-surfaced fibre is just as warm as a more wiry, coarse wool. Merino is a fantastic choice for wearing against the skin, and is often treated to make it suitable for machine-washing. Good for soft scarves, armwarmers, and children's garments.

Alpaca This fibre has a luxurious feel and is one of the warmest natural fibres you can knit with. Even a fine, 4-ply garment provides sufficient insulation in bitterly cold weather. The alpaca is related to the llama. Alpaca yarn is perfect for ski hats, and thick, cosy jumpers and socks. You will also find baby alpaca yarn available, which is softer still.

Mohair This fibre is the hair of the angora goat, and it produces a unique natural "halo" when knitted up. Working with it is quite challenging, as its frizzy appearance makes it difficult to see the structure of the knitting and any mistakes made. Mohair makes particularly interesting oversized jumpers or accessories. It is not advisable to use it for babywear as it may shed hair when newly made, which could be dangerous if inhaled.

Mohair

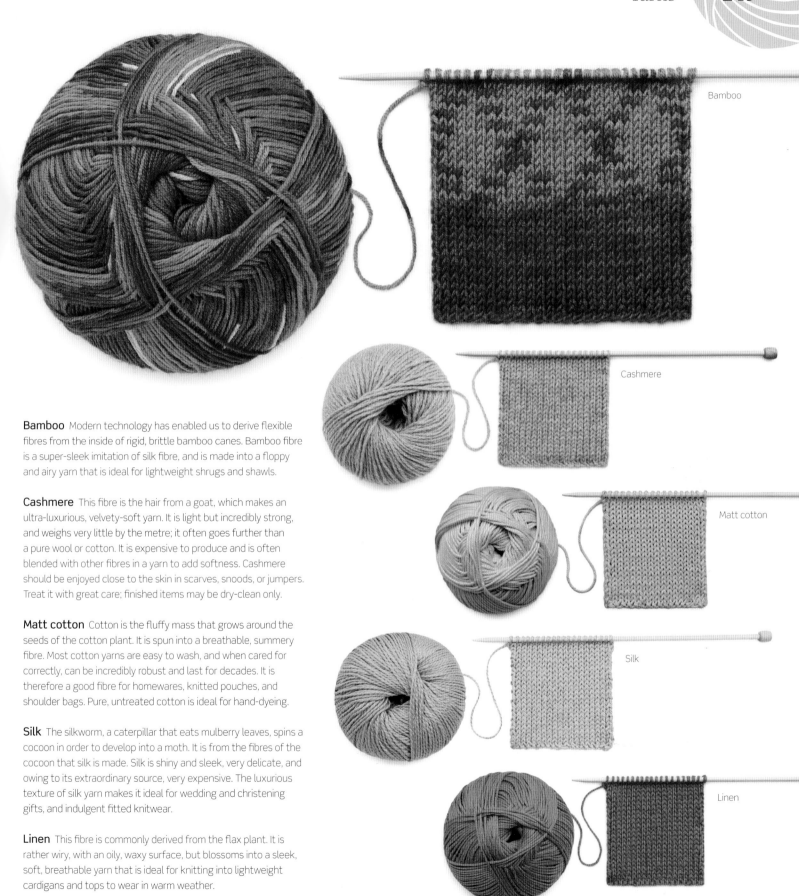

Bamboo

Cashmere

Matt cotton

Silk

Linen

Bamboo Modern technology has enabled us to derive flexible fibres from the inside of rigid, brittle bamboo canes. Bamboo fibre is a super-sleek imitation of silk fibre, and is made into a floppy and airy yarn that is ideal for lightweight shrugs and shawls.

Cashmere This fibre is the hair from a goat, which makes an ultra-luxurious, velvety-soft yarn. It is light but incredibly strong, and weighs very little by the metre; it often goes further than a pure wool or cotton. It is expensive to produce and is often blended with other fibres in a yarn to add softness. Cashmere should be enjoyed close to the skin in scarves, snoods, or jumpers. Treat it with great care; finished items may be dry-clean only.

Matt cotton Cotton is the fluffy mass that grows around the seeds of the cotton plant. It is spun into a breathable, summery fibre. Most cotton yarns are easy to wash, and when cared for correctly, can be incredibly robust and last for decades. It is therefore a good fibre for homewares, knitted pouches, and shoulder bags. Pure, untreated cotton is ideal for hand-dyeing.

Silk The silkworm, a caterpillar that eats mulberry leaves, spins a cocoon in order to develop into a moth. It is from the fibres of the cocoon that silk is made. Silk is shiny and sleek, very delicate, and owing to its extraordinary source, very expensive. The luxurious texture of silk yarn makes it ideal for wedding and christening gifts, and indulgent fitted knitwear.

Linen This fibre is commonly derived from the flax plant. It is rather wiry, with an oily, waxy surface, but blossoms into a sleek, soft, breathable yarn that is ideal for knitting into lightweight cardigans and tops to wear in warm weather.

Yarn weights

The yarn "weight" refers to the thickness of a yarn. Some yarns are spun by manufacturers to fall into what are considered as "standard" yarn weights, such as UK double-knitting and aran, and US sport or worsted. These standard weights have long histories and will probably be around for some time to come. However, even within these standard weights there is slight variation in thickness, and textured novelty yarns are not easy to categorize by thickness alone.

Visual yarn thickness is only one indicator of a yarn-weight category. A yarn can look thicker than another yarn purely because of its loft, the air between the fibres, and the springiness of the strands. By pulling a strand between your hands you can see how much loft it has by how much the thickness diminishes when the yarn is stretched. The ply of a yarn is also not an indication of yarn thickness. Plies are the strands spun together around each other to form the yarn. A yarn with four plies can be very thick or very thin depending on the thickness of each individual ply.

In order to help knitters attempting to match like for like when looking for a substitute yarn for their knitting pattern, yarn manufacturers have created a table of yarn weights. This table (right) demonstrates how to find the nearest yarn substitute if you are unable to purchase the yarn specified in a knitting pattern. The very best indication of a yarn weight is the manufacturer's recommended tension and needle size for the yarn. (These will produce a knitted fabric that is loose enough to be soft and flexible but not so loose that it loses its shape.) Two yarns with the same fibre content and the same recommended tension and needle size will be ideal substitutes for each other.

TOP TIP

A ply is a single twisted strand – the more plies, the thicker the yarn.

Yarn labels

Yarn is usually packaged with a label that provides all the information you need to knit successfully. Before you buy, always read the label carefully to establish the type of yarn, suggested needle size, care instructions, and ball length.

Decide whether you require an easy-care yarn and check the care instructions. Fibre content will indicate whether the yarn is synthetic, natural, or a mix of fibres. The ball length will enable you to calculate how many balls are required especially when substituting yarn. Check the dye lot number if you are purchasing several balls, as variations in colour can occur across different dye lots.

Lace/2-ply Extremely light and often sold in a plentiful quantity. If worked on needles of the recommended size, the yarn produces a very fine-knit, delicate result. It can be more pleasurable to use the yarn with slightly larger needles for a more open fabric and a quicker knit.

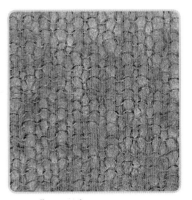

Superfine/3-ply An ideal choice for lightweight lace work. It goes a long way per ball, and requires very slim needles. A gossamer yarn such as this one, above, highlights stitch definition and fine detail, which is why intricate lace work looks stunning in superfine yarn.

Fine/4-ply Many knitters prefer fine to superfine yarn as it uses a more comfortable needle size yet still produces a lightweight knit. It is ideal for socks and baby clothes. The small stitches and neat appearance also suit delicate texture and colourwork items.

Standard yarn weight chart

Yarn symbol		**0** Lace	**1** Superfine	**2** Fine	**3** Light	**4** Medium	**5** Bulky	**6** Super bulky
Recommended needle sizes	Metric	2mm 2.5mm	2.75mm 3mm 3.25mm	3.5mm 3.75mm 4mm	4.5mm	5mm 5.5mm	6mm 6.5mm 7mm 8mm	9mm 10mm
	Old UK	14 13	12 11 10	n/a 9 8	7	6 5	4 3 2 0	00 000
	US	0 1	2 n/a 3	4 5 6	7	8 9	10 10½ n/a 11	13 15
Yarn weight		Lace, 2-ply, fingering	Superfine, 3-ply, fingering, baby	Fine, 4-ply, sport, baby	Double knit (DK), light worsted, 5–6-ply	Aran, medium, worsted, Afghan, 12-ply	Bulky, chunky, craft, rug. 14-ply	Super bulky, super chunky, bulky, roving, 16-ply and upwards
What do you want to knit?		Lace	Fine-knit socks, shawls, babywear	Light sweaters, babywear, socks, accessories	Sweaters, light-weight scarves, blankets, toys	Sweaters, cables menswear, blankets, hats, scarves, mittens	Rugs, jackets, blankets, hats, legwarmers, winter accessories	Heavy blankets, rugs, thick scarves

Double knit (DK)/Light worsted/ 5–6-ply DK yarn is used for anything from blankets and toys to jumpers and cardigans. It is commonly associated with 4mm (UK8/US6) needles, and knits up quickly. Many projects in this book are knitted in DK yarn.

Aran/Worsted/12-ply A thick, warm yarn that requires 5mm (UK6/US8) needles. It is good for men's garments with thick cabled detail, and functional items. Many yarns in this thickness employ a variety of fibres to make them machine-washable.

Bulky/chunky/14-ply Although bulky, the yarn consists mainly of lightweight fibres to prevent garments from misshaping. Commonly worked on 7mm (UK2/USn/a) needles, it makes a chunky knitted fabric perfect for outerwear, hats, and legwarmers.

Super bulky/Super chunky/ 16-ply+ The yarn thickness varies, but it is mostly used with large needles from 10mm (UK000/US15) upwards. A great choice for beginners as stitches are so large that mistakes are easily visible. Good for rugged scarves.

Straight needles

If you are new to knitting, start with straight needles because they give a great deal of support to the hand when knitting. Short needles are recommended for small projects; longer needles are more suitable for wider knits such as a pullover or a baby's blanket, and for knitters who like to work by holding the needles underneath their arms or elbows.

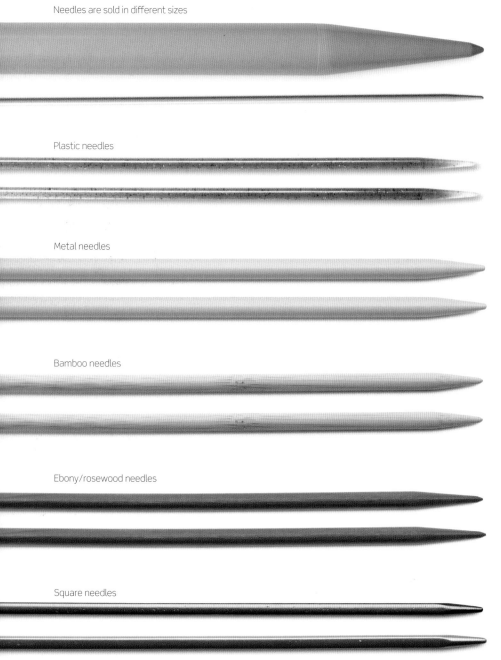

Needles are sold in different sizes

Plastic needles

Metal needles

Bamboo needles

Ebony/rosewood needles

Square needles

Size Knitting needles vary in diameter, from just 1.5mm (¹⁄₁₆in) thick to over 25mm (1in). There are three common needle-sizing systems: European metric, old British sizes, and American sizes. If you have older needles, use a knitting needle gauge (see p.255) to find their equivalent modern size. Needles are also available in various lengths to suit different projects and different ways of holding needles.

Plastic needles For needles with a surface that is halfway between that of metal and that of bamboo, choose plastic. It remains at a steady temperature during use, which may suit people who have arthritis. Avoid plastic needles of 4mm (UK8/US6) or smaller, as heavy projects may bend or break them.

Metal needles When working with hairy fibres such as mohair or wool, which may stick, slippery metal needles are great. If you find that you tend to knit too tightly, the slippery surface can help as it will cause a knitter's tension to loosen. Needles of more than 8mm (UK0/US11) in diameter can be clunky to work with, so are rarely available.

Bamboo needles Bamboo is a lightweight, flexible material, and makes excellent knitting needles. It helps to keep stitches regularly spaced, creating an even knitted fabric with a good tension. Great for slippery fibres such as silk and bamboo yarn. Recommended for arthritis sufferers. Thin needles will gradually warp slightly with use, to fit the curvature of your hand.

Ebony/rosewood needles These wooden needles feel luxurious to work with, and can be quite expensive. They often have a waxy surface, which becomes smooth with wear, creating a soft and tactile surface. Like bamboo needles, they help to create an even tension; they hold their shape and remain straight when used, giving them a solid feel.

Square needles Most needles are cylindrical with a pointed tip; these unusual new needles have a faceted surface and a pointed tip. Made from metal, they lie over each other better, which is particularly useful when working with double-pointed needles, and cause less strain on the hands, making them especially suitable for arthritis sufferers.

Double-pointed and circular needles

Some projects are "knitted in the round" (see pp.290–291), to produce a tube of knitting without a seam. You can use both double-pointed needles and circular needles to do this, but the choice of needles is usually down to length. Most circular needles are too large to knit socks on, so double-pointed needles, which can knit a narrow tube, are used instead. Your tension and style will change according to which you use.

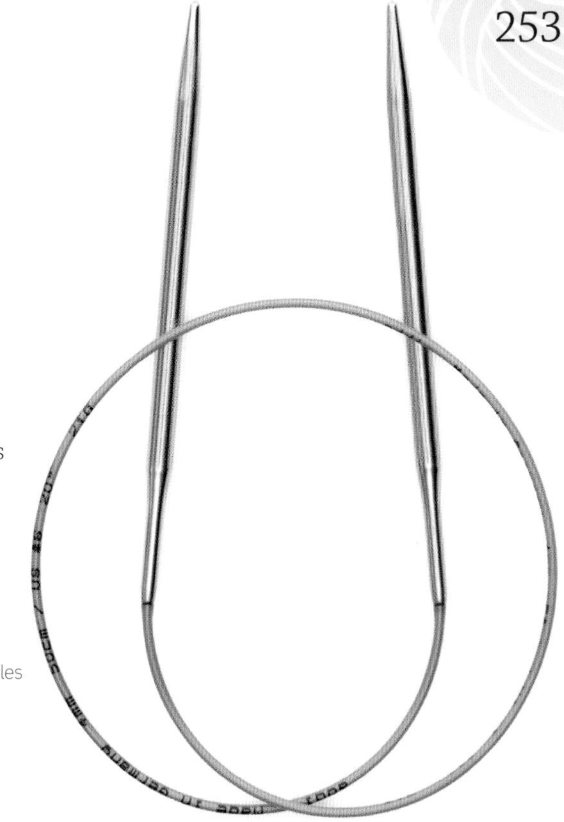

Double-pointed needles (DPNs) The recommended option for socks and gloves. These needles are short and do not accommodate a large number of stitches. At first, some knitters may find that ladders form on each corner between the needles; however, this problem will disappear over time through practise. DPNs are less slippery when made of bamboo or wood.

Circular needles A flexible tube joins two needles to make a pair of circular needles. These come in a selection of different lengths and thicknesses. Choose ones appropriate to your project – they should match the anticipated diameter of the knitted tube. Knitting patterns usually specify the size required. A piece of flat knitting can also be worked on circular needles; just turn your needles around after each row instead of working in the round.

Interchangeable circular needles These are a worthwhile investment if you frequently knit in the round. The set comes with a connecting wire in various lengths, and a selection of tips. Attach your chosen tip to each end of the wire to build a pair of needles to a specific length and size. Some sets allow you to attach several wires together to create very long circular needles.

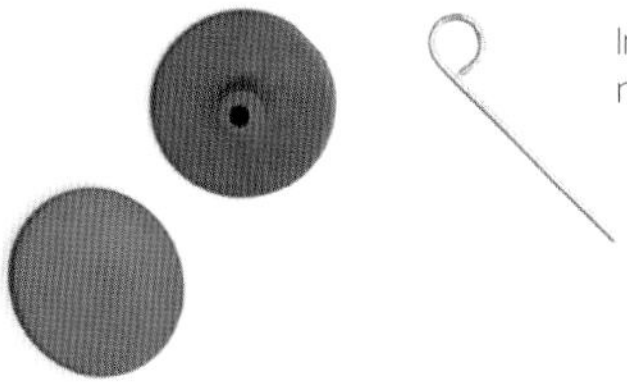

Circular needles

Double-pointed needles

Interchangeable circular needles with set of tips, left

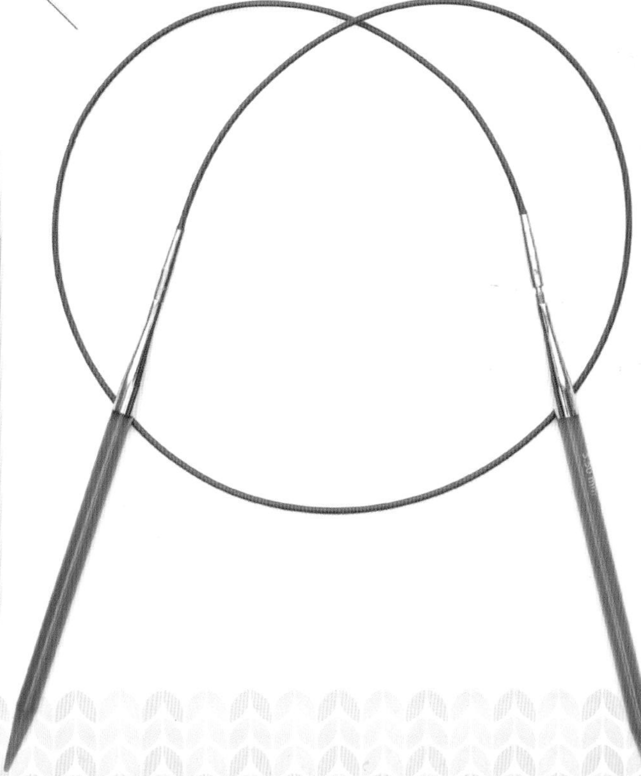

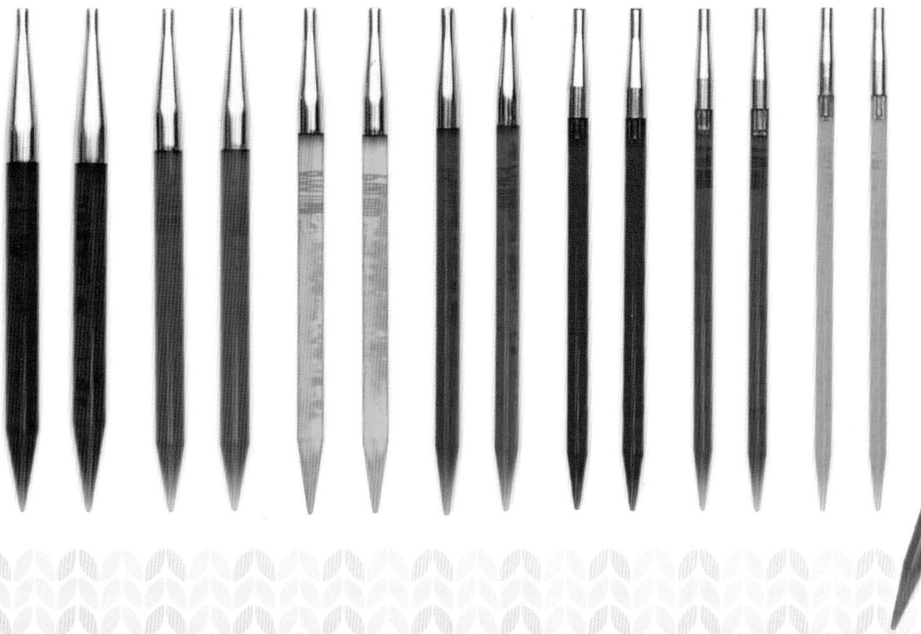

Other equipment

Hundreds of different gadgets are available to knitters. Some are merely for convenience, whereas others are absolutely vital and perform specific tasks. Here are the basics, to which you can add more advanced items as you progress. These basic items should always be at hand when you are working on a project. Most knitters have a portable knitting bag or case to keep them in, so that it is easy to take everything to wherever they want to sit and knit. The tools below are relatively inexpensive, and can be purchased from haberdashery stores and knitting suppliers.

Tape measure Use this to accurately gauge sizing, to check tension, and to measure your knitting. Stick to using either metric or imperial measures.

Stitch holder Use it to hold stitches that you will return to later. Make your own stitch holder from a length of lightweight cotton yarn, or a safety pin.

Cable needle A kinked or v-shaped cable needle is used when working cables; this shape prevents cable stitches from sliding away. Choose a size that is closest to that of the needles used for the main body of the knitting.

Crochet hook A crochet hook makes it much easier to pick up previously dropped stitches. You can also use a crochet hook for inserting tassels.

Tapestry needle This has a blunt tip that will not damage yarn. Make sure that the eye is an appropriate size for the type of yarn you are using.

Stitch markers Use these to mark the beginning and end of a panel of stitches, and to identify the end of each row when working in the round. As you arrive at a marker, transfer it with the stitches and continue working the row as normal.

Knitting bag Bags for knitters often have many compartments, perfect for storing equipment and materials for your current project.

Tape measure

Stitch holder

Cable needles

Crochet hook

Tapestry needle

Stitch markers

Knitting bag

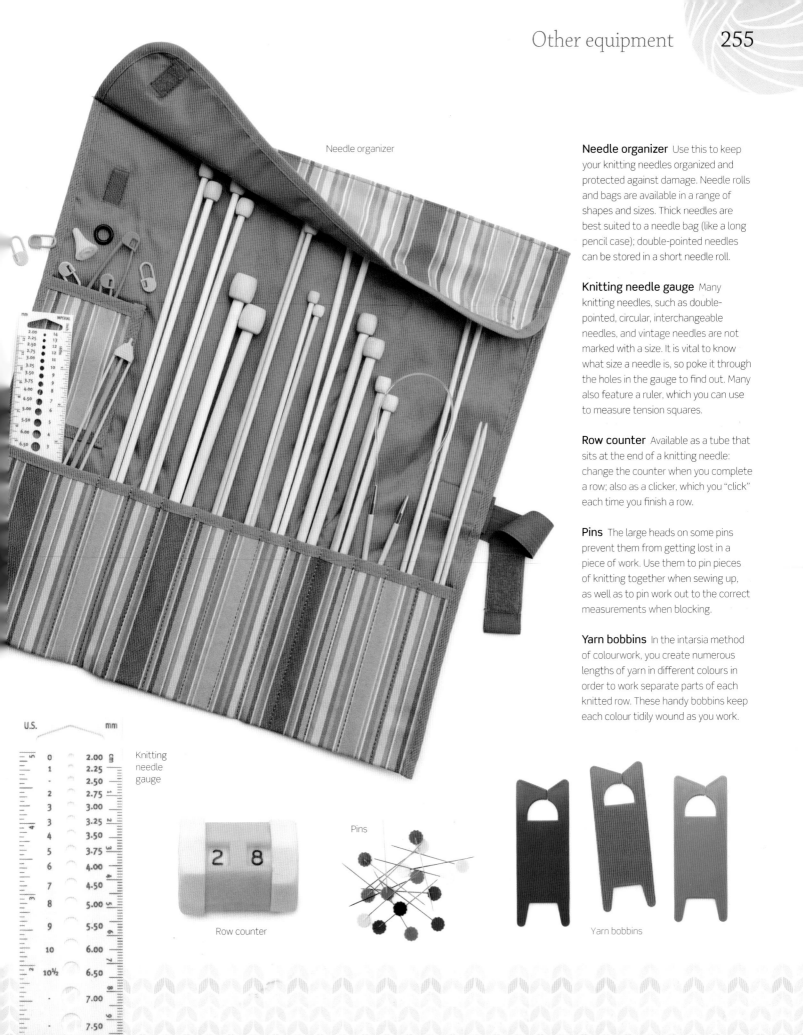

Needle organizer

Needle organizer Use this to keep your knitting needles organized and protected against damage. Needle rolls and bags are available in a range of shapes and sizes. Thick needles are best suited to a needle bag (like a long pencil case); double-pointed needles can be stored in a short needle roll.

Knitting needle gauge Many knitting needles, such as double-pointed, circular, interchangeable needles, and vintage needles are not marked with a size. It is vital to know what size a needle is, so poke it through the holes in the gauge to find out. Many also feature a ruler, which you can use to measure tension squares.

Row counter Available as a tube that sits at the end of a knitting needle: change the counter when you complete a row; also as a clicker, which you "click" each time you finish a row.

Pins The large heads on some pins prevent them from getting lost in a piece of work. Use them to pin pieces of knitting together when sewing up, as well as to pin work out to the correct measurements when blocking.

Yarn bobbins In the intarsia method of colourwork, you create numerous lengths of yarn in different colours in order to work separate parts of each knitted row. These handy bobbins keep each colour tidily wound as you work.

Knitting needle gauge

Row counter

Pins

Yarn bobbins

Embellishments

Add dazzle and give your knitting an edge by adding embellishments, from embroidery to beads, sequins, ribbons, pretty trimmings, as well as fastenings, and attractive handles. These can completely change the feel of a project, depending on the way that you use them. Embellishment gives you an opportunity to express your creativity: try some of the ideas here.

Trimmings

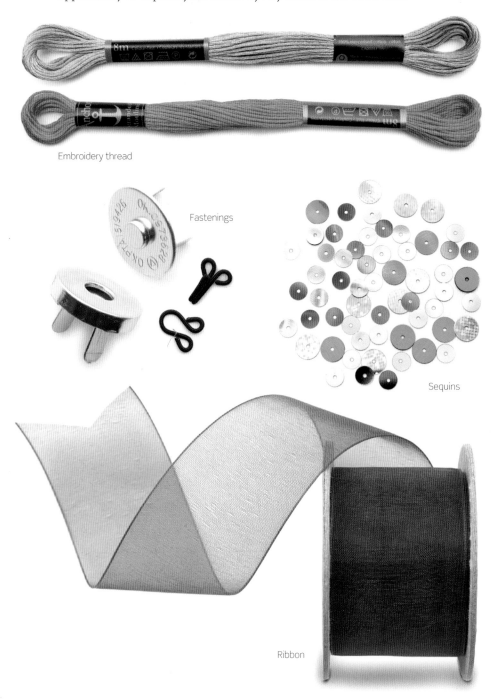

Embroidery thread

Fastenings

Sequins

Ribbon

Trimmings There is a huge range of trimmings that you can choose from to customize and personlize your knitted projects. Fringes, broderie anglaise, and feathers, to name just a few, can add interest to clothing and home accessories. Look in haberdashery shops for inspiration.

Embroidery thread Silky, shiny embroidery threads come in a mixture of colours and styles. Metallic threads are particularly interesting and will jazz up a solid knitted background. Use a tapestry needle to embroider knitting, remembering that most embroidery threads stipulate that they must be hand-washed.

Fastenings Choose fastenings with care, according to the type of project and the yarn you are using, and make sure they are not too heavy or they will pull the knitting out of shape. Buttons usually double as a feature, but other fastenings are more discreet, such as a hook-and-eye or a press-stud. Stitch these on with knitting yarn or sewing thread. Use push-on press-studs for felted work.

Sequins Knit sequins into your work as you go, or embroider them on afterwards. If you're going to knit them in, look for pailettes, which have a larger hole than regular sequins, and are best suited to fine yarns. Choose flat sequins, which will sit flat against the work and each other, and are less inclined to get scratched and lose surface colour.

Ribbon When choosing ribbon, take the project with you to colour-coordinate effectively (although you may feel able to remember a colour, this is unreliable). Among the vast choice available, you could try organza, patterned, striped, or metallic ribbons. Thread them through your work, trim an edge, or form them into bows or rosettes.

Machine embroidery thread This thread is very fine, and is sold on cones or small reels. It is intended for machine embroidery, but you could try double-stranding a metallic one (check its meterage) with a knitting yarn for a subtle hint of sparkle. Alternatively, use variegated threads, or several at the same time, with the yarn.

Buttons The choice of buttons for a garment is an important one. They are decorative as well as serving a practical purpose; make sure you select them to suit the garment's cleaning instructions, or they may have to be removed beforehand. Coconut, shell, wooden, and metallic buttons are fairly neutral and work with many colours. Take your project with you when choosing buttons.

Bag handles Knitted bags are given added strength when carried on solid bag handles. These will take the weight of the bag's contents without stretching out of shape or breaking. There are jazzy coloured plastic handles, wood, or metal versions available, which can be used to make a bag look classic, contemporary, or quirky.

Knitting beads Most knitting beads are specially manufactured to be washable, and retain their colour over time, whereas other types may not withstand wear and washing. They come in various sizes to match the different yarn weights available.

Machine embroidery thread

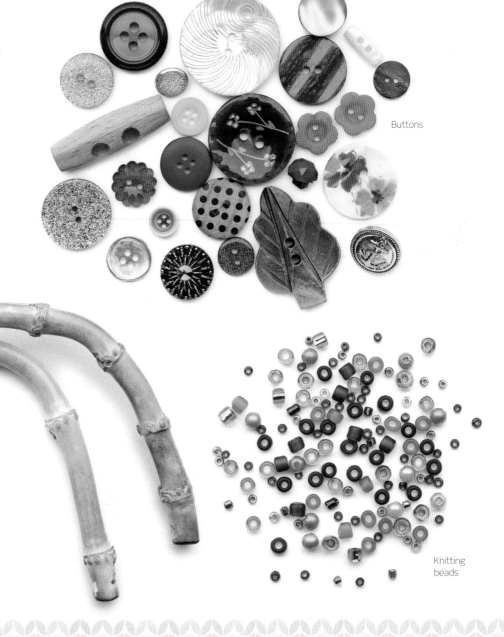

Buttons

Bag handles

Knitting beads

Following a pattern

Knitting patterns can look daunting to a beginner knitter, but if approached step by step they are easy to understand. This section provides an explanation of how to follow simple knitting patterns and gives tips for finishing details and seams. The best advice for a beginner wanting to knit a first project from a knitting pattern is to start with a simple accessory. Cushion covers are especially good practice as the instructions are straightforward and usually the only finishing details are seams. This is an example of a pattern for a simple, striped, stocking stitch cushion cover.

At the beginning of most patterns you will find the skill level required for the knitting. Make sure you are confident that the skill level is right for you.

Check the size of the finished item. If it is a simple square like this cushion, you can adjust the size easily by adding or subtracting stitches and rows.

Use the yarn specified, but if you are unable to obtain this yarn, choose a substitute yarn of the same weight.

Make a tension swatch before starting to knit and change the needle size if necessary (see opposite page).

Consult the abbreviations list with your pattern for the meanings of abbreviations (see also p.261).

The back of a cushion cover is sometimes exactly the same as the front or it has a fabric back. In this case, the stripes are reversed on the back for a more versatile cover.

After all the knitted pieces are complete, follow the Making up (or Finishing) section of the pattern.

See p.300 for how to darn in loose ends.

See pp.300–302 for seaming options. Take time with seams on knitting. Practise on odd pieces of knitting before starting your main project.

Summer cushion cover

Skill level
Easy

Size of finished cushion
40.5 x 40.5cm (16 x 16in)

Materials
3 x 50g (1³⁄₄oz)/125m (137yd) balls in each of branded Pure Wool DK in Lavender 039 (A) and Avocado 019 (B). Pair of 4mm (US size 6) knitting needles. Cushion pad to fit finished cover.

Tension
22sts and 30 rows to 10cm (4in) over stocking stitch on 4mm (UK8/US6) needles or size necessary to achieve correct tension. To save time, take time to check tension.

Front
Using 4mm (UK8/US6) needles and A, cast on 88sts. Beg with a K row, work in st st until work measures 14cm (5¹⁄₂in) from cast on edge, ending with RS facing for next row.
Cut off A and change to B.
Cont in st st until work measures 26.5cm (10¹⁄₂in) from cast on edge, ending with RS facing for next row.
Cut off B and change to A.
Cont in st st until work measures 40.5cm (16in) from cast on edge, ending with RS facing for next row.
Cast off.

Back
Work as for Front, but use B for A, and A for B.

Making up
Darn in loose ends.
Block and press lightly on wrong side, following instructions on yarn label. With wrong sides facing, sew three sides of back and front together. Turn right-side out, insert cushion pad, and sew remaining seam.

Always purchase the same total amount in metres/yards of a substitute yarn; not the same amount in weight.

If desired, select different colours to suit your décor; the colours specified are just suggestions.

Extra items needed for your project will usually be listed under Notions or Additional materials.

Instructions for working a piece of knitted fabric always start with how many stitches to cast on and what yarn or needle size to use. If there is only one needle size and one yarn, these may be absent here.

Work in the specified stitch pattern, for the specified number of rows or cm/in.

Colours are usually changed on a right-side row, so end with the right side facing for the changeover row.

If no stitch is specified for the cast off, always cast off knitwise (see p.269).

Make sure you look at the yarn label instructions before attempting to press any piece of knitting. The label may say that the yarn cannot be pressed or to press it only with a cool iron. (See p.300 for blocking tips.)

Garment patterns

Choosing the right size and knitting a tension swatch are the two most important things to get right if you want to create a successful garment. It is also possible to make simple alterations to patterns worked in plain garter or stocking stitch.

Choosing a garment size

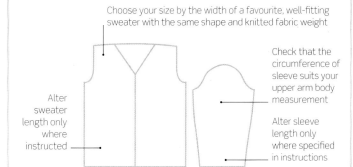

Choose your size by the width of a favourite, well-fitting sweater with the same shape and knitted fabric weight

Alter sweater length only where instructed

Check that the circumference of sleeve suits your upper arm body measurement

Alter sleeve length only where specified in instructions

Rather than looking at specific "sizes" when choosing which size to knit, select the one nearest to how you want the garment to fit. The best way to do this is to find a similar garment that fits you. Lay it flat and measure its width – choose the width on the pattern that is the closest match to your body shape.

Photocopy your pattern and highlight the figures for your size throughout. Start with the number of balls of yarn, then the number of stitches to cast on, the length to knit to the armhole, and so on. The smallest size is given first and larger sizes follow in parentheses. Where only one figure is given, this applies to all sizes.

Measuring tension

Always knit a swatch before starting your project to make sure that you achieve the recommended stitch size (tension). Only if you achieve the correct tension will your knitting have the correct measurements.

1 Using the specified needle size, knit a 13cm (5in) square. Mark 10cm (4in) across the centre with pins and count the number of stitches between the pins.

2 Count the number of rows to 10cm (4in) in the same way. If you have fewer stitches and rows than you should, try again with a smaller needle size; if you have more, change to a larger needle. Use the needle size for your knitting that best matches the correct tension. (Matching stitch width is more important than matching row height.)

Altering patterns

Alter the length of garment patterns worked in plain garter or stocking stitch, but avoid altering armholes, necklines, or sleeve heads. As sleeves and some bodies have shaping, this must also be adjusted. In this example, length is added to a sleeve:

1 Photocopy or draw out the pattern diagram. Write the new required length on the diagram (eg 48cm (19in)).

2 Find the number of rows to 10cm (4in) in the tension note. Divide number by 10 to calculate how many rows there are in 1cm. For example, 30 rows per 10cm (4in). 30 ÷ 10 = 3 rows per 1cm (½in).

3 Multiply the required new length by the number of rows in 1cm (½in). The resulting figure is the total number in the new length. For example, 48 × 3 = 144 rows.

4 Any increasing will also have to be re-calculated. From the pattern, note the number of stitches to cast on at the cuff and how many there will be on the needle just before the start of the underarm shaping (this figure should be shown at the end of the written instruction for the increases).

5 Subtract the smallest from the largest amount of stitches. The answer is the total number of stitches to be increased. Divide the answer by two (because a sleeve has two sides), to give the number of stitches to increase on each side. For example. 114 - 60 = 54 sts. 54 ÷ 2 = 27 sts.

6 To calculate the number of rows between each increase, divide the new number of rows found in Step 3 by the number of increases calculated in Step 5. If you have a fraction in this answer, round the number down. For example, 144 ÷ 27 = 4.22. Increase one stitch each side every 4 rows. Knit the remaining rows straight before underarm cast offs.

Understanding written instructions

Anyone who can cast on, knit and purl, and cast off will be able to work from simple knit-and-purl-combination stitch pattern instructions with little difficulty. It is just a question of following the instructions one step at a time and getting used to the abbreviations. A list of common knitting abbreviations is given opposite, but for simple knit and purl textures all you need to grasp is that "k1" means "knit one stitch", "k2" means "knit two stitches", and so on. And the same applies for the purl stitches – "p1" means "purl one stitch", "p2" means "purl two stitches", and so on.

To begin a stitch pattern, cast on the number of stitches that it tells you to, using your chosen yarn and the yarn manufacturer's recommended needle size. Work the stitch row by row, then repeat the rows as instructed and the stitch pattern will grow beneath the needles. When your knitting is the desired size, cast off in pattern (see pp.269–272).

The best tips for first-timers are to follow the rows slowly; mark the right side of the fabric by knotting a coloured thread onto it; use a row counter to keep track of where you are; and pull out your stitches and start again if you get in a muddle. If you love the stitch pattern you are trying out, you can make a scarf, blanket, or cushion cover with it – no need to buy a knitting pattern.

The principles for following stitch patterns are the same for cables and lace (see p.287 and p.288–289). Some stitch patterns will call for "slipping" stitches and knitting "through the back of the loop". These useful techniques are given in the glossary (see p.314) as a handy reference, as well as consulting the abbreviations and terminology list (right).

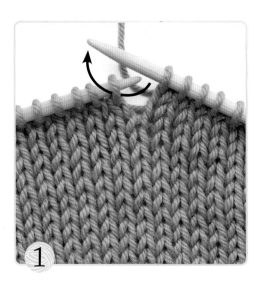

Slipping stitches purlwise

1 Always slip stitches purlwise, for example when slipping stitches onto a stitch holder, unless instructed otherwise. Insert the tip of the right needle from right to left through the front of the loop on the left needle.

2 Slide the stitch onto the tip of the right needle and off the left needle without working it. The slipped stitch now sits on the right needle with the right side of the loop at the front just like the worked stitches next to it.

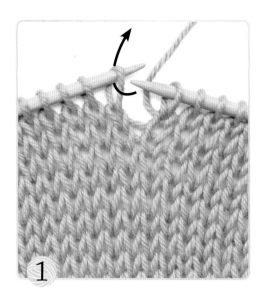

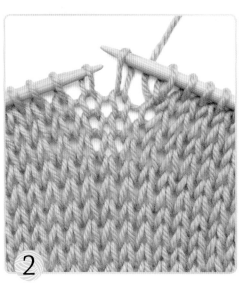

Slipping stitches knitwise

1 Slip stitches knitwise only if instructed to do so, or if working decreases (see pp.282-285), as it twists the stitch. First insert the tip of the right needle from left to right through the front of the loop on the left needle.

2 Slide the stitch onto the right needle and off the left needle without working it. The slipped stitch now sits on the right needle with the left side of the loop at the front of the needle unlike the worked stitches next to it.

Symbols, charts, and abbreviations

Knitting instructions for stitch patterns can also be given in chart form. Some knitters prefer working with stitch-symbol charts because they are easy to read, and they build up a visual image of the stitch repeat that is quick to memorize.

Even with charted instructions, there are usually written directions for how many stitches to cast on. If not, you can calculate the cast on from the chart, where the number of stitches in the pattern "repeat" are clearly marked. Cast on a multiple of this number, plus any edge stitches, three stitches are shown on the example chart, below, outside the six-stitch repeat.

Each square represents one knitted stitch and each horizontal line of squares represents a row on your knitted fabric. After casting on, work from the bottom of the chart upwards to start creating the knitted fabric. Read odd-numbered rows (usually RS rows) from right to left and even-numbered rows (usually WS rows) from left to right. Work the edge stitches, then work the stitches inside the repeat as many times as required. Some symbols may mean one thing on a RS row and another on a WS row (see below).

Once you have worked all the charted rows, start again at the bottom of the chart to begin the "row repeat" once more.

Charts

❸ Read row 2 and all other WS rows from left to right

❹ After completing row 16, start again at row 1

Rep = 16 rows

❷ Read row 1 and all other RS rows from right to left

❶ Cast on a multiple of 6 stitches, plus 3 extra stitches at each end

3 edge sts   Rep = 6sts

Start at the bottom

Stitch symbols

These are some of the commonly used knitting symbols in this book. Any unusual symbols will be explained in the pattern. Symbols can vary, so follow the explanations in your pattern.

☐	K on RS rows, p on WS rows
●	P on RS rows, k on WS rows
Ｏ	Yarnover
⟋	K2tog
⟍	Ssk
⟋\	S1 k2tog psso (sk2p)
/⟋\	Sk2 k1 p2sso (s2kpo)

Knitting abbreviations

These are the most frequently used knitting abbreviations found both in this book and in popular knitting patterns throughout the world. Any special abbreviations in knitting instructions are always explained within the pattern.

alt alternate

beg begin(ning)

cm centimetre(s)

cont continu(e)(ing)

dec decreas(e)(ing)

foll follow(s)(ing)

g gram(s)

g st garter stitch

in inch(es)

inc increas(e)(ing)

k knit

k1 tbl knit st through back of loop

k2tog (or dec 1) knit next 2sts together (see p.282)

kfb (or inc 1) knit into front and back of next st

LH left hand

m metre(s)

M1 (or M1k) make one stitch (see pp.278–279)

mm millimetre(s)

oz ounce(s)

p purl

p2tog (or dec 1) purl next 2sts together (see p.282)

patt pattern, or work in pattern

Pfb (or inc 1) purl into front and back of next st (see p.277)

psso pass slipped stitch over

rem remain(s)(ing)

rep repeat(ing)

rev st st reverse stocking stitch

RH right hand

RS right side (of work)

s1 k1 psso (skpo) slip one, knit one, pass slipped st over (see p.283)

s1 k2tog psso (or sk2p) slip one st, knit 2sts together, pass slipped sts over (see p.284)

ssk slip, slip, knit (see p.283)

s slip stitch(es)

s2 k1 p2sso (or s2kpo) slip 2, knit one, pass slipped stitches over (see p.284)

st(s) stitch(es)

st st stocking stitch

tbl through back of loop(s)

tog together

WS wrong side (of work)

yd yard(s)

yfwd yarn forward (US yo; see p.280)

yfrn yarn forward round needle (US yo; see p.281)

yon yarn over needle (US yo; see p.281)

yrn yarn round needle (US yo; see p.280)

[ ] * Repeat the instructions between the brackets, or after or between the asterisks, as many times as instructed in the pattern

Holding yarn and needles

Learning to knit is a very quick process. There are only a few initial techniques to pick up before you are ready to make simple shapes, such as scarves, blankets, and cushion covers. Basics include casting stitches onto the needles, knit and purl stitches, and casting stitches off the needles. Before starting to knit, familiarize yourself with how to hold the yarn and needles. See below for two common methods.

Knitting English style

1 Wrap yarn around fingers on your right hand. The aim is to control the yarn firmly but with a relaxed hand. Release the yarn to flow through fingers as the stitches are formed.

2 You need to be able to tension the yarn just enough with your fingers to create even stitches that are neither too loose nor too tight.

3 Hold the needles with the stitches about to be worked in the left hand and the working needle in the right hand. Use the right forefinger to wrap the yarn around the needle.

Knitting Continental style

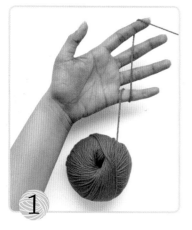
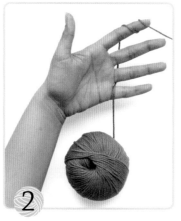

1 Wrap the yarn around the fingers of your left hand in any way that feels comfortable. Try this technique to see if you can both release and tension the yarn easily to create uniform loops.

2 This alternative tensioning technique may suit you better. Here the yarn is wrapped twice around the forefinger.

3 Hold the needle with the unworked stitches in the left hand and the working needle in the right. Position the yarn with the left forefinger and pull it through the loops with the right needle.

Making a slip knot

After reading about the two knitting styles on the previous page you are now ready to place the first loop of yarn on your needle and start creating a piece of knitting. This initial loop is called the slip knot and it is the first stitch formed when casting on stitches.

1 Begin by crossing the yarn coming from the ball over the yarn end (called the yarn tail) to form a large circle, or loop, of yarn.

2 Insert the tip of a knitting needle through the circle of yarn, then wrap the needle tip around the ball end of the yarn and pull the yarn through the circle.

3 This forms a loop on the needle and a loose, open knot below the loop.

4 Pull both ends of the yarn firmly to tighten the knot and the loop on the needle.

5 Make sure the completed slip knot is tight enough on the needle that it will not fall off but not so tight that you can barely slide it along the needle.

6 The yarn tail on the slip knot should be at least 10–15cm (4–6in) long so it can be threaded onto a blunt-ended yarn needle and darned in later. Your knitting pattern, however, may instruct you to leave an extra-long yarn tail (called a long loose end) to use for seams or other purposes.

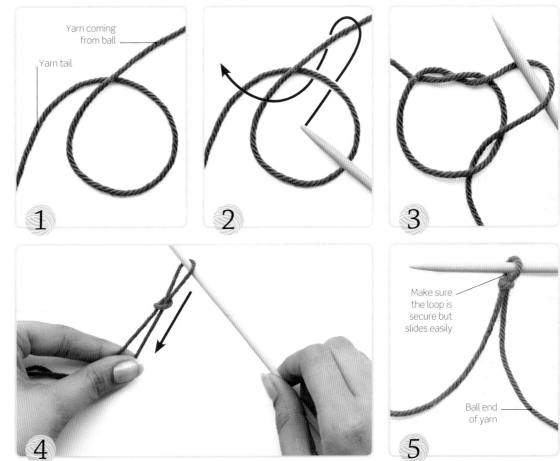

Yarn coming from ball

Yarn tail

1

2

3

4

Make sure the loop is secure but slides easily

Ball end of yarn

5

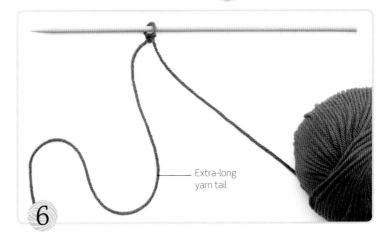

Extra-long yarn tail

6

Single strand cast ons

Casting on gives a closed edge to your knitting that won't unravel. There are several methods of casting on, but the basic techniques shown here are the quickest and simplest ways to get started.

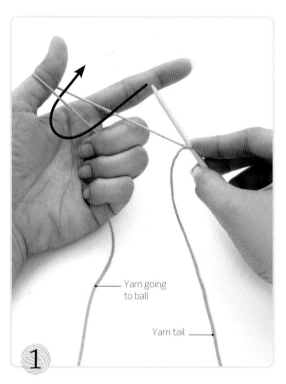

Yarn going to ball

Yarn tail

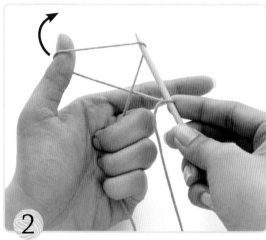

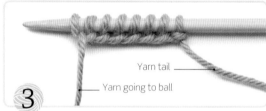

Yarn tail

Yarn going to ball

Single cast on
(also called thumb cast on)

1 This is the easiest cast on technique. Hold the needle with the slip knot in your right hand. Then wrap the yarn around your left thumb as shown and hold the yarn in place in the palm of your left hand. Insert the needle tip under and up through the loop on your thumb following the arrow.

2 Release the loop from your thumb and pull the yarn to tighten the new cast on loop on the needle, sliding it up close to the slip knot.

3 Loop the yarn around your thumb again and continue making loops in the same way until the required number of stitches is on the needle.

Knit on cast on
(also called knit stitch cast on)

1 Place the needle with the slip knot in your left hand. Insert tip of right needle from left to right through centre of loop on left needle. With yarn behind needles, wrap it under and around tip of right needle. (While casting on, use your left forefinger to hold loops on left needle in position.) Using tip of right needle, carefully draw yarn through loop on left needle.

2 Transfer the loop on the right needle to the left needle by inserting the left needle from right to left through the front of the loop. Pull both yarn ends to tighten the new cast on loop on the needle, sliding it up close to the slip knot.

3 Continue casting on stitches in the same way for the required number of stitches. For a looser cast on, hold two needles together in your left hand while casting on.

Yarn going to ball

Long yarn tail

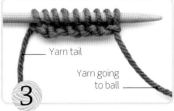

Yarn tail

Yarn going to ball

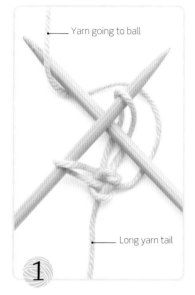

Yarn going to ball

Long yarn tail

1

2

3

Cable cast on

1 Begin by working Steps 1–2 of the knit on cast on (opposite). Then insert the tip of the right needle between the two loops on the left needle and wrap the yarn under and around the tip of the right needle.

2 With the tip of the right needle, draw the yarn through to form a loop on the right needle.

3 Transfer the loop on the right needle to the left needle (see Step 2 Knit on cast on). Continue, inserting the needle between the first two loops on the left needle when beginning each new cast on stitch.

1

2

3

Finger loop cast on

1 This gives a soft cast on. Hold the needle with the slip knot in your right hand. Lift the yarn from underneath with your left index finger pointing away from you. Bend and turn your finger to point towards you.

2 Insert the needle into the loop that lies on top of your finger from behind.

3 Release your index finger and tighten the stitch on the needle.

TOP TIP   *If your casting on is always too tight, use a needle one size larger.*

Two strand cast ons

These cast on techniques all use two strands of yarn, but generally only one needle, and are strong, elastic, and versatile. They are usually followed by a wrong side row, unless the reverse is the right side. As with double cast on, start all these with a slip knot made after a long tail at least three times as long as the planned knitting width.

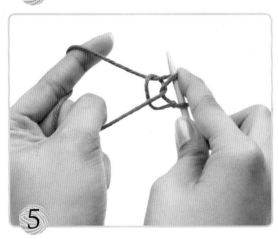

Long yarn tail   Yarn going to ball

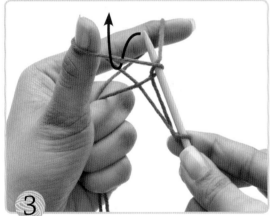

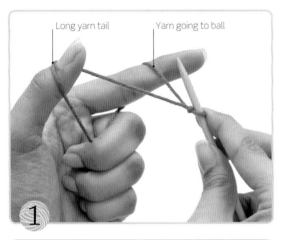

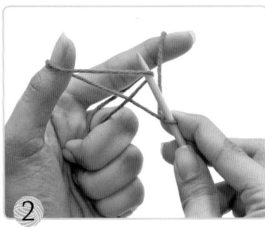

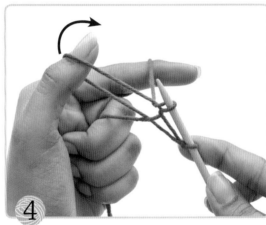

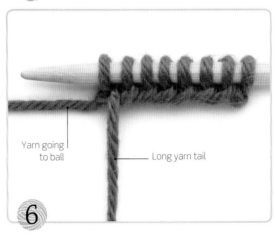

Yarn going to ball   Long yarn tail

Double cast on
(also called long-tail cast on)

1 Make a slip knot on the needle, leaving a long yarn tail – allow about 3.5cm (1³⁄₈in) for each stitch being cast on. Hold the needle in your right hand. Loop the yarn tail over your left thumb and the ball yarn end over your left forefinger as shown. Hold both strands in the palm of your left hand.

2 Insert the tip of the needle under and up through the loop that is around your left thumb.

3 Wrap the tip of the needle around the loop on your forefinger from right to left and use it to pull the yarn through the loop on your thumb as shown by the arrow.

4 Gently release the loop by bending down the thumb and sliding the yarn off.

5 Pull both yarn ends to tighten the new cast on loop on the needle, sliding it up close to the slip knot.

6 Loop the yarn around the thumb again and cast on another stitch in the same way. Make as many stitches as you need.

Twisted double cast on

This cast on is very stretchy, so is useful before a rib. It can be made even stretchier by working it over two needles held together.

1 Hold the yarn and needle as for double cast on. Bring the needle towards you and then back under both thumb loops.

2 Bring the needle towards you over the top of the furthest thumb loop and down between both thumb strands. The thumb loop is now a figure of eight.

3 Take the needle over the first loop on your index finger.

4 Bring the needle towards you. Drop the end of your thumb away from you and let the loop slide down towards the end to open the thumb loop. Bring the needle down through the open thumb loop.

5 Release the thumb loop keeping the yarn around your index finger ready to start the next cast on loop. Pull the short strand to tighten the stitch. Loop the yarn around the thumb again and repeat to this point to cast on another stitch in the same way. The stitches will create a stretchy double twist effect.

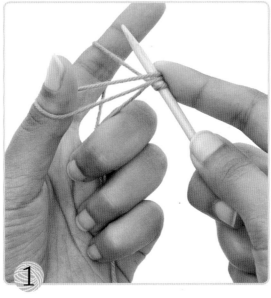

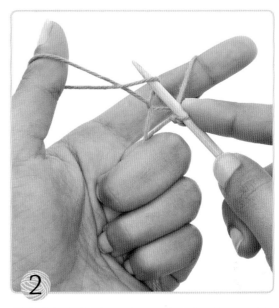

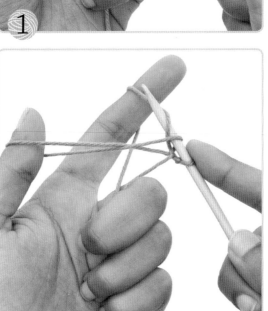

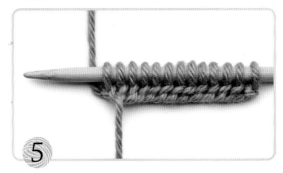

TOP TIP   *It is important to use the correct method of casting on.*

Contrast edge cast on

1 Cut strand of contrast yarn three times length of cast on, and tie end onto main yarn. Hold both strands in left hand, with contrast yarn towards you. Slide needle between yarns so that knot sits on right side of needle. Hold in place. Loop contrast yarn over thumb and main colour over index finger. Insert needle from below under front strand of contrast yarn on thumb.

2 Move needle towards index finger and take tip up and over front index finger loop, pulling back towards you. Pull this main colour loop through contrast-coloured thumb loop.

3 Release contrast yarn thumb loop. Pull both yarn ends to hold needle snugly, and slide cast on stitch close to slip knot.

4 Cast on required stitches. Knit next row in main yarn and continue working in garter stitch as shown.

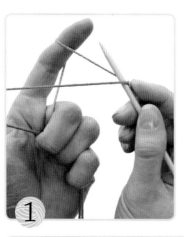

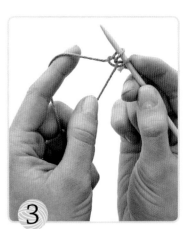

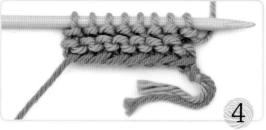

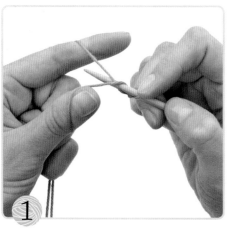

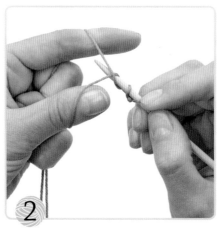

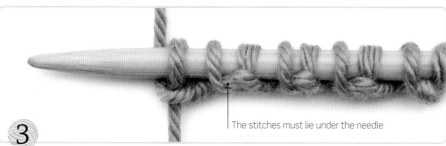

The stitches must lie under the needle

Tubular cast on
(also called invisible cast on)

This is a good method for single rib knitting, but can become wavy if over-stretched. Use needles at least two sizes smaller to cast on than those used for the rest of the pattern.

1 Hold needle and yarn as for double cast on (see p.266). Bring needle forwards, passing over and back under thumb strand. Catch index-finger strand, going over and back towards you.

2 Flick thumb strand over needle. Bring left hand back to original position, passing yarn under needle. Ensure stitch goes all the way around needle, and lies centrally under needle. Take needle back over and under index finger strand. With needle towards you, take it over and back under thumb strand.

3 Move index finger towards you passing yarn over needle, and return hand to its original position, making sure stitch goes all way around needle. Repeat to cast on an even number of stitches. At end, tie the two strands together under needle. Knit first row by knitting into back of first stitch, bring yarn to front and slip next stitch purlwise. Repeat along row. For second row, repeat without knitting into back of stitch.

Simple cast off

When your piece of knitted fabric is complete you need to close off the loops so that they cannot unravel. This is called casting off the stitches. Although casting off is shown here worked across knit stitches, the principle is the same for purl stitches. If instructed to retain stitches for future use, slip your stitches onto a spare needle or a stitch holder.

Casting off knitwise

1 Begin by knitting the first two stitches. Then insert the tip of the left needle from left to right through the first stitch and lift this stitch up and over the second stitch and off the right needle.

2 To cast off the next stitch, knit one more stitch and repeat Step 1. Continue until only one stitch remains on the right needle. If your pattern says "cast off in pattern", work the stitches in the specified pattern as you cast off.

3 To stop the last stitch from unravelling, cut the yarn, leaving a yarn tail 20cm (8in) long, which is long enough to darn into the knitting later. (Alternatively, leave a much longer yarn end to use for a future seam.) Pass the yarn end through the remaining loop and pull tight to close the loop. This is called fastening off.

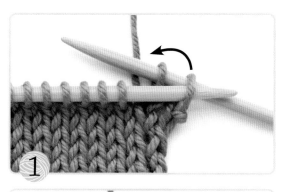

Slipping stitches off needle

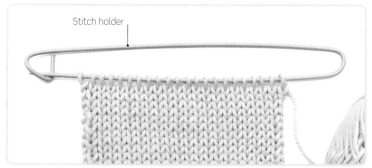

Using a stitch holder: If you are setting stitches aside to work on later, your instructions will tell you whether to cut the yarn or keep it attached to the ball. Carefully slip your stitches onto a stitch holder large enough to hold all the stitches. If you are only slipping a few stitches, use a safety pin.

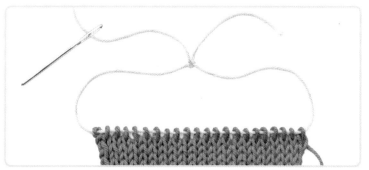

Using a length of yarn: If you do not have a stitch holder or do not have one large enough, use a length of cotton yarn instead. Using a blunt-ended yarn needle, pass the yarn through the stitches as you slip them off the knitting needle. Knot the ends of the cotton yarn together.

Alternative cast offs

Try using one of these casting off techniques to complement your project. Consider using a contrast colour, either in the basic cast off or combined with a decorative style. Cast offs are included that give more stretch to ribs or loosen an edge, and an adaptation of the three needle cast off can be used to join pockets and hems.

Purl cast off

1 Purl two stitches, then take the yarn to the back. Insert the tip of the left needle into the first stitch and pass it over the second stitch and off the right needle.

2 Bring the yarn to the front, repeat Steps 1 and 2 across row, but purl only one stitch in Step 1. Pull the end stitch through itself as for casting off knitwise (see p.269).

Casting off in rib effect

Use after a single rib fabric to maintain the rib corrugations. This method adds a little more stretch than casting off in either all knit or all purl.

1 Work one knit and one purl. Move the yarn to the back. Insert the left needle into the first stitch. Pass over the second and off the right needle.

2 Knit the next stitch then pass the first stitch over the second and off the right needle as before.

3 Yarn to front and purl next stitch. Repeat Steps 2 and 3 across the row. Pull the final stitch through itself to fasten off.

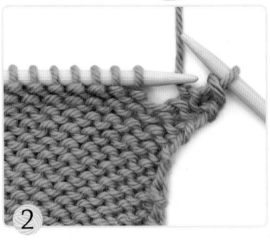

Three needle cast off

This seam can be worked on the right side of the knitting (as here) to form a decorative seam, or on the wrong side.

1 Hold the needles with the stitches to be joined together with the wrong sides facing each other. Insert a third needle through the centre of the first stitch on each needle and knit these two stitches together.

2 Continue to knit together one stitch from each needle as you cast off the stitches in the usual way. (A contrasting yarn is used here to show the seam clearly.)

3 When the pieces of knitting are opened out, you will see that this technique forms a raised chain along the seam.

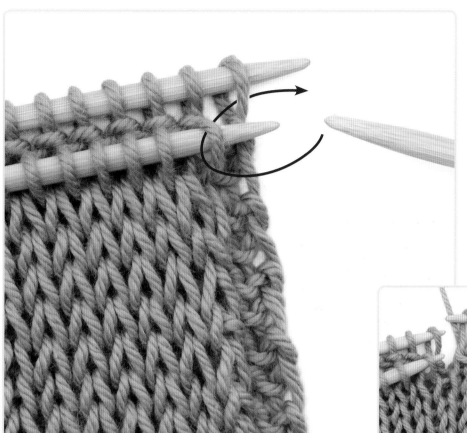

Decrease cast off

A decorative cast off, this method is better for single ribs than plain casting off knitwise. Insert the tip of the right needle into the front of the first two stitches on the left needle and knit them together. Slip the new stitch on the right needle back onto the left without twisting it. Repeat across the row, pulling the thread through the last stitch to secure the end.

Tubular cast off

1 In preparation, and over an even number of stitches, work two rows as follows: knit the first stitch, bring yarn to front and slip the purl stitch that follows without twisting it (purlwise), take yarn to back. Repeat across row.

2 Stretch your ribbing out and cut the yarn end to about four times the length of the required cast off edge. Thread onto a blunt-ended yarn needle. Hold the knitting with the tip to the right. Insert the yarn needle into the first stitch knitwise. Pull the yarn through and drop the stitch.

3 Bring the yarn across the front and insert the needle purlwise into the third (knit) stitch. Pull the yarn through but not too tightly. Take it to the right and insert purlwise into the second (purl) stitch, taking the yarn through to the back.

4 Take the yarn behind the third (knit) stitch, bring it to the front between the third and fourth stitch and insert it as shown into the fourth (purl) stitch. Then insert the needle through the centre of the preceding knit stitch, and out to the front around the left leg.

5 Repeat Steps 3–4. Tension the stitches evenly as you work.

TOP TIP *Thread the yarn gently for a straight edge.*

Knit and purl stitches

All knitting is made up of only two basic stitches – knit and purl. These examples are shown on stocking stitch. The purl stitch is a little more difficult, but becomes effortless with practise. Once you are a seasoned knitter, your hands will know how to work these basic stitches in your sleep. Work your first purl row after you have cast on and knitted a few rows of garter stitch (see p.274).

Knit stitch (abbreviation: k)

1 Hold needle with unworked stitches in your left hand and other needle in your right hand. With yarn at back of knitting, insert right needle from left to right under front loop and through centre of next stitch to be worked on left needle.

2 Wrap yarn under and around right needle, keeping an even tension as the yarn slips through your fingers.

3 With right needle, draw yarn through stitch on left needle. Hold yarn reasonably firmly. Let old loop drop off left needle to complete knit stitch on right needle. Work all stitches on left needle onto right needle in same way. To start new row, turn work and transfer right needle to left hand.

Yarn at back of knitting

Purl stitch (abbreviation: p)

1 With yarn at front of knitting, insert right needle from right to left through centre of next stitch to be worked on left needle. Wrap yarn over and around right needle. Keep an even tension on yarn as you release it.

2 With needle, draw yarn through stitch on left needle. Keep your hands relaxed and allow yarn to slip through fingers in a controlled manner.

3 Let old loop drop off left needle to complete purl stitch. Work all stitches on left needle onto right needle in the same way. To start next row, turn work and transfer the knitting to your left hand.

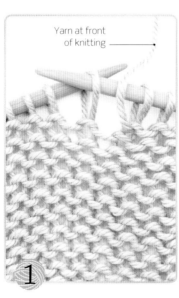
Yarn at front of knitting

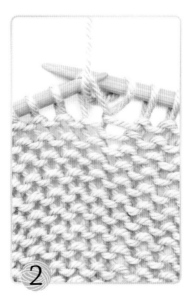

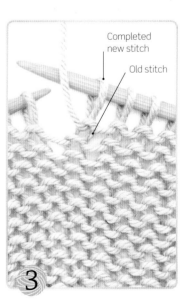
Completed new stitch

Old stitch

Basic pattern stitches

Once you know how to work knit and purl stitch with ease, you will be able to work the most frequently used stitch patterns – garter stitch and stocking stitch. Stocking stitch and reverse stocking stitch are commonly used for plain knitted garments and many more complicated patterns are based on these stitches.

Garter stitch (abbreviation: g st)

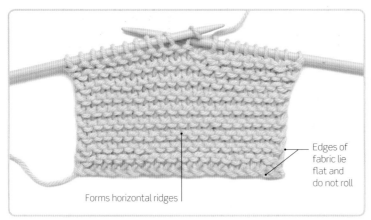

Forms horizontal ridges

Edges of fabric lie flat and do not roll

Knit right side (RS) rows: Garter stitch is the easiest of all knitted fabrics because whichever side is facing you, all rows are worked in knit stitch. When the right side of the fabric is facing you, knit all the stitches in the row. Both sides look the same. The resulting fabric is soft, textured, and slightly stretchy. More rows are needed than in stocking stitch to make the same length of fabric.

Single ribbing (abbreviation: k1, p1 rib)

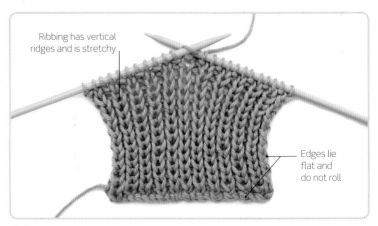

Ribbing has vertical ridges and is stretchy

Edges lie flat and do not roll

Right side (RS) rows: Single ribbing is formed by working alternating knit and purl stitches over an even number of stitches. Bring the yarn forwards before working the second (purl) stitch, and take it backwards before the third (knit) stitch, and so on. Both sides look the same and are worked in the same way. Refer to p.308 for single rib and double rib, and p.310 for English rib stitch patterns.

Stocking stitch (abbreviation: st st)

Side edges roll slightly to back

Right side is smooth

Bottom edge naturally rolls up at front

Knit right side (RS) rows: Stocking stitch is formed by working alternate rows of knit and purl stitches. When the right side is facing you, knit all the stitches in the row.

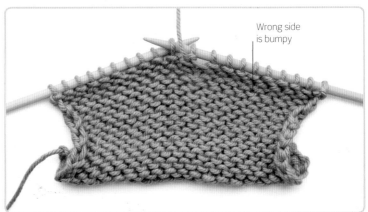

Wrong side is bumpy

Purl wrong side (WS) rows: When the wrong side is facing you, purl all the stitches in the row. The wrong side is often referred to as the "purl side".

Joining yarn

To calculate if there is sufficient yarn to complete two rows, fold the remaining yarn in half and make a slip knot at the fold. Knit the first row. If the knot comes before the end of the row you do not have enough yarn and need to join on a fresh ball.

End of old ball

New ball

Knot close to knitting

New ball joined on

Joining on a new ball

1 Always join on a new ball at the beginning of a row. Knot the new end of yarn onto the old yarn.

2 Slide the knot up very close to the edge of the knitting. The knot can be hidden in the seam later. If you are knitting a scarf or blanket, tie the knot loosely so you can undo it later and darn in the ends.

Weaver's knot

Use this knot when joining yarns of different thickness.

1 Make a loop of the thick yarn and pinch the neck together. Thread a longish end of the thin yarn through the loop from above, and wrap it over the neck of the loop from back to front, pinch this to the loop with your fingers.

2 Take the thin yarn end that is wrapped around the loop under the front thread of the thick yarn loop. Pass it over itself as you take it towards the back and then pass it under the rear thread of the thick yarn loop.

3 Holding both thick yarns in one hand and both thin in the other, gently pull the short ends apart with your fingers to close the knot.

Square knot

This is made like a granny knot, but take left over right, then right over left. This is best made at the point where it is needed in the knitting so you can make sure it goes to the back.

Correcting mistakes

The best thing to do if you make a mistake in your knitting is to unravel it back to the mistake by unpicking the stitches one by one. If you drop a stitch, be sure to pick it up quickly before it comes undone right back to the cast on edge.

Unpicking a knit row

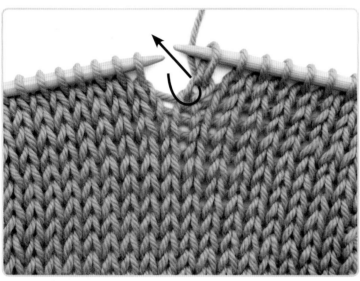

Unravelling on RS: Hold the needle with the stitches in your right hand. To unpick each stitch individually, insert the tip of the left needle from front to back through the stitch below the first knit stitch on the right needle, then drop the old knit stitch off the needle and pull out the loop.

Unpicking a purl row

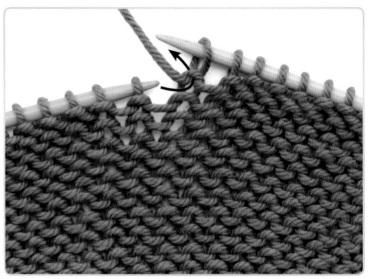

Unravelling on WS: Hold the needle with the stitches in your right hand. Unpick each purl stitch individually with the tip of the left needle in the same way as for the knit stitch. When unpicking stitches, do not split the yarn or you will add two stitches to your needle. Count the stitches before you start knitting again.

Picking up a dropped stitch

Reclaim a dropped stitch on st st: You can easily reclaim a dropped stitch with a crochet hook. With the right side of the knitting facing you, insert the hook through the dropped loop. Grab the strand between the stitches and pull a loop through the loop on the hook. Continue up the rows in this way until you reach the top. Then slip the stitch back onto your needle.

Simple increases

Increasing the number of stitches on the needle is one way knitting is shaped, changing the edges from straight vertical sides to curves and slants. The following techniques are simple increases used for shaping knitting.

Knit into front and back of stitch

(abbreviation: kfb or inc 1)

This popular invisible increase for a knit row is also called a bar increase because it creates a little bar between the stitches.

1 Knit the next stitch, leaving the stitch being worked on the left needle. Insert the right needle through the back of the loop from right to left.

2 Wrap the yarn around the tip of the right needle, draw the yarn through the loop to form the second stitch and drop the old stitch off the left needle.

3 Knitting into both the front and the back of the stitch creates two new stitches out of one, and increases one stitch overall in the row.

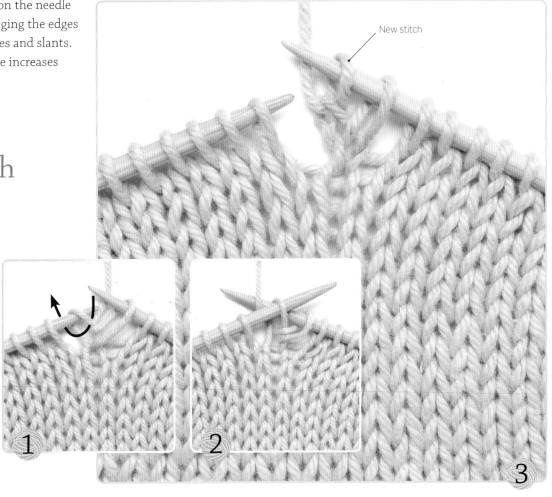

New stitch

Purl into front and back of stitch (abbreviation: pfb or inc 1)

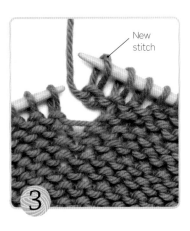

New stitch

1 Purl the next stitch, leaving the stitch being worked on the left needle. Insert the right needle through the back of the loop from left to right.

2 Wrap the yarn around the tip of the right needle, draw the yarn through the loop to form the second stitch and drop the old stitch off the left needle.

3 Purling into the front and the back of the stitch like this creates two stitches out of one and increases one stitch in the row.

Lifted increase on knit row (abbreviation: inc 1)

1 Insert the tip of the right needle from front to back through the stitch below the next stitch on the left needle. Knit this lifted loop.

2 Knit the next stitch (the stitch above the lifted stitch on the left needle) in the usual way.

3 This creates two stitches out of one and increases one stitch in the row. (The purl version of this stitch is worked using the same principle.)

"Make one" left cross increase on a knit row (abbreviation: M1 or M1k)

1 Insert the tip of the left needle from front to back under the horizontal strand between the stitch just knit and the next stitch. Then insert the right needle through the strand on the left needle from right to left behind the left needle.

2 Wrap the yarn around the tip of the right needle and draw the yarn through the lifted loop. (This is called knitting through the back of the loop.)

3 This creates an extra stitch in the row. (Knitting through the back of the loop twists the base of the new stitch to produce a crossed stitch that closes up the hole it would have created.)

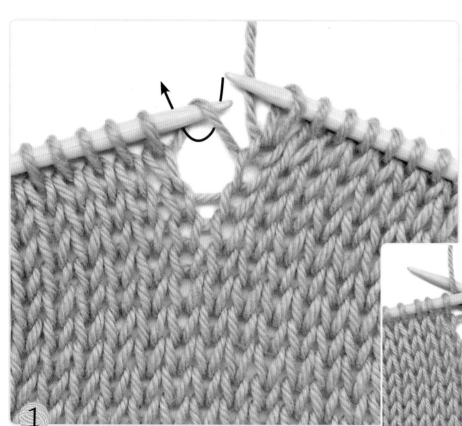

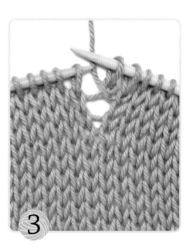

"Make one" right cross increase on a knit row (abbreviation: M1 or M1k)

Knitting patterns do not always differentiate between left and right "make one" increases. Choose the most suitable increase for your project.

1 Insert the tip of the left needle from back to front under the horizontal strand between the knitted stitch and the next one. Insert the right needle from left to right into the front of this new loop, twisting the stitch.

2 Wrap the yarn around the tip of the needle and draw the yarn through the lifted loop, knitting into the front of the stitch.

3 This action crosses the lifted stitch, and closes the hole made by picking up the loop. The resulting increase slants to the right and is normally worked at the end of a knit row.

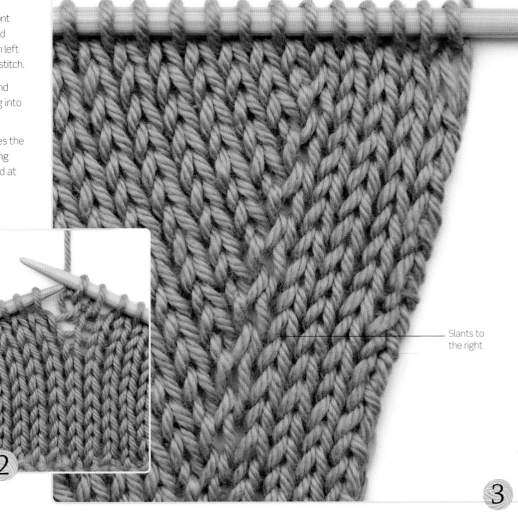

Slants to the right

TOP TIP *M1 means to make a new, separate stitch between two stitches.*

Yarnover increases

Also known as "visible increases", yarnover increases add stitches to a row and create holes at the same time. They are used to produce decorative lace patterns. A yarnover is made by looping the yarn around the right needle to form an extra stitch. It is important to wrap the loop around the needle in the correct way or it will become crossed when it is worked in the next row, which closes the hole.

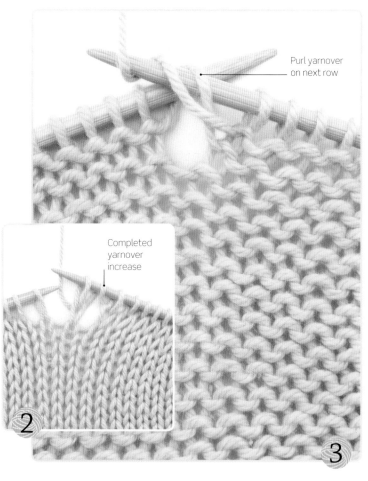

Purl yarnover on next row

Yarnover between knit stitches

(abbreviation: UK yfwd; US yo)

1 Bring the yarn forwards (yfwd) to the front of the knitting between the needles. Take the yarn over the top of the right needle to the back and work the next knit stitch in the usual way.

2 When the knit stitch is complete, the yarnover is correctly formed on the right needle with the right leg of the loop at the front.

3 On the following row, when you reach the yarnover, purl it through the front of the loop. This will create an open hole under the purl stitch.

Completed yarnover increase

Yarnover between purl stitches (abbreviation: UK yrn; US yo)

Completed yarnover increase

Knit yarnover on next row

1 Bring the yarn to the back of the work over the top of the right needle, then to the front between the needles. Work the next purl stitch in the usual way.

2 When the purl stitch is complete, the yarnover is correctly formed on the right needle with the right leg of the loop at the front of the needle.

3 On the following row, when you reach the yarnover, knit it through the front of the loop in the usual way. This creates an open hole under the knit stitch.

Yarnover between knit and purl stitches (abbreviation: UK yfrn and yon; US yo)

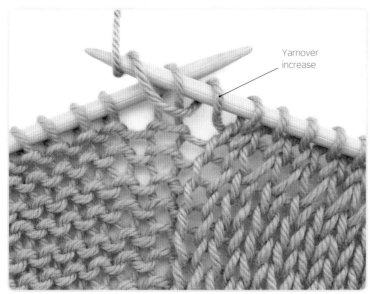

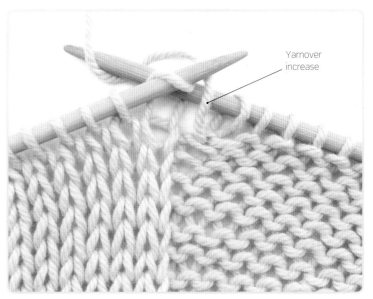

After a knit stitch and before a purl stitch (yfrn): Bring the yarn to the front between the needles, then over the top of the right needle and to the front again. Purl the next stitch. On the following row, work the yarnover through the front of the loop in the usual way to create an open hole.

After a purl stitch and before a knit stitch (yon): Take the yarn over the top of the right needle and to the back of the work, then knit the next stitch. On the following row, work the yarnover through the front of the loop in the usual way to create an open hole.

Yarnover at the beginning of a row (abbreviation: UK yfwd and yrn; US yo)

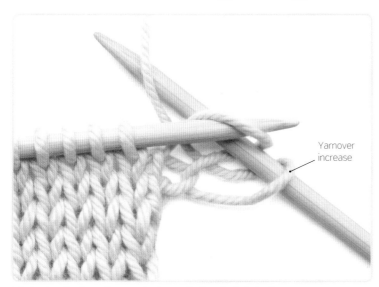

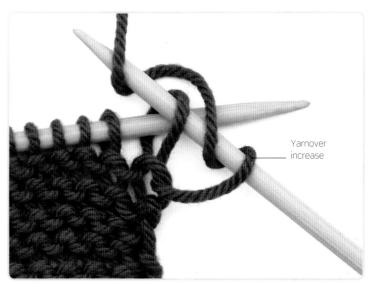

At the beginning of a row before a knit stitch (yfwd): Insert the right needle behind the yarn and into the first stitch knitwise. Take the yarn over the top of the right needle to the back and complete the knit stitch. On the following row, work yarnover through front of loop to create an open scallop at the edge.

At the beginning of a row before a purl stitch (yrn): Wrap the yarn from front to back over the top of the right needle and to the front again between the needles. Then purl the first stitch. On the following row, work the yarnover through the front of the loop in the usual way to create an open scallop at the edge.

Simple decreases

To shape knitting, and for creating textured stitches, when paired with increases, decreases are essential. Complicated decreases are always explained in knitting instructions. Most of the decreases that follow are single decreases that subtract only one stitch from the knitting, but the most common double decreases are included.

Completed decrease slants right

Knit two together
(abbreviation: k2tog or dec 1)

1 Insert the tip of the right needle from left to right through the second stitch then the first stitch on the left needle.

2 Wrap the yarn around the tip of the right needle, draw the yarn through both loops and drop the old stitches off the left needle.

3 This makes two stitches into one and decreases one stitch in the row. The completed stitch slants to the right.

Purl two together (abbreviation: p2tog or dec 1)

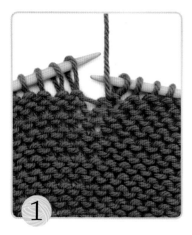

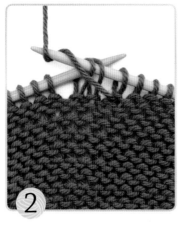

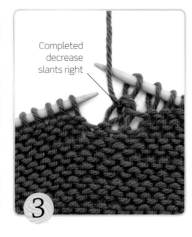

Completed decrease slants right

1 Use the p2tog decrease where a pattern specifies "decrease 1" on a purl row. Insert the tip of the right needle from right to left through the first, then the second stitch on the left needle.

2 Wrap the yarn around the tip of the right needle, draw the yarn through both loops and drop the old stitches off the left needle.

3 This makes two stitches into one and decreases one stitch in the row.

Slip one, knit one, pass slipped stitch over (abbeviation: s1 k1 psso or skpo)

1 Slip the first stitch on the left needle knitwise onto the right needle without working it. Then knit the next stitch.

2 Pick up the slipped stitch with the tip of the left needle and pass it over the knit stitch and off the right needle.

3 This makes two stitches into one and decreases one stitch in the row.

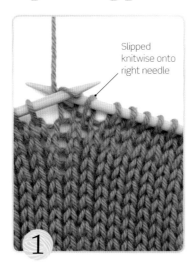

Slipped knitwise onto right needle

Completed decrease slants left

Slipped knitwise onto right needle

Slip, slip, knit

(abbreviation: ssk)

1 Slip the next two stitches on the left needle knitwise, one at a time, onto the tip of the right needle without working them.

2 Insert the tip of the left needle from left to right through the fronts of the two slipped stitches (the right needle is now behind the left). Knit these two stitches together.

3 This makes two stitches into one and decreases one stitch in the row.

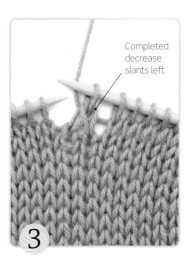

Completed decrease slants left

Slip, slip, purl (abbreviation: ssp)

1 Keeping yarn at the front, slip two stitches, one at a time, knitwise onto the right needle without working them as for ssk decrease (see p.283). Holding needles tip to tip, insert left needle into both stitches and transfer back to left needle without twisting.

2 Holding the right needle at the back, bring the tip upwards from left to right through the back of the two stitches. Bring the right needle in front of left as it comes through the stitches.

3 Lay the yarn between the needles as for purl. Take the right needle down and back through both loops, then slide them off the left needle together. This makes one stitch out of the two, and decreases one stitch.

Double decreases

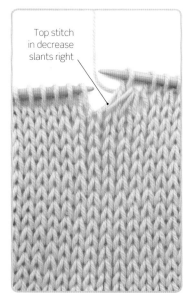

Top stitch in decrease slants right

k3tog: Insert the tip of the right needle from left to right through the third stitch on the left needle, then the second, then the first. Knit these three together. This decreases two stitches at the same time.

Top stitch in decrease slants left

s1 k2tog psso: Slip one stitch knitwise onto the tip of the right needle, knit the next two stitches together, then pass the slipped stitch over the k2tog and off the right needle. This decreases two stitches at once.

Top stitch in decrease is upright

s2 k1 p2sso: Slip two stitches knitwise together onto the right needle, knit the next stitch, then pass the two slipped stitches together over the knit stitch and off the right needle. This instantly decreases two stitches.

Paired edge decreases

k2tog slants to the right on left edge

skp slants to the left on right edge

skp and k2tog: This example has slip1, knit1, pass slipped stitch over (skp) at start of RS row. At other end of RS row, knit to two stitches from end and knit two stitches together (k2tog)(see p.282).

Paired increases and decreases

Increases or decreases at each end of a row can be worked to slant left or right so that the edges mirror each other. Paired shapings should be worked at consistent intervals, and are easier if worked on a knit row. When working a pattern, one or two edge stitches can be worked plain so that the shaping does not affect the pattern.

Paired increases

When made at end of a row	Abbreviation	When made at start of a row	Abbreviation
Slants left – increases the left edge of the knit side of stocking stitch		Slants right – shapes the right edge of the knit side of stocking stitch	
Knit (or purl) in front and back of stitch	kfb or inc 1	Knit (or purl) in front and back of stitch	kfb or inc 1
Purl in front and back increases: ● on a purl row seen from knit side, bar to the right of the stitch into which increase is made		Knit in front and back increases: ● on a knit row seen from knit side, bar to the left of the stitch into which increase is made	
Make one knit (or purl) left cross	M1k (M1p)	Make one knit (or purl) right cross	M1k (M1p)
● virtually invisible ● must have rows between or will pull ● made between stitches, so shows where placed ● slants the stitch worked after it to the left		● virtually invisible ● must have rows between or will pull ● made between stitches, so shows where placed ● slants the stitch worked before it to the right	

Paired decreases

When made at end of a row	Abbreviation	When made at start of a row	Abbreviation
Right slant – decreases the left of the knit side of stocking stitch		Left slant – decreases the right of the knit side of stocking stitch	
Knit (or purl) two together	k2tog (p2tog)	Slip, slip, knit (or slip, slip, purl)	ssk (ssp)
Knit (or purl) two together	k2tog (p2tog)	Slip1, knit1, pass slipped stitch over	skp, s1 k1 psso, or skpo
Knit (or purl) two together	k2tog (p2tog)	Knit (or purl) two together through back of loops	k2tog tbl (p2tog tbl) or k-b2tog (p-b2tog)

TOP TIP *Use increase and decrease stitches to shape your knitted garment.*

Simple twists

If you desire textures with relief and sculptural qualities, cables and twists are the techniques to learn. The following twists are worked in stocking stitch on a stocking stitch background, called a "ground", but they can also be worked with one knit and one purl stitch.

Right twist
(abbreviation: T2R)

1 With yarn at the back of the right needle and in front of the left, knit the second stitch leaving the first and second stitches on the left needle.

2 Knit the first stitch on the left needle and drop both old stitches off the left needle at the same time.

3 Without the use of a cable needle, this creates a "one-over-one" two-stitch cable slanting to the right — called a right twist.

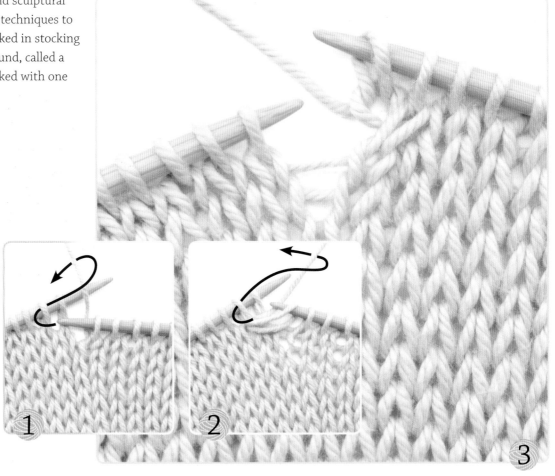

Left twist (abbreviation: T2L)

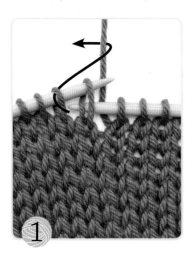

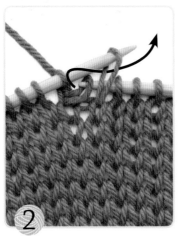

1 Insert the tip of the right needle behind the first stitch on the left needle and through the second stitch knitwise. Then wrap the yarn around the right needle.

2 Pull the loop through the second stitch behind the first stitch. Be careful not to drop either the first or second stitches off the left needle yet.

3 Knit the first stitch on the left needle and drop both old stitches off the left needle. This creates a two-stitch cable slanting to the left — called a left twist.

Cables

These are traditionally worked in stocking stitch on a reverse stocking stitch (or garter stitch) ground. They are made by crossing two, three, four, or more stitches over other stitches in the row.

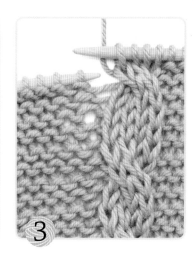

Cable 4 front
(abbreviation: C4F)

1 Work to position of four stocking stitches that form the cable and slip first two stitches onto cable needle. With cable needle at front, knit next two stitches on the left needle.

2 Next, knit the two stitches that have been placed on the cable needle.

3 This creates a cable crossing that slants to the left. For this reason, a "front" cable is also called a "left" cable.

Cable 4 back
(abbreviation: C4B)

1 Work as for Step 1 of Cable 4 front (above), but knit the first two stitches from the left needle with the cable needle at the back of the knitting.

2 Then knit the two stitches that are on the cable needle.

3 This creates a cable crossing that slants to the right. For this reason, a "back" cable is also called a "right" cable.

Cable and twist stitch chart symbols

K on RS rows, p on WS rows	C4B	MB = make bobble / K2tog	Sk2p / CR4L
P on RS rows, p on WS rows	C4F	Yarnover (yon) / Ssk	S2kpo / CR4R
C2F	C6B	C8B	CR2R
C2B	C6F	C8F	CR2L

Lace knitting

The airy openwork texture of knitted lace is formed by combining yarnovers and decreases to create holes (called eyelets) over the fabric. Although lace knitting looks complicated, the techniques are relatively easy. Choose a lace stitch with a short row repeat and knit the openwork fabric quickly to produce impressive, delicate textures.

Tips for lace knitting

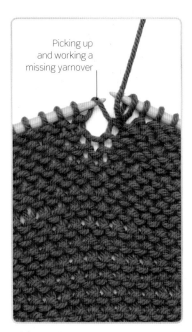

Picking up and working a missing yarnover

Eyelets arranged in various ways around each other are the basis of all lace stitches. Eyelets are made up of yarnovers, which produce the holes in the fabric, and decreases, which frame the eyelets and compensate for these increases in the row to keep the knitting the same width. The techniques for two simple eyelets are given here. Methods for producing alternative eyelet stitches will be explained in full in your pattern instructions.

● Cast on loosely for lace patterns. This is best achieved not by trying to make loose loops but by spacing the cast on stitches farther apart on the knitting needle, with at least 3mm (⅛in) between the loops. If you find this difficult to do evenly, then use a needle one or two sizes larger than the size you are using for the lace and switch to the correct needle size on the first row. Depending on your yarn, metal needles may be easier to work with than wooden ones when knitting fine-weight lace.

● Lace stitch patterns sometimes have yarnovers and decreases in the very first row. These are not easy to work on cast on loops, so you can start with a plain knit or purl row then begin the lace pattern on the following row.

● Use a row counter when working lace stitches to keep track of which pattern row you are on. This is especially important for intricate lace worked over a long row-repeat. If you do get lost in your pattern, stop and start again. Use stitch markers to separate each pattern repeat until you are confident that you know it by heart.

● Count your stitches frequently when knitting lace to make sure you still have the right number of stitches. If you are missing a stitch you may have left out a yarnover. There is no need to undo stitches all the way back to the missing yarn. Simply work to the position of the missing yarnover on the following row, then insert the left needle from front to back under the strand between the stitch just worked and the next stitch on the left needle (see left). Work this stitch through the front of the loop in the usual way.

Chain eyelet

1 For a chain eyelet on a stocking stitch ground, begin by creating a yarnover on the right needle (see p.280). Then knit the next two stitches together (see p.282).

2 The yarnover creates a hole in the knitting and the k2tog decrease compensates for the extra loop so that the knitting remains the same width.

3 On the following row, purl the yarnover in the usual way. A single chain eyelet is shown here so that its structure is clear, but eyelets can be arranged separated by several rows and several stitches or sitting side by side.

Yarnover

1

2

3

Open eyelet

1 For an open eyelet on a stocking stitch ground, work a yarnover on the right needle (see p.280). Then work a "s1 k1 psso" decrease (see p.283) after the yarnover.

2 The yarnover creates a hole and the decrease compensates for the extra loop so that the knitting remains the same width.

3 On the following row, purl the yarnover in the usual way. Open eyelets can be arranged in various ways to create any number of different lace textures and patterns. An open eyelet makes a simple, small buttonhole.

Yarnover

Mohair lace

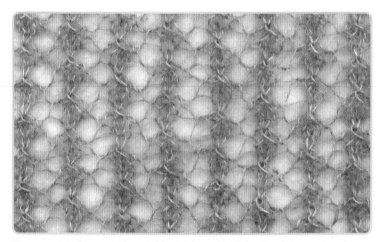

Fine 2- and 4-ply yarn: Using a lightweight yarn highlights the delicacy of the lacy stitches. Try easy lace patterns when starting, as mohair is more difficult to knit with than smooth yarn, and complicated lace does not show up clearly in textured yarns.

Traditional-style knitted lace

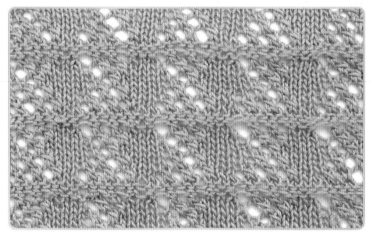

Fine cotton thread: Traditional-style knitted lace, which has been popular with knitters for centuries, is worked using cotton thread on very thin needles. Lace knitting is a satisfying challenge for more experienced knitters.

Lace stitch chart symbols

☐ K on RS rows, p on WS rows	⭕ Yarnover (yon)	◁ Sk2p	
⬛ P on RS rows, k on WS rows	⟋ K2tog	⧄ S2kpo	
	⟍ Ssk		

Knitting in the round

Circular knitting, or knitting in the round, is worked on a circular needle or with a set of four double-pointed needles. With the right side facing, the knitting is worked to form a tube or flat medallion. It is ideal for knitting seamless projects, such as bags, hats, and socks. A circular needle is easy to master, while working with double-pointed needles is best suited to intermediate knitters.

Working with a circular knitting needle

1 Cast on the required number of stitches. Ensure that the stitches are untwisted and they all face inwards, then slip a stitch marker onto the end of the right needle to mark the beginning of the round.

2 Hold one needle end in each hand and bring the right needle up to the left needle to work the first stitch. Knit round and round on the stitches. When the stitch marker is reached, slip it from the left needle to the right needle.

3 If you are working a stocking stitch tube on a circular needle, the right side of the work will always be facing you and every round will be a knit round.

Stitch marker

1

Knit first stitch of first round tightly

2

3

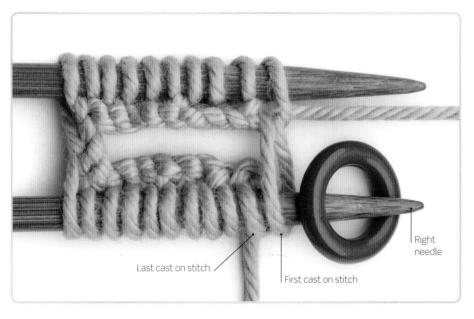

Last cast on stitch

First cast on stitch

Right needle

Joining the circle of stitches

Close the circle in circular knitting: Cast on the required number of stitches, plus one stitch. Slip the first cast on stitch onto the right needle next to the last cast on stitch. Place the join marker after this stitch. Knit the round, and when you reach the end, knit the last two stitches before the marker together (this will be the first cast on stitch and the extra stitch).

Working with a set of four double-pointed needles

1 Your knitting instructions will specify how many double-pointed needles to use for the project you are making — either a set of four or a set of five. When working with a set of four needles, first cast on all of the stitches required onto a single needle.

2 Slip some of the stitches off onto two other needles — your knitting pattern will tell you precisely how many to place on each needle. Ensure that the bottoms of the cast on loops are all facing inwards.

3 Place a stitch marker between the first and second stitches on the first needle to mark the beginning of the round. Then pull the first and third needles close together and start to knit with the fourth needle. Knit round and round in this way as for knitting with a circular needle.

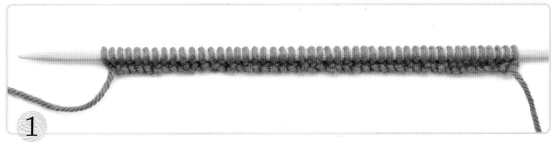

1

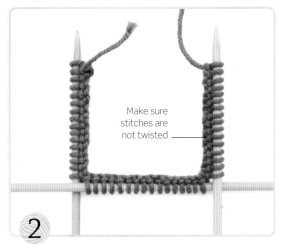

Make sure stitches are not twisted

2

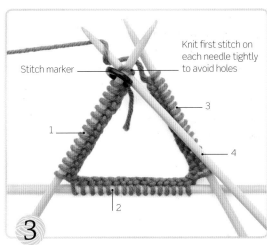

Stitch marker

Knit first stitch on each needle tightly to avoid holes

1

3

4

2

3

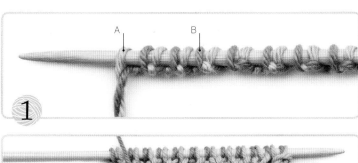

A   B

1

B side

A side

2

Tubular knitting

Although associated with circular knitting, tubular knitting can be worked on straight needles by slipping every other stitch. Both sides are knitted at the same time and shown here in colours A and B for clarity.

1 Tie the ends of yarns A and B together. Holding knot on right side of needle, with colour A over your index finger and colour B over your thumb, cast on an even number of stitches (not counting the slip knot) using tubular cast on (see p.268). Twist yarns before knitting first stitch.

2 With colour B, knit a B stitch, then bring yarn to front, and slip one A stitch purlwise, take yarn to back, repeat along row. Drop the slip knot and tie the ends together under the needle. With colour B, purl the B stitches of the last row, taking yarn to back to slip the A stitches purlwise. Yarn to front and repeat along row. With colour A, purl the A stitches, take yarn to back and slip B stitches purlwise, bring yarn to front and repeat along row. With colour A, knit the purled A stitches of the last row, bringing yarn forwards to slip the B stitches. Using two colours in this way results in open sides.

Selvedges

Whether you require a decorative edge or a neat, straight finish, selvedge stitches will make all the difference to your knitted garment or accessory. Loose edges can be tightened with chain or slipped garter selvedge and rolling edges can be controlled with a garter selvedge. Both selvedges do not have to be worked the same.

Garter selvedge

1 This makes a bumpy seam, and so is best for edges that will not be sewn together. It encourages the edge of stocking stitch to lie flat. Each "bump" equals two rows.

2 On stocking stitch, knit the first and last stitch of every row.

Slipped garter selvedge

1 Slipped garter selvedge gives a firmer and smoother finish than garter selvedge (see above). Slip the first stitch knitwise and knit the last stitch on all rows.

2 The slipped stitches can aid picking up on some projects.

Double slipped garter selvedge

1 Use this selvedge for slightly decorative, free edges. Knit all rows identically. Insert the right needle into the back of the first stitch from right to left, as indicated by the arrow, and slip the stitch.

2 Knit the second stitch. Work as pattern to two stitches from the end of the row and knit the last two stitches. The slipped stitches will aid picking up stitches on some projects.

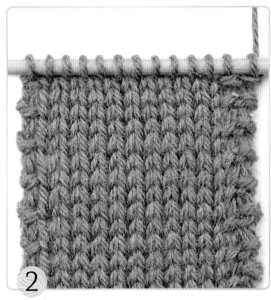

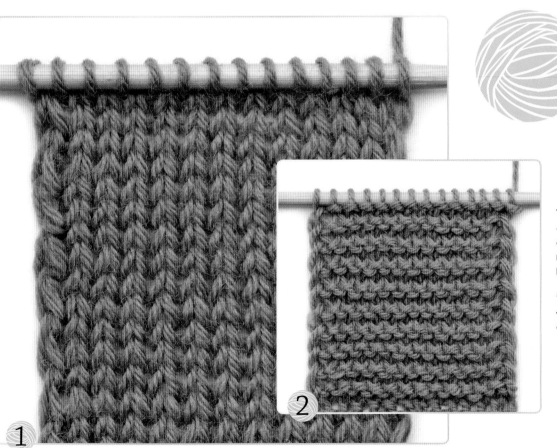

Chain selvedge

1 On stocking stitch, all right side rows slip first stitch knitwise, and knit last stitch. On all wrong side rows, slip first stitch purlwise, and purl last stitch.

2 On garter stitch, with yarn in front slip first stitch purlwise, yarn back and knit to end.

Buttonholes and zips

The simplest form of buttonhole is an eyelet, and for larger ones, horizontal is the most common technique.
When choosing fastenings, such as buttons and zips, select an appropriate size and material for your project.
Plastic is light and unobtrusive but metal and contrasting coloured items can make a bold statement.

Positioning buttons and buttonholes

First decide on the number of buttons: Mark holes to match button size. Top and bottom buttons are usually positioned between 1cm (1/2in) and 3cm (11/4in) from neck and hem edge. Mark the top and bottom button position with thread, see left. Start buttonholes at least three stitches from the edge. Count rows and stitches, as measuring may be inaccurate. For vertically worked bands, knit and attach the buttonband first.

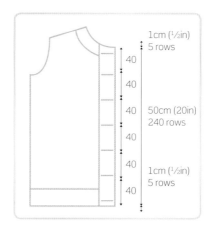

1cm (1/2in)
5 rows
40
40
40   50cm (20in)
      240 rows
40
40
1cm (1/2in)
40   5 rows

Knit the buttonhole band: Work the holes to match button size, and work the calculated number of rows between buttonholes, allowing two rows for a two-row buttonhole (see left). Work vertical buttonhole rows so that they centre on the button position marker. For a horizontally worked picked up buttonband, count the stitches rather than the rows to calculate the spacing.

1

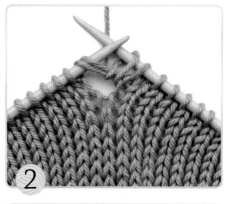
2

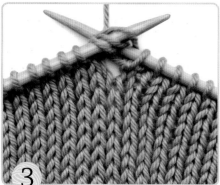
3

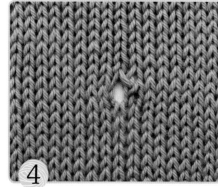
4

Reinforced eyelet buttonhole

1 On a knit row, work to position of buttonhole. Make a yarnover (see p.280). Work to end of row. On the next row, slip the yarnover purlwise and make another front to back yarnover. Work to end of row.

2 On the next row, slip the stitch before the yarnovers knitwise. Knit both yarnovers together but do not drop them from the left needle.

3 Pass the slipped stitch over the newly made stitch. Knit three stitches together (the yarnovers and the following stitch). Work to end of row.

4 The resulting buttonhole is strong and neat. Afterwards, sew on the corresponding buttons, making sure that they fit through each buttonhole without stretching the fabric.

One row horizontal buttonhole

1 Knit to the buttonhole position (this should be a knit row on reverse stocking stitch). Move the yarn to the front. Slip one stitch purlwise and move the yarn to the back.

2 Slip one stitch purlwise and pass the previous stitch over. Repeat this method across the number of buttonhole stitches required on your knitted garment or accessory.

3 Slip the last stitch on the right needle back to the left. Turn work. Yarn back. Cast on the number of stitches for the buttonhole using cable cast on (see p.265). Cast on one more stitch, bring yarn forwards after making stitch but before placing it on left needle. Turn work.

4 Slip one stitch knitwise and pass the last cast on stitch over it. Knit the rest of the row. The result will be a strong buttonhole (worked on stocking stitch in this example), but which works equally well on a garter stitch or a reverse stocking stitch garment or accessory.

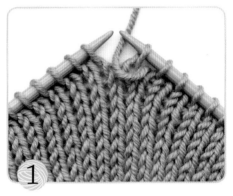

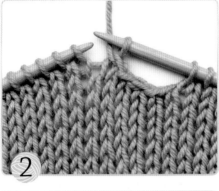

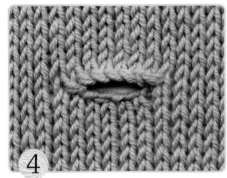

Sewing in a zip

1 Match the colour and weight of the zip to your yarn. Knit the length of garment to match the zip lengths available. Work a garter selvedge (see p.292) at the zip edge.

2 Close the zip. With right side facing, pin the top and bottom of the knitting to the zip first, making sure the teeth are covered by the knitted edge. Pin the centre, then the centres of the remaining sections, easing the rows so they are evenly distributed. Pin horizontally rather than vertically. Do one side at a time and use plenty of pins.

3 Tack the zip in place with contrast sewing thread, sewing between the same vertical lines of stitches. With a sharp large-eyed needle and knitting yarn (or matching sewing thread), backstitch neatly upwards from the hem, sewing between the same vertical lines of stitches.

4 Turn garment inside out. With knitting yarn, or matching sewing thread, slip stitch outer edges of zip to knitting, sewing into the back of the same vertical lines of stitches.

Beaded knitting

Plain knitting sometimes calls for embellishment. Embroidery, beads, or a decorative edging are good candidates for the perfect finishing touch. Pockets, collars, hems, and cuffs are ideal positions for these. Choose beads carefully, glass beads are attractive, but can weigh knitting down. Make sure that the bead hole is large enough for the yarn.

Threading beads onto yarn

Count the beads: Make sure you have the right beads before starting to thread them onto the yarn. Consider their size and weight. If your knitting is to be entirely covered with scattered beads, large heavy beads will be unsuitable as they would weigh the knitting down too much. Adding a little weight to the knitting can, however, produce the extra drape needed for a graceful shawl, scarf, or evening knit.

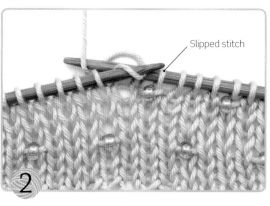

Knitting yarn

Sewing thread

Yarn going to ball

Thread on the beads: The last bead to be used is threaded on first and the first bead to be used is threaded on last. Fold a short length of sewing thread in half, thread both cut ends together through the eye of an ordinary sewing needle, and pass the end of the yarn through the sewing-thread loop. Thread the beads onto the sewing needle, over the thread and onto the yarn.

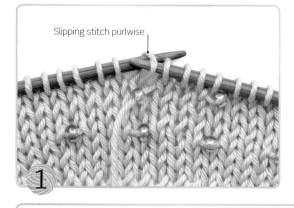

Slipping stitch purlwise

1

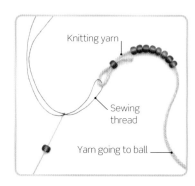

Slipped stitch

2

Slip stitch beading

1 The beads are placed on knit (right side) rows. Knit to the position of the bead, then bring the yarn to the front (right side) of the work between the two needles. Slide the bead up close to the knitting and slip the next stitch purlwise from the left needle to the right needle.

2 Take the yarn to the wrong side between the two needles, leaving the bead sitting on the right side in front of the stitch just slipped. Knit the next stitch firmly to tighten the strand holding the bead at the front.

Beading chart

Sometimes, there is a chart provided for positioning the beads on slip stitch beading, unless only a few beads are to be added, in which case the bead placements will be within the written instructions. The sample chart here illustrates how slip stitch beads are staggered. This is because the slipped stitches at the bead positions pull in the knitting and alternating the bead placements evens out the fabric.

☐ k on RS rows, p on WS rows

⦿ place bead and slip stitch

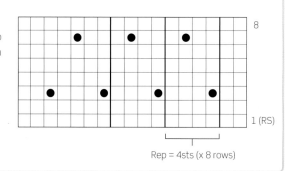

8

1 (RS)

Rep = 4sts (x 8 rows)

Simple garter stitch beading

1 This method can be used to create bands of beads along borders or at intervals for beaded stripes. Start with a right side row and work at least three rows of plain garter stitch before adding any beads. On the next row (a wrong side row), knit two edge stitches before adding a bead. Push a bead up close to the knitting before working each stitch. At the end of the row, add the last bead when two stitches remain on the left needle, then knit the last two stitches.

2 Knit the next row with no beads. Alternate a bead row and a plain row to form a band of beads of the desired depth. Use this technique to create a piece entirely covered with beads for a small bag, such as the Beaded party clutch (see pp.222–223).

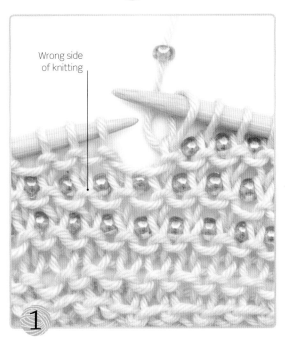

Wrong side of knitting

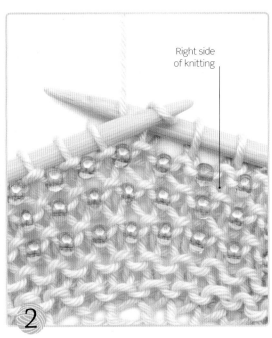

Right side of knitting

Reverse stitch beading

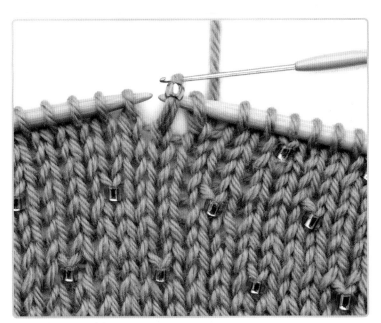

Hold bead in position

Thread beads onto knitting yarn: Working in stocking stitch, knit to one stitch before bead position. Yarn to front. Purl one. The bead must sit tight against the right needle, so slide it along the yarn to this position and hold it there. Purl the next stitch. Yarn to back and work to next bead position.

Inset bead with a hook

Knit to bead position: Place bead on a fine crochet hook. Pick the next stitch off the left needle with the hook. Slide bead onto stitch and return it to left needle. Knit or purl the stitch. Needle and thread can be used instead of a crochet hook by making a loop of thread through stitch and sliding bead down the thread.

Close beading

1 Work at a tight tension so the beads stay at the front. Thread the beads on the yarn. Slide the bead along close to the needle. On a knit row: knit into back of stitch, draw loop, and bead through stitch, with bead behind right needle. Tighten the stitch with the bead at the front.

2 On a purl row: slide a bead along close to the needle. Purl into the back of the stitch, positioning the right needle above the bead from the previous row.

3 Draw both the loop and bead through the stitch, with the bead behind the right needle. Tighten to ensure the bead stays on the right side.

Beaded cast off

1 Cut a piece of main colour yarn five times the width of the knitting. Thread one bead for each stitch to be beaded, less one, onto the yarn. Tie the last bead (which will not be worked) to the end of the yarn to prevent beads sliding off. With beaded yarn, knit first two stitches of cast off. Pass second over first as normal. This leaves a selvedge stitch for seaming. Push a bead close to back of fabric. For a firm edge (as shown here), knit stitch drawing both bead and yarn through stitch. To alter lie of bead, change which side of the bead the stitch is passed over in Step 2. For a dangling bead, knit the next stitch leaving bead at back as new loop is formed.

2 For either method, pass second stitch on right needle over first and off tip of needle. Repeat the process along the cast off, either working one bead per stitch or some plain cast offs in between, depending on the size of bead and effect required. The last stitch should not be beaded if it will be seamed, so remove and discard the end bead, work last stitch plain, and pull end through as normal.

Decorative edgings

Add a quick and easy finishing touch to a child's sweater, a winter scarf or hat, or a comfy cushion with woollen pom-poms and tassels. Make these decorations in the same yarn as your knitted project or try a contrasting colour.

Pom-poms

1 Draw two 8cm (3¼in) diameter circles on stiff card. Draw another 2.5cm (1in) diameter circle in the centre. The diameter of the outer circle minus that of the inner will be the size of the pom-pom. A smaller centre circle makes a denser pom-pom. Cut out circles. Cut a few 1m (1yd) lengths of yarn and wind together into a small ball. Put the circles together. Hold yarn ends at the edge of the circle, and insert ball into centre, winding yarn through the circles. Continue winding. When the first ball runs out make another. If the centre becomes too tight, thread as many strands of yarn as possible onto a large-eyed needle, and use this to complete the winding. Cut through the wraps with scissors.

2 Slide a long doubled strand of yarn between the circles, wrap and knot it tightly around the core.

3 Thread the yarn onto a needle and make a few stitches through the knot. Remove the circles. Shake and trim the pom-pom, but do not cut the tie strands. Suspend the pom-pom in steam to make it fuller (hang it from a long needle for safety).

Tassels

1 Cut a template, such as a piece of thick card, to the desired length of your finished tassel, for instance 10cm (4in) makes a good length. Holding the end with your thumb, wrap the yarn repeatedly around the template using single or varied colours. Fifty wraps is average, but use more to make a thicker tassel. With a threaded needle, pull a long doubled strand of yarn between yarn and template, and slide it up to the end. Tie tightly around strands, leaving long ends.

2 Carefully insert scissors at the base of the wraps and cut across all strands of yarn. Then remove the template. Wrap another strand of yarn tightly around the top, a short distance below the head, then tie securely and sew the ends through the wraps and into the tassel head a few times.

3 Trim the ends of the tassel and sew it to your project with the remaining long strand at the head. A light pressing or steaming makes the tassel sleeker.

Seams and blocking

After you have finished knitting, and before you sew it togehter, your project will need blocking. This means to pin out and set the knitted shape using steam, or by wet-pressing. Always refer to the yarn label, or pattern instructions beforehand. Textured stitches may lose their shape when steam blocked.

Wet blocking

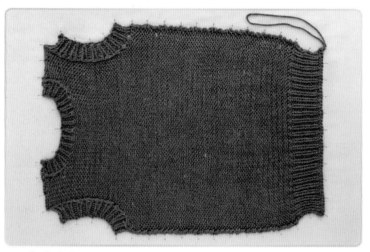

Wet the knitting: Wet blocking is the best way to even out your knitting on certain yarns (see ballband). Using lukewarm water, either wash the piece or simply wet it. Squeeze and lay it flat on a towel, then roll the towel to squeeze out more moisture. Pin the piece into shape on layers of dry towels covered with a sheet. Leave to dry.

Steam blocking

Steam the knitting: Only steam block if your yarn allows. Pin the piece to the correct shape, then place a clean damp cloth on top. Use a warm iron to create steam, barely touching the cloth. Do not rest the iron on the knitting, and avoid any garter stitch or ribbed areas. Before removing the pins, let the piece dry completely.

Darning in an end

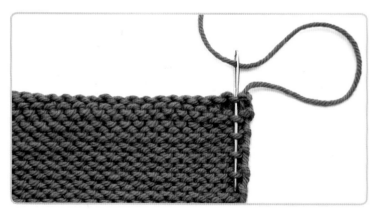

A professional finish: Completed knitting will have at least two yarn ends – one at the cast on and one at the cast off edges. For every extra ball used, there will be two more ends. Thread each end separately onto a large-eyed needle and weave it vertically or horizontally through stitches on the wrong side of your work.

Edge-to-edge seam

Suitable for most stitch patterns: Align the pieces of knitting with the wrong sides facing upwards. Using a large-eyed needle and matching yarn, sew the seam together through the little pips formed along the edges of knitting, as shown. Do not pull the seam too tight.

Backstitch seam

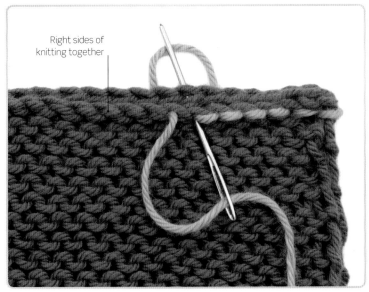

Right sides of
knitting together

Suitable for almost any seam on knitting: Align the pieces of knitting with the right sides together. Make one stitch forwards, and one stitch back into the starting point of the previous stitch as shown. Work the stitches as close to the edge of the knitting as possible. A backstitch seam is not suitable for super-bulky yarns.

Overcast seam

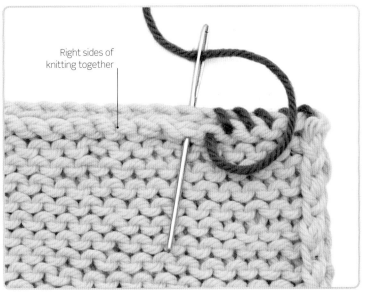

Right sides of
knitting together

Oversewn seam (or whipped stitch seam): With the right sides facing each other, insert the needle from back to front through both layers of knitted fabric, working through the centres of the edge stitches and not through the pips at the edge of the fabric. Create each stitch in the same way as you sew the seam together.

Grafted seam

This seam is worked along two pieces of knitting that have not been cast off or along two cast off edges as shown here; the principle for both is the same.

1 With the right sides facing you, follow the path of a row of knitting along the seam as shown. Do not pull the stitches too tight.

2 When worked in a matching yarn as here, the seam blends in completely and makes it look like a continuous piece of knitting.

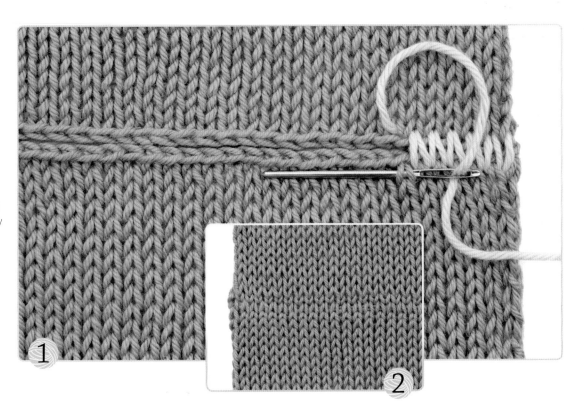

Figure of eight start for seams

1 Lay the pieces to be joined side by side, right sides facing you. Thread your needle with knitting yarn then bring the needle from back to front through the bottom stitch of the right piece, as close to both edges as possible. Take the needle under the left piece, and insert it from back to front through the bottom edge stitch.

2 Move the needle to the right piece and repeat the process of bringing the needle from back to front through the bottom stitch of the right piece. This makes a figure of eight which is a strong, neat start to a seam.

3 To use before mattress stitch (see below), and after making a figure of eight, take the needle back under the left piece and bring it through the same place as before. This will position the first stitch in the correct place.

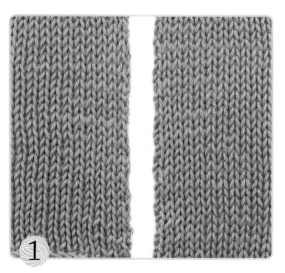

Mattress stitch

1 The best seam technique for ribbing and stocking stitch, mattress stitch is practically invisible. Start by aligning the edges of the pieces to be seamed with both right sides facing.

2 Insert the needle from front through centre of the first knit stitch on one piece of knitting and up through centre of stitch two rows above. Repeat on other piece, working up seam and pulling edges together every few stitches.

Embroidery on knitting

Swiss darning, running stitch, satin stitch, lazy daisies, and chain stitch are the most commonly used decorative stitches worked on knitting. Use a smooth yarn that is the same weight as that used for the knitting, or slightly thicker, together with a large-eyed needle to avoid splitting the yarn.

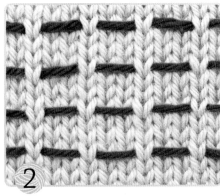

Running stitch

1 Secure the yarn on the wrong side of your work with a knot. Bring the needle through to the front between two stitches, at the end of the line to be worked. Take the needle through to the back between two stitches to get the length of stitch you want. Count the number of stitches or rows to the right (or left).

2 Repeat Step 1, spacing the stitches in an even pattern as required, being careful not to pucker the fabric.

Satin stitch

1 Secure the yarn on the wrong side. Bring the needle through to the front between two stitches, at one side of the shape to be worked. Take needle to the back between two stitches at the opposite side of the shape.

2 Bring needle to front again at the original side. Space it a yarn width away by angling the needle while at back of work. The stitches should lie flat and parallel to each other. Continue to work the shape in long smooth stitches that do not pucker the fabric.

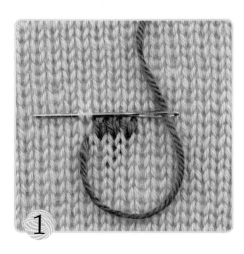

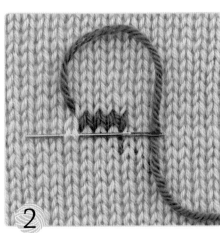

Swiss darning

1 This example is for horizontal Swiss darning. Secure the embroidery yarn to the wrong side of the stocking stitch. Pass the needle from back to front through the centre of a knit stitch, and pull the yarn through. Next, insert the needle from right to left behind the knit stitch above as shown and pull the yarn through gently so it "mirrors" the knit stitch size.

2 Insert the needle from right to left into the knit stitch below and out at the centre of the next knit stitch to the left to complete the stitch as shown. Continue in this way, tracing the path of the knitting horizontally.

Knitted toys

Toys are fun to knit and can be rewarding to complete. Start with a simple pattern, such as the Cheeky monkey (see p.240); instructions for how to sew together each part and complete your toy are shown here.

Choosing materials

Start your toy project by choosing the yarns and needles. Lightweight or medium-weight yarns are best when knitting toys. One ball of each shade is often enough for a small toy, but your pattern will specify a yarn quantity. For striped toys, small amounts of leftover yarns are ideal, as long as they are all the same weight.

Use a pair of knitting needles that are one or two sizes smaller than the size recommended on the yarn label. This will ensure a close-textured knitted fabric that you will be able to fill. You will also need six-stranded embroidery thread for facial features, such as eyes, a nose and mouth, plus additional details such as the embroidery stitches used for

the Knitted bunnies (see p.244). Small (10mm (¼in) in diameter) buttons make a quick pair of eyes but bear in mind that if you are making the toy for a small child, you should select manufactured eyes that meet health and safety regulations. Safety eyes have a shank that is pushed through the fabric and held by a metal backing that clamps onto the shank. Attach buttons using strong button thread to avoid them becoming detached.

Choose an environmentally, fire-retardant brand of filling. Most are made from polyester but capoc or a natural stuffing is also suitable. Toys can also be stuffed with pulses to weigh them down.

Knitting body parts

1 Work toy pieces in the order given; the body and head are usually knitted first, followed by arms and legs, and then smaller items. Knit tightly and count your stitches regularly to ensure that you have the correct number. Knitted toy pieces only take on their final shape once the seams are sewn and they are fully stuffed, so do not be surprised if they look unlike how you imagined.

2 After the body and head, the legs and arms are usually the next pieces to knit for a toy and are often worked from the foot/hand upwards. If the pattern calls for long, loose ends at the cast on and/or cast off edges, this is to use for stitching when assembling the toy. If you leave too little extra yarn, you can join on a new length, but it is easier to use a strand already attached to the knitted piece.

3 After the main pieces of your toy are knitted, there are usually other items to make, for example, ears, hair, and possibly clothes. Make sure you leave long yarn tails to darn into the knitting (see p.300).

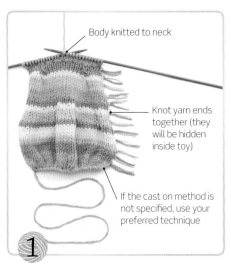

Body knitted to neck

Knot yarn ends together (they will be hidden inside toy)

If the cast on method is not specified, use your preferred technique

1

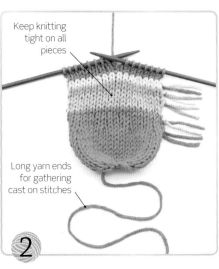

Keep knitting tight on all pieces

Long yarn ends for gathering cast on stitches

2

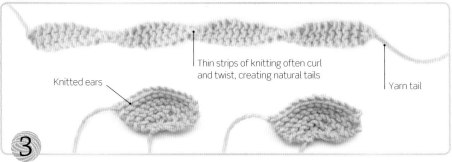

Thin strips of knitting often curl and twist, creating natural tails

Knitted ears

Yarn tail

3

Stuffing and assembling the toy pieces

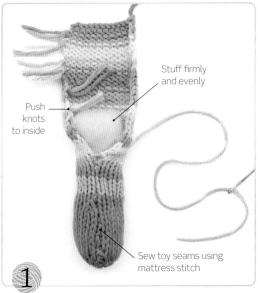

Push knots to inside

Stuff firmly and evenly

Sew toy seams using mattress stitch

1

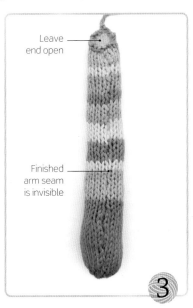

Leave end open

Finished arm seam is invisible

3

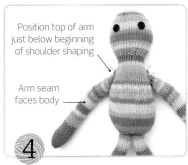

Facial features applied first

Back seam

Position cast off edge of legs inside the body

Leg seams face back of body

2

Position top of arm just below beginning of shoulder shaping

Arm seam faces body

4

Fill firmly and evenly with toy filling

5

Use thick enough thread to make the features stand out boldly

6

1 Using the long yarn ends, weave in and out of the cast on stitches using mattress stitch (see p.302) and pull the knitted limbs to gather. Sew up the seams, stuffing each segment as you go. Pinch the end of each limb together, with the seam at the centre, and usually at the back, then sew the ends closed with overcast stitches.

2 Before sewing up the seams on main items, as shown here, attach facial features. Position eyes about three or four stitches apart at the centre of the head. Starting at the cast on edge and using mattress stitch, sew 2.5cm (1in) of the back seam on the body. Next, sew the lower body seam with overcast stitches. Continue sewing the back body seam, stuffing the toy firmly with filling. Continue the seam up the back of the head. Make sure each segment is packed with toy filling before completing the seam. Secure the yarn with two or three small stitches.

3 Look at the photograph of the toy in your pattern to see how to position the arms. Unless stated otherwise, keep the arm ends open so that they meet the body in a circle and slant downwards.

4 Pin the arms (and legs) in position, and then sew them in place, turning the edge of the arm inside the arm as you stitch. Remove the pins as you stitch.

5 For small body pieces, such as ears and muzzle, use the yarn end to stitch in and out of the cast on stitches and pull to gather. Sew the seam, starting at the cast on end. Trim the seam yarn to 5cm (2in) long and hide inside the item before stuffing with toy filling. Pin each body piece to the head or body and sew in place with short overcast stitches. Make widely spaced overcast stitches along the straight edge of flat body parts and gather to form a cup shape. Using the gathering yarn, sew the ears to the sides of the head. Sew on additional items, such as a tail or a tongue.

6 Use a blunt-ended yarn needle and all six strands of embroidery thread for facial features. Embroider the mouth and any other features in backstitch. To personalize your toy, alter the position and size of the eyes, and add a mouth and eyebrows.

Charted colourwork

The techniques for charted stocking stitch colourwork – Fair Isle and intarsia – open up a world of richly coloured designs. In Fair Isle, a yarn colour is carried across the wrong side of the work until it is required. In intarsia, a separate length of yarn is used for each colour and the yarns are twisted together at the colour change junctures.

Following a colourwork chart

The first step in understanding charted colourwork is to grasp how easy the charts are to follow. As an alternative method to writing out how many stitches in each colour you need to work across a row, your knitting pattern provides a chart with the colours marked on it in symbols or in blocks of colour.

If a knitting pattern covers the whole garment back, front, and sleeve and cannot be repeated,

a large chart is provided for each of these elements rather than written instructions. Where a pattern is a simple repeat, the repeat alone is charted. Each square on a stocking stitch colourwork chart represents one stitch of your knitting and each horizontal row of squares represents an entire knitted row. Follow the chart from the bottom to the top, just as your knitting forms on the needles.

The key provided with the chart tells you which colour to use for each stitch. All odd-numbered rows on a colourwork chart are usually RS (knit) rows and are read from right to left. All even-numbered rows on a colourwork chart are usually WS (purl) rows and are read from left to right. Always read your knitting pattern instructions carefully to make sure that the chart follows these general rules before you start.

Fair Isle chart

□ background colour
● motif colour

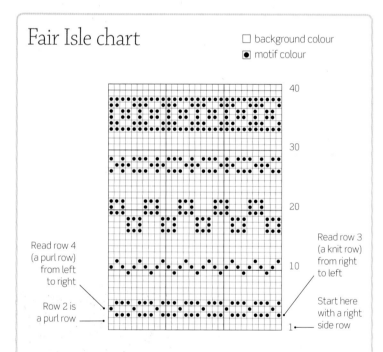

This example of a Fair Isle chart with symbols illustrates how easy it is to knit simple Fair Isle patterns. Each symbol represents a colour while the plain squares represent the background colour. On colour charts, each coloured square represents a difficent shade, usually the actual yarn colours of the knitted project. A key always accompanies a Fair Isle chart.

No more than two colours are used in a row, which makes it ideal for beginners. The colour not in use is stranded across the back of the knitting until it is needed. To identify if a colourwork chart should be worked in the Fair Isle technique, check that both colours in a row are used across the entire row.

Intarsia chart

□ background colour   ● motif colour 2
● motif colour 1   ⊠ motif colour 3

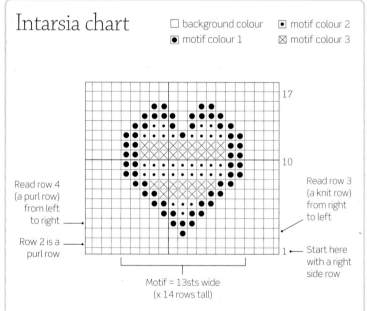

This heart motif is a typical example of a simple intarsia colourwork chart. Each colour on the chart is represented by a different symbol. The blank square (the background) also represents a colour.

You can tell that a charted design should be worked in the intarsia technique if a colour appears only in a section of a row and is not needed across the entire row. Use a separate long length of yarn, or yarn on a bobbin, for each area of colour in intarsia knitting (including separated background areas). Twist the colours where they meet (see opposite). Avoid knitting straight from the ball because the twisting will cause the yarn to tangle.

Fair Isle stranding technique

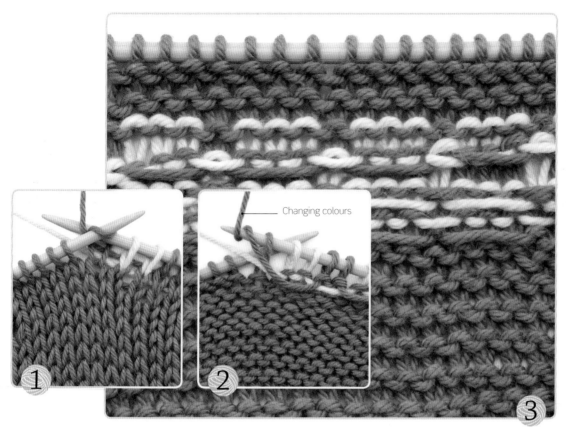

Changing colours

1 Fair Isle is usually worked on stocking stitch. On the knit rows, knit the stitches in the first colour, then drop it at the back and knit the stitches in the second colour. Strand the colour not in use across the back of the work until required. To prevent long strands catching, weave them into the back.

2 Work the purl rows in the same way, but strand the colour not in use across the front (wrong side). Keep one colour on top and the other underneath so they do not twist around each other.

3 The trick to Fair Isle knitting is to learn to keep the yarns tensioned evenly, as shown here. The stranding should not be too loose or too tight or the colour patterning will look stretched. With continued practise the correct tensioning of the yarns will become automatic.

Intarsia technique

Right-slant colour change: To avoid holes, twist the colours around each other only on the knit rows.

Left-slant colour change: To avoid holes, twist the colours around each other only on the purl rows.

Vertical colour change: To avoid holes, twist the colours around each other on both knit and purl rows.

Moss stitch

This knit and purl stitch is one of the best known, creating an attractive textured finish.

Instructions
For an even number of sts:
ROW 1: *K1, p1, rep from *.
ROW 2: *P1, k1, rep from *.
Rep rows 1 and 2 to form patt.

For an odd number of sts:
ROW 1: *K1, p1, rep from * to last st, k1.
Rep row 1 to form patt.

Single rib

Ribbed knitting is stretchy and great for cuffs and hems on sweaters and cardigans.

Instructions
For an even number of sts:
ROW 1: *K1, p1, rep from * to end.
Rep row 1 to form patt.

For an odd number of sts:
ROW 1: *K1, p1, rep from * to last st, k1.
ROW 2: *P1, k1, rep from * to last st, p1.
Rep rows 1 and 2 to form patt.

Double rib

More defined than single rib, this stitch is ideal for edging hats and gloves where a ribbed band creates an "elasticated" but tight fit around the head or wrists.

Instructions
Cast on a multiple of 4sts.
ROW 1: *K2, p2, rep from *.
Rep row 1 to form patt.

Basketweave stitch

A traditional textured stitch that looks lovely on children's garments and blankets. Work it in a single colour to make the pattern stand out.

Instructions
Cast on a multiple of 8sts.
ROWS 1–5: *K4, p4, rep from *.
ROWS 6–10: *P4, k4, rep from *.
Rep rows 1–10 to form patt.

Textured check stitch

This stitch is great for beginners who want a reversible fabric, such as for a throw. Try this as an alternative stitch for the Chequered cot blanket (see p.192).

Instructions
Cast on a multiple of 4sts plus 3 extra sts.
ROW 1: K3, *p1, k3, rep from *.
ROW 2: K1, *p1, k3, rep from * to last 2sts, p1, k1.
ROWS 3–6: [Rep rows 1 and 2] twice.
ROW 7: K1, *p1, k3, rep from * to last 2sts, p1, k1.
ROWS 9–12: [Rep rows 7 and 8] twice.
Rep rows 1–12 to form patt.

Striped check stitch

Looking rather like bricks on a house, the horizontal stripes are formed by garter stitch with the squares tucked in between. Use it as an alternative pattern for the Button-neck child's sweater (see p.88).

Instructions
Cast on a multiple of 6sts plus 3 extra sts.
ROW 1 AND ALL ODD-NUMBERED ROWS (RS): K.
ROW 2: K.
ROWS 4 AND 6: P3, *k3, p3, rep from *.
ROWS 12 AND 14: K3, *p3, k3, rep from *.
ROW 16: K.
Rep rows 1–16 to form patt.

Little check stitch

A textured stitch that works well when matched with a plain stitch such as garter stitch to create a simple pattern.

Instructions

Cast on a multiple of 10sts plus 5 extra sts.

ROW 1: *K5, p5, rep from * to last 5sts, k5.

ROW 2: P.

Repeat last 2 rows twice more, then row 1 again.

ROW 8: K5, *p5, k5, rep from * to end.

ROW 9: K.

Rep last 2 rows twice more, then row 8 once more.

Diamond stitch

A reversible stitch that adds texture and can turn a plain garment or cushion into an eye-catching project. It is easy to work but looks very impressive.

Instructions

Cast on a multiple of 9sts.

ROW 1 (RS): K2, *p5, k4, rep from * to last 7sts, p5, k2.

ROW 2: P1, *k7, p2, rep from * to last 8sts, k7, p1.

ROW 3: P.

ROW 4: Rep row 2.

ROW 5: Rep row 1.

ROW 6: P3, *k3, p6, rep from * to last 6sts, k3, p3.

ROW 7: K4, *p1, k8, rep from * to last 5sts, p1, k4.

ROW 8: Rep row 6.

Rep rows 1–8 to form patt.

English rib

A traditional ridged pattern that creates a thick fabric for winter woollies.

Instructions

Cast on an odd number of sts.

ROW 1: S1, *p1, k1, rep from * to end.

ROW 2: S1, *k1 tbl, p1, rep from * to end.

Rep rows 1 and 2 to form patt.

Fisherman's rib

Ribbed knitted fabric encompasses a vertically ridged pattern. It is often used for socks and sweaters because it is stretchy and sturdy.

Instructions

Cast on an odd number of sts and knit 1 row.
ROW 1 (RS): S1, *k1 tbl, p1, rep from * to end.
ROW 2: S1, *p1, k1 tbl, rep from * to last 2sts, p1, k1.
Rep rows 1 and 2 to form patt.

Cable effect

For beginner knitters who find cable stitches too daunting, try this look-alike stitch.

Instructions

Cast on a multiple of 5sts plus 7 extra sts.
NOTE: The stitch count varies from row to row.
ROW 1 (RS): P2, *yarn to back of work between 2 needles, s1 purlwise, k2, pass slipped st over last 2 k sts and off RH needle, p2, rep from *.
ROW 2: K2, *p1, yrn, p1, k2, rep from *.
ROW 3: P2, *k3, p2, rep from *.
ROW 4: K2, *p3, k2, rep from *.
Rep rows 1–4 to form patt.

Subtle sparkles

An alternative pattern to add a touch of glamour to the Beaded party clutch (see p.222).

Instructions

Cast on a multiple of 6sts, plus 2 extra sts.
ROW 1 (RS): K.
ROW 2: P.
ROW 3: K1, *pb, k5, rep from *to last st, k1.
ROW 4: P.
ROW 5: K.
ROW 6: P.
ROW 7: K1, *k3, pb, k2, rep from * to last st, k1.
ROW 8: P.
Rep rows 1–8 to form patt.

Special abbreviations
PB Place bead

Travelling rib

An ideal pattern for plain sweaters. Maintain the tension of the stitches as the rib travels across the fabric to form neat and tidy knitting.

Instructions

Cast on a multiple of 4sts.

ROW 1 (RS): *K2, p2, rep from * to end.

ROW 2: As row 1.

ROW 3: *K1, p2, k1, rep from * to end.

ROW 4: *P1, k2, p1, rep from * to end.

ROW 5: *P2, k2, rep from * to end.

ROW 6: As row 5.

ROW 7: As row 4.

ROW 8: As row 3.

Rep rows 1–8 to form patt.

Broken rib

This is actually a false rib — only every other row is ribbed, making it a quick and easy stitch for beginners. It is not stretchy like real ribs.

Instructions

Cast on a multiple of 4sts plus 2 extra sts.

ROW 1 (RS): *K3, p1, rep from * to last 2sts, k2.

ROW 2: P1, *k3, p1, rep from * to last st, k1.

Rep rows 1 and 2 to form patt.

Broken moss stitch

This pattern makes a non-curling fabric and is easy to knit because every other row is knit straight across.

Instructions

Cast on an odd number of sts.

ROW 1 (RS): K.

ROW 2: *P1, k1, rep from * to last st, k1.

Rep rows 1 and 2 to form patt.

Grand eyelet mesh

Try this as an alternative stitch for the Spiral lace sweater (see p.46). When blocking a garment knitted in grand eyelet mesh stitch, stretch the fabric vertically to open the eyelets.

Instructions

Cast on a multiple of 3sts plus 4 extra sts.

ROW 1: K2, *s1 k2tog psso, yfwd twice, rep from * to last 2sts, k2.

ROW 2: K2, *[p1, k1] into double yfwd, p1, rep from * to last 2sts, k2.

ROW 3: K.

Rep rows 1–3 to form patt.

Victory lace stitch

Lace is where the holes made by increases and decreases form a pattern. Use this pattern as an alternative stitch for the Women's lace hoodie (see p.50).

Instructions

Cast on a multiple of 8sts plus 6 extra sts.

ROW 1: K5, *s1 k1 psso, yon, k6, rep from * to last st, k1.

ROW 2 AND ALL FOLL ALT ROWS: P.

ROW 3: K4, *s1 k1 psso, yon, k1, yon, k2tog, k3, rep from * to last st, k1.

ROW 5: K3, *s1 k1 psso, yon, k3, yon, k2tog, k1, rep from * to last st, k1.

ROW 7: K.

ROW 8: P.

Rep rows 1–8 to form patt.

Openwork diamonds

Use openwork diamonds to create a delicate shawl, wrap, or baby hat.

Instructions

Cast on a multiple of 12sts plus 7 extra sts.

ROW 1 (RS): *K2, k2tog, yon, k8, rep from * to last 7sts, k2, k2tog, yon, k3.

ROW 2 AND ALL FOLL ALT ROWS: P.

ROW 3: *K1, k2tog, yon, k2tog, yon, k7, rep from * to last 7sts, k1, k2tog, yon, k2tog, yon, k2.

ROW 5: As row 1.

ROW 7: K.

ROW 9: *K8, k2tog, yon, k2, rep from * to last 7sts, k7.

ROW 11: *K7, k2tog, yon, k2tog, yon, k1, rep from * to last 7sts, k7.

ROW 13: As row 9.

ROW 15: K.

ROW 16: P.

Rep these 16 rows to form patt.

Glossary

Aran yarn Also called medium, 12-ply, worsted, or Afghan (yarn symbol 4). A medium yarn suitable for sweaters, cabled menswear, blankets, hats, scarves, and winter mittens.

Backstitch A sewing stitch used for firm, straight seams, which is worked from the wrong side of the knitted fabric.

Ballband The wrapper around a ball or donut of yarn, which usually details fibre content, weight, length, needle size, tension, and cleaning instructions.

Ball-winder A device for winding hanks of yarn into balls; also to wind two or more strands together to make a double-stranded yarn. Often used in conjunction with a swift.

Bias knitting A diagonally shaped piece of knitting that slopes to the left or right due to decreases on one side and increases on the other.

Blocking The finishing process for a piece of knitting, in which it is set in shape using water or steam.

Blocking wire Wire for insertion around the edge of a piece of very fine lace work, which is left in to keep it in shape.

Bulky or chunky yarn Also called 14-ply, craft, or rug (yarn symbol 5). A chunky yarn that is suitable for rugs, jackets, blankets, hats, legwarmers, and winter accessories.

Cable A design made by crossing one or more stitches over other stitches in a row; it frequently resembles a rope or cable. Twist stitches belong to the same family.

Cable cast on A method of casting on that produces a firm, cord-like edge, which holds a neat and defined border.

Cable needle A short double-pointed needle, usually with a kink or U-shape, used when working cables.

Carrying up the side A method for keeping the edges of a two-coloured, even-row stripe pattern tidy. The yarns are twisted around each other and carried up the side of the knitting.

Casting off/binding off Completing a piece of knitting by finishing off the loops of the stitches so that they cannot unravel or drop from knitting needle (US: bind off).

Casting off knitwise/purlwise Casting off while working stitches in the knit/purl method of knitting.

Casting off in pattern Casting off stitches while working stitches in the pattern used in the previous row.

Casting off in ribbing A method of casting off a piece of knitting within a rib pattern, while working stitches that are in the ribbing used in the previous row.

Casting on Forming an initial number of stitches on a needle to form the foundation for the piece of knitting. There are various methods, depending on the effect you want to achieve.

Circular knitting Working on circular needles or double-pointed needles (DPNs) to produce a seamless item such as a hat, sock, or sleeve. There is no need to turn the work and no wrong-side row. Sometimes called tubular knitting.

Circular needles A pair of short straight needles that are connected by a flexible nylon wire, usually used for circular knitting and very wide projects that do not fit on conventional straight needles.

Colourwork A variety of techniques for incorporating colour into your knitting. Methods include stripes, Fair Isle, intarsia, and slipped stitch patterns.

Continental-style knitting A way of holding the yarn as you knit, lacing it around your left hand and using these fingers to position the yarn to make a stitch.

Darning in ends The process of completing a piece of knitting by weaving yarn tails (such as from the cast on and cast off edges) into the knitted fabric with a large-eyed needle to disguise them and create a neat finish.

Decreases/decreasing Techniques that subtract stitches. Used to shape knitting, and to form textures in combination with other stitches.

Double cast on See Two-strand cast on and Long-tail cast on.

Double knit yarn (DK) A medium-weight yarn. Also called DK, 5–6-ply, or (US) light worsted (yarn symbol 3). DK yarn is suitable for sweaters and cardigans, lightweight scarves and hats, blankets, and toys.

Double-pointed needles (DPNs) Knitting needles with a tip at each end. A set of four or five is used for the circular knitting of small items, such as mittens and socks.

Double-sided or double knitting See Tubular knitting.

English-style knitting A way of holding the yarn as you knit, lacing it around your right hand and using the right forefinger to wrap the yarn around the needle.

Fair Isle patterns Various multicoloured, stranded, geometric patterns originating from Fair Isle, in northern Scotland, and latterly the Shetland Islands.

Fair Isle knitting A method in which yarn colours not being worked are carried across the back of the knitting until required. This unworked yarn can also be woven in.

Faux colourwork Adding yarn in another colour without having to knit with two different yarns in each row. It involves manipulating stitches from previous rows.

Fibres Yarn is made up of fibres, such as the hair from an animal, man-made (synthetic) fibres, or fibres derived from a plant. The fibres are processed and spun into a yarn.

Fine yarn Also called 4-ply, sport, or baby (yarn symbol 2). A fine yarn suitable for lightweight sweaters and shawls, babywear, socks, and accessories.

Fisherman's rib A pattern of knit and purl stitches in which alternating stitches are double knitted, making a thick, warm, textured fabric.

Fully fashioned shaping An attractive method for increasing or decreasing when working stocking stitch, in which a line of stitches is preserved to follow the edge of the piece.

Garter stitch A basic knitting stitch worked in just knit stitches on every row, whichever side of the knitting is facing you. It produces a thick fabric that is identical on both sides and will not curl at the edges.

Hank A loose, twisted ring of yarn that needs to be wound into one or more balls or donuts before it can be used. Several luxury and hand-dyed yarns are sold in hanks as they are easy to ship and store.

I-cord A narrow tube of knitting that is created on a knitting dolly or cord-maker, or knitted on double-pointed needles. Used as cords, straps, ties, or as a trimming.

Increases/increasing Creating stitches during knitting. Increases can be combined with other stitches in order to form shapes and textures.

Intarsia A method for working with different-coloured yarns to create blocks of colour. A separate length of yarn is used for each colour of the motif and twisted where the colour changes to prevent a hole; yarns are not stranded across the reverse of the work. Intarsia designs use less yarn than Fair Isle knitting.

Knit-on cast on This cast on uses two needles to combine a cast on with the knitting of the first row. If worked through the front of the loops, it produces a soft edge. If knitted through the back of the loops, the edge is firmer.

Knit stitch One of the two basic stitches used to form a piece of knitted fabric.

Knitting beads Beads with a central hole in various sizes for specific thicknesses of yarn. Most are washable and colourfast. Your pattern will tell you how many, and what size, beads you will need.

Knitting needle gauge A tool used for identifying needle sizes by pushing the tip of a needle through holes.

Knitting through back of loop Stitches that twist the stitch in the row below so that the legs of the stitch cross at the base.

Knitwise Working with knit stitches facing you, inserting the right-hand needle into a stitch as if to knit it. *See also* purlwise.

Lace cast on method A cast on that produces a looser, more open effect than other cast ons, and is particularly suitable for lacy designs.

Lace yarn Also called 2-ply or fingering (yarn symbol 0). A very fine yarn for knitting lace projects.

Lanolin An oily substance contained in a sheep's wool.

Live stitches Stitches that are currently being worked.

Long-tail cast on method *See also* two-strand cast on. This method is also known as a double cast on. It produces a sturdy, reinforced edge and so is good for ribbing.

Mattress stitch A seaming stitch that is almost invisible. It is used to sew pieces of knitting together with the right side facing. It only forms a small seam on the wrong side of the work.

Medallion A circular, hexagonal, octagonal, or square flat shape made from knitted fabric. Medallions are knitted from the centre outwards.

Mercerized cotton Cotton thread, fabric, or yarn that has been treated in order to strengthen it and add a sheen. The yarn is a good choice for items that need to be strong and hold a shape, such as a bag.

Organic wool Wool produced from sheep that graze on land that is not treated with herbicides, pesticides, or artificial fertilizers. The wool is not given any man-made chemical treatments.

Oversewing/overcasting Stitches used to seam two pieces of knitting by placing them right sides together and then sewing through the edge stitches. It is also known as whip stitch.

Pick up and knit To draw loops through the edge of the knitting and place them on the needle.

Pilling When the surface of a knitted item rubs up into unsightly tiny balls, due to wear and friction.

Plied yarn A yarn made from more than one strand of spun fibre, so 4-ply is four strands plied together. Most knitting yarns are plied, as plying prevents the yarn twisting and resulting fabric slanting diagonally.

Pom-pom A small fluffy ball, made from numerous strands of yarn wrapped around a cardboard template and then cut, that is used as a trimming or decoration.

Purl stitch One of the two basic stitches used in knitting.

Purlwise Working with stitches that are facing you, inserting the right-hand needle into a stitch as if to purl it. *See also* knitwise.

Put-up A specific quantity of yarn packaged for sale, such as a ball, donut, hank, or skein.

Reverse stocking stitch An easy method of knitting where all RS rows are purled and all WS rows are knitted. (US: reverse stockinette stitch).

Ribbing/rib/rib stitch Knitting with great elasticity, used where fabric needs to hold tightly to the body, but is capable of expanding. Single ribbing or 1x1 rib is knit 1, purl 1; 2x2 rib is knit 2, purl 2; 3x3 rib is knit 3, purl 3 etc.

Short-row shaping Used for shaping shoulders, curving hems, making darts, and turning sock heels. Rows are added in only one part of the fabric by knitting part of a row instead of knitting it to the end. It uses one of three turning methods to close holes.

Single rib/ribbing *See* Ribbing.

Single strand cast on A group of methods for casting on, using one strand of yarn. Tends to produce a soft edge, but this can be made firmer by twisting the stitches.

Skein Yarn sold wound into a long oblong shape, which is ready to knit. Several hand-dyed or organic yarns are packaged in skeins.

Slip knot A knot that you form when you place the first loop on the needle as you start casting on stitches.

Slip stitch Sliding a stitch from the left-hand needle to the right-hand needle without working it. The usual method is to slip stitches purlwise; less frequently, stitches are slipped knitwise. Slipped stitches at the beginning of each row – slipped selvedge – can help to create a very neat edge.

Sock blocker A flat plastic or wooden shape that is inserted into a finished sock and used to mould it to shape in conjunction with moisture.

Stock stoppers Plastic caps used to stop stitches falling off double-pointed needles.

Stocking stitch A stitch formed by knitting all stitches when the right side of the work is facing you, and purling all stitches when the wrong side of the work is facing you. (US: stockinette stitch).

Stranded beading method A process for streamlining the knitting-in of beads by threading them on yarn before you begin, using a needle and thread looped through the yarn. Beads are later arranged in the knitting when brought to the front of the work and wrapped around a slipped stitch.

Super bulky or super chunky yarn Also called 16-ply (and upwards), bulky, or roving (yarn symbol 6). A chunky yarn suitable for heavy blankets, rugs, and thick scarves.

Superfine yarn Also called 3-ply, fingering, or baby (yarn symbol 1). A very fine yarn suitable for fine-knit socks, lace shawls, and delicate babywear.

Swift A wooden frame used with a ball-winder to transform a hank of yarn into convenient balls.

Tape yarn A wide, flat, or tubular yarn, flattened when wound into a ball. Tape yarn can be knitted to produce a nubbly or smooth result.

Tension The size of the stitches in a piece of knitting (US: gauge), measured by the number of stitches and rows to 10cm (4in), or to 2.5cm (1in) on fine knitting.

Tension square A square knitted to the required number of stitches and rows to match the stated tension of a project, usually 10cm (4in) square. A knitter must achieve the tension stated in a pattern, or else the knitted item will not end up the correct size.

Three-needle cast off/bind off A method of casting off that binds two sets of stitches together, whilst casting off simultaneously. This creates a firm, neat seam, with a smooth finish on the right side of the work. It is a good way of finishing the toe of a sock or the fingertip area of a mitten or fingerless glove.

Tubular cast on/cast off Also known as an invisible cast-on/off. Produces a good edge for a single rib; best to use needles that are at least two sizes smaller than the main fabric in order to prevent the ribbing stretching out of shape.

Tubular knitting Also known as double knitting or double-sided knitting. It is worked on straight needles by slipping every other stitch and produces a double-sided fabric. See also circular knitting.

Twist Two stitches twisted together to form a narrow cable, which slants to the right or left. A cable needle is not used.

Two strand cast on A variety of different methods used for casting on with two strands of yarn. It tends to produce a strong, elastic edge.

Work straight Work in specified pattern without increasing or decreasing.

Yarn Fibres that have been spun into a long strand in order for you to knit with them. Yarns may be made of natural fibres, man-made fibres, a blend of the two, or even non-standard materials.

Yarn bobbins Small plastic shapes used for holding yarn when working an intarsia pattern, where there are many yarns in different colours.

Yarnover (yon) An instruction to increase by adding stitches and creating holes at the same time. Yarnovers (yons) are used for decorative purposes, such as producing lace knitting. There are various types: yfwd (US yo), yarnover between knit stitches; yrn (US yo), yarnover between purl stitches; yfrn and yon (US yo), yarnover between knit and purl stitches; and yfwd (US yo), yarnover at the beginning of a row.

Index

Acknowledgments

Dorling Kindersley UK would like to thank the following people for their hard work and contributions towards *Big Book of Knitting*:

Knitting consultant Dr Vikki Haffenden
Pattern checker Carol Ibbetson
Proofreader Angela Baynham
Indexer Marie Lorimer
Editorial assistance Becky Alexander, Kathryn Meeker
Yarn photographer in India Deepak Aggarwal
Location for photography 1st Option
Props George & Beth, Backgrounds

Knitting designers Caroline Birkett, Shirley Bradford, Sian Brown, Tessa Dennison, Lara Evans, Julie Ferguson, Vikki Haffenden, Amanda Jones, Courtney Kelley, Pat Menchini, Woolly Wormhead.

Knitters Ruth Bridgeman, Pauline Buck, Grace Coombs, Sally Cuthbert, Ursula Doherty, Joan Doyle, Eva Hallas, Jill Houghton, Dolly Howes, Karen Howie, Brenda Jennings, Ann McFaull, Elaine Morris, Daphne Moyce, Mrs Parsons, Doreen Payne, Karen Tattersall, Jane Wales, Brenda Willows.

Yarn manufacturers and distributors for supplying yarn for the projects Artesano Ltd, Coats Crafts UK, Designer Yarns, Kelbourne Woolens, King Cole Ltd, Rico Design, Sirdar Yarns, Sublime Yarns, Texere Yarns Ltd for providing yarn for the projects. Also Dutton for Buttons for supplying buttons for projects on pp.14–17, pp.26–27, pp.28–31, and pp.58–59.

Models Sophie Adams, Abigail Ashford, George Ayre, Louis Claridge, Oliver Claridge, Isabel de Cordova, Natasha Hall, Martha Jenkinson, Nathan Jenkinson, Kyle Johnson, Heidi Lockwood, Kate Meeker, Julie Stewart, Eden White.